D0036328

WOMEN AND RELIGION

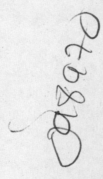

WOMEN AND RELIGION

∿ *The Original Sourcebook
of Women in Christian Thought*

NEW REVISED AND EXPANDED EDITION

Elizabeth A. Clark and Herbert Richardson, *Editors*

Gary Brower and Randall Styers, *Assistant Editors*

HarperSanFrancisco
An Imprint of HarperCollins*Publishers*

Permissions acknowledgments begin on page 385 and constitute a continuation of this copyright page.

WOMEN AND RELIGION: *The Original Sourcebook of Women in Christian Thought*. Copyright © 1977 by Elizabeth Clark and Herbert Richardson. Newly revised and expanded edition copyright © 1996 by Elizabeth Clark and Herbert Richardson. All rights reserved. Printed in the United States of America. No part of this book may be used or reproduced in any manner whatsoever without written permission except in the case of brief quotations embodied in critical articles and reviews. For information address HarperCollins Publishers, 10 East 53rd Street, New York, NY 10022.

HarperCollins Web Site: http://www.harpercollins.com

HarperCollins®, ▄ ®, and HarperSanFrancisco™ are trademarks of HarperCollins Publishers Inc.

FIRST HARPERCOLLINS REVISED EDITION PUBLISHED IN 1996

Library of Congress Cataloging-in-Publication Data

Women and religion : the original sourcebook of women in Christian thought / edited by Elizabeth A. Clark and Herbert Richardson ; Gary Brower and Randall Styers, assistant editors.—New rev. and expanded ed.
   Rev. ed. of: Women and religion / Elizabeth Clark and Herbert Richardson. 1st ed. c 1977.
   "First HarperCollins revised edition"
   Includes bibliographical references.
   ISBN 0–06–061409–9 (pbk.)
   1. Woman (Christian theology) 2. Women in Christianity—History. 3. Feminist theology—History.
   I. Clark, Elizabeth A. (Elizabeth Ann). II. Richardson, Herbert Warren.
  BT704.C53 1996
  270'. 082—dc20   96–10959

96 97 98 99 00 ❖ RRD (H) 10 9 8 7 6 5 4 3 2 1

For Gay Trotter

∿ Contents

⌒ Preface

The first edition of *Women and Religion* (1977) was published at an exciting moment in twentieth-century women's history. By the early 1970s, the "second wave" of feminism had inspired countless Americans to work toward equal treatment for women in all areas of life. The social fervor of the movement spilled over to the academy, where scholars began to question the seeming exclusion of women from the historical record. Although courses concerning women multiplied rapidly across the country, few published sources were available in the early 1970s for classroom use. The first edition of this book was thus a response to that ferment and to the academic needs it generated.

Two decades later, studies of women and gender have found an established place in most college, university, and seminary curricula. The research of hundreds of scholars has extended our knowledge and deepened our understanding of women's history. The mass of new material the editors confronted in preparing the second edition of this book contrasts sharply with the paucity of sources with which they dealt in the early and middle 1970s. Nonetheless, the recent "backlash" against gains women have made in the intervening decades stands as a sobering reminder that the feminist agenda of our foremothers has yet to be realized. Hence the publication of this revised edition of *Women and Religion* is timely.

In the first edition of the book, we thanked the following people for their assistance: Nathaniel Brown, David Cain, Kate Dickson, Frank Flinn, Susan Hanna, Mary Beth Iskat, William Kemp, Elizabeth Kirk, Warren Lewis, George Oliver, Elaine Pagels, Georgiane Perret, William Phipps, Wayne Smith, and Rose Yunker. We now expand our list to include Judith Bennett, Carol Bleser, Ann Burlein, Mary McClintock Fulkerson, Barbara Harris, Cynthia Herrup, Kelly Jarrett, Evelyn Kirkley, Lucas Lamadrid, Dale Martin, Ruth Drucilla Richardson, and the students in our various "women and religion" classes who have contributed much to the rethinking of this book. Elizabeth Clark wishes to thank three teaching assistants in Religion 125 at Duke ("Women and Sexuality in the Western Christian Tradition") for their marvelous colleagueship during the past decade: Blake Leyerle, Gary Brower, and Randall Styers. Several Duke graduate students served as research assistants during the period when the volume was being compiled: Beth Kreitzer, Lucas Lamadrid, Michael Rackett, and Stephen Shoemaker. We are also grateful for the assistance of Lynda Harrison and Sandra Woods, staff members of Duke's Department of Religion. At HarperSanFrancisco, John Loudon and Karen Levine must be thanked for their encouragement of this project.

Last, all four editors wish to single out the one person without whom this book could not have been produced: Gay Trotter, staff assistant of Duke's Graduate Program in Religion. In addition to her invaluable work in the preparation of this manuscript, her efficiency and good cheer in the running of Duke's Graduate Program in Religion are much appreciated by students and faculty alike. She daily demonstrates her devotion to the future of graduate education in religion. To her this book is dedicated.

Elizabeth A. Clark
John Carlisle Kilgo Professor of Religion
Duke University

Herbert Richardson
Editor-in-Chief
The Edwin Mellen Press

Gary Brower
Episcopal Chaplain
The University of California—Berkeley

Randall Styers
Duke University

ᜬ Introduction

This volume contains readings that cover both male representations of women in the Western Christian tradition and women's own religious experiences and theological formulations. Since the first edition of this book was published in 1977, scholarship on women in Western history has burgeoned: unknown or little-known sources have been brought to light; editions and translations of women's writings have multiplied; scholarly articles and monographs have vastly expanded our knowledge of past women. (Given the multiplication of sourcebooks on women in antiquity, we no longer include material on ancient Greece and Israel in the second edition of this volume.) "Gender" is now recognized as a central category of analysis by almost all historians, and the history of sexuality is a fast-growing area of study.

Our increasing knowledge of women in Western history, however, has not confirmed that there was a steady improvement in women's status from antiquity to the present. Nor has it suggested that Christianity should be unequivocally heralded as a liberating force. As D. S. Bailey put it some decades ago, "Christianity displayed from the first a marked inclination toward conservatism" on issues pertaining to women and marriage.[1] Like many contemporary historians, the editors of this volume have adopted an historiographical model that seeks to emphasize both the mechanisms through which male power has been exercised *and* the resistances to that domination by women.

Judith Bennett, an historian of women in medieval England, has recently argued that the term *patriarchy* can be usefully employed by feminist historians. She cites a broad definition of the word formulated by the feminist poet and critic Adrienne Rich:

> a familial-social, ideological, political system in which men—by force, direct pressure, or through ritual, tradition, law, and language, customs, etiquette, education, and the division of labor, determine what part women shall or shall not play, and in which the female is everywhere subsumed under the male.[2]

As used by historians such as Bennett, "patriarchy" does not signify an amorphous, transhistorical entity but instead addresses the specifics of time, place, religion, race, sexuality, and class. The term, Bennett argues, "highlights the pervasiveness and durability of women's oppression, without denying the differences generated by such other oppressions as imperialism, racism, feudalism, capitalism, and heterosexism."[3] Although we will never resolve the futile search for the origins of patriarchy, "we can reconstruct *how* patriarchy has adapted, changed, and survived over time and place." Patriarchy, then, is a topic amenable to a thoroughly historical analysis, one in which women emerge as agents as well as victims.[4]

With respect to the first Christian millennium, we are hampered in our investigations by the paucity of source material on women. Thus, the early chapters of this volume include writings by male authors only. This very fact, however, should prompt reflection on the reasons for women's exclusion from so many early Christian sources. Bernadette Brooten, a scholar of the early Christian period, has succinctly expressed the problem: "The lack of sources on women is part of the history of women."[5]

The New Testament, where we begin our exploration, itself illustrates how promising beginnings were compromised in the name of social expediency. Some New Testament books show women finding expanded opportunities within the new religion (in missionary activity, for example), but subsequent parts of Christian Scripture restrict women's roles to the household and preach a message of female subordination. In the early Christian centuries, we hear of groups of widows and deaconesses—but women's attempts to assume priestly roles were associated with "heresy" by "mainstream" churchmen from the second century onward. Women were effectively excluded from the official ministry of most Christian churches until the nineteenth and twentieth centuries.

One avenue that Christianity opened to women in the early centuries was that of asceticism, particularly involving sexual renunciation. Feminist scholars of early Christianity have debated whether the adoption of celibacy should be seen as an "advance" for women: was the absence of sexual life and children compensated for by the greater opportunities for study, devotion, and religious leadership?[6] Early Christian believers explored diverse forms of ascetic living, but from the late fourth century onward, residence in a monastery was deemed to be the proper mode of life for ascetically inclined females. Asceticism and monasticism offered the only viable alternative to family life for most women. In the absence of reliable methods of contraception (coupled with the church fathers' denunciation of both contraception and abortion), marriage could well involve submission to a husband and repeated dangerous pregnancies. It is in this context that we should understand the "propaganda" for the ascetic life offered by the early Christian writers, such as Jerome, excerpted in this volume. Christian writers such as Clement of Alexandria and Augustine, on the other hand, defended the goodness of marriage against the attacks of allegedly heretical groups of their time.

Many more documents remain from the Middle Ages that provide evidence about the lives of women, especially women in monastic life. As convents developed in the medieval period, they often became influential forces in Christian society. Some abbesses exerted power far beyond that permitted to most married women of their day. Women's monasteries, however, catered mainly to elite women, although some groups, such as the Beguines of the later Middle Ages, provided a haven of celibate living for women of less than elite status.

Medieval women mystics have also been the subject of much recent scholarship. Their distinctive religious experiences and practices prompted them (or male admirers) to record their experiences for their own contemporaries and for posterity. Many of these women claimed to have experienced direct encounters with God or Jesus, unmediated by male priests or monastic authorities. Selections in this volume from Angela of Foligno, Julian of Norwich, Catherine of Siena, and Margery Kempe indicate the diverse experiences of these women. Nonetheless, the high theological traditions of the Middle Ages—represented here by Thomas Aquinas—continued to affirm women's secondary status on the basis of earlier Christian tradition, bolstered now by the biological theories of the Greek philosopher Aristotle, which had been newly recovered in the West.

The misogyny we encounter in theological texts, however, pales before the direct evidence of the witchcraft persecutions, which saw the torture and execution of untold numbers of women in the late medieval and early modern period. In this sourcebook, we include selections from the *Malleus Maleficarum*, a manual written for inquisitors at witchcraft trials, and from materials detailing the outbreak of witchcraft accusations in Salem, Massachusetts, in the late seventeenth century. Why women were the principal targets of witchcraft accusations is a question that remains unresolved.

Another much-contested question is the Protestant Reformation's contribution to women's advancement. With the advent of Protestantism, the celibate life fell into disfavor and marriage was enjoined for (almost) all Protestants as God's command—but did women's fortunes improve? Did the new theological status accorded marriage by Protestant leaders result in a more favorable position for women? Although partisans of the Protestant Reformation have often thought so, some recent historians, such as Lyndal Roper, reject the claim that Protestantism brought any substantive amelioration to women's lives.[7] With the coming of Protestantism, women were stationed in patriarchal families and lost the one option outside of marriage, the monastic profession, in which some had been able to exert leadership and to live in a sisterhood largely independent of men. As the excerpted comments of the sixteenth-century Catholic nun Jeanne de Jussie suggest, not all Catholic women found the Reformation message liberating.

Within a few centuries, Western perceptions of marriage coming from the Reformation prompted other disputes. For example, the seventeenth-century English poet and civil libertarian John Milton argued in his divorce treatises that emerging notions of marriage based on compatibility necessitated changes in the then-restrictive divorce laws. More radically, eighteenth- and nineteenth-century religious groups such as the Shakers, the Oneida Community, and the Mormons sought new ways to configure the male/female relationship, through celibacy (with the Shakers), in "complex marriage" (with the Oneida Community), and in "plural marriage" (with the Mormons).

Theology, too, changed ground with the rise of modernity. Concerned to assert religion's relevance to intellectuals in a newly rational and scientific world, theologians such as Friedrich Schleiermacher in the early nineteenth century shifted the domain of theology from the realm of "rational knowledge" to that of "feeling." Such reconceptualizations were significant in loosening the claims of institutional religious authority and in placing religion within the realm of individual perception. Contemporary feminist theologians acknowledge this development as beneficial, since it initiated a movement, more fully realized in our time, in which women could claim authority for their own religious experience.

Without doubt, the feminist movements of the nineteenth and twentieth centuries have been of signal importance for reconstruing the Christian tradition. In this volume, selections from Sarah Grimké and Elizabeth Cady Stanton demonstrate how nineteenth-century feminists challenged traditional interpretations of the Bible and of ecclesiastical authority. Claiming the right to interpret the Bible in ways that challenged patriarchy, Grimké and Stanton pressed for women to gain access to educational opportunities that would permit them to become authoritative interpreters of the Bible, as well as knowledgeable citizens and activists in movements for social reform. In the twentieth century, feminist theologians such as Mary Daly and Carter Heyward have reformulated earlier traditions to accent the features most productive for women and to critique the detrimental effects of a patriarchal construction of Christianity. The feminist call for equal opportunity has also challenged traditional church policies and practices that forbid (or make difficult) the ordination of women and that seek to restrict women's access to contraception and abortion. In this volume, selections from papal documents and from Christian advocates of reproductive reform, such as Beverly Wildung Harrison, illustrate these debates.

Finally, one of the most laudable developments of recent decades has been the proliferation of diverse female voices contributing to academic and religious dialogue. The dramatic increase of works by and about Christian women of color has contributed greatly to the development of a richer historical record; thus, for example, we include a discussion of the nineteenth-century African-American woman preacher Jarena Lee. Nowhere is this proliferation of voices more apparent than in the development of liberation theology. In addition to excerpts from white liberation theologians Mary Daly and Rosemary Radford Ruether, we here excerpt selections from African-American theologian Jacquelyn Grant and Latina theologian Ada María Isasi-Díaz.

Although the editors of this volume do not claim that Christianity has been unreservedly a liberating force for women, they do believe that there are certain liberating themes that can be identified. For example, changed ways of understanding the Bible have come to benefit Christian women. Early Christian writers tended to concentrate on Eve's secondary status at creation (Genesis 2) and her primacy in the first sin (Genesis 3) to justify their views of the subordination of women. Christian reformers of the nineteenth and twentieth centuries urged their sisters to reclaim the Bible as their own, to raise up the liberating passages rather than to accept submissively the message of female subordination that many males had derived from the Bible. Now, feminist commentators are more apt to cite the Genesis 1 story of creation, which represents woman and man as created simultaneously, "in the image and likeness of God." They emphasize the female disciples of Jesus and the female coworkers of Paul in the early Christian mission. They look to such passages as Galatians 3:28 (that in Christ Jesus there is "no male and female") rather than to the Pastoral Epistles, which counsel women to marry, raise children, and accept their subordinate position as divinely ordained.

A second important issue on which to focus throughout the readings in this volume is where various authors locate the source and norm of religious authority. For example, conservative Catholics who hold the pope's words as binding and authoritative for their lives have found little in recent papal decrees to encourage a feminist message. Likewise, Protestant women who bow to the authority of male pastors and church synods in formulating their religious and moral views often find themselves bound by traditions and conventions that restrict their activities. But directly claiming God as one's source of authority has often proved liberating, as the women mystics of the Middle Ages discovered. Moreover, women who belong to religious movements that rest their ultimate claim on the activity of the Holy Spirit, rather than on ecclesiastical authority or the words of the Bible, often find religious grounding for greater freedom (as did some Montanist and Gnostic women in the early Christian centuries, as well as Shakers, Quakers, and Pentecostals in more recent times).

Finally, recent attention to the rhetorical and power-laden dimensions of language has served to liberate women (and others) from reading practices that automatically assumed the fixed "truth" of texts. Today, we are more keenly aware of how language, in its seeming innocence, seeks to persuade and shape us. Readers of this volume may well be struck by the rhetorical strength of many of these selections. One interesting example that occurs throughout these readings is the appeal to "nature." Today we can see that an author's appeal to "nature" or "the natural" is usually a way to claim objective moral authority for the author's own views. Recently, feminists and other social critics have demonstrated the ideological force of such appeals in Christian writings reinforcing traditional or conservative values.[8] One of the principal tasks awaiting the readers of this volume is to unravel such workings of patriarchal texts.

Although there are few in late twentieth-century America who would seriously repeat the words of the early church father Tertullian to women—"*You* are the devil's gateway"[9]—there are still many who oppose the feminist agenda of securing equal access and opportunity for women. We hope that this sourcebook will be of value to all who seek to understand not only the workings of patriarchy in Christian history but also the aspirations and activities of Christian women, past and present, with a different vision.

I.

∾ The New Testament and Christian Origins

THE GOSPELS

The New Testament Gospels, all of which were written about forty years or more after Jesus' death, present four different pictures of him. They were composed not as biographies but as confessions of faith, witnessing to their authors' conviction that the risen Lord was still guiding the Christian community. (We have no firsthand material from Jesus himself, as we do from Paul.)

The Gospels, as far as we know, were all composed by men or groups of men, and their readers and hearers were not part of a world in which women had equal rights with men. Yet the Gospels give us a picture of Jesus as a man who talked with women, who was not afraid of becoming ritually defiled by them, and who apparently did not think that their only function consisted of household and childbearing duties. All of the Gospels mention the female followers of Jesus and stress their roles in the resurrection events. The Gospel of Luke, in particular, stresses Jesus' friendship with Mary and Martha (Luke 10:38–42), mentions Jesus' female traveling companions (Luke 8:1–3), and even analogizes God to a woman in the parable of the lost coin (Luke 15:8–10). Although Jesus is represented as dealing with women in a kindly fashion, he is also shown treating other outcasts—lepers, tax collectors, the poor—with similar benevolence. Some have even suggested that the depiction of Jesus in the Bible gives us the right to claim him as a "feminist."[1]

It is not just the gaps and silences in the Gospels that make an investigation of the topic "Jesus and Women" difficult; centuries of Christian readers who come to the text with their interests and biases have construed the Gospels in ways that have supported their own assumptions about the nature of early Christianity. Scholarship of recent decades has done much to uncover these assumptions and explode the myth of the objective, neutral observer who approaches texts that are imagined to speak for themselves. Today, interpreters are more sensitive to the claim that history "is never simply 'history of' but always 'history for'"—in other words, writers produce their works with certain audiences, as well as their own ideological objectives, in mind.[2] Thus we must always question not only the ancient social settings within which biblical texts were produced, as well as the audiences with their particular interests to which those texts were directed, but also the interests and audiences of *modern* commentators on biblical texts. The fact that even much modern scholarship operates within an androcentric framework that assumes men to have been the "actors" in early Christianity and that makes maleness the norm against which women appear as deviations has become increasingly clear to women scholars of the New Testament.[3] As feminist scholars have approached the New Testament tradition, they have learned to read against the grain of a text, to note its silences; these interpretive techniques are aimed at uncovering not so much what men *thought* of women or what prescriptions men made for them but what women may plausibly be expected to have done. Ancient reports by men about women have been assigned to the category of an "artistic rendering"[4]—or, in more politically oriented language, of ideology.[5]

A major theme of late twentieth-century New Testament interpretation that has been useful to feminist scholars is the understanding of early Christianity as a renewal movement within Judaism.[6] In keeping with its devotees' expectation of an imminent end to the world, leaders of the new movement may have tolerated or even encouraged forms of behavior that would be considered bizarre by standards of a later, more established Christianity: itinerant preachers, women prophets, an emphasis on charismatic gifts. Enthusiastic bursts of new religious spirit are often accompanied by a loosening of societal structures, allowing more freedom of expression for marginal groups such as women—although it is also typical that as women's power and status increase, prescriptions (by men) attempting to limit their activities and behavior *also* increase.[7] Scholars who believe that the Gospels and Paul's letters contain a liberating message argue that by the turn of the second century the freedoms that attended the earliest decades of Christianity were in the process of restriction. This model of interpretation often stresses (for example) the early Christian missionary movement as providing an avenue of female equality.[8] Other scholars—equally feminist in their contemporary commitments—argue that Paul is a dubious ally for feminists.[9]

THE PAULINE EPISTLES

Paul's letters are the earliest materials preserved in the New Testament, dating to the middle of the first century. Most scholars now believe that Paul himself did not compose the letters to Timothy, Titus, the Ephesians, and probably the Colossians, which are assigned to later decades; this reduction of the traditional Pauline canon eliminates from Pauline authorship some of the more problematic passages about women in the New Testament. But even if we limit our investigation to those of Paul's letters that are still considered authentic, there is considerable disagreement over their interpretation.

Gaps in our historical knowledge hinder our ability to understand the place of women in Paul's missionizing activities. Using
the examples of two women who figure in New Testament accounts pertaining to Paul, Junia and Prisca, New Testament
scholar Bernadette Brooten suggests the kinds of historical questions which arise as we attempt to grasp their roles more fully:

> What are the sources for first-century Jewish women in Rome?
> What do we know about women and the Roman penal code? What
> do we know about Jewish women's education and about non-
> Jewish Roman women's education in this period? Are there other
> examples of wives and husbands practicing a trade together? What
> would have been the income from such a trade? How much do we
> know about women and travel in this period? Did women serve as
> delegates or missionaries in other religious movements or in civic
> contexts? What can we know of the size, layout, and cost of a
> house in which a house church could have met? These questions
> are rather straightforward historical questions, unusual only be-
> cause they simply presuppose that women, like men, are historical
> beings, and that the historical study of women is a worthwhile en-
> terprise.[10]

Turning to the evidence provided by Paul's letters themselves, we find little agreement among scholars on how it should
be construed. Some feminists take Galatians 3:28 ("There is
neither Jew nor Greek, there is neither slave nor free, there is
neither male nor female;[11] for you are all one in Christ Jesus")
to mean that Paul was urging the equality of women. Others
argue, however, that Paul was not speaking of "social reality"
but of how things might be in the Christian future and that he
had no more interest in women's "freedom" than he did in the
freedom of slaves.[12] Yet Paul in his letters does send greetings to
women who are leaders in the early Christian churches. In
1 Corinthians 11:5, he acknowledges (without complaint) that
women are praying and prophesying along with men in worship. In Romans 16:1, he refers to Phoebe as a *diakonos*,[13]

which perhaps suggests that she held a recognized church of-fice.[14]

Since the 1970s, New Testament scholars have disagreed strongly over the degree to which Paul can be considered a "protofeminist," centering their attention especially on two pas-sages, 1 Corinthians 7 and 11:2–16.[15] Do Paul's words on mar-riage in 1 Corinthians 7 take us in the direction of "liberation" or of "bondage"? Are Paul's injunctions in I Corinthians 11 that women keep their heads covered during public worship a char-acteristically repressive gesture, a "backsliding" from a more tol-erant stance, or an indication of women's new freedom in the Christian faith?[16] Did Paul think that "freedom" was linked to ascetic renunciation (i.e., freedom from marriage), in which case he may have placed more restrictions on married women than on the unmarried? Such interpretations have attempted to bring greater coherence to what otherwise seem like contradictory rec-ommendations. And 1 Corinthians 14:34–36 (which instructs women to keep silent in the churches) is such an embarrassment to advocates of Paul's feminism that the verses are often taken to be an interpolation by a later editor or are interpreted so as to seek to exonerate Paul from allegations of misogyny.[17]

Another topic generating considerable discussion among New Testament scholars is that of Paul's allusions to same-sex relations, which he holds in Romans 1:18–32 to be a particular manifestation of the bad behavior resulting from the Gentiles' "idolatry." Although conservative Christians have often ap-pealed to this passage (along with condemnations of male same-sex relations found in Hebrew Scripture) to claim that gays and lesbians of the present deserve God's wrathful punishment, re-cent discussions of Romans 1 that contextualize Paul's words in his religious and social setting argue that the Apostle here is actually discussing not the consequences of general human fallenness, but the consequences of particular Gentile forms of polytheism and idolatry that are not readily applicable to modern debates.[18]

LATER NEW TESTAMENT LITERATURE

Most scholars agree that attitudes of male Christian writers toward women became increasingly restrictive around the end of the first century C.E., as Christians gradually relinquished their hope for the early arrival of the kingdom of God and strove to reconcile their faith with the mores and customs of the world; now, a Christian matron's subservience to her husband could be used as propaganda to convince Gentile audiences that Christianity was not subversive of traditional domestic life.[19] The post-Pauline epistles bear witness to this change. In these letters, it is presumed that women will stay at home, bear children, obey their husbands, and keep silent. No more missionary journeys to advance the Christian cause!

Particularly problematic for feminist interpreters have been the passages called "the Household Codes" (Col. 3:18–4:1; 1 Pet. 2:11–3:7; Eph. 5:22–6:9; 1 Tim. 2:11–15, 5:3–8, 6:1–2; Titus 2:2–10, 3:1–2). These texts, which order authority in the household (husbands over wives, parents over children, masters over slaves), have been much analyzed as to their social setting and philosophical provenance; for example, are they related to Stoic or to Aristotelian ethical injunctions?[20] Their effects—whatever the authors' intention—were to "tame" any more egalitarian possibilities the early Christian movement might have developed. Also problematic for later feminist interpreters are the passages in the Pastoral Epistles that attempt to limit the number of widows enrolled as an ecclesiastically sponsored group and restrict their activities (1 Tim. 5:3–16);[21] that "permit no woman to teach or to have authority over men" (1 Tim. 2:12); and that urge wives to be subject to their husbands, on the model of the (female) church, which subordinates herself to the male bridegroom, Christ (Eph. 5:22–33). The ambivalence occasioned by the presence of both progressive and traditional currents within the canon of the New Testament had serious consequences for Christianity in the next centuries—indeed, up to the present—as Constance Parvey has well described:

> The later Church, when it lost the vision that the Kingdom was coming, also lost the theology that enabled it to live as though the Kingdom were at hand. As a consequence, it inherited two seemingly divergent messages: the theology of equivalence in Christ; the practice of women's subordination. In attempting to reconcile them, it maintained a status-quo ethics on the social level through the subordination of women, and it affirmed the vision of equivalence on the spiritual level by projecting it as an otherworldly reality. Throughout the history of the Church this has led to complex and confused theological arguments, with their consequent social distortions.[22]

THE BIRTH STORIES

One pair of Gospel stories—the stories of Jesus' birth recounted in Matthew and Luke—had enormous significance for the veneration of Mary and of virginity. Although the stories differ in many details, they both agree that Mary was a virgin at the time she conceived Jesus. Already in the second century these accounts—preserved nowhere else in the New Testament and presumably unknown to Paul and other New Testament writers—had been elaborated to stress that Mary never lost the physiological evidence of her virginal status, not even after she had given birth to Jesus. An apocryphal gospel called *The Protevangelium of James* was one of the first to expound this point. According to this work, after Jesus had been born in a cave, the midwife who had attended the birth met her friend Salome:

> And she said to her: "Salome, Salome, I have a new sight to tell you; a virgin has brought forth, a thing which her nature does not allow." And Salome said: "*As the Lord my God lives, unless I put (forward) my finger* and test her condition, I will not believe that a virgin has brought forth."

And the midwife went in and said to Mary: "Make yourself ready, for there is no small contention concerning you." And Salome put (forward) her finger to test her condition. And she cried out, saying: "Woe for my wickedness and my unbelief; for I have tempted the living God; and behold, my hand falls away from me, consumed by fire!"[23]

Salome is soon healed by touching the infant Jesus, and she affirms her belief in Mary's virginity.

THE VIRGIN MARY IN THE EARLY CHRISTIAN TRADITION

The theme of Mary's virginal conception of Jesus assumed further significance as early Christian theologians such as Augustine asserted that there was a link between sexual intercourse and the transfer of original sin. Jesus was held to be exempt from sin not only because he was the Son of God but also because he was born of a virgin.

By the eleventh century, it was popularly believed that Mary also had a sin-free status, although it was not until 1854 that the Vatican decreed as a dogmatic pronouncement that Mary was "immaculately conceived" by her parents.[24] Thus Mary gradually came to be depicted in Catholic teaching as a sinless woman, a notion that is sometimes held to be of importance for raising the status of women. Feminists often challenge this interpretation, claiming that the figure of Mary cannot serve as a role model for ordinary women, who can never aspire to her divinely given freedom from original sin any more than they can hope to achieve simultaneous motherhood and virginity.[25] Nonetheless, Mary played an important part in Christian thinking from at least the fourth century, due to the fact that she was taken by the church as the exemplar of lifelong virginity, and by that time such chastity was the preferred mode of existence for Christians.[26]

WOMEN IN THE APOCRYPHAL ACTS

One trajectory developing from New Testament material that has received much recent comment involves the traditions of the Apocryphal Acts of the Apostles. These works, which take the names of the various apostles for their titles, contain some of the most liberating material for women from the early Christian period. Thoroughly ascetic in worldview, these tales recount how exemplary women reject husbands and fiancés upon hearing the message of Christian renunciation preached by the apostles. Scholars have speculated whether women could have produced these stories, or at least have been their prime audience.[27]

One of the most celebrated of the Apocryphal Acts recounts the story of Thecla, a highborn young woman from Iconium, who was swiftly converted to an ascetic form of Christianity by hearing the message preached by Paul. Against her mother's will, Thecla breaks her engagement and defies male authorities who attempt to force her to reject her ascetic commitment. After many adventurous exploits—including baptizing herself in a pool of ferocious seals—Thecla crops her hair, dons clothing disguising her femaleness, and begins a mission of preaching and teaching that lasts until her death.[28] Although Thecla became a popular heroine from the late second century on, her independent behavior was worrisome to the church fathers, who did not want "mainstream" Christian women to imagine (for example) that they had the right to teach and baptize on the basis of Thecla's reported action.[29] Several scholars of early Christian women's history see the trajectory from Paul's writings to the Apocryphal Acts as substantially different from (and, some would say, earlier than) that to the Pastoral Epistles, which contain a restrictive message regarding Christian women's roles.[30] Indeed, the New Testament's "message" about women may have been variously interpreted in antiquity, as it is now.

Passages appropriate to be read in conjunction with this chapter include:

Matthew 5:31–32 = Matthew 19:9 = Mark 10:1–12 = Luke 16:18
Matthew 9:18–26 = Mark 5:21–43 = Luke 8:40–56
Matthew 10:34–36 = Luke 12:51–53
Matthew 10:37–39 = Luke 14:26–27
Matthew 12:46–50 = Mark 3:31–35 = Luke 8:19–21
Matthew 15:21–28 = Mark 7:24–30
Matthew 19:1–15 = Mark 10:1–16 = cf. Luke 18:15–18
Matthew 22:23–33 = Mark 12:18–27 = Luke 20:27–40
Matthew 26:6–13 = Mark 14:3–9
Matthew 27:55–28:10 = cf. Mark 15:40–16:11 = cf. Luke 23:49–24:11
Mark 12:41–44 = Luke 21:1–4
Matthew 1–2, 5:27–30, 25:1–13
Mark 3:19b–22
Luke 1–3, 7:11–17, 7:36–50, 8:1–3, 10:38–42, 11:27–28, 13:10–17, 15:8–10
John 2:1–11, 4:1–42, 8:1–11, 11:1–44, 12:1–8, 19:25–20:18
Acts 9:36–43, 12:12–17, 16:11–15, 18:1–3, 18:24–28, 21:8–9
Romans 1, 7:1–3, 16
1 Corinthians 5–7, 11:1–16, 14:33–36
Galatians 3:26–28
Ephesians 5:21–33
Colossians 3:18–19, 4:15
1 Thessalonians 4:1–8
1 Timothy 2:8–15, 3:11, 5:3–16
Titus 2:3–5
Hebrews 13:4
1 Peter 3:1–7

2.

∾ Clement of Alexandria and the Gnostics: Women, Sexuality, and Marriage in Orthodoxy and Heterodoxy

Standing outside the bounds of the "orthodox"[1] church, the Gnostic movement provided a foil for the early church's affirmation of the goodness of marriage and reproduction. As described by Hans Jonas, Gnosticism was a "dualistic transcendent religion of salvation" that formed part of the broader religious foment that swept the late Hellenistic world.[2] Clement of Alexandria, a Christian instructor of the Alexandrian church who wrote and taught at the turn of the third century, composed his treatise on marriage,[3] one of the most positive statements on marriage and sexuality in early Christian literature, to combat Gnostic views and to affirm that the created order had received God's blessing. By the fourth century, however, the burgeoning of ascetic theory and practice within the Christian community would call into question even the lukewarm affirmation of marriage given by Clement.

GNOSTICISM

We can here suggest a few of the features of Gnosticism with which Clement was concerned. According to the church fathers, Gnosticism encompassed a large variety of sects, each of which had its own mythology and ethic. Many of the second- and third-century church fathers wrote against various Gnostic teachers and sects; today we are fortunate also to possess the Gnostic treatises that were discovered at Nag Hammadi in Egypt several decades ago.[4] Some Gnostics posited that the universe was tainted,[5] created either through the malicious intent of a wicked deity or through an accident that occurred within the realm of the spiritual powers. In either case, the material world was seen as the unfortunate result of divine mismanagement. The "spark" or "spirit" (*pneuma*) within humans—or true Gnostics, at least—was trapped in the fleshly covering of the body. To bring enlightenment to humans regarding their heavenly origin and destiny was a central aim of the Gnostic religion.

According to the church fathers, Gnostic hostility to the physical universe and to the powers responsible for its creation stimulated diverse ethical outlooks.[6] Some Gnostics took an ascetic approach to the material world and denied themselves food, drink, and sexual intercourse. Others (again, according to the church fathers) took the opposite stance of libertinism: if the God who made the universe and gave us the Old Testament commandments was not the redeemer who brings us knowledge *(gnosis),* we should show our contempt by defying the Creator's laws and standards of goodness. It appears, however, that the majority of Gnostics adopted an ascetic rather than a libertine ethic.[7] We also know from the Gnostics' own writings that some of them approved of human marriage, thinking it reflected the union of male and female spiritual powers above.[8]

Many Gnostics believed that people's "salvation" or "damnation" depended on whether they received the *gnosis*. True Gnostics were the elect who could not forfeit their salvation. The church fathers were suspicious of this "predestinarian" element in Gnostic thinking and frequently asserted that righteous behavior resulting from a person's free choice was essential for salvation. The praise and blame assigned to a person's deeds must be related to volition; righteousness was, in the words of Hellenistic philosophy, "up to us." It is easy to understand how, in this context, neither the predestinarian elements of Paul's teaching nor his emphasis on God's grace would be much stressed by church leaders until years after the first wave of Gnosticism had subsided. Clement was one of the church fathers most vociferous in his attack on Gnostic "determinism." His stress on the free will of human beings was, as W. E. G. Floyd has put it, his "trump card."[9]

CLEMENT'S RESPONSE

In the selections that follow, Clement demonstrates his opposition to both the ascetic and the libertine forms of Gnostic ethics. It is blasphemy to abstain from sexual relations out of hostility to the Creator and the world he made, Clement argues. Sexual desire is implanted in us by God and hence must be good. Clement is so eager to affirm the positive worth of marriage that he even asserts that Paul married![10]

Clement believes that Christians should be taught that abstinence can be a good if—and only if—it is undertaken from the motivation of the love of God and with constant dependence on divine help. Mere physical continence by itself, such as that practiced by athletes, would not meet Clement's standards. Clement himself probably would have preferred that more Christians embrace the old Stoic ideal of *apatheia,* freedom from passion, but since this goal did not seem to be a realistic one for the large mass of "simple believers," marriage should be affirmed as a kind of "middle way."[11] Even within marriage, Clement enjoins restraint regarding sexual relations, which ought to be undertaken solely for the sake of begetting children.[12] Nonetheless, marriage as well as celibacy can be approved as a kind of "service and ministry to the Lord."

GNOSTIC VIEWS OF THE FEMININE

Later in this chapter we shall examine some Gnostic material. The selection from Clement gives us few clues about the distinctive beliefs and practices of the Gnostics regarding femaleness. In two different ways, the Gnostics indicated that their view of women might sometimes be at variance with "orthodox" Christianity's. First, in contrast to the unremittingly "male" imagery associated with the fullness of the Godhead by the church fathers, there are many references in Gnostic literature to female aspects of divinity. Some Gnostic systems describe the Godhead *(pleroma)* as composed of male and female principles. In the Valentinian Gnostic scheme, for example, the Forefather, Abyss, mates with a primordial female, Thought (also called Grace and Silence), to bring forth a male aeon, Mind, and a female one, Truth—and the "begetting" continues from that point, with male and female principles bringing forth new offspring.[13] The last female aeon, Sophia (Wisdom), disrupts the *pleroma* with her passion to know Father Abyss; because of the disturbance she causes, the entire universe (and humankind) is created.[14] Although a female principle here receives much attention, her activities, it should be noted, are cast in a negative light. In other Gnostic texts, such as the *Apocryphon of John,* instead of the conventional description of the Trinity as Father, Son, and Holy Spirit, we hear of the Father, the Son, and the Mother: "John" is given a vision in which God informs him, "I am the Father, I am the Mother, I am the Son."[15] Such references to a female component of the Godhead are almost nonexistent in "orthodox" Christian circles of this era, but they reemerge later in some Christian mystical literature and in Shaker piety.[16]

Second, the church fathers alleged that some Gnostic sects allowed women to take on leadership roles that "mainstream" Christians deemed inappropriate. One example of the church fathers' horror at female leadership among the Gnostics is Tertullian's famous outcry: "How bold these heretical women are! They have no modesty; they are bold enough to teach, to argue, to perform exorcisms, to undertake cures, and maybe even to baptize!"[17] The selection that follows from the Gnostic *Gospel of Mary* also indicates an approval of roles for females that orthodox Christianity did not sanction. The reproval of Mary by Peter and Andrew—exemplars of "orthodox" Catholicism—suggests that the Gnostic writer of this gospel was aware that roles for women were a contested point between his group and the "mainstream" church. It has been much debated whether one attraction for women to the so-called heretical and schismatic groups (such as the Gnostics and the Montanists) lay in the expanded field of activity and responsibility that these groups allowed them.[18]

ON MARRIAGE*

It is not our aim to pursue this subject in further detail and to mention further senseless heresies. To put them to shame we should be forced to deal with each one, and to state our objections to each point, which would extend these notes to an unconscionable length. Accordingly we may divide all the heresies into two groups in making answer to them. Either they teach that one ought to live on the principle that it is a matter of indifference whether one does right or wrong, or

---

* From Clement of Alexandria, "On Marriage," *Stromateis* 3 in *Alexandrian Christianity,* eds. J. E. L. Oulton and H. Chadwick, vol. 3 of *The Library of Christian Classics* (Philadelphia: Westminster Press, 1954), 58–65, 66–67, 76–77, 88–90.

they set a too ascetic tone and proclaim the necessity of continence on the ground of opinions which are godless and arise
from hatred of what God has created. First we may discuss the
former group. If it is lawful to live any sort of life one likes,
obviously one may live in continence; or if any kind of life has
no dangers for the elect, obviously one of virtue and self-control is far less dangerous. If the "lord of the sabbath" (Matt.
12:8) has been given the right to pass uncorrected if he lives an
immoral life, *a fortiori* there will be no correction for him who
behaves decently. "All things are lawful, but all things are not
expedient" (1 Cor. 6:12, 10:23) says the apostle. If all things
are lawful, obviously this includes self-control. . . .

But how is it possible to become like the Lord and have
knowledge of God if one is subject to physical pleasures? . . .
We must not live as if there were no difference between right
and wrong, but, to the best of our power, must purify ourselves from indulgence and lust and take care for our soul
which must continually be devoted to the Deity alone. For
when it is pure and set free from all evil the mind is somehow capable of receiving the power of God and the divine
image is set up in it. "And everyone who has this hope in the
Lord purifies himself," says the Scripture, "even as he is
pure" (1 John 3:3).

To attain the knowledge of God is impossible for those
who are still under the control of their passions. Therefore
they cannot attain the salvation they hope for as they have
not obtained any knowledge of God. He who fails to attain
this end is clearly subject to the charge of being ignorant of
God, and ignorance of God is shown by a man's manner of
life. It is absolutely impossible at the same time to be a man
of understanding and not to be ashamed to gratify the
body. . . .

It is the manner of life which shows up those who know
the commandments; for as a man's word is, so is his life. The
tree is known by its fruit (Matt. 7:16), not by its blossom

and leaves. Knowledge, then, comes from the fruit and from behaviour, not from talk and from blossom. We say that knowledge is not mere talk, but a certain divine knowledge, that light which is kindled in the soul as a result of obedience to the commandments, and which reveals all that is in a state of becoming, enables man to know himself and teaches him to become possessed of God. What the eye is in the body, knowledge is in the mind. Let them not call bondage to pleasure freedom, as if bitterness were sweet. We have learnt to recognize as freedom that which the Lord alone confers on us when he liberates us from lusts and desires and the other passions. "He who says, I know the Lord, and does not keep his commandments, is a liar and the truth is not in him," says John (1 John 2:4).

To those, on the other hand, who under a pious cloak blaspheme by their continence both the creation and the holy Creator, the almighty, only God, and teach that one must reject marriage and begetting of children, and should not bring others in their place to live in this wretched world, nor give any sustenance to death, our reply is as follows. . . .

The task of the law is to deliver us from a dissolute life and all disorderly ways. Its purpose is to lead us from unrighteousness to righteousness, so that it would have us self-controlled in marriage, in begetting children, and in general behaviour. The Lord is not "come to destroy the law but to fulfill it" (Matt. 5:17). "To fulfill" does not imply that it was defective, but that by his coming the prophecies of the law are accomplished, since before the law the demand for right conduct was proclaimed by the Logos to those also who lived good lives. The multitude who know nothing of continence live for the body, not for the spirit. But the body without spirit is "earth and ashes" (Gen. 18:27). Now the Lord judges adultery which is only committed in thought (Matt. 5:28). What then? Is it not possible to remain continent even in the married state and not to seek to "put asunder what

God has joined together" (Matt. 19:6)? For such is the teaching of those who divide the yoke of marriage, by reason of whom the Christian name is blasphemed. If it is the view of these people who themselves owe their existence to sexual relations that such relations are impure, must not they be impure? But I hold that even the seed of the sanctified is holy. . . .

If, as they say, they have already attained the state of resurrection, and on this account reject marriage let them neither eat nor drink. For the apostle says that in the resurrection the belly and food shall be destroyed. Why then do they hunger and thirst and suffer the weaknesses of the flesh and all the other needs which will not affect the man who through Christ has attained to the hoped for resurrection? Furthermore those who worship idols abstain both from food and from sexual intercourse. "But the kingdom of God does not consist in eating and drinking" (Rom. 14:17), he says. And indeed the Magi make a point of abstaining from wine and the meat of animals and from sexual intercourse while they are worshipping angels and daemons. But just as humility consists in meekness and not in treating one's body roughly, so also continence is a virtue of the soul which is not manifest to others, but is in secret.

There are some who say outright that marriage is fornication and teach that it was introduced by the devil. They proudly say that they are imitating the Lord who neither married nor had any possession in this world, boasting that they understand the gospel better than anyone else. The Scripture says to them: "God resists the proud but gives grace to the humble" (James 4:6; 1 Pet. 5:5). Further, they do not know the reason why the Lord did not marry. In the first place he had his own bride, the Church; and in the next place he was no ordinary man that he should also be in need of some helpmeet (Gen. 2:18) after the flesh. Nor was it necessary for him to beget children since he abides eternally and was born the only Son of God. It is the Lord himself who says: "That which God has joined together, let no man put asunder" (Matt. 19:6). And again: "As it was in the days of Noah, they were marrying, and giving in marriage, building and planting, and as it was in the days of Lot, so shall be the coming of the Son of man" (Matt. 24:37–39). And to show that he is not referring to the heathen he adds: "When the Son of man is come, shall he find faith on the earth?" (Luke 18:8). And again: "Woe to those who are with child and are giving suck in those days" (Matt. 24:19), a saying, I admit, to be understood allegorically. The reason why he did not determine "the times which the Father has appointed by his own power" (Acts 1:7) was that the world might continue from generation to generation.

Concerning the words, "Not all can receive this saying. There are some eunuchs who were born so, and some who were made eunuchs by men, and some who have made themselves eunuchs for the sake of the kingdom of heaven; let him receive it who can receive it" (Matt. 19:11f.), they do not realize the context. After his word about divorce some asked him whether, if that is the position in relation to woman, it is better not to marry; and it was then that the Lord said: "Not all can receive this saying, but those to whom it is granted." What the questioners wanted to know was whether, when a man's wife has been condemned for fornication, it is allowable for him to marry another.

It is said, however, that several athletes abstained from sexual intercourse, exercising continence to keep their bodies in training, as Astylos of Croton and Crison of Himera. Even the cithara-player, Amoebeus, though newly married, kept away from his bride. And Aristotle of Cyrene was the only man to disdain the love of Lais when she fell for him.

As he had sworn to the courtesan that he would take her to his home country if she rendered him some assistance against his antagonists, when she had rendered it, he kept his oath in an amusing manner by painting the closest possible likeness of her and setting it up in Cyrene. The story is told by Istros in his book on *The Peculiarity of Athletic Contests*. Therefore there is nothing meritorious about abstinence from marriage unless it arises from love to God. At any rate the blessed Paul says of those who revile marriage: "In the last times some shall depart from the faith, turning to spirits of error and doctrines inspired by daemons, forbidding to marry and commanding abstinence from food" (1 Tim. 4:1, 3). And again he says: "Let no one disqualify you by demanding self-imposed ascetic practices and severe treatment of the body" (Col. 2:18, 23). And the same writer has this also: "Are you bound to a wife? Do not seek to be separated from her. Are you free from any wife? Do not seek to find one." And again: "Let every man have his own wife lest Satan tempt you" (1 Cor. 7:27, 2, 5).

How then? Did not the righteous in ancient times partake of what God made with thanksgiving? Some begat children and lived chastely in the married state. To Elijah the ravens brought bread and meat for food (1 Kings 17:6). And Samuel the prophet brought as food for Saul the remnant of the thigh, of which he had already eaten (1 Sam. 9:24). But whereas they say that they are superior to them in behaviour and conduct, they cannot even be compared with them in their deeds. "He who does not eat," then, "let him not despise him who eats; and he who eats let him not judge him who does not eat; for God has accepted him" (Rom. 14:3). Moreover, the Lord says of himself: "John came neither eating nor drinking, and they say, He has a devil. The Son of man came eating and drinking and they say, Behold a gluttonous man and a wine-bibber, a friend of publicans and a sinner" (Matt. 11:18f.).

Or do they also scorn the apostles? Peter and Philip had children, and Philip gave his daughters in marriage.

Even Paul did not hesitate in one letter to address his consort.* The only reason why he did not take her about with him was that it would have been an inconvenience for his ministry. Accordingly he says in a letter: "Have we not a right to take about with us a wife that is a sister like the other apostles?" (1 Cor. 9:5). But the latter, in accordance with their particular ministry, devoted themselves to preaching without any distraction, and took their wives with them not as women with whom they had marriage relations, but as sisters, that they might be their fellow-ministers in dealing with housewives. It was through them that the Lord's teaching penetrated also the women's quarters without any scandal being aroused. We also know the directions about women deacons which are given by the noble Paul in his second letter to Timothy (1 Tim. 5:9f. [cf. 1 Tim. 3:11]). Furthermore, the self-same man cried aloud that "the kingdom of God does not consist in food and drink," not indeed in abstinence from wine and meat, "but in righteousness, peace, and joy in the Holy Spirit" (Rom. 14:17). Which of them goes about like Elijah clad in a sheepskin and a leather girdle? Which of them goes about like Isaiah, naked except for a piece of sacking and without shoes? Or clothed merely in a linen loincloth like Jeremiah? (1 Kings 19:13; 2 Kings 1:8; Isa. 20:2; Jer. 13:1). Which of them will imitate John's gnostic way of life? The blessed prophets also lived in this manner and were thankful to the Creator. . . .

The human ideal of continence, I mean that which is set forth by Greek philosophers, teaches that one should fight desire and not be subservient to it so as to bring it to practical effect. But our ideal is not to experience desire at all. Our aim is not that while a man feels desire he should get the better of it, but that he should be continent even respecting

---

* Does Clement have in mind Philippians 4:3?

desire itself. This chastity cannot be attained in any other way except by God's grace. That was why he said "Ask and it shall be given you" (Matt. 7:7). This grace was received even by Moses, though clothed in his needy body, so that for forty days he felt neither thirst nor hunger (Exod. 24:18). Just as it is better to be in good health than for a sick man to talk about health, so to be light is better than to discuss light, and true chastity is better than that taught by the philosophers. Where there is light there is no darkness. But where there is inward desire, even if it goes no further than desire and is quiescent so far as bodily action is concerned, union takes place in thought with the object of desire, although that object is not present.

Our general argument concerning marriage, food, and other matters, may proceed to show that we should do nothing from desire. Our will is to be directed only towards that which is necessary. For we are children not of desire but of will (cf. John 1:13). A man who marries for the sake of begetting children must practise continence so that it is not desire he feels for his wife, whom he ought to love, and that he may beget children with a chaste and controlled will. For we have learnt not to "have thought for the flesh to fulfill its desires." We are to "walk honourably as in the day," that is in Christ and in the enlightened conduct of the Lord's way, "not in revelling and drunkenness, not in debauchery and lasciviousness, not in strife and envy" (Rom. 13:13–14). . . .

If by agreement marriage relations are suspended for a time to give opportunity for prayer (1 Cor. 7:5), this teaches continence. He adds the words "by agreement" lest anyone should dissolve his marriage, and the words "for a time" lest a married man, brought to continence by force, should then fall into sin; for if he spares his own wife he may fall into desire for another woman. On this principle he said that the man who thinks he is not behaving properly if he brings up his daughter to be unmarried, does right to give her in marriage (1 Cor. 7:36). Whether a man becomes a celibate or whether he joins himself in marriage with a woman for the sake of having children, his purpose ought to be to remain unyielding to what is inferior. If he can live a life of intense devotion, he will gain to himself great merit with God, since his continence is both pure and reasonable. But if he goes beyond the rule he has chosen to gain greater glory, there is a danger that he may lose hope. Both celibacy and marriage have their own different forms of service and ministry to the Lord; I have in mind the caring for one's wife and children. For it seems that the particular characteristic of the married state is that it gives the man who desires a perfect marriage an opportunity to take responsibility for everything in the home which he shares with his wife. The apostle says that one should appoint bishops who by their oversight over their own house have learned to be in charge of the whole church (1 Tim. 3:4f.). Let each man therefore fulfill his ministry by the work in which he was called (1 Cor. 7:24), that he may be free (1 Cor. 7:22) in Christ and receive the proper reward of his ministry. . . .

If birth is something evil, let the blasphemers say that the Lord who shared in birth was born in evil, and that the virgin gave birth to him in evil. Woe to these wicked fellows! They blaspheme against the will of God and the mystery of creation in speaking evil of birth. This is the ground upon which Docetism is held by Cassian and by Marcion also, and on which even Valentine indeed teaches that Christ's body was "psychic." They say: Man became like the beast when he came to practise sexual intercourse. But it is when a man in his passion really wants to go to bed with a strange woman that in truth such a man has become a wild beast. "Wild horses were they become, each man whinnied after his neighbour's wife" (Jer. 5:8). And if the serpent took the use of intercourse from the irrational animals and persuaded Adam to agree to have sexual union with Eve, as though the couple first created did not have such union by nature, as some think, this again is blasphemy against the creation. For it makes human nature weaker than that of the brute beasts if in this matter those who were first created by God copied them.

But if nature led them, like the irrational animals, to procreation, yet they were impelled to do it more quickly than was proper because they were still young and had been led away by deceit. Thus God's judgment against them was just, because they did not wait for his will. But birth is holy. By it were made the world, the existences, the natures, the angels, powers, souls, the commandments, the law, the gospel, the knowledge of God. And "all flesh is grass, and all the glory of man as the flower of grass. The grass withers, the flower falls; but the word of the Lord abides" (Isa. 40:6–8) which anoints the soul and unites it with the spirit. Without the body how could the divine plan for us in the Church achieve its end? Surely the Lord himself, the head of the Church (Eph. 1:22; 5:23), came in the flesh, though without form and beauty (Isa. 53:2), to teach us to look upon the formless and incorporeal nature of the divine Cause. "For a tree of life" says the prophet, "grows by a good desire" (Prov. 13:12), teaching that desires which are in the living Lord are good and pure.

Furthermore they wish to maintain that the intercourse of man and wife in marriage, which is called knowledge, is a sin; this sin is referred to as eating of the tree of good and evil, and the phrase "he knew" (Gen. 2:9) signifies transgression of the commandment. But if this is so, even knowledge of the truth is eating of the tree of life (Gen. 2:9; 3:22). It is possible for a sober-minded marriage to partake of that tree. We have already observed that marriage may be used rightly or wrongly; and this is the tree of knowledge, if we do not transgress in marriage. What then? Does not the Saviour who heals the soul also heal the body of its passions? But if the flesh were hostile to the soul, he would not have raised an obstacle to the soul by strengthening with good health the hostile flesh. "This I say, brethren, that flesh and blood cannot inherit the kingdom of God nor corruption incorruption" (1 Cor. 15:50). For sin being corruption cannot have fellowship with incorruption which is righteousness. "Are you so foolish?" he says; "having begun in the Spirit are you now to be made perfect by the flesh?" (Gal. 3:3).

Some, then, as we have shown, have tried to go beyond what is right and the concord that marks salvation which is holy and established. They have blasphemously accepted the ideal of continence for reasons entirely godless. Celibacy may lawfully be chosen according to the sound rule with godly reasons, provided that the person gives thanks for the grace God has granted (cf. 1 Cor. 7:7), and does not hate the creation or reckon married people to be of no account. For the world is created: celibacy is also created. Let both give thanks for their appointed state, if they know to what state they are appointed. But others have kicked over the traces and waxed wanton, having become indeed "wild horses who whinny after their neighbour's wives" (Jer. 5:8). They have abandoned themselves to lust without restraint and persuade their neighbours to live licentiously; as wretches they follow the Scripture: "Cast your lot in with us; let us all have a common purse and let our moneybag be one" (Prov. 1:14).

THE GNOSTICS' GOSPEL OF MARY

The Coptic *Gospel of Mary* is a Gnostic writing of an undetermined sect composed probably in the second century. In the first part of the gospel,[19] the risen Christ instructs his disciples. After his departure, they remain perplexed as to his intention for their future activities; Mary Magdalene (a favorite character in Gnostic literature) comforts them and shares with them the private revelations given her by Jesus. Some of the male disciples, especially Peter,[20] refuse to believe that Jesus gave such revelations to a woman rather than to them. The disciple Levi mediates the dispute, and the disciples depart to undertake their religious missions. Thus the worth of a woman is vindicated; a female has instructed male associates, much as some Gnostic women presumably preached to and taught men. Evidence for women's role in church leadership remains scanty—although not nonexistent—in early orthodox Christianity, but is much fuller in such spiritualistic sects as the Quakers, Shakers, and Christian Scientists many centuries later.

THE GOSPEL OF MARY*

The Saviour said, "Sin as such does not exist, but you make sin when you do what is of the nature of fornication, which is called 'sin.' For this reason the Good came into your midst, to the essence of each nature, to restore it to its root." He went on to say, "For this reason you come into existence and die (...) whoever knows may know (...) a suffering which has nothing like itself, which has arisen out of what is contrary to nature. Then there arises a disturbance in the whole body. For this reason I said to you, Be of good courage (cf. Matt. 28:9), and if you are discouraged, still take courage over against the various forms of nature. He who has ears to hear, let him hear." When the Blessed One had said this, he greeted all of them, saying "Peace be with you (cf. John 14:27). Receive my peace for yourselves. Take heed lest anyone lead you astray with the words, 'Lo, here!' or 'Lo, there!' (cf. Matt. 24:5, 23; Luke 17:21) for the Son of Man is within you (cf. Luke 17:21). Follow him; those who seek him will find him (cf. Matt. 7:7). Go, therefore, and

* From *The Gospel of Mary*, in *Gnosticism: A Sourcebook of Heretical Writings from the Early Christian Period*, ed. Robert M. Grant (New York: Harper & Bros., 1961), 65–68.

34

preach the Gospel of the Kingdom (cf. Matt. 4:23; 9:15; Mark 16:15). I have left no commandment but what I have commanded you, and I have given you no law, as the law-giver did, lest you be bound by it."

When he had said this, he went away. But they were grieved and mourned greatly, saying, "How shall we go to the Gentiles and preach the Gospel of the Kingdom of the Son of Man? If even he was not spared, how shall we be spared?"

Then Mary stood up and greeted all of them and said to her brethren, "Do not mourn or grieve or be irresolute, for his grace will be with you all and will defend you. Let us rather praise his greatness, for he prepared us and made us into men." When Mary said this, their hearts changed for the better, and they began to discuss the words of the (Saviour).

Peter said to Mary, "Sister, we know that the Saviour loved you more than other women (cf. John 11:5, Luke 10:38–42). Tell us the words of the Saviour which you have in mind since you know them; and we do not, nor have we heard them."

Mary answered and said, "What is hidden from you I will impart to you." And she began to say the following words to them. "I," she said, "I saw the Lord in a vision and I said to him, 'Lord, I saw you today in a vision.' He answered and said to me, 'Blessed are you, since you did not waver at the sight of me. For where the mind is, there is your countenance' (cf. Matt. 6:21). I said to him, 'Lord, the mind which sees the vision, does it see it through the soul or through the spirit?' The Saviour answered and said, 'It sees neither through the soul nor through the spirit, but the mind, which is between the two, which sees the vision, and it is . . .'"

[At this point, pages 11–14 of the papyrus are lost.]

". . . and Desire said, 'I did not see you descend; but now I see you rising. Why do you speak falsely, when you belong to me?' The soul answered and said, 'I saw you, but you did not see me or recognise me; I served you as a garment and you did not recognise me.' After it had said this, it went joyfully and gladly away. Again it came to the third power, Ignorance. This power questioned the soul: 'Whither are you going? You were bound in wickedness, you were bound indeed. Judge not' (cf. Matt. 7:1). And the soul said, 'Why do you judge me, when I judged not? I was bound, though I did not bind. I was not recognised, but I recognised that all will go free, things both earthly and heavenly.' After the soul had left the third power behind, it rose upward, and saw the fourth power, which had seven forms. The first form is darkness, the second desire, the third ignorance, the fourth the arousing of death, the fifth is the kingdom of the flesh, the sixth is the wisdom of the folly of the flesh, the seventh is wrathful (?) wisdom. These are the seven participants in wrath. They ask the soul, 'Whence do you come, killer of men, or where are you going, conqueror of space?' The soul answered and said, 'What seizes me is killed; what turns me about is overcome; my desire has come to an end and ignorance is dead. In a world I was saved from a world, and in a "type," from a higher "type" and from the fetter of the impotence of knowledge, the existence of which is temporal. From this time I will reach rest in the time of the moment of the Aeon in silence.'"

When Mary had said this, she was silent, since the Saviour had spoken thus far with her. But Andrew answered and said to the brethren, "Say what you think concerning what she said. For I do not believe that the Saviour said this. For certainly these teachings are of other ideas."

Peter also opposed her in regard to these matters and asked them about the Saviour. "Did he then speak secretly with a woman (cf. John 4:27), in preference to us, and not openly? Are we to turn back and all listen to her? Did he prefer her to us?"

Then Mary grieved and said to Peter, "My brother Peter, what do you think? Do you think I thought this up myself in my heart or that I am lying concerning the Saviour?"

Levi answered and said to Peter, "Peter, you are always irate. Now I see that you are contending against the woman like the adversaries. But if the Saviour made her worthy, who are you to reject her? Surely the Saviour knew her very well (cf. Luke 10:38–42). For this reason he loved her more than us (cf. John 11:5). And we should rather be ashamed and put on the Perfect Man, to form us (?) as he commanded us, and proclaim the gospel, without publishing a further commandment or a further law than the one which the Saviour spoke." When Levi had said this, they began to go out in order to proclaim him and preach him.

～ Jerome: The Exaltation of Christian Virginity

Jerome (c. 342–420) was one of the foremost advocates and practitioners of the celibate life in fourth-century Christianity.[1] Jerome moved to Rome in the year 382 where he served as secretary and adviser to Pope Damasus until 386. Upon Damasus's death, Jerome fell out of favor with many Roman Christians and left Rome for Palestine. Known as the most learned Christian interpreter and translator of Scripture in his day, Jerome was a staunch advocate of ascetic renunciation.

THE ASCETIC MOVEMENT

Two reasons are sometimes advanced for the burgeoning popularity of ascetic practice in the period after the emperor Constantine's conversion to Christianity in 312. One explanation notes that before the fourth century, some Christians had been able to demonstrate their extraordinary devotion by giving themselves as martyrs; once the persecutions ended and the Roman empire became nominally Christian under Constantine, this means of displaying loyalty to Christianity ended. A second argument notes that when Christianity became a legally protected religion, many flocked to the church who were of less than heroic fiber. How, under these circumstances, could some Christians show their superior commitment? Asceticism became a popular way to manifest one's ardent devotion to Christianity. Although scholars do not agree on why early Christian theology and practice developed a strong ascetic bent, they acknowledge the power that asceticism exerted in the first centuries of the religion.

As the fourth century progressed, thousands of men and women chose lives of renunciation in the hope of transcending the frailty of human nature and coming closer to God. Jerome himself spent two or three years in the desert near Antioch.[2] Nonetheless, he tells one of his numerous correspondents that despite his deprivations, he could never reach the height of Christian perfection since he had already forfeited the crown of virginity in his youth.[3] And he reports that even when as a hermit he denied his body physical comforts, he was still plagued with visions of dancing girls.[4] Jerome spent his mature years as the head of a monastery for men in Bethlehem, where he died in the year 420.

JEROME AND WOMEN

In his writings, Jerome frequently sounds extremely misogynist. Indeed, he incorporated the pagan antifeminist tradition derived from such authors as Juvenal and Horace into his own literary productions.[5] Both of the selections we have included here reveal this bias. "To Eustochium," in fact, has been called "the greatest slander of women since Juvenal's sixth satire,"[6] while Jerome's treatise *Against Jovinian* has been cited as influential on the misogynist strain in literary traditions of the Middle Ages.[7]

Although Jerome often wrote disparagingly of women in general, he was extremely supportive of those who accepted his ascetic tutelage. While he resided at Rome in the early 380s, he acquired a circle of wealthy Roman women among his devotees.[8] To these women he taught Scripture—even organizing Hebrew classes[9]—and encouraged their adoption of celibacy; two of them followed him to Bethlehem and set up a convent near the monastery he established there for men. How to reconcile Jerome's personal devotion to and friendships with women and the misogynist tone of his satiric writings remains a puzzle.[10]

Eustochium, whom he addresses in our first selection, was the teenage daughter of his favorite Roman woman friend and patron, Paula. While still an adolescent, Eustochium decided to embrace the "virgin's profession"; Jerome wrote at length commending her resolution to do so. He tells Eustochium that she is the first highborn Roman Christian woman to devote herself to virginity. He stresses how fortunate she is to be escaping the trials of marriage—which he paints in the blackest of colors—and to be winning the love of the heavenly bridegroom, Jesus. (Jerome does not hesitate to use overtly sexual metaphors derived from the Song of Songs to describe Eustochium's relationship with Jesus.)[11] Virginity will give her a foretaste of the angelic afterlife as well as a means of recapturing the innocence of Eden before the Fall. Although the virginal life is rigorous, Jerome is confident that Eustochium will succeed if she follows his advice, which includes shunning the "sham" virgins who not only associated with men but who were (according to Jerome) sometimes found to be pregnant by their supposedly "spiritual brothers."[12]

JEROME AND ASCETICISM

Our second selection is taken from Jerome's *Against Jovinian,* a treatise repudiating the theories of a former monk who had, in about 390, argued against an excessive exaltation of virginity that he deemed quasi-heretical. Jovinian argued against Jerome that a virgin was no better than a wife in the eyes of God nor would she receive a higher reward after death, basing his opinion on the belief that baptism makes all Christians equal before God. Jovinian marshaled much scriptural evidence to demonstrate that marriage was commended in the sacred writings. When Jerome undertook to answer Jovinian's arguments, he was surprised to discover that the Roman public considered parts of *Against Jovinian* offensive, even shocking; Jerome later had to defend his intentions in writing the treatise.[13] He had clearly underestimated the extent to which Roman Christians supported traditional views of marriage. Despite his claim that he held a more favorable view of marriage than some other Christian writers,[14] and his effort to dissociate himself from the opinions of "heretics" who denigrated marriage, he did not succeed in persuading his Roman audience. Certainly Jerome's inclusion in *Against Jovinian* of a long section of the biting and misogynist treatise *On Marriage,* which he attributes to the earlier Aristotelian writer Theophrastus, did not help his defense.[15]

THE PERPETUAL VIRGINITY OF MARY

As part of his pro-virginity campaign, Jerome championed the notion of the perpetual virginity of Mary, the mother of Jesus, devoting a whole treatise *(Against Helvidius)* to this subject. Helvidius, a Roman layman, had argued that although Mary was a virgin at the time of Jesus' conception, she did not remain one afterward—a view espoused by many Protestant writers of later centuries. Helvidius drew his evidence from the wording of the birth stories, which implies that Joseph and Mary engaged in sexual relations after Jesus' birth, as well as from the biblical passages mentioning Jesus' brothers and sisters. Jerome applied his talents as an exegete to the task of interpreting the passages Helvidius had singled out so that Mary was instead represented as devoted to the ideal of lifelong virginity; thus he asserts that the brothers and sisters of Jesus were actually cousins or other relatives.[16] Jerome was so eager to advance the cause of virginity that he also depicted Joseph as a devotee of lifelong celibacy.[17]

Jerome's treatise on Mary's virginity was part of a rising interest at the end of the fourth century in the notion of the virgin birth and in Mary.[18] In 649, a Lateran Council declared the perpetual virginity of Mary to be a doctrine of the Catholic church. Catholicism's devotion to Mary and to virginity has continued through the ages, as is evidenced in several of the selections that follow.[19]

LETTER TWENTY-TWO ("TO EUSTOCHIUM")*

...I am writing this to you, Lady Eustochium (I am bound to call my Lord's bride "Lady"), that from the very beginning of my discourse you may learn that I do not today intend to sing the praises of the virginity which you have adopted and proved to be so good. Nor shall I now reckon up the disadvantages of marriage, such as pregnancy, a crying baby, the tortures of jealousy, the cares of household management, and the cutting short by death of all its fancied blessings. Married women have their due allotted place, if they live in honourable marriage and keep their bed undefiled. My purpose in this letter is to show you that you are fleeing from Sodom and that you should take warning by Lot's wife. There is no flattery in these pages. A flatterer is a smooth-spoken enemy. Nor will there be any pomp of rhetoric in expounding the beatitude of virginity, setting you among the angels and putting the world beneath your feet....

---

* From Jerome, Letter Twenty-Two, "To Eustochium: The Virgin's Profession," *Select Letters of St. Jerome,* trans. F. A. Wright (Cambridge, Mass.: Harvard University Press, Loeb Classical Library, 1933), 57, 67–69, 75–77, 79–83, 91–93, 94, 95, 99–101, 109.

Oh, how often, when I was living in the desert, in that lonely waste, scorched by the burning sun, which affords to hermits a savage dwelling-place, how often did I fancy myself surrounded by the pleasures of Rome! I used to sit alone; for I was filled with bitterness. My unkempt limbs were covered in shapeless sackcloth; my skin through long neglect had become as rough and black as an Ethiopian's. Tears and groans were every day my portion; and if sleep ever overcame my resistance and fell upon my eyes, I bruised my restless bones against the naked earth. Of food and drink I will not speak. Hermits have nothing but cold water even when they are sick, and for them it is sinful luxury to partake of cooked dishes. But though in my fear of hell I had condemned myself to this prison-house, where my only companions were scorpions and wild beasts, I often found myself surrounded by bands of dancing girls. My face was pale with fasting; but though my limbs were cold as ice my mind was burning with desire, and the fires of lust kept bubbling up before me when my flesh was as good as dead.

And so, when all other help failed me, I used to fling myself at Jesus' feet; I watered them with my tears, I wiped them with my hair; and if my flesh still rebelled I subdued it by weeks of fasting. I do not blush to confess my misery; nay, rather, I lament that I am not now what once I was. I remember that often I joined night to day with my wailings and ceased not from beating my breast till tranquillity returned to me at the Lord's behest. I used to dread my poor cell as though it knew my secret thoughts. Filled with stiff anger against myself, I would make my way alone into the desert; and when I came upon some hollow valley or rough mountain or precipitous cliff, there I would set up my oratory, and make that spot a place of torture for my unhappy flesh. There sometimes also—the Lord Himself is my witness—after many a tear and straining of my eyes to heaven, I felt myself in the presence of the angelic hosts and in joy and gladness would sing: "Because of the savour of thy good ointments we will run after thee" (Song of Sol. 1:3).

If such are the temptations of men whose bodies are emaciated with fasting so that they have only evil thoughts to withstand, how must it fare with a girl who clings to the enjoyment of luxuries?. . .

You may choose perhaps to answer that a girl of good family like yourself, accustomed to luxury and down pillows, cannot do without wine and tasty food and would find a stricter rule of life impossible. To that I can only say: "Live then by your own rule, since you cannot live by God's." Not that God, the Lord and Creator of the universe, takes any delight in the rumbling of our intestines or the emptiness of our stomach or the inflammation of our lungs; but because this is the only way of preserving chastity. . . .

It wearies me to tell how many virgins fall daily, what notabilities Mother Church loses from her bosom: over how many stars the proud enemy sets his throne, how many hollow rocks the serpent pierces and makes his habitation. You may see many women who have been left widows before they were ever wed, trying to conceal their consciousness of guilt by means of a lying garb. Unless they are betrayed by a swelling womb or by the crying of their little ones they walk abroad with tripping feet and lifted head. Some even ensure barrenness by the help of potions, murdering human beings before they are fully conceived. Others, when they find that they are with child as the result of their sin, practise abortion with drugs, and so frequently bring about their own death, taking with them to the lower world the guilt of three crimes: suicide, adultery against Christ, and child murder. Yet these are the women who will say: "To the pure all things are pure. My conscience is enough for me. A pure heart is what God craves. Why should I refrain from the food which God made for enjoyment?" When they wish to appear bright and merry, they drench themselves with wine, and then joining profanity to drunkenness they cry: "Heaven forbid that I should abstain from the blood of Christ." When they see a woman with a pale sad face, they call her "a miserable Manichaean": and quite logically too, for on their principles fasting is heresy. As they walk the streets they try to attract attention and with stealthy nods and winks draw after them troops of young men. Of them the prophet's words are true: "Thou hast a whore's forehead: thou refusest to be ashamed" (Jer. 3:3). Let them have only a little purple in their dress, and loose bandeau on their head to leave the hair free; cheap slippers, and a Maforte fluttering from their shoulders; sleeves fitting close to their arms, and a loose-kneed walk: there you have all their marks of virginity. Such women may have their admirers, and it may cost more to ruin them because they are called virgins. But to such virgins as these I prefer to be displeasing.

There is another scandal of which I blush to speak; yet, though sad, it is true. From what source has this plague of "dearly beloved sisters" found its way into the Church? Whence come these unwedded wives, these new types of concubines, nay, I will go further, these one-man harlots? They live in the same house with their male-friend; they occupy the same room and often even the same bed; and yet they call us suspicious if we think that anything is wrong. A brother leaves his virgin sister; a virgin, scorning her unmarried brother, seeks a stranger to take his place. Both alike pretend to have but one object: they are seeking spiritual consolation among strangers: but their real aim is to indulge at home in carnal intercourse. About such folk as these Solomon in Proverbs speaks the scornful words: "Can a man take fire in his bosom and his clothes not be burned? Can one go upon hot coals and not burn his feet?" (Prov. 6:27)

Let us therefore drive off and expel from our company such women as only wish to seem and not to be virgins: Now I would direct all my words to you who, inasmuch as you have been at the beginning the first virgin of high rank at Rome, will now have to labour the more diligently so as not to lose your present and your future happiness. As for the troubles of wedded life and the uncertainties of marriage, you know of them by an example in your own family. Your sister Blesilla, superior to you in age but inferior in firmness of will, has become a widow seven months after taking a husband. How luckless is our mortal state, how ignorant of the future! She has lost both the crown of virginity and the pleasures of wedlock. Although the widowed state ranks as the second degree of chastity, can you not imagine the crosses which every moment she must bear, seeing in her sister daily that which she herself has lost? It is harder for her than for you to forgo the delights that she once knew, and yet she receives a less reward for her present continence. Still, she too may rejoice and be not afraid. The fruit that is an hundredfold and that which is sixtyfold both spring from one seed, the seed of chastity. . . .

Some one may say: "Do you dare to disparage wedlock, a state which God has blessed?" It is not disparaging wedlock to prefer virginity. No one can make a comparison between two things, if one is good and the other evil. Let married women take their pride in coming next after virgins. "Be fruitful," God said, "and multiply and replenish the earth" (Gen. 1:28). Let him then be fruitful and multiply who intends to replenish the earth: but your company is in heaven. The command to increase and multiply is fulfilled after the expulsion from Paradise, after the recognition of nakedness, after the putting on of the fig leaves which augured the approach of marital desire. Let them marry and be given in marriage who eat their bread in the sweat of their brow, whose land brings forth thorns and thistles, and whose crops are choked with brambles. My seed produces fruit a hundredfold.

. . . Eve in Paradise was a virgin: it was only after she put on a garment of skins that her married life began. Paradise is your home. Keep therefore as you were born, and say: "Return unto thy rest, O my soul" (Ps. 116:7). . . .

I praise wedlock, I praise marriage; but it is because they produce me virgins. I gather the rose from the thorn, the gold from the earth, the pearl from the oyster. Shall the ploughman plough all day? Shall he not also enjoy the fruit of his labour? Wedlock is the more honoured when the fruit of wedlock is the more loved. Why, mother, grudge your daughter her virginity? She has been reared on your milk, she has come from your body, she has grown strong in your arms. Your watchful love has kept her safe. Are you vexed with her because she chooses to wed not a soldier but a King? She has rendered you a high service: from to-day you are the mother by marriage of God. . . .

In the old days, as I have said, the virtue of continence was confined to men, and Eve continually bore children in travail. But now that a virgin has conceived in the womb a child, upon whose shoulders is government, a mighty God, Father of the age to come, the fetters of the old curse are broken. Death came through Eve: life has come through Mary. For this reason the gift of virginity has been poured most abundantly upon women, seeing that it was from a woman it began. As soon as the Son of God set foot on earth, He formed for Himself a new household, that as He was adored by angels in heaven He might have angels also on earth. . . .

Let the seclusion of your own chamber ever guard you; ever let the Bridegroom sport with you within. If you pray, you are speaking to your Spouse: if you read, He is speaking to you. When sleep falls on you, He will come behind the wall and will put His hand through the hole in the door and will touch your flesh. And you will awake and rise up and cry: "I am sick with love" (Song of Sol. 5:8). And you will hear Him answer: "A garden inclosed is my sister, my spouse; a spring shut up, a fountain sealed" (Song of Sol. 4:12). Go not from home nor visit the daughters of a strange land, though you have patriarchs for brothers and rejoice in Israel as your father. Dinah went out and was seduced (Gen. 34:1). I would not have you seek the Bridegroom in the public squares; I would not have you go about the corners of the city. You may say: "I will rise now and go about the city: in the streets and in the broad ways I will seek Him whom my soul loveth" (Song of Sol. 3:2). But though you ask the watchmen: "Saw ye Him whom my soul loveth?" no one will deign to answer you. The Bridegroom cannot be found in the city squares. "Strait and narrow is the way that leadeth unto life" (Matt. 7:14). And the Song goes on: "I sought him but I could not find him: I called him but he gave me no answer."

AGAINST JOVINIAN *

... For ourselves, we do not follow the views of Marcion and Manichaeus, and disparage marriage; nor, deceived by the error of Tatian, the leader of the Encratites, do we think all intercourse impure; he condemns and rejects not only marriage but also food which God created for the use of man. ... We are not ignorant of the words (Heb. 13:4), "Marriage is honourable among all, and the bed undefiled." We have read God's first command (Gen. 1:28), "Be fruitful, and multiply, and replenish the earth"; but while we honour marriage we prefer virginity which is the offspring of marriage. Will silver cease to be silver, if gold is more precious than silver? Or is despite done to tree and corn, if we prefer the fruit to root and foliage, or the grain to stalk and ear? Virginity is to marriage what fruit is to the tree, or grain to the straw. Although the hundred-fold, the sixty-fold, and the thirty-fold spring

---

* From Jerome, *Against Jovinian*, in *St. Jerome: Letters and Select Works, Nicene and Post-Nicene Fathers*, 2nd ser., vol. 6, ed. Philip Schaff (New York: Christian Literature Co., 1893), 347–48, 371–72, 373–74, 383–84.

from one earth and from one sowing, yet there is a great difference in respect of number. The thirty-fold has reference to marriage. . . . The sixty-fold applies to widows, because they are placed in a position of difficulty and distress. . . . [And the hundred-fold applies to virgins.]. . .

He [Jovinian] says that "virgins, widows, and married women, who have been once passed through the laver of Christ, if they are on a par in other respects, are of equal merit.". . .

. . . I entreat virgins of both sexes and all such as are continent, the married also and the twice married, to assist my efforts with their prayers. Jovinian is the common enemy. For he who maintains all to be of equal merit, does no less injury to virginity in comparing it with marriage than he does to marriage, when he allows it to be lawful, but to the same extent as second and third marriages. But to digamists and trigamists also he does wrong, for he places on a level with them whoremongers and the most licentious persons as soon as they have repented; but perhaps those who have been married twice or thrice ought not to complain, for the same whoremonger if penitent is made equal in the kingdom of heaven even to virgins. . . .

First of all, he says, God declares that (Gen. 2:24), "therefore shall a man leave his father and his mother, and shall cleave unto his wife: and they shall be one flesh." And lest we should say that this is a quotation from the Old Testament, he asserts that it has been confirmed by the Lord in the Gospel (Matt. 19:5)—"What God hath joined together, let not man put asunder": and he immediately adds (Gen. 1:28; 9:1), "Be fruitful, and multiply, and replenish the earth." He next repeats the names of Seth, Enos, Cainan, Mahalalel, Jared, Enoch, Methuselah, Lamech, Noah, and tells us that they all had wives and in accordance with the will of God begot sons, as though there could be any table of descent or any history of mankind without wives and children. . . .

[Jovinian here lists numerous Old Testament and New Testament characters who were married yet favored by God. Jerome acknowledges these cases, but cites examples of biblical virgins, widows, and widowers. Jovinian then takes up the issue of married clergy, to which Jerome responds.]

All that goes for nothing, says Jovinianus, because even bishops, priests, and deacons, husbands of one wife, and having children, were appointed by the Apostle. Just as the Apostle (1 Cor. 7:25) says he has no commandment respecting virgins, and yet gives his advice, as one who had obtained mercy from the Lord, and is anxious throughout the whole discussion to give virginity the preference over marriage, and advises what he does not venture to command, lest he seem to lay a snare, and to put a heavier burden upon man's nature than it can bear; so also in establishing the constitution of the Church, inasmuch as the elements of the early Church were drawn from the Gentiles, he made the rules for fresh believers somewhat lighter that they might not in alarm shrink from keeping them. . . . For he does not say: Let a bishop be chosen who marries one wife and begets children; but who marries one wife, and (1 Tim. 3:2–4, Titus 1:6) has his children in subjection and well disciplined. You surely admit that he is no bishop who during his episcopate begets children. The reverse is the case—if he be discovered, he will not be bound by the ordinary obligations of a husband, but will be condemned as an adulterer. Either permit priests to perform the work of marriage with the result that virginity and marriage are on a par: or if it is unlawful for priests to touch their wives, they are so far holy in that they imitate virgin chastity. But something more follows. A layman, or any believer, cannot pray unless he abstain from sexual intercourse. Now a priest must always offer sacrifices for the people: he must therefore always pray. And if he must always pray, he must always be released from the duties of marriage. For even under the old law they who used to offer sacrifices for the people not only remained in their houses, but purified themselves for the occasion by separating from their wives, nor would they drink wine or strong drink which are wont to stimulate lust. That married men are elected to the priesthood, I do not deny: the number of virgins is not so great as that of the priests required. Does it follow that because all the strongest men are chosen for the army, weaker men should not be taken as well? All cannot be strong. If an army were constituted of strength only, and numbers went for nothing, the feebler men might be rejected. As it is, men of second- or third-rate strength are chosen, that the army may have its full numerical complement. How is it, then, you will say, that frequently at the ordination of priests a virgin is passed over, and a married man taken? Perhaps because he lacks other qualifications in keeping with virginity, or it may be that he is thought a virgin, and is not: or there may be a stigma on his virginity, or at all events virginity itself makes him proud, and while he plumes himself on mere bodily chastity, he neglects other virtues; he does not cherish the poor: he is too fond of money. It sometimes happens that a man has a gloomy visage, a frowning brow, a walk as though he were in a solemn procession, and so offends the people, who, because they have no fault to find with his life, hate his mere dress and gait. Many are chosen not out of affection for themselves, but out of hatred for another. In most cases the election is won by mere simplicity, while the shrewdness and discretion of another candidate elicit opposition as though they were evils. Sometimes the judgement of the commoner people is at fault, and in testing the qualities of the priesthood, the individual inclines to his own character, with the result that he looks not so much for a good candidate as for one like himself. Not unfrequently it happens that married men, who form the larger portion of the people, in approving married candidates seem to approve themselves, and it does not occur to them that the mere fact that they prefer a married person to a virgin is evidence of their inferiority to virgins. What I am going to say will perhaps offend many. Yet I will say it, and good men will not be angry with me, because they will not feel the sting of conscience. Sometimes it is the fault of the bishops, who choose into the ranks of the clergy not the best, but the cleverest, men, and think the more simple as well as innocent ones incapable: or, as though they were distributing the offices of an earthly service, they give posts to their kindred and relations; or they listen to the dictates of wealth. And, worse than all, they give promotion to the clergy who besmear them with flattery. . . .

But you will say: "If everybody were a virgin, what would become of the human race?" Like shall here beget like. If everyone were a widow, or continent in marriage, how will mortal men be propagated? . . . You are afraid that if the desire for virginity were general there would be no prostitutes, no adulteresses, no wailing infants in town or country. Every day the blood of adulterers is shed, adulterers are condemned, and lust is raging and rampant in the very presence of the laws and the symbols of authority and the courts of justice. Be not afraid that all will become virgins: virginity is a hard matter, and therefore rare, because it is hard: "Many are called, few chosen." Many begin, few persevere. And so the reward is great for those who have persevered. If all were able to be virgins, our Lord would never have said (Matt. 19:12): "He that is able to receive it, let him receive it," and the Apostle would not have hesitated to give his advice (1 Cor. 7:25),—"Now concerning virgins I have no commandment of the Lord." Why then, you will say, were the organs of generation created, and why were we so fashioned by the all-wise creator, that we burn for one another, and long for natural intercourse? . . . Are we never then to forego lust, for fear that we may have members of this kind for nothing? Why then should a husband keep himself from his wife? Why should a widow persevere in chastity, if we were only born to live like beasts? Or what harm does it do me if another man lies with my wife? For as the teeth were made for chewing, and the food masticated passes into the stomach, and a man is not blamed for giving my wife bread: similarly if it was intended that the organs of generation should always be performing their office, when my vigour is spent let another take my place, and, if I may so speak, let my wife quench her burning lust where she can. But what does the Apostle mean by exhorting to continence, if continence be contrary to nature? What does our Lord mean when He instructs us in the various kinds of eunuchs? (Matt. 19:12) Surely (1 Cor. 7:7) the Apostle who bids us emulate his own chastity, must be asked, if we are to be consistent, Why are you like other men, Paul? Why are you distinguished from the female sex by a beard, hair, and other peculiarities of person? How is it that you have not swelling bosoms, and are not broad at the hips, narrow at the chest? Your voice is rugged, your speech rough, your eyebrows more shaggy. To no purpose you have all these manly qualities, if you forego the embraces of women. I am compelled to say something and become a fool: but you have forced me to dare to speak. Our Lord and Savior (Phil. 2:6–8), Who though He was in the form of God, condescended to take the form of a servant, and became obedient to the Father even unto death, yea the death of the cross—what necessity was there for Him to be born with members which He was not going to use? He certainly was circumcised to manifest His sex. Why did he cause John the Apostle and John the Baptist to make themselves eunuchs through love of Him, after causing them to be born men? Let us then who believe in Christ follow His example. And if we knew Him after the flesh, let us no longer know Him according to the flesh. The substance of our resurrection bodies will certainly be the same as now, though of higher glory. For the Saviour after His descent into hell had so far the selfsame body in which He was crucified, that (John 20:20) He showed the disciples the marks of the nails in His hands and the wound in His side. Moreover, if we deny the identity of His body because (John 20:19) He entered though the doors were shut, and this is not a property of human bodies, we must deny also that Peter and the Lord had real bodies because they (Matt. 14:28) walked upon the water, which is contrary to nature. "In the resurrection of the dead they will neither marry nor be given in marriage, but will be like the angels" (Matt. 22:30). What others will hereafter be in heaven, that virgins begin to be on earth. If likeness to the angels is promised us (and there is no difference of sex among the angels), we shall either be of no sex as are the angels, or at all events, which is clearly proved, though we rise from the dead in our own sex, we shall not perform the functions of sex. . . .

. . . A book *On Marriage,* worth its weight in gold, passes under the name of Theophrastus. In it the author asks whether a wise man marries. And after laying down the conditions—that the wife must be fair, of good character, and honest parentage, the husband in good health and of ample means, and after saying that under these circumstances, a wise man sometimes enters the state of matrimony, he immediately proceeds thus: "But all these conditions are seldom satisfied in marriage. A wise man therefore must not take a wife. For in the first place his study of philosophy will be hindered, and it is impossible for anyone to attend to his books and his wife. Matrons want many things, costly dresses, gold, jewels, great outlay, maid-servants, all kinds of furniture, litters and gilded coaches. Then come curtain-lectures the livelong night: she complains that one lady goes out better dressed than she: that another is looked up to by all: 'I am a poor despised nobody at the ladies' assemblies.' 'Why did you ogle that creature next door?' 'Why were you talking to the maid?' 'What did you bring from the market?' 'I am not

allowed to have a single friend, or companion.' She suspects
that her husband's love goes the same way as her hate. There
may be in some neighbouring city the wisest of teachers; but
if we have a wife we can neither leave her behind, nor take
the burden with us. To support a poor wife, is hard: to put
up with a rich one, is torture. Notice, too, that in the case of
a wife you cannot pick and choose: you must take her as you
find her. If she has a bad temper, or is a fool, if she has a
blemish, or is proud, or has bad breath, whatever her fault
may be—all this we learn after marriage. Horses, asses, cattle, even slaves of the smallest worth, clothes, kettles,
wooden seats, cups, and earthenware pitchers, are first tried
and then bought: a wife is the only thing that is not shown
before she is married, for fear she may not give satisfaction.
Our gaze must always be directed to her face, and we must
always praise her beauty: if you look at another woman, she
thinks that she is out of favour. . . . If a woman be fair, she
soon finds lovers; if she be ugly, it is easy to be wanton. It is
difficult to guard what many long for. It is annoying to have
what no one thinks worth possessing. But the misery of having an ugly wife is less than that of watching a comely one.
Nothing is safe, for which a whole people sighs and longs.
One man entices with his figure, another with his brains, another with his wit, another with his open hand. Somehow, or
sometime, the fortress is captured which is attacked on all
sides. Men marry, indeed, so as to get a manager for the
house, to solace weariness, to banish solitude; but a faithful
slave is a far better manager, more submissive to the master,
more observant of his ways, than a wife who thinks she
proves herself mistress if she acts in opposition to her husband, that is, if she does what pleases her, not what she is
commanded. But friends, and servants who are under the
obligation of benefits received, are better able to wait upon
us in sickness than a wife who makes us responsible for her
tears (she will sell you enough to make a deluge for the hope

of a legacy); who boasts of her anxiety, yet drives her sick husband to the distraction of despair. But if she herself is poorly, we must fall sick with her and never leave her bed-side. Or if she be a good and agreeable wife (how rare a bird she is!), we have to share her groans in childbirth, and suffer torture when she is in danger. . . . Then again, to marry for the sake of children, so that our name may not perish, or that we may have support in old age, and leave our property without dispute, is the height of stupidity. For what is it to us when we are leaving the world if another bears our name, when even a son does not all at once take his father's title, and there are countless others who are called by the same name. Or what support in old age is he whom you bring up, and who may die before you, or turn out a reprobate? Or at all events when he reaches mature age, you may seem to him long in dying. Friends and relatives whom you can judi-ciously love are better and safer heirs than those whom you must make your heirs whether you like it or not. Indeed, the surest way of having a good heir is to ruin your fortune in a good cause while you live, not to leave the fruit of your labour to be used you know not how."

4.

∾ Augustine: Sinfulness and Sexuality

AUGUSTINE'S LIFE AND RELIGIOUS CONTROVERSIES

Augustine's writings on marriage and sexuality, more than those of any other church father, contributed to the development of later Roman Catholic theory regarding those topics; his words are quoted with as much approval by twentieth-century popes as they were by medieval theologians. Unlike many churchmen of the early Christian era, Augustine (354–430) had engaged in a long sexual relationship in his youth, fathering a son by a nameless concubine while he himself was still an adolescent in the 370s.[1] He became convinced that the renunciation of sexual life was essential for his own espousal of Christianity; his *Confessions* reveal how enormously difficult this decision was for him.[2] About Augustine's concubine, who was cast off when his mother decided that he should embark on a respectable married career,[3] we are told little. About his mother, Monica, on the other hand, who worried much about her son's prospects in life, we hear a great deal. Augustine reports that Monica believed that a proper wife should serve her husband.[4] Far from countering her view, Augustine admired his mother's willing acceptance of a humble female role and remarked that her patient submissiveness had served her well, for she, unlike her more assertive friends, had escaped being beaten by her husband.[5]

Many of Augustine's most important ideas on sexuality were developed in reaction to opposing religious movements. For nine years in his youth, Augustine belonged to the Manichaean sect,[6] a movement that had originated in third-century Persia and had spread to North Africa in the fourth century. Manichaean ethical teaching opposed procreation: bringing new humans into the world only further dispersed the "sparks of light" that had become entangled with matter as a result of the defeat of Light by Darkness in a primeval battle. Although the higher rank of the Manichaeans, the "Elect," apparently avoided sexual intercourse altogether, the "Auditors" of the lower level, to which Augustine belonged, married and engaged in sexual relations, but tried to ensure that these would be nonprocreative through the use of contraceptive measures. In his adult writings against the Manichaeans, Augustine formulated "an ethic which bound intercourse to procreation and found marital procreation good."[7] Augustine's view that procreation was the chief justification for sexual relations thus stemmed in part from his rejection of Manichaean sexual theory and practice. On the other hand, Augustine did not stress the joys of family life, as did later Protestant Reformers. In the *Confessions,* he asserts that marriage inhibits the contemplation, study, and friendships that men might be able to enjoy together if they were left unencumbered by women.[8]

A second religious movement that Augustine confronted was Pelagianism.[9] As part of their defense of God's justice in his dealings with humans, Pelagius and his followers emphasized humans' capacity to will and do the good. Those Christians who complained that they were morally too weak to keep God's commandments were enjoined to summon up their willpower and try harder. Pelagius thought that rational adults were responsible for their own sins; neither Adam, Eve, nor the devil could be blamed for our wrongdoing. Infants did not enter the world in a state of sin, but were "blank slates" awaiting moral development. Pelagius did not think that child baptism eradicated sinfulness, although he believed that it initiated the infant into the Christian community.[10]

In opposition to Pelagius, Augustine elaborated the doctrine of original sin. Although Adam and Eve had been created with free will and in Eden had possessed the ability to keep from sinning, once they erred they lost the ability to choose the good. Moreover, they implicated not just themselves but all their descendants in sin, two central effects of which were death and lust. Augustine thought that through the sacraments, especially baptism, the worst effects of original sin are mitigated, but the body remains resistant to rational control while we are on this earth; only in heaven will true perfection be attained. There the blessed saints will be granted God's prerogative, the inability to sin.[11]

Augustine's opponents argued that the theory of original sin implied a condemnation of sexuality and marriage. Although Augustine was careful not to say that there was a "biological" transfer of the parents' sinfulness to the child, the suggestion nonetheless remained that the sexual act was necessarily tainted, if the child so conceived was born under the influence of original sin. Earlier, Paul in his Epistle to the Romans had written about the sin of Adam and the disobedience of the members of our bodies, but it lay with Augustine to make a firm connection between the transmission of original sin and sexual intercourse.[12]

AUGUSTINE'S VIEWS ON MARRIAGE

Despite Augustine's view that the sex act was tainted by lust, he set himself up as the *defender* of marriage against such contemporaries as Jerome. In fact, Augustine reports that he felt impelled to write about marriage and sexuality since no one (that is, not even Jerome) had given a satisfactory answer to Jovinian.[13] Augustine thought that Jerome had presented too negative a view of marriage, one out of keeping with the Christian faith. Also unlike Jerome, Augustine did not belittle or mock women. He shared the common views of his day regarding women's inferiority to men,[14] but he did not stress the evils of women as a justification for the celibate life. Virginity he indeed held to be higher than marriage, but marriage had its own "goods," including a "bond" that held the partners together until death. Even the sex act itself would have been part of the innocent life in Eden had Adam and Eve not sinned—although intercourse would not have involved lust.[15] Yet Augustine's view of the "ideal" sexual relation in Eden does not suggest a notion of women that would be compatible with modern sentiments. Rosemary Radford Ruether has called Augustine's picture of Eve "depersonalized" and "unfeeling"; the woman for Augustine becomes virtually a "baby-making machine."[16] And despite the fact that Augustine can refer to Eve as Adam's "companion," he himself (unlike Jerome) seems not to have sustained friendships with women.[17]

Augustine's attitudes on sexuality and marriage became a central part of the teaching of the Catholic church. The notion that sexual relations are best engaged in for the sake of procreation alone and that children are the first "good" of marriage became commonplaces of Catholic teaching. Augustine's words on contraception and abortion became central to all later Christian debates on these topics,[18] while his understanding of what was "natural" in sexual relations contributed to the church's rejection of any sexual practice that by definition did not involve the possibility of conception, such as oral or anal intercourse.[19]

Because of limitations of space, selections from *The City of God* are not included in this volume. For readings illustrative of Augustine's views on humans' original righteousness, the entrance of sin into the world, and the relation of both to sexuality, see *The City of God,* Book 13, Chapters 3 and 13, and Book 14, Chapters 16, 18, 21–24, and 26.

ON MARRIAGE AND CONCUPISCENCE*

Book 1, Chap. 5 no. 4. *The natural good of marriage. All society naturally repudiates a fraudulent companion. What is true conjugal purity? No true virginity and chastity, except in devotion to true Faith.*

The union, then, of male and female for the purpose of procreation is the natural good of marriage. But he makes a bad use of this good who uses it bestially, so that his intention is on the gratification of lust, instead of the desire of offspring. Nevertheless, in sundry animals unendowed with reason, as, for instance, in most birds, there is both preserved a certain kind of confederation of pairs, and a social combination of skill in nest-building; and their mutual division of the periods for cherishing their eggs and their alternation in the labor of feeding their young, give them the appearance of so acting, when they mate, as to be intent rather on securing the continuance of their kind than on gratifying lust. Of these two, the one is the likeness of man in a brute; the other, the likeness of the brute in man. With respect, however, to what I ascribed to the nature of marriage, that the male and the female are united together as associates for procreation, and consequently do not defraud each other (forasmuch as every associated state has a natural abhorrence of a fraudulent companion), although even men without faith possess this palpable blessing of nature, yet, since

---

* From Augustine, *On Marriage and Concupiscence,* in *Augustine: Anti-Pelagian Writings, Nicene and Post-Nicene Fathers,* 1st ser., vol. 5, ed. Philip Schaff (New York: Christian Literature Society, 1893), 265–66, 270–71, 297.

they use it not in faith, they only turn it to evil and sin. In like manner, therefore, the marriage of believers converts to the use of righteousness that carnal concupiscence by which "the flesh lusteth against the Spirit" (Gal. 5:17). For they entertain the firm purpose of generating offspring to be regenerated—that the children who are born of them as "children of the world" may be born again and become "sons of God." Wherefore all parents who do not beget children with this intention, this will, this purpose, of transferring them from being members of the first man into being members of Christ, but boast as unbelieving parents over unbelieving children,—however circumspect they be in their cohabitation, studiously limiting it to the begetting of children,—really have no conjugal chastity in themselves. For inasmuch as chastity is a virtue, having unchastity as its contrary vice, and as all the virtues (even those whose operation is by means of the body) have their seat in the soul, how can the body be in any true sense said to be chaste, when the soul itself is committing fornication against the true God? Now such fornication the holy psalmist censures when he says: "For, lo, they that are far from Thee shall perish: Thou hast destroyed all them that go a whoring from Thee" (Ps. 73:27). There is, then, no true chastity, whether conjugal, or vidual, or virginal, except that which devotes itself to true faith. For though consecrated virginity is rightly preferred to marriage, yet what Christian in his sober mind would not prefer catholic Christian women who have been even more than once married, to not only vestals, but also to heretical virgins? So great is the avail of faith, of which the apostle says, "Whatsoever is not of faith is sin" (Rom. 14:23); and of which it is written in the Epistle to the Hebrews, "Without faith it is impossible to please God" (Heb. 11:6).

Book 1, chap. 16, no. 14. *A certain degree of intemperance is to be tolerated in the case of married persons; the use of mat-*

rimony for the mere pleasure of lust is not without sin, but because of the nuptial relation the sin is venial.

But in the married, as these things are desirable and praiseworthy, so the others are to be tolerated, that no lapse occur into damnable sins; that is, into fornications and adulteries. To escape this evil, even such embraces of husband and wife as have not procreation for their object, but serve an overbearing concupiscence, are permitted, so far as to be within range of forgiveness, though not prescribed by way of commandment (1 Cor. 7:6): and the married pair are enjoined not to defraud one the other, lest Satan should tempt them by reason of their incontinence (1 Cor. 7:5). For thus says the Scripture: "Let the husband render unto the wife her due: and likewise also the wife unto the husband. The wife hath not power of her own body, but the husband: and likewise also the husband hath not power of his own body, but the wife. Defraud ye not one the other; except it be with consent for a time, that ye may have leisure for prayer; and then come together again, that Satan tempt you not for your incontinency. But I speak this by permission, and not of commandment" (1 Cor. 7:3–6). Now in a case where permission must be given, it cannot by any means be contended that there is not some amount of sin. Since, however, the cohabitation for the purpose of procreating children, which must be admitted to be the proper end of marriage, is not sinful, what is it which the apostle allows to be permissible, but that married persons, when they have not the gift of continence, may require one from the other the due of the flesh—and that not from a wish for procreation, but for the pleasure of concupiscence? This gratification incurs not the imputation of guilt on account of marriage, but receives permission on account of marriage. This, therefore, must be reckoned among the praises of matrimony; that, on its own account, it makes pardonable that which does not essentially appertain to itself. For the nuptial embrace, which subserves the demands of concupiscence, is so effected as not to impede the child-bearing, which is the end and aim of marriage.

Book 1, chap. 17, no. 15. *What is sinless in the use of matrimony? What is attended with venial sin, and what with mortal?*

It is, however, one thing for married persons to have intercourse only for the wish to beget children, which is not sinful: it is another thing for them to desire carnal pleasure in cohabitation, but with the spouse only, which involves venial sin. For although propagation of offspring is not the motive of the intercourse, there is still no attempt to prevent such propagation, either by wrong desire or evil appliance. They who resort to these, although called by the name of spouses, are really not such; they retain no vestige of true matrimony, but pretend the honourable designation as a cloak for criminal conduct. Having also proceeded so far, they are betrayed into exposing their children, which are born against their will. They hate to nourish and retain those whom they were afraid they would beget. This infliction of cruelty on their offspring so reluctantly begotten, unmasks the sins which they had practised in darkness, and drags it clearly into the light of day. The open cruelty reproves the concealed sin. Sometimes, indeed, this lustful cruelty, or, if you please, cruel lust, resorts to such extravagant methods as to use poisonous drugs to secure barrenness; or else, if unsuccessful in this, to destroy the conceived seed by some means previous to birth, preferring that its offspring should rather perish than receive vitality; or if it was advancing to life within the womb, should be slain before it was born. Well, if both parties alike are so flagitious, they are not husband and wife; and if such were their character from the beginning, they have not come together by wedlock but by debauchery. But if the two are not alike in such sin, I boldly declare either that the woman is, so to say, the husband's harlot; or the man, the wife's adulterer.

Book 1, chap. 19, no. 17. *Blessings of matrimony.*

In matrimony, however, let these nuptial blessings be the objects of our love—offspring, fidelity, the sacramental bond. Offspring, not that it be born only, but born again; for it is born to punishment unless it be born again to life. Fidelity, not such as even unbelievers observe one towards the other, in their ardent love of the flesh. For what husband, however impious himself, likes an adulterous wife? Or what wife, however impious she be, likes an adulterous husband? This is indeed a natural good in marriage, though a carnal one. But a member of Christ ought to be afraid of adultery, not on account of himself, but of his spouse; and ought to hope to receive from Christ the reward of that fidelity which he shows to his spouse. The sacramental bond, again, which is lost neither by divorce nor by adultery, should be guarded by husband and wife with concord and chastity. For it alone is that which even an unfruitful marriage retains by the law of piety, now that all that hope of fruitfulness is lost for the purpose of which the couple married. Let these nuptial blessings be praised in marriage by him who wishes to extol the nuptial institution. Carnal concupiscence, however, must not be ascribed to marriage: it is only to be tolerated in marriage. It is not a good which comes out of the essence of marriage, but an evil which is the accident of original sin.

Book 2, chap. 35, no. 20. *He answers the arguments of Julianus. What is the natural use of the woman? What is the unnatural use?*

My answer to this challenge is, that not only the children of wedlock, but also those of adultery, are a good work in so far as they are the work of God, by whom they are created: but as concerns original sin, they are all born under condemnation of

the first Adam; not only those who are born in adultery, but
likewise such as are born in wedlock, unless they be regenerated in the second Adam, which is Christ. As to what the
apostle says of the wicked, that "leaving the natural use of
the woman, the men burned in their lust one toward another:
men with men working that which is unseemly" (Rom. 1:27);
he did not speak of the conjugal use, but the "natural use,"
wishing us to understand how it comes to pass that by means
of the members created for the purpose the two sexes can
combine for generation. Thus it follows, that even when a
man unites with a harlot to use these members, the use is
a natural one. It is not, however, commendable, but rather
culpable. But as regards any part of the body which is
not meant for generative purposes, should a man use even
his own wife in it, it is against nature and flagitious. Indeed,
the same apostle had previously (Rom. 1:26) said concerning women: "Even their women did change the natural use
into that which is against nature;" and then concerning
men he added, that they worked that which is unseemly by
leaving the natural use of the woman. Therefore, by the
phrase in question, "the natural use," it is not meant to
praise conjugal connection; but thereby are denoted those
flagitious deeds which are more unclean and criminal than
even men's use of women, which, even if unlawful, is nevertheless natural.

5.

∾ Thomas Aquinas and the Scholastic Woman

Ꜣ

THOMAS AND ARISTOTLE ON WOMEN

Feminist interpreters of medieval theologian Thomas Aquinas (c. 1225–74) note with regret that elements in his theology that *could* have resulted in a different evaluation of womanhood were not developed. For example, Thomas's names for God are abstract and nonsexual (Being Itself, the First Mover, and Pure Act), and such gender-neutral terminology could have contributed to the formulation of a theological system not biased toward "maleness."[1] In addition, Thomas believed that woman, like man, was created directly by God (rather than through the mediation of angels, as other theologians had posited),[2] so that she, too, was in God's "image." When we ask why the more progressive implications of these theological positions did not triumph, we are thrown back on such explanations as Thomas's acceptance of Aristotelian biological theories.[3] Aristotle's works, which had not been known to Western Christians in the early Middle Ages, were translated into Latin in Thomas's era. The combination of Aristotelian biological theory and patristic teaching on women thus formed the intellectual background in which Thomas developed his own views. The historian Eleanor Commo McLaughlin sums up the problem in this way:

> Although the medieval centuries saw some amelioration of the patristic sexual pessimism in admitting a more positive view of Christian marriage, ultimately our medieval commentators deepened the androcentric and antifemale character of the tradition under the influence of a strongly patriarchal Germanic society and with the scientific support of the wholly androcentric Aristotelian biology. Aristotle's intellectualistic definition of human nature combined with the inherited ascetic tradition to further strengthen the limitation of the female human being to the auxiliary and instrumental role of sexual procreation, defining the woman as a misbegotten and wholly subordinate creature, hedged about with fear and loathing as an embodiment of the sensuality that threatens the purity of male mind and spirit. By giving a "scientific" basis to the earlier patristic attitudes, the Middle Ages guaranteed the survival of this antifemale anthropology long after rigorist ascetic attitudes had ceased to dominate Western society.[4]

Nor did Aquinas's life provide much incentive for the development of different views on women. As a younger son born into a large family, Thomas was presented by his parents as an oblate at the Italian monastery of Monte Cassino in 1230, when he was only five years old. Thomas's life span of half a century was taken up with study, teaching, and religious duties mostly among celibate men (he joined the Dominican order in 1244). His direct interactions with women were thus extremely limited. Of his personal life and interests, we know almost nothing.

Thomas's male-centeredness seems to have been influenced by Aristotelian philosophy. Yet while Aristotle had defined the female as a "misbegotten male," the result of a defective conception[5] (perfect humanity was humanity in its male form[6]), Thomas qualified Aristotle's definition in a way that mitigated some of its harshness. As a Christian, Thomas affirmed that God had created woman—and God, for Thomas, was not a Being prone to make mistakes. Rather, God had a specific purpose in making the female: she was to be a useful partner in procreation. Besides, Thomas argued, females are not conceived simply due to a defective male force; a variety of neutral and natural factors, such as the weather, could also determine the conception of a female child, as Aristotle himself had admitted.[7] Perhaps the strongest indication Thomas gives that the production of woman was not an unhappy error is his speculation regarding the reproductive process that would have occurred in Eden had the first couple not sinned: the sex of the fetus would have been determined by the will of the parents, and females, he asserts, would have been born in equal numbers to males.[8] Critics nonetheless point out that Thomas affirmed each woman's *individual* defectiveness, even if she is needed to perpetuate the species.[9] Moreover, Thomas justifies the creation of females on the grounds that even lesser grades of perfection contribute to the completeness of the world.[10] The latter argument—that even defects enlarge the fullness of God's universe—was traditionally used to explain the presence of evil in a world created by an omnipotent and benevolent deity and hence is not much consolation to feminist readers of our era.

In addition, Thomas's use of the Aristotelian categories of form and matter, actuality and potentiality, as they were applied to the concepts of maleness and femaleness, resulted in a further depreciation of women. For Aristotle, form and matter were the two "metaphysical constitutive elements of bodies."[11] Matter was not a particular physical entity but an abstract principle of potentiality, while form was the determining principle that shaped matter, gave it definition. In human beings, for example, the form is the rational soul, the particular characteristic that makes us human. In discussing conception, Aristotle had postulated that the male supplied the form for the process and the female the matter;[12] the matter, contributed by the woman, "lacks soul,"[13] which deficiency is corrected by the male. Thomas accepts Aristotle's analysis but qualifies it in an important way: he claims that it is God alone who is the author of all souls and who infuses them into the developing fetus. The male force "prepares" the matter contributed by the female so that it is ready to accept the soul,[14] but the man himself does not donate the soul that the fetus receives. In Thomas's explanation, men cannot claim that they are the ones who endow their offspring with "humanity." Nonetheless, it is still loftier to be a shaper rather than a mere provider of matter—and for Thomas,[15] as for Aristotle, the woman contributes nothing but the matter. Thomas further asserts that although both men and women were granted rational souls by God, woman's was weakened by being associated with a feeble female body: the soul in a female is often unable to "keep a firm grip on things" and hence sins, due to its relation with female physicality.[16] Women's lowly role in the reproductive process appears even more disparaged when we recall that Thomas explicitly states that conception and birth are the two unique "helps" that wives can give their husbands; for any other tasks, another man would be better suited.[17] Even in the sex act, the husband is assigned the "more noble" function, activity, whereas the wife exhibits the passive receptivity of womanhood.[18]

Woman's fragility of mind and will, Thomas thought, had serious consequences in human history. It was her weakness that led the serpent to approach Eve first and trick her so easily; Adam, more intellectually alert, would at least have been able to spot the temptation. Although the man also was at fault, according to Thomas the woman's sin was greater.[19] Moreover, Thomas attributes woman's subjection to the male to her inferior reasoning. Even before the Fall, Eve was subordinated to Adam, and although she did not yet experience the harsh subjection she would suffer later as a penalty for her sin, she knew the subjugation "whereby the superior makes use of his subjects for their own benefit and good." Order would not have been maintained, Thomas taught, unless some (in this case, women) were destined to be "governed by others wiser than themselves," for in the male, "the discretion of reason predominates."[20] Her lack of wisdom relegates woman to subordinate status.[21]

Woman's weakness and subjection are also the reasons Thomas gives for her exclusion from the priesthood. The problem for him is not merely that the church has forbidden the ordination of women:[22] ordination simply does not "take" if it is performed on a woman, he argues. Even if she were to undergo an ordination ceremony, it would be to no avail; her subjection to the male prevents her from receiving holy orders, for she lacks the "eminence of degree" necessary for ordination. Thomas acknowledges that women past and present have exerted political rulership, but he is not willing to admit them to the priestly care of minds and souls.[23] Likewise, he does not deny that women have received spiritual gifts such as prophecy—in fact, he concedes that some women exhibit spiritual gifts to a greater degree than men, but these endowments do not make them fit candidates for clerical office.[24] Thomas's views have heavily influenced the Catholic church's exclusion of women from the priesthood. And since, in 1879, Pope Leo XIII declared that Thomas Aquinas's teaching was authoritative for Catholic theology, Thomas's words are taken with great seriousness by many contemporary Catholic intellectuals and writers.

To these traditional attitudes, derived in part from the Aristotelian estimate of woman's mental and physical defectiveness, Thomas added androcentric themes from biblical and patristic Christianity. The New Testament contributed metaphors that gave religious sanction to male superiority. Ephesians 5, for example, described the husband-wife relation as analogous to Christ's with the subordinate church. Thomas adopts this image,[25] adding that Eve's creation from Adam's rib was symbolic of the church's derivation from Christ (the water and blood that flowed from his side on the cross represent the church's sacraments).[26] Thomas also used the Genesis 2 story to justify male supremacy: Adam's being made first mirrors God's role as Lord of the universe. Just as God rules over all creation, so Adam heads the whole human race, including Eve.[27]

MARRIAGE AND SEXUALITY

We suspect that the ascetic tone prevalent in early Christian writings also contributed to Thomas's depreciation of women. Since the only irreplaceable function women fulfill is childbearing, and children are the products of sexual intercourse, women's status gets tied to the moral evaluation of the sexual act. Married intercourse, Thomas holds, is not itself evil. Following Augustine, he argues that even if Adam and Eve had remained innocent, sexual intercourse would have taken place in Eden.[28] There would, however, have been several differences had the Fall not occurred. Because of Eve's sin, women must forfeit their virginity and suffer "corruption" in order to engage in intercourse; their bodies are injured and they lose their original condition of wholeness. In Eden, on the other hand, the breaking of the woman's hymen would not have been needed for intercourse to take place.[29] Likewise, there would have been no lust associated with sex.[30]

At this point, however, Thomas takes a step beyond Augustine. Not only would the couple have felt pleasure, asserts Thomas; the pleasure would have been an even greater one because it would have been rational[31]—a view that he may have derived from his teacher, Albertus Magnus, who is credited with more "humane" views of the marital relation than many other medieval theologians.[32] The controlled manner in which Thomas pictures Edenic sex contrasts sharply with the state of affairs in the post-Fall world, in which humans are overcome by sexual desire. Some men, raging with lust, embrace their mates too ardently, sinfully forgetting that they are to be treated as wives, not as "just another woman."[33] Despite his nuanced views on sexual pleasure, Thomas nonetheless writes that in intercourse man "becomes flesh and nothing more."[34] This evaluation contrasts sharply with that of a thinker whom we will consider later in this volume,[35] John Humphrey Noyes, who saw in the "amative function of sex" (the expression of the love relation) its highest meaning.

NATURAL LAW

In another section of the *Summa Theologica* not included in this volume, Thomas sets forth his theory of natural law; it remains to this day the chief philosophical base on which the Vatican grounds its prohibition of contraception. The concept of natural law originated in classical Greek philosophy. In early Christianity, the notion of the "natural" acquired further significance as a moral injunction. God as the creator of nature, it was held, had established certain values and standards for human life; when we contravene them, we defy both our own "natures" and God's will.

Thomas gave a more systematic expression to the concept of natural law. He defined it as humankind's rational participation in God's eternal law.[36] Because humans have been endowed with reason, they can reflect on the various inclinations implanted within them by God and recognize God's purposes for those inclinations.[37] The desire for sexual intercourse, for example, is one that humans share with the animals, but because humans are rational, they can understand that intercourse has as its purpose the birth of offspring.[38] The church has always taught that humans need not be totally governed by "lower" inclinations but can choose to refrain from engaging in sexual relations altogether.[39] If humans decide to marry and engage in sexual relations, however, the couple must allow sexual desire to lead to the goal God intended—conception. Any attempt to thwart this purpose of intercourse is a grave evil. Without doubt, a major reinterpretation of natural law insofar as it relates to sexuality will have to be undertaken before the Vatican modifies its opposition to contraception.[40]

THOMAS'S METHOD

One last note: although Thomas's literary method may strike the reader as strange, even impenetrable, it was a common one in the medieval Scholastic tradition. For each issue, Thomas first raises a question and lists the objections to it. The objections represent both imaginary arguments and, more frequently, positions actually espoused by philosophers and theologians of the past or of Thomas's own day. After the objections, Thomas inserts a (usually brief) section identified as "on the contrary," to indicate to the reader that there *is* another point of view— usually his own. The "I answer that" section is Thomas's own response to the former arguments. Finally, he specifically responds to each objection. Thus, Thomas does not just inform the reader of his own opinions; his immense erudition also makes available to us the variety of approaches medieval thinkers might have taken to various problems.

SUMMA THEOLOGICA*

Part 1, Question 92
The Production of the Woman
(In Four Articles)

We must next consider the production of the woman. Under this head there are four points of inquiry: (1) Whether the woman should have been made in that first production of things? (2) Whether the woman should have been made from man? (3) Whether of man's rib? (4) Whether the woman was made immediately by God?

FIRST ARTICLE
Whether the woman should have been made in the first production of things?

We proceed thus to the First Article:
Objection 1. It would seem that the woman should not have been made in the first production of things. For the

---

* From Thomas Aquinas, *Summa Theologica,* ed. Fathers of the English Dominican Province (London: Burns, Oates and Washbourne, Ltd., 1914), IV: 274–81, 344–54; XIX: 51–53, 156–58.

Philosopher says (*De Gener. Animal.* 2.3), that the *female is a misbegotten male.* But nothing misbegotten or defective should have been in the first production of things. Therefore woman should not have been made at that first production.

Objection 2. Further, subjection and limitation were a result of sin, for to the woman was it said after sin (Gen. 3:16): *Thou shalt be under the man's power;* and Gregory says that, *Where there is no sin, there is no inequality.* But woman is naturally of less strength and dignity than man; *for the agent is always more honourable than the patient,* as Augustine says (*Gen. ad lit.* 12.16). Therefore woman should not have been made in the first production of things before sin.

Objection 3. Further, occasions of sin should be cut off. But God foresaw that the woman would be an occasion of sin to man. Therefore He should not have made woman.

On the contrary, It is written (Gen. 2:18): *It is not good for man to be alone; let us make him a helper like to himself.*

I answer that, It was necessary for woman to be made, as the Scripture says, as *a helper* to man; not, indeed, as a helpmate in other works, as some say, since man can be more efficiently helped by another man in other works; but as a helper in the work of generation. This can be made clear if we observe the mode of generation carried out in various living things. Some living things do not possess in themselves the power of generation, but are generated by some other specific agent, such as some plants and animals by the influence of the heavenly bodies, from some fitting matter and not from seed: others possess the active and passive generative power together; as we see in plants which are generated from seed; for the noblest vital function in plants is generation. Wherefore we observe that in these the active power of generation invariably accompanies the passive power. Among perfect animals the active power of generation belongs to the male sex, and the passive power to the female. And as among animals there is a vital operation nobler than generation, to which their life is principally directed; therefore the male sex is not found in continual union with the female in perfect animals, but only at the time of coition; so that we may consider that by this means the male and female are one, as in plants they are always united; although in some cases one of them preponderates, and in some the other. But man is yet further ordered to a still nobler vital action, and that is intellectual operation. Therefore there was greater reason for the distinction of these two forces in man; so that the female should be produced separately from the male; although they are carnally united for generation. Therefore directly after the formation of woman, it was said: *And they shall be two in one flesh* (Gen. 2:24).

Reply Objection 1. As regards the individual nature, woman is defective and misbegotten, for the active force in the male seed tends to the production of a perfect likeness in the masculine sex; while the production of woman comes from a defect in the active force or from some material indisposition, or even from some external influence; such as that of a south wind, which is moist, as the Philosopher observes (*De Gener. Animal.* 4.2). On the other hand, as regards human nature in general, woman is not misbegotten, but is included in nature's intention as directed to the work of generation. Now the general intention of nature depends on God, Who is the universal Author of nature. Therefore, in producing nature, God formed not only the male but also the female.

Reply Objection 2. Subjection is twofold. One is servile, by virtue of which a superior makes use of a subject for his own benefit; and this kind of subjection began after sin. There is another kind of subjection, which is called economic or civil, whereby the superior makes use of his subjects for their own benefit and good; and this kind of subjection existed even before sin. For good order would have been wanting in the human family if some were not governed by others wiser than themselves. So by such a kind of subjection woman is naturally subject to man, because in man the discretion of reason predominates. Nor is inequality among men excluded by the state of innocence, as we shall prove (Q. 96, A. 3).

Reply Objection 3. If God had deprived the world of all those things which proved an occasion of sin, the universe would have been imperfect. Nor was it fitting for the common good to be destroyed in order that individual evil might be avoided; especially as God is so powerful that He can direct any evil to a good end.

SECOND ARTICLE
Whether woman should have been made from man?

We proceed thus to the Second Article: ...

I answer that, When all things were first formed, it was more suitable for the woman to be made from the man than (for the female to be from the male) in other animals. First, in order thus to give the first man a certain dignity consisting in this, that as God is the principle of the whole universe, so the first man, in likeness to God, was the principle of the whole human race. Wherefore Paul says that *God made the whole human race from one* (Acts 17:26). Secondly, that man might love woman all the more, and cleave to her more closely, knowing her to be fashioned from himself. Hence it is written (Gen. 2:23, 24): *She was taken out of man, wherefore a man shall leave father and mother, and shall cleave to his wife.* This was most necessary as regards the human race, in which the male and female live together for life; which is not the case with other animals. Thirdly, because, as the Philosopher says (*Ethic.* 8.12), the human male and female are united, not only for generation, as with other animals, but also for the purpose of domestic life, in which each has his or her particular duty, and in which the man is the head of the woman. Wherefore it was suitable for the woman to be made out of man, as out of her principle. Fourthly, there is a sacramental reason for this. For by this is signified that the Church takes her origin from Christ. Wherefore the Apostle says (Eph. 5:32): *This is a great sacrament; but I speak in Christ and in the Church.* . . .

THIRD ARTICLE
Whether the woman was fittingly made from the rib of man?

We proceed thus to the Third Article: . . .

I answer that, It was right for the woman to be made from a rib of man. First, to signify the social union of man and woman, for the woman should neither *use authority over man,* and so she was not made from his head; nor was it right for her to be subject to man's contempt as his slave, and so she was not made from his feet. Secondly, for the sacramental signification; for from the side of Christ sleeping on the Cross the Sacraments flowed—namely, blood and water—on which the Church was established. . . .

FOURTH ARTICLE
Whether the woman was formed immediately by God?

We proceed thus to the Fourth Article: . . .

Objection 2. Further, Augustine (*De Trin.* 3.4) says that corporeal things are governed by God through the angels. But the woman's body was formed from corporeal matter. Therefore it was made through the ministry of the angels, and not immediately by God. . . .

I answer that, As was said above (A. 2, *ad* 2), the natural generation of every species is from some determinate matter. Now the matter whence man is naturally begotten is the human semen of man or woman. Wherefore from any other matter an individual of the human species cannot naturally be generated. Now God alone, the Author of nature, can produce an effect into existence outside the ordinary course of nature. Therefore God alone could produce either a man from the slime of the earth, or a woman from the rib of man. . . .

Reply Objection 2. As Augustine says (*Gen. ad lit.* 9.15), we do not know whether the angels were employed by God in the formation of the woman; but it is certain that, as the body of man was not formed by the angels from the slime of the earth, so neither was the body of the woman formed by them from the man's rib.

Part 1, Question 98
Of the Preservation of the Species
(In Two Articles)

We next consider what belongs to the preservation of the species; and, first, of generation; secondly, of the state of the offspring. Under the first head there are two points of inquiry: (1) Whether in the state of innocence there would have been generation? (2) Whether generation would have been through coition?

FIRST ARTICLE
Whether in the state of innocence generation existed?

We proceed thus to the First Article: ...

I answer that, In the state of innocence there would have been generation of offspring for the multiplication of the human race; otherwise man's sin would have been very necessary, for such a great blessing to be its result. We must, therefore, observe that man, by his nature, is established, as it were, midway between corruptible and incorruptible creatures, his soul being naturally incorruptible, while his body is naturally corruptible. We must also observe that nature's purpose appears to be different as regards corruptible and incorruptible things. For that seems to be the direct purpose of nature, which is invariable and perpetual; while what is only for a time is seemingly not the chief purpose of nature, but, as it were, subordinate to something else; otherwise, when it ceased to exist, nature's purpose would become void.

Therefore, since in things corruptible none is everlasting and permanent except the species, it follows that the chief

purpose of nature is the good of the species; for the preservation of which natural generation is ordained. On the other
hand, incorruptible substances survive, not only in the
species, but also in the individual; wherefore even the individuals are included in the chief purpose of nature.

Hence it belongs to man to beget offspring, on the part of
the naturally corruptible body. But on the part of the soul,
which is incorruptible, it is fitting that the multitude of individuals should be the direct purpose of nature, or rather of
the Author of nature, Who alone is the Creator of the human
soul. Wherefore, to provide for the multiplication of the
human race, He established the begetting of offspring even in
the state of innocence. . . .

SECOND ARTICLE
*Whether in the state of innocence there would have been
generation by coition?*

We proceed thus to the Second Article:

Objection 1. It would seem that generation by coition
would not have existed in the state of innocence. For, as
Damascene says (*De Fid. Orth.* 2.2: 4.25), the first man in
the terrestrial Paradise was *like an angel.* But in the future
state of the resurrection, when men will be like to the angels,
they shall neither marry nor be married, as it is written in
Matt. 22:30. Therefore neither in Paradise would there have
been generation by coition.

Objection 2. Further, our first parents were created at the
age of perfect development. Therefore, if generation by
coition had existed before sin, they would have had intercourse while still in Paradise: which was not the case according to Scripture (Gen. 4:1).

Objection 3. Further, in carnal intercourse, more than at
any other time, man becomes like the beasts, on account of
the vehement delight which he takes therein; whence conti-
nency is praiseworthy, whereby man refrains from such pleasures. But man is compared to beasts by reason of sin,

according to Psalm 48:13: *Man, when he was in honour, did not understand; he is compared to senseless beasts, and is become like to them.* Therefore, before sin, there would have been no such intercourse of man and woman.

Objection 4. Further, in the state of innocence there would have been no corruption. But virginal integrity is corrupted by intercourse. Therefore there would have been no such thing in the state of innocence.

On the contrary, God made man and woman before sin (Gen. 1 and 2). But nothing is void in God's works. Therefore, even if man had not sinned, there would have been such intercourse, to which the distinction of sex is ordained. Moreover, we are told that woman was made to be a help to man (Gen. 2:18, 20). But she was not fitted to help man except in generation, because another man would have proved a more effective help in anything else. Therefore there would have been such generation also in the state of innocence.

I answer that, Some of the earlier doctors, considering the nature of concupiscence as regards generation in our present state, concluded that in the state of innocence generation would not have been effected in the same way. Thus Gregory of Nyssa says (*De Hom. Opif.* 17) that in Paradise the human race would have been multiplied by some other means, as the angels were multiplied without coition by the operation of the Divine Power. He adds that God made man male and female before sin, because He foreknew the mode of generation which would take place after sin, which He foresaw. But this is unreasonable. For what is natural to man was neither acquired nor forfeited by sin. Now it is clear that generation by coition is natural to man by reason of his animal life, which he possessed even before sin, as above explained (Q. 97, A. 3), just as it is natural to other perfect animals, as the corporeal members make it clear. So we cannot allow that these members would not have had a natural use, as other members had, before sin.

Thus, as regards generation by coition, there are, in the present state of life, two things to be considered. One, which comes from nature, is the union of man and woman; for in every act of generation there is an active and a passive principle. Wherefore, since wherever there is distinction of sex, the active principle is male and the passive is female; the order of nature demands that for the purpose of generation there should be concurrence of male and female. The second thing to be observed is a certain deformity of excessive concupiscence, which in the state of innocence would not have existed, when the lower powers were entirely subject to reason. Wherefore Augustine says (*De Civ. Dei* 14.26): *We must be far from supposing that offspring could not be begotten without concupiscence. All the bodily members would have been equally moved by the will, without ardent or wanton incentive, with calmness of soul and body.*

Reply Objection 1. In Paradise man would have been like an angel in his spirituality of mind, yet with an animal life in his body. After the resurrection man will be like an angel, spiritualized in soul and body. Wherefore there is no parallel.

Reply Objection 2. As Augustine says (*Gen. ad lit.* 9.4), our first parents did not come together in Paradise, because on account of sin they were ejected from Paradise shortly after the creation of the woman; or because, having received the general Divine command relative to generation, they awaited the special command relative to the time.

Reply Objection 3. Beasts are without reason. In this way man becomes, as it were, like them in coition, because he cannot moderate concupiscence. In the state of innocence nothing of this kind would have happened that was not regulated by reason, not because delight of sense was less, as some say (rather indeed would sensible delight have been the greater in proportion to the greater purity of nature and the greater sensibility of the body), but because the force of concupiscence would not have so inordinately thrown itself into such pleasure, being curbed by reason, whose place it is not to lessen sensual pleasure, but to prevent the force of concupiscence from cleaving to it immoderately. By *immoderately* I mean going beyond the bounds of reason, as a sober person does not take less pleasure in food taken in moderation than the glutton, but his concupiscence lingers less in such pleasures. This is what Augustine means by the words quoted, which do not exclude intensity of pleasure from the state of innocence, but the ardour of desire and restlessness of the mind. Therefore continence would not have been praiseworthy in the state of innocence, whereas it is praiseworthy in our present state, not because it removes fecundity, but because it excludes inordinate desire. In that state fecundity would have been without lust.

Reply Objection 4. As Augustine says (*De Civ. Dei* 14.26): In that state *intercourse would have been without prejudice to virginal integrity; this would have remained intact, as it does in the menses. And just as in giving birth the mother was then relieved, not by groans of pain, but by the instigations of maturity; so in conceiving, the union was one, not of lustful desire, but of deliberate action. . . .*

Part 1, Question 99
Of the Condition of the Offspring as to Body

SECOND ARTICLE
Whether, in the primitive state, women would have been born?

We proceed thus to the Second Article:

Objection 1. It would seem that in the primitive state woman would not have been born. For the Philosopher says (*De Gener. Animal.* 2.3) that woman is a *misbegotten male,* as though she were a product outside the purpose of nature: But in that state nothing would have been unnatural in human generation. Therefore in that state women would not have been born.

Objection 2. Further, every agent produces its like, unless prevented by insufficient power or ineptness of matter; thus a small fire cannot burn green wood. But in generation the active force is in the male. Since, therefore, in the state of innocence man's active force was not subject to defect, nor was there inept matter on the part of the woman, it seems that males would always have been born.

Objection 3. Further, in the state of innocence generation is ordered to the multiplication of the human race. But the race would have been sufficiently multiplied by the first man and woman, from the fact that they would have lived for ever. Therefore, in the state of innocence, there was no need for woman to be born.

On the contrary, nature's process in generation would have been in harmony with the manner in which it was established by God. But God established male and female in human nature, as it is written (Gen. 1 and 2). Therefore also in the state of innocence male and female would have been born.

I answer that, Nothing belonging to the completeness of human nature would have been lacking in the state of innocence. And as different grades belong to the perfection of the universe, so also diversity of sex belongs to the perfection of human nature. Therefore in the state of innocence, both sexes would have been begotten.

Reply Objection 1. Woman is said to be a *misbegotten male,* as being a product outside the purpose of nature considered in the individual case: but not against the purpose of universal nature, as above explained (Q. 92, A. 1, *ad* 2).

Reply Objection 2. The generation of woman is not occasioned either by a defect of the active force or by inept matter, as the objection supposes; but sometimes by an extrinsic accidental cause; thus the Philosopher says (*De Animal. Histor.* 6.19): *The northern wind favours the generation of males, and the southern wind that of females:* sometimes also by some impression in the soul (of the parents) which may easily have some effect on the body (of the child). Especially was this the case in the state of innocence, when the body was more subject to the soul; so that by the mere will of the parent the sex of the offspring might be diversified.

Reply Objection 3. The offspring would have been begotten to an animal life, as to the use of food and generation. Hence it was fitting that all should generate, and not only the first parents. From this it seems to follow that males and females would have been in equal number.

Part 3 Supplement, Question 39
Of the Impediments to This Sacrament
(In Six Articles)

FIRST ARTICLE
Whether the female sex is an impediment to receiving Orders?

We proceed thus to the First Article:

Objection 1. It would seem that the female sex is no impediment to receiving Orders. For the office of prophet is greater than the office of priest, since a prophet stands midway between God and priests, just as the priest does between God and people. Now the office of prophet was sometimes granted to women, as may be gathered from 2 Kings 22:14. Therefore the office of priest also may be competent to them.

Objection 2. Further, Just as Order pertains to a kind of pre-eminence, so does a position of authority as well as martyrdom and the religious state. Now authority is entrusted to women in the New Testament, as in the case of abbesses, and in the Old Testament, as in the case of Debbora, who judged Israel (Judg. 2). Moreover martyrdom and the religious life are also befitting to them. Therefore the Orders of the Church are also competent to them.

Objection 3. Further, The power of Orders is founded in the soul. But sex is not in the soul. Therefore difference in sex makes no difference to the reception of Orders.

On the contrary, It is said (1 Tim. 2:12): *I suffer not a woman to teach (in the Church),** nor to use authority over the man.*

Further, The crown is required previous to receiving Orders, albeit not for the validity of the sacrament. But the crown or tonsure is not befitting to women according to 1 Corinthians 11. Neither therefore is the receiving of Orders.

I answer that, Certain things are required in the recipient of a sacrament as being requisite for the validity of the sacrament, and if such things be lacking, one can receive neither the sacrament nor the reality of the sacrament. Other things, however, are required, not for the validity of the sacrament, but for its lawfulness, as being congruous to the sacrament; and without these one receives the sacrament, but not the reality of the sacrament. Accordingly we must say that the male sex is required for receiving Orders not only in the second, but also in the first way. Wherefore even though a woman were made the object of all that is done in conferring Orders, she would not receive Orders, for since a sacrament is a sign, not only the thing, but the signification of the thing, is required in all sacramental action; thus it was stated above (Q. 32, A. 2) that in Extreme Unction it is necessary to have a sick man, in order to signify the need of healing. Accordingly, since it is not possible in the female sex to signify eminence of degree, for a woman is in the state of subjection, it follows that she cannot receive the sacrament of Order. Some, however, have asserted that the male sex is necessary for the lawfulness and not for the validity of the sacrament, because even in the Decretals (cap. *Mulieres,* dist. 32; ca. *Diaconissam,* 27, qu. 1)** mention is made of deaconesses and

---

* The words in parentheses are from 1 Corinthians 14:34, *Let women keep silence in the churches.*

** Gratian's *Decretals* is a twelfth-century collection of church law.

priestesses. But *deaconess* there denotes a woman who shares in some act of a deacon, namely who reads the homilies in the Church; and *priestess (presbytera)* means a widow, for the word *presbyter* means elder.

Reply Objection 1. Prophecy is not a sacrament but a gift of God. Wherefore there it is not the signification, but only the thing which is necessary. And since in matters pertaining to the soul woman does not differ from man as to the thing (for sometimes a woman is found to be better than many men as regards the soul), it follows that she can receive the gift of prophecy and the like, but not the sacrament of Orders.

And thereby appears the *Reply* to the *Second* and *Third Objections.* However, as to abbesses, it is said that they have not ordinary authority, but delegated as it were, on account of the danger of men and women living together. But Debbora exercised authority in temporal not in priestly matters, even as now woman may have temporal power.

Part 3 Supplement, Question 49
Of the Marriage Goods

SIXTH ARTICLE
Whether it is a mortal sin for a man to have knowledge of his wife, with the intention not of a marriage good but merely of pleasure?

We proceed thus to the Sixth Article:

Objection 1. It would seem that whenever a man has knowledge of his wife, with the intention not of a marriage good but merely of pleasure, he commits a mortal sin. For according to Jerome (*Comment in* Eph. 5:25), as quoted in the text (4. *Sent.* D.31), *the pleasure taken in the embraces of a wanton is damnable in a husband.* Now nothing but mortal sin is said to be damnable. Therefore it is always a mortal sin to have knowledge of one's wife for mere pleasure.

Objection 2. Further, Consent to pleasure is a mortal sin, as stated in the Second Book (2 *Sent.* D.24). Now whoever knows his wife for the sake of pleasure consents to the pleasure. Therefore he sins mortally.

Objection 3. Further, Whoever fails to refer the use of a creature to God enjoys a creature, and this is a mortal sin. But whoever uses his wife for mere pleasure does not refer that use to God. Therefore he sins mortally.

Objection 4. Further, No one should be excommunicated except for a mortal sin. Now according to the text *(loc. cit.)* a man who knows his wife for mere pleasure is debarred from entering the Church, as though he were excommunicated. Therefore every such man sins mortally.

On the contrary, As stated in the text *(loc. cit.),* according to Augustine (*Contra Jul.* 2.10; *De Decem Chord.* 11; *Serm.* 41., *de Sanct.*), carnal intercourse of this kind is one of the daily sins, for which we say the *Our Father.* Now these are not mortal sins. Therefore, etc.

Further, It is no mortal sin to take food for mere pleasure. Therefore in like manner it is not a mortal sin for a man to use his wife merely to satisfy his desire.

I answer that, Some say that whenever pleasure is the chief motive for the marriage act it is a mortal sin; that when it is an indirect motive it is a venial sin; and that when it spurns the pleasure altogether and is displeasing, it is wholly void of venial sin; so that it would be a mortal sin to seek pleasure in this act, a venial sin to take the pleasure when offered, but that perfection requires one to detest it. But this is impossible, since according to the Philosopher (*Ethic.* 10.3, 4) the same judgment applies to pleasure as to action, because pleasure in a good action is good, and in an evil action, evil; wherefore, as the marriage act is not evil in itself, neither will it be always a mortal sin to seek pleasure therein. Consequently the right answer to this question is that if pleasure be sought in such a way as to exclude the honesty of marriage, so that, to wit, it is not as a wife but as a woman that a man treats his wife, and that he is ready to use her in the same way if she were not his wife, it is a mortal sin; wherefore such a man is said to be too ardent a lover of his wife, because his ardour carries him away from the goods of marriage, so that it would not be sought in another than his wife, it is a venial sin.

Reply Objection 1. A man seeks wanton pleasure in his wife when he sees no more in her than he would in a wanton.

Reply Objection 2. Consent to the pleasure of the intercourse that is a mortal sin is itself a mortal sin; but such is not the consent to the marriage act.

Reply Objection 3. Although he does not actually refer the pleasure to God, he does not place his will's last end therein; otherwise he would seek it anywhere indifferently. Hence it does not follow that he enjoys a creature; but he uses a creature actually for his own sake, and himself habitually, though not actually, for God's sake.

Reply Objection 4. The reason for this statement is not that man deserves to be excommunicated for this sin, but because he renders himself unfit for spiritual things, since in that act he becomes flesh and nothing more.

6.

⌁ Women Religious
of the Middle Ages

THE HISTORIOGRAPHY OF
WOMEN IN THE MIDDLE AGES

This chapter is notable since it is the first in which we offer selections from books and letters that women themselves have written. During recent decades, the proliferation of scholarship on medieval women has greatly increased our knowledge of them as workers, as mothers and wives, and as brokers of power within (and occasionally outside of) the family. Our expanded knowledge derives in part from the historiographical swing away from models of history writing that concentrate on public events and offices, military ventures, and the growth of nationhood (all areas in which women had diminished roles as agents) to more socially oriented models.[1] Fortunately for our purposes, one of the topics pertaining to medieval women that has received a good deal of attention is that of women religious.[2]

The results of this expanded scholarship, however, have not borne out the hypothesis cherished by earlier generations of historians that the Middle Ages were a "high" period for women. Concentrating on literary evidence pertaining to courtly love and to the developing cult of the Virgin Mary, earlier scholars often posited that women in the "real" world of the Middle Ages were similarly exalted. By contrast, medievalists now soberly note the limitations on women and their activities in this era. In historian Barbara Hanawalt's words, recent research "has diminished enthusiastic searches for a medieval El Dorado."[3]

WOMEN IN RELIGIOUS LIFE

Among the questions that have caught the imaginations of both past and present scholars, however, is why so many medieval women wished to enter religious life. Was there a surplus of females in medieval society that resulted in unmarried—and unmarriageable—females being siphoned off to monasteries?[4] Feminist historians tend to react against this view: nunneries should not be seen as "holding tanks."[5] As the selections included in this chapter make clear, numerous medieval women actively chose religious life as preferable to marriage, even when husbands were in ready supply. In addition to freedom from marriage, nunneries offered women some limited degree of autonomy and a chance for education that would likely have been denied them in the world outside the monastery.

Recent scholarship on medieval women's religious options focuses on particular geographical areas and subperiods. Thus, female monasticism in Frankish society flourished in the sixth century but declined under the Carolingians—a "golden age" for intellectual male religious, but not for women.[6] By the ninth century, nunneries had often lost their earlier auras of sanctity and served as refuges for the old and outcast or were used by princesses and queens as a source of income. In twelfth-century England, on the other hand, there was a great expansion of religious opportunities for women (about 120 new communities for women religious were founded in England during the twelfth century alone), but monasteries for English women declined in the fourteenth century and beyond.[7] In medieval France, male monastics in the late twelfth and thirteenth centuries tried to suppress, compress, and absorb monastic houses for women so as to rid themselves of the responsibility of supervising and caring for nuns, while the wider church at the same time tried to limit nuns' participation in public ceremonies. All evidence suggests that medieval French nuns lived in noticeably greater poverty than did their male counterparts.[8] Thus, women's monasticism in various areas flourished and declined in different centuries.

Most historians agree that with the tighter cloistering of women religious in the High Middle Ages, their opportunities and activities were curtailed; cloistering had been instituted during the early medieval period of invasions as a protective device for nuns, but it gradually became a practice that limited their activities. Moreover, the increased clericalization of the church from the late eleventh century onward, with its strong emphasis on sexual chastity, meant that all women—even nuns—were seen increasingly as threats to men's power and purity. A distinctive sign of this trend was the gradual abandonment of an arrangement often called "double monasteries," in which male and female monastics lived in proximity, both groups sometimes governed by the abbess. With the demise of double monasteries, religious women were denied contact with their male counterparts and found that the "privileges and responsibilities which the abbess and her nuns had previously assumed were removed to the authority of the bishop or abbot."[9] In addition, Jane Tibbetts Schulenburg, studying monastic developments in Britain and France from 500–1100 A.D., has discovered that less than 10 percent of the monastic houses founded in this period were for women;[10] male religious appear to have outnumbered female religious by a wide margin.

The waxing and waning of nuns' fortunes also varied among different religious orders. The Premonstratensian order, for example, reached out to accept women's houses in the twelfth century, but their zeal for the task had diminished completely by the thirteenth—whereas the Cistercians, who had earlier refused to take in women's houses, in the thirteenth century began to accept them at a great rate.[11] Dominicans and Franciscans, in

Germany at least, were hospitable to the inclusion of women's houses: of the fifty-eight Dominican cloisters for women that we know existed in the late thirteenth century, forty were in Germany.[12] Benedictines, on the other hand, had minimal provisions for accepting female monastics and, by the twelfth and thirteenth centuries, not only numbered far fewer houses for women than for men but their women's houses were not deemed strict enough by women dedicated to a rigorously ascetic life. Even for the wealthy, who could afford to pay the sometimes steep entrance fees, there was a shortage of nunneries and spaces within them.[13] In England, both the founding of the Gilbertine order and the Premonstratensians' opening of three new houses in the twelfth century expanded the monastic options for women religious.[14]

ALTERNATIVES TO THE CONVENT

By the twelfth century, in light of the hostility women sometimes faced from male monastics, the impediments they encountered in finding a suitable convent, and the expense of entering it,[15] alternative forms of ascetic living became popular among women. Women (such as Angela of Foligno, whose writings appear here) might attach themselves to convents without taking formal vows; others, such as Margery Kempe, remained married yet tried to practice intense religious devotion. Yet another choice, increasingly prevalent by the late eleventh century, was to adopt the life of an anchorite, or recluse. Female renunciants in towns and cities might be literally walled up against the side of a church in a cramped cell with small openings facing into the church (so that they could see the mass and receive the Eucharist) and facing the outside (so that they could speak with those seeking spiritual advice). If a woman could enlist a monastery or a church to provide minimal food for her, she could adopt an anchoritic way of life, which was thought to imitate that of the early desert fathers. Although a mass for the dead was sometimes said when an anchoress was enclosed, she nonetheless was able to speak to those who sought her holy instruction and counsel.[16]

One famous early female anchorite was the twelfth-century Christina of Markyate, whose struggles to escape marriage and sexual involvement provide lively reading; her mother is reported to have said that she didn't care who deflowered her recalcitrant daughter, just so she *got* deflowered! Befriended by abbots and male recluses, Christina became famous for her solitary confinement—although in the 1140s, considerably before her death, she became head of a nunnery that was established on the spot where she once had been a recluse.[17] In this volume, the anchorite tradition is represented by selections from Julian of Norwich.

Another alternative to the enclosed life of the convent was provided by the Beguines, who were not cloistered and did not take monastic vows. These women banded together especially in the urban centers of the Low Countries, northern France, and the Rhineland. Sharing a house, they often earned their own money by manual labor in the cloth industry, giving as much as they could to charity. As the number of Beguines grew, they came to be recognized by the church in the thirteenth century as a semiofficial organization, although this recognition brought with it increased supervision and restriction by church authorities. Along with the fame they accrued for their simple living and their poverty, the Beguines were also known for their great devotion to Christ's physical presence in the Eucharist.[18] Their freer style of life, however, attracted suspicion, and Beguines sometimes found themselves accused of heresy, a charge they shared with other groups who were committed to apostolic poverty and who entrusted themselves to the Holy Spirit's—rather than the church hierarchy's—guidance.[19] Before the church moved to curtail them, the Beguines provided a popular alternative to the cloister: it is reported that in their heyday, from the midthirteenth to the midfourteenth century, Frankfurt am Main had as many as fifty-seven Beguinages, and Strasbourg claimed sixty.[20]

ACTIVITIES OF WOMEN RELIGIOUS

Just as there were multiple forms of pious existence for medieval women religious, so their lives and activities exhibit considerable diversity. Some early medieval women religious functioned effectively as missionaries, as did Lioba, an eighth-century Anglo-Saxon nun who went to missionize Germany at the request of Boniface.[21] With the gradual enclosure of women religious, however, such a life of traveling and exposure to the "outside" world would be deemed highly dangerous. As the cloistering of nuns became more restrictive, their power and fame came to derive increasingly from their ascetic practices and mystic visions. The ascetic discipline that they inflicted on themselves was for them a sign of their penitence and their desire to share the suffering of Jesus, with whom they felt united as "brides." Especially prominent among the nuns' ascetic practices was extreme fasting—so severe that in recent years it has been compared to the modern phenomenon of anorexia.[22] Rigorous fasting appears to have been more characteristic of women's piety than of men's, and some women religious were reported to live on nothing but the Eucharist.[23]

Yet the mystic's very pain (as Laurie Finke has argued) was what gave her "the authority to speak and be heard, to have followers, to act as a spiritual advisor, to heal the sick, and to found convents and hospitals."[24] Inasmuch as such nuns usually claimed to have special revelations from and visions of God or Jesus—and were believed—they enjoyed an authority that was more "public" than we might assume.[25] Their unmediated relation with the divine suggests that they were not so likely to be controlled by priests and bishops.

Women religious became famous in their own times and later through writings (either penned by them or dictated to scribes) that recorded their mystical visions and spiritual experiences. In addition to the large number of writings now designated as "mystical,"[26] women such as Hildegard of Bingen (1098–1179)

wrote on a wide variety of topics. According to one of Hildegard's most recent commentators, Barbara Newman, she composed "three major theological works, a scientific and medical
encyclopedia, a liturgical song cycle, two saints' lives, the first
European morality play, and a vast correspondence."[27] So extensive was Hildegard's literary production and her range of interests that Peter Dronke, in his book *Women Writers of the
Middle Ages,* compares her to the polymath Islamic philosopher
and scientist of the Middle Ages, Avicenna.[28] A few centuries
after Hildegard, universities were established throughout Europe
to provide higher education for men; the fact that, with only the
rarest of exceptions, their doors remained closed to women underscores the importance of the monastery as a center for female
education.

THE MEDIEVAL CULT
OF THE VIRGIN MARY

In this chapter, we will offer some selections from four religious
women of the Middle Ages: Angela of Foligno, Julian of Norwich, Catherine of Siena, and Margery Kempe. But even a brief
introduction such as this would be incomplete without a few
words on the developing cult of the Virgin Mary in the Middle
Ages. From the time that the Lateran Council of 649 had pronounced as dogma that Mary was to be revered as a perpetual
virgin, Mary's fortunes rose steadily in the medieval church. Devotion to Mary was a theme in which all strata of society could
take religious interest, from highly educated ecclesiastical authors to ordinary working men and women. Morality plays re-
counting stories of the conception and birth of Jesus were a
popular form of entertainment centering on Mary.[29] Even as male
monastics were calling Jesus their "Mother,"[30] Mary was represented as an intercessor with God for penitents and was given
the title "Mediatrix" ("female Mediator"). The "Hail Mary"
prayer is thought to date from the middle of the eleventh century.[31] Since no Gospel traditions detailed Mary's death or bur-

ial place, speculation arose early that she had been assumed bodily into heaven—a view that was pronounced to be a dogma of the Catholic church in 1950. Likewise, learned theologians debated whether Mary had been sinless from the time of her conception—that is, that no original sin had been transmitted to her, a teaching declared true dogma for all Catholics in 1854.[32] It was believed that Mary spoke directly from heaven to some women religious of the Middle Ages, such as Birgitta of Sweden, who claimed to receive instructions for the behavior of friars and how they should reply to heretics.[33] Through such claims to revelation, medieval women religious could develop an authoritative voice.

ANGELA OF FOLIGNO

Angela of Foligno (an Italian town near Assisi) lived from around 1248 to 1309. In her youth, she married and had children—only to see her entire family die. Grateful to be freed from familial obligations that had posed obstacles to her renunciation, Angela sought a more intense ascetic life and became a Franciscan tertiary, a layperson who attached herself to a Franciscan convent without taking the formal vows of a nun. She lived thereafter as a recluse. Her *Book* consists of two main works: a *Memorial* that details her spiritual journey, especially the stages of her penitence (that is, the "steps" she describes), and a set of *Instructions,* her spiritual teaching and advice. The fact that twenty-eight manuscripts of her work remain suggests that her writings were quite widely read and copied.[34]

Angela was one of the first medieval mystics to depict in graphic terms her marriage to Christ. In her visions, she experienced herself as drinking the blood that flowed from the wounds of Christ; as part of her penitential devotion, she drank the water with which she had washed a leper's sores. Like Margery Kempe after her, Angela's outbursts of screaming annoyed some, who suspected that she was possessed by a demon rather than overcome with love of Jesus.[35]

MEMORIAL *

Once I was back home, I felt so peaceful and was so filled with divine sweetness that I find no words to express my experience; and there was also in me a desire to die. The thought that I had to go on living was a great burden because of that inexpressible sweetness, quiet, peace, and delight which I felt; and because I wanted to attain the source of this experience and not lose it—that is why I wanted to leave this world. The thought of continuing to live was a greater burden for me to bear than the pain and sorrow I had felt over the death of my mother and my sons, and beyond any pain that I could imagine. I lay at home enthralled by this great consolation and in a state of languor for eight days. And my soul cried out: "Lord, take pity on me and do not allow me to remain any longer in this world." On the road going to Assisi, he had predicted that I would experience this delectable and indescribable consolation in these terms: "Once back in your home, you will feel a sweetness different from any you have ever experienced. And I will not speak to you then as I have until now; but you will feel me." True enough I did feel this sweet and ineffable consolation in which I felt so peaceful and quiet that I cannot find words to describe it. I lay in bed for eight days hardly able to speak, say the Our Father, or get up to move around. He had also told me on the road to Assisi: "I was with the apostles many times, and they saw me with their bodily eyes but they did not feel what you feel. You do not see me but you feel me."

I realized at this point that this experience was coming to an end, for he began to withdraw from me and he did so very gently while telling me: "My daughter, you are sweeter to me

---

* From Angela of Foligno, *Complete Works*, trans. Paul Lachance, preface by Romana Guarnieri (New York/Mahwah: Paulist Press, 1993), 142–44, 125–26, 182, 128, 162–63, 126–27, 131.

than I am to you." And he repeated what he had already said: "My temple, my delight." At these words I realized that he did not want me to be lying down while he was leaving so I stood up. He then said to me: "You are holding the ring of my love. From now on you are engaged to me and you will never leave me. May the blessing of the Father, the Son, and the Holy Spirit be upon you and your companion." He said this at the moment of departure because I had asked him for a special grace for my companion.[36] In response to this request he simply said: "The grace I will give to your companion will be a different one from yours." I must add that when he said: "You shall never leave me again," my soul cried out: "Oh, that I may never sin mortally." To this he replied: "These are your words, not mine."

Thereafter, I often smelled scents of extraordinary fragrances. But these experiences and others were so powerful that I cannot find words to describe them. I can say something about them, but my words are inadequate to transmit the sweetness and the delight I experienced. Many more times did I hear God speak to me with words such as the above but never at such length, nor with the same depth or with such sweetness. . . .

~

In the eighth step, while looking at the cross, I was given an even greater perception of the way the Son of God had died for our sins. This perception made me aware of all my sins, and this was extremely painful. I felt that I myself had crucified Christ. But I still did not know which was the greatest gift he had bestowed—whether it was the fact that he had withdrawn me from sin and hell and converted me to the way of penance or that he had been crucified for me. Nonetheless, this perception of the meaning of the cross set me so afire that, standing near the cross, I stripped myself of all my clothing and offered my whole self to him. Although very fearful, I promised him then to maintain perpetual chastity and not to offend him again with any of my bodily members, accusing each of these one by one. I prayed that he himself keep me faithful to this promise, namely, to observe chastity with all the members of my body and all my senses. On the one hand, I feared to make this promise, but on the other hand, the fire of which I spoke drew it out of me, and I could not do otherwise.

In the ninth step, it was given to me to seek the way of the cross, that I too might stand at the foot of the cross where all sinners find refuge. I was instructed, illumined, and shown the way of the cross in the following manner: I was inspired with the thought that if I wanted to go to the cross, I would need to strip myself in order to be lighter and go naked to it. This would entail forgiving all who had offended me, stripping myself of everything worldly, of all attachments to men and women, of my friends and relatives, and everyone else, and, likewise, of my possessions and even my very self. Then I would be free to give my heart to Christ from whom I had received so many graces, and to walk along the thorny path, that is, the path of tribulations.

I then decided to put aside my best garments, fine food, and fancy headdress. But this was still a very shameful and burdensome thing for me to do, for at this point I was not feeling any love. During this period I was still living with my husband, and it was bitter for me to put up with all the slanders and injustices leveled against me. Nonetheless, I bore these as patiently as I could. Moreover, it came to pass, God so willing, that at that time my mother, who had been a great obstacle to me, died. In like manner my husband died, as did all my sons in a short space of time. Because I had already entered the aforesaid way, and had prayed to God for their death, I felt a great consolation when it happened. I thought that since God had conceded me this aforesaid favor, my heart would always be within God's heart, and God's heart always within mine. . . .

❧

On Holy Saturday, after what has just been related, Christ's faithful one told me the wonderful and joy-filled experiences of God which were now hers. Among other things, she related to me, brother scribe,[37] that on that very day, in a state of ecstasy, she found herself in the sepulcher with Christ. She said she had first of all kissed Christ's breast—and saw that he lay dead, with his eyes closed—then she kissed his mouth, from which, she added, a delightful fragrance emanated, one impossible to describe. This moment lasted only a short while. Afterward, she placed her cheek on Christ's own and he, in turn, placed his hand on her other cheek, pressing her closely to him. At that moment, Christ's faithful one heard him telling her: "Before I was laid in the sepulcher, I held you this tightly to me." Even though she understood that it was Christ telling her this, nonetheless she saw him lying there with eyes closed, lips motionless, exactly as he was when he lay dead in the sepulcher. Her joy was immense and indescribable. . . .

❧

In the fourteenth step, while I was standing in prayer, Christ on the cross appeared more clearly to me while I was awake, that is to say, he gave me an even greater awareness of himself than before. He then called me to place my mouth to the wound in his side. It seemed to me that I saw and drank the blood, which was freshly flowing from his side. His intention was to make me understand that by this blood he would cleanse me. And at this I began to experience a great joy, although when I thought about the passion I was still filled with sadness.

I then prayed to God to enable me to shed all my blood for love of him just as he had done for me. I was even disposed, because of his love, to wish that all the parts of my body suffer a death not like his, that is, one much more vile. I imagined and desired that if I could find someone who was willing to kill me—provided of course that it was licit to be killed on account of one's faith and love of God—then I would beg him to grant me this grace, namely, that since Christ had been crucified on the wood of the cross, that I be crucified in a gully, or in some very vile place, and by a very vile instrument. Moreover, since I did not desire to die as the saints had died, that he make me die a slower and even more vile death than theirs. I could not imagine a death vile enough to match my desire. I even grieved deeply that I could not discover a death which would have nothing in common with those of any of the saints. I felt totally unworthy of dying as they did. . . .

⌒

This is what she told me: On Maundy Thursday, I suggested to my companion that we go out to find Christ: "Let's go," I told her, "to the hospital and perhaps we will be able to find Christ there among the poor, the suffering, and the afflicted." We brought with us all the head veils that we could carry, for we had nothing else. We told Giliola, the servant at that hospital, to sell them and from the sale to buy some food for those in the hospital to eat. And, although initially she strongly resisted our request, and said we were trying to shame her, nonetheless, because of our repeated insistence, she went ahead and sold our small head veils and from the sale bought some fish. We had also brought with us all the bread which had been given to us to live on.

And after we had distributed all that we had, we washed the feet of the women and the hands of the men, and especially those of one of the lepers which were festering and in an advanced stage of decomposition. Then we drank the very water with which we had washed him. And the drink was so sweet that, all the way home, we tasted its sweetness and it was as if we had received Holy Communion. As a small scale of the leper's sores was stuck in my throat, I tried to swallow it. My conscience would not let me spit it out, just as if I had received Holy Communion. I really did not want to spit it out but simply to detach it from my throat.

❧

In the tenth step, while I was asking God what I could do to please him more, in his mercy, he appeared to me many times, both while I was asleep and awake, crucified on the cross. He told me that I should look at his wounds. In a wonderful manner, he showed me how he had endured all these wounds for me; and he did this many times. As he was showing me the sufferings he had endured for me from each of these wounds, one after the other, he told me: "What then can you do that would seem to you to be enough?" Likewise, he appeared many times to me while I was awake, and these appearances were more pleasant than those which occurred while I was asleep, although he always seemed to be suffering greatly. He spoke to me just as he had while I was sleeping, showing me his afflictions from head to toe. He even showed me how his beard, eyebrows, and hair had been plucked out and enumerated each and every one of the blows of the whip that he had received. And he said: "I have endured all these things for you."

After this, I was given an astonishing remembrance of all my sins and became aware that I was the one who had wounded him afresh with my sins and because of this, great should be my sorrow. And I did grieve more for my sins than ever before. He continued to show me the sufferings of his passion and repeated: "What indeed can you do for me that would satisfy you?" I wept much, shedding such hot tears that they burned my flesh. I had to apply water to cool it. . . .

❧

Afterward, this fire of the love of God in my heart became so intense that if I heard anyone speak about God I would scream. Even if someone had stood over me with an axe ready to kill me, this would not have stopped my screaming. This happened to me for the first time when I sold my country villa to give to the poor. It was the best property that I owned. Before I used to make fun of a certain Pietruccio, but now I could not do otherwise than follow his example. Moreover, when people said that I was possessed by the devil because I had no control over my inordinate behavior—for which I was greatly ashamed—I would concur with their judgment and likewise think of myself as very sick and possessed. I could not answer those who spoke ill of me.

JULIAN OF NORWICH

Dame Julian of Norwich (1342–1416) was a subtle theologian whose book *The Revelations of Divine Love* (sometimes called *Showings*) recounts sixteen visions she experienced while deathly ill, together with her interpretations of them. Julian was an anchorite whose cell was a room attached to the side of a church in Norwich, England. One of her visitors was Margery Kempe, who sought Julian's guidance and support. As we shall see in the selection from Kempe, Julian confirmed that Margery's emotional outbursts were a sign of the Spirit's indwelling.

The following selections from the *Revelations of Divine Love* expound Julian's teaching about "Christ as Mother" and the "Motherhood of God," as well as her experience of the suffering Christ and her teaching on the Trinity.[38] For Julian, the church's confession that the Second Person of the Trinity (the Son) took flesh in Jesus meant that this aspect of the Godhead has a special role in nurturing and preserving human beings, as well as in creating them in his own image. In Julian's writing, the gracious protection and care of our humanity, which she describes in maternal imagery, are special attributes of the Son. To depict the Second Person of the Trinity as female was highly unusual in theological treatises of this era.

REVELATIONS OF DIVINE LOVE*

And when I was thirty years and a half, God sent me a bodily sickness; in which I lay three days and three nights. And on the fourth night I received all the rites of Holy Church, and thought not to have lived till day. . . . And I understood in my reason, and by the pains I felt, that I was going to die. . . . Thus I endured until day; and by then my body, as regards feeling, was dead from the middle downwards. . . .

My curate was sent for to be present at my end. . . . He set the cross before my face, and said: "I have brought the image of thy Saviour; look thereupon, and comfort thee therewith. . . ."

And in this time, suddenly I saw the red blood running down from under the garland, hot and fresh, plenteous and life-like, just as it was in the time that the garland of thorns was pressed down on his blessed head. Even so I conceived truly that it was himself, God and man, the same that suffered for me, who shewed it to me—without any intermediary.

In the same showing, suddenly the Trinity filled full my heart with the utmost joy (thus I understood it shall be in heaven without end unto all that come thither). For the Trinity is God, and God is the Trinity. The Trinity is our Maker. The Trinity is our Keeper. The Trinity is our everlasting Lover. . . .

And then I saw that God rejoiceth that he is our Father: and God rejoiceth that he is our Mother: and God rejoiceth that he is our true Spouse, and our soul his beloved wife. And Christ rejoiceth that he is our Brother: and Jesus rejoiceth that he is our Saviour. These are five high joys. . . .

And thus, in our making, God almighty is our kindly Father: and God all-wisdom is our kindly Mother; with the love and goodness of the Holy Ghost; which is all one God,

---

* From Julian of Norwich, *The Revelations of Divine Love*, trans. James Walsh (New York: Harper & Row, 1961), 49, 51, 144, 158–67.

one Lord. And in the knitting and the oneing he is our very true Spouse, and we his loved wife and his fair maiden. With which wife he was never displeased; for he saith: "I love thee, and thou lovest me, and our love shall never be parted in two."

I beheld the working of all the blessed Trinity. In which beholding I saw and understood these three properties: the property of the Fatherhood, and the property of the Motherhood, and the property of the Lordship—in one God. In our Father almighty we have our keeping and our bliss, in respect of our kindly substance (which is applied to us by our creation), from without-beginning. And in the second Person [i.e., of the Trinity], in understanding and wisdom, we have our keeping in respect of our sensuality, our restoring and our saving. (For he is our Mother, Brother and Saviour.) And in our good Lord the Holy Ghost we have our rewarding and our enrichment for our living and our travail: which, of his high plenteous grace, and in his marvellous courtesy, endlessly surpasses all that we desire. . . .

And furthermore, I saw that the second Person, who is our Mother substantially—the same very dear Person is now become our Mother sensually. For of God's making we are double: that is to say, substantial and sensual. Our substance is that higher part which we have in our Father, God almighty. And the second Person of the Trinity is our Mother in kind, in our substantial making—in whom we are grounded and rooted; and he is our Mother of mercy in taking our sensuality. And thus "our Mother" meaneth for us different manners of his working, in whom our parts are kept unseparated. For in our Mother Christ, we have profit and increase; and in mercy he re-formeth and restoreth us: and by the power of his passion, his death and his uprising, oned us to our substance. Thus worketh our Mother in mercy to all his beloved children who are docile and obedient to him. . . .

Thus Jesus Christ, who doeth good against evil, is our very Mother. We have our being of him, there, where the ground of Motherhood beginneth; with all the sweet keeping of love that endlessly followeth. As truly as God is our Father, so truly is God our Mother. And that shewed he in all, and especially in these sweet words where he sayeth "I it am . . . the might and the goodness of the Fatherhood. I it am: the wisdom and the kindness of Motherhood. I it am: the light and the grace that is all blessed love. I it am, the Trinity. . . ."

And thus is Jesus our true Mother in kind, of our first making; and he is our true Mother in grace by his taking of our made kind. All the fair working and all the sweet kindly offices of most dear Motherhood are appropriated to the second Person. For in him we have this godly will whole and secure without end, both in kind and in grace, of his own proper goodness. I understand three types of beholding of Motherhood in God. The first is the ground of making of our kind. The second is the taking of our kind—and there beginneth the Motherhood of grace. The third is Motherhood in working. And therein is a forth-spreading, by the same grace, of a length and breadth, of a height and a deepness without end. And all is one love. . . .

Our kind Mother, our gracious Mother—for he would all wholly become our Mother in all things—he made the ground of his work to be full low and full mildly in the Maiden's womb. . . . That is to say: our high God, the sovereign Wisdom of all, in this lowly place he arrayed him and made him all ready; in our poor flesh, himself to do the service and office of Motherhood, in all things.

The mother's service is nearest, readiest and surest; nearest: for it is most of kind; readiest: for it is most of love; surest: for it is most of truth. This office no one might nor could ever do to the full, except he alone. We know that all our mothers beareth us to pain and to dying; a strange thing, that! But our true Mother Jesus, he alone beareth us to joy and to endless living; blessed may he be! Thus he sustaineth us within him, in love and in travail unto the full time in which he willed to suffer the sharpest throes and most grievous pains that ever were, or ever shall be; and he died at the last. Yet all this might not fully satisfy his marvellous love. And that shewed he in these high overpassing words of love: "If I could suffer more, I would suffer more." He could no more die, but he would not cease working.

Wherefore it behoveth him to feed us; for the very dear love of motherhood hath made him our debtor. The mother can give her child to suck of her milk. But our precious Mother Jesus, he can feed us with himself; and doeth, full courteously and tenderly, with the Blessed Sacrament, that is the precious food of true life. . . .

The mother can lay her child tenderly to her breast. But our tender Mother Jesus can lead us . . . into his blessed breast, by his sweet open side; and shew us there, in part, the Godhead and the joys of heaven, with a ghostly* sureness of endless bliss. . . .

This fair lovely word *Mother,* it is so sweet and so kind in itself, that it cannot truly be said to any nor of any, but to him and of him who is very Mother of life and of all. To the property of Motherhood belongeth kind love, wisdom and knowing; and it is God. For though it is true that our bodily forthbringing is but little, lowly and simple in comparison with our ghostly forthbringing; yet it is he that doeth the first in the creatures by whom it is done. The kind loving mother understandeth and knoweth the need of her child. She keepeth it full tenderly, as the kind and condition of motherhood will. And ever as it waxeth in age and in stature, she changeth her way of working, but not her love. And when it is come to a more advanced age, she suffereth it to be chastised, for the breaking down of vices, and to make the child receive virtues and grace. This work, with all that is fair and good, our Lord doeth it, in those by whom it is done.

Thus he is our Mother in kind by the working of grace in the lower part, for the sake of the higher. And he willeth that

---

* Ghostly = spiritual.

we know it. For he willeth to have all our love fastened to
him. And in this I saw that all the debts that we owe, by
God's bidding, to fatherhood and motherhood is fulfilled in
true loving of God. . . .

And though, possibly, an earthly mother may suffer her
child to perish, our heavenly Mother Jesus can never suffer us
who are his children to perish. For he is almighty, all-wisdom
and all-love: and so is none but he. Blessed may he be!

But oftentimes, when our falling and our wretchedness is
shewed to us, we are so sore adread, and so greatly ashamed
of ourselves, that we scarcely know where to put ourselves.
Yet even then our courteous Mother willeth not that we flee
away: nothing could be more displeasing to him. Rather, he
willeth us to behave as a child. For when it is distressed and
afraid, it runneth hastily to the mother. And if it can do
naught else, it crieth to the mother for help, with all its
might. So will he have us behave as the meek child, saying
thus: "My kind Mother, my gracious Mother, my most dear
Mother, have mercy on me. I have made myself foul and unlike to thee; and I cannot or may not amend it but with thine
help and grace." . . . The sweet gracious hands of our
Mother are ready and diligent about us.

CATHERINE OF SIENA

Catherine of Siena (1347–80) was a far more public figure than
many of the other women religious of the Middle Ages. In her
brief life (she was thirty-three when she died), she not only concerned herself with ascetic devotions but also believed that her
visions and her mystical marriage to Christ gave her the power
to instruct prelates on the reform of the church. She was a Dominican tertiary and for several years lived as a recluse in her
parents' home.

In 1305, a French pope had moved the seat of the papacy
from Rome to Avignon, France, where it became aligned with

the French king and court. Catherine made it her task in the 1370s to encourage Pope Gregory XI to return to Rome and to the reform of the church, which she thought had sunk into degeneracy and become far too occupied with the "worldly" concerns of money, war, and the state. She believed that through her penitential devotion she could serve to expiate the sins of the church. Catherine wrote a *Dialogue,* which contains her spiritual teaching, as well as letters and prayers. Her energetic activity on behalf of church reform is suggested in the following selection from her *Letters,* in which she makes her first approach to Pope Gregory XI at Avignon. The Pope had recently (1376) suffered the defection of the republic of Bologna, which had been under the jurisdiction of the papacy. Due in part to Catherine's insistent pleas, the Pope returned to Rome in early 1377.

LETTER 63 TO POPE GREGORY XI*

In the name of Jesus Christ crucified and of gentle Mary.

Dearest, most holy and gracious father in Christ Jesus,

Your poor unworthy daughter Caterina, servant and slave of the servants of Jesus Christ, is writing to you in his precious blood. With desire have I desired to see you so filled with divine grace that you may be the instrument and means, by divine grace, of bringing peace to the whole world. So I beg you, my dear father, to use your authority and power diligently and with hungry longing for peace, God's honor, and the salvation of souls. And if you should say to me, father, "The world is in such a sorry state—how can I bring it peace?" I tell you in the name of Christ crucified that you must use your authority to do three essential things. You are

---

* From Catherine of Siena, "Letter 63 to Pope Gregory XI," in *The Letters of St. Catherine of Siena,* trans. Suzanne Noffke (Binghamton, N.Y.: Medieval and Renaissance Texts and Studies, 1988), 1: 200–203 (footnotes deleted).

in charge of the garden of holy Church. So [first of all] uproot from that garden the stinking weeds full of impurity and avarice, and bloated with pride (I mean the evil pastors and administrators who poison and corrupt the garden). Ah, *use* your authority, you who are in charge of us! Uproot these weeds and throw them out where they will have nothing to administer! Tell them to tend to administering themselves by a good holy life. Plant fragrant flowers in this garden for us, pastors and administrators who will be true servants of Jesus Christ crucified, who will seek only God's honor and the salvation of souls, who will be fathers to the poor.

Ah, what a shame this is! They ought to be mirrors of freely chosen poverty, humble lambs, giving out the Church's possessions to the poor. Yet here they are, living in worldly luxury and ambition and pretentious vanity a thousand times worse than if they belonged to the world! In fact, many layfolk put them to shame by their good holy lives. But it seems supreme eternal Goodness is making us do under coercion what we haven't done for love. It seems he is permitting his bride to be stripped of prestige and luxury, as if to show that he wants holy Church to return to being poor, humble, and meek as she was in those holy early days, when she was concerned only with God's honor and the salvation of souls, taken up not with material things but with the spiritual. For ever since the Church has paid more attention to the material than to the spiritual, things have gone from bad to worse.

This is why you have seen God in his just judgment permitting the Church to suffer so many persecutions and trials. But take heart, father, and don't be afraid, no matter what has happened or may yet happen. God is doing it to make the Church perfect once again, so that lambs may feed in this garden instead of the wolves who are devouring the honor that belongs to God by stealing it for themselves. Take heart in Christ gentle Jesus, for I trust that his help, the fullness of divine grace, will come soon to your support and aid. If you do as I've told you, you will emerge from war into the greatest peace, from persecution to complete unity—not by human power but by holy virtue—and you will defeat the devils we can see (evil people) as well as those we cannot see—though they never take their eyes off us.

But just think, my dear father, how difficult it will be to do what I've been talking about unless you do the other two essential things. I mean your return [to Rome] and the raising of the standard of the most holy cross. Don't let your holy desire falter on account of any dissent or rebellion you might see or hear about on the part of the cities. Rather, let your holy desire be fired the more to act soon. Don't put off your coming because of it. Don't believe the devil. He knows he is the loser, and so he is trying to put obstacles in your way to make you give up what is yours. He wants to make you lose love and charity, and prevent your coming. I tell you, father in Christ Jesus, to come soon, like a gentle lamb. Respond to the Holy Spirit, who is calling you! I tell you: come! come! come! Don't wait for time, because time isn't waiting for you. Then you will be acting like the slain Lamb, whose place you hold. With unarmed hand he slew our enemies. He came as a gentle Lamb, using the power of love as his only weapon, looking only to care for spiritual things and to the restoration of grace to humankind, who had lost it through sin.

Ah, my dear father! I am begging you, I am *telling* you: come, and conquer our enemies with the same gentle hand. In the name of Christ crucified I am telling you. Don't choose to listen to the devil's advisors. They would like to block your holy and good resolution. Be a courageous man for me, not a coward. Respond to God, who is calling you to come and take possession of the place of the glorious shepherd, Saint Peter, whose representative you still are. And there raise the standard of the holy cross. For as we were freed through the cross (as said our dear Paul), so by raising this standard (which I see as the refuge of Christians) we shall be freed—we from war and divisions and many sins, and the unbelievers from their unbelief. And by doing these [two] things you will come to see the reform of holy Church in the persons of good pastors. You will bring back to her faded face the color of blazing charity—for so much blood has been sucked from her by wicked gluttons that she is all pale.

But take heart and come, father! Don't make God's servants, tormented with desire, wait any longer. I, poor wretch, *cannot* wait any more. Though I am alive, I feel as if I am dying of anguish, seeing God so insulted. Don't back off from making peace because of what happened in Bologna. Just come, for I tell you, the ferocious wolves will lay their heads in your lap meek as lambs, and will ask you for mercy.

Father, I'll say no more. I beg you to hear and listen to what Frate Raimondo my father and my other sons who are in his company have to say to you. They come in the name of Christ crucified and in mine, for they are true servants of God and sons of holy Church.

Pardon my foolishness, father, and let the love and sorrow that make me speak be my excuse in the presence of your kindness. Give me your blessing.

Keep living in God's holy and tender love.

Jesus, gentle Jesus!

MARGERY KEMPE

The final selection concerning medieval religious women is from *The Book of Margery Kempe,* the text usually considered to be the first autobiography written in the English language (1426).[39] Margery lived from around 1373 until at least 1439. After almost twenty years of marriage, during which she had borne fourteen children, Margery began to have visions of Christ; she decided to break off sexual relations with her husband and undertake a pilgrimage to Jerusalem. Receiving confirmation of her spiritual quest from Julian of Norwich, Margery left her husband to make several pilgrimages to the Holy Land and

Italy, to the pilgrim site of Santiago de Compostela in Spain, and to Norway and Danzig.

In the course of these pilgrimages, Margery met with religious leaders and theologians to discuss her experiences. Sometimes—as when she visited Constance in 1414–15, while the Council of Constance was in session—she received confirmation that her revelations were from God, not from the devil. But occasionally she was accused of heresy—a charge closely connected with that of witchcraft in this period. Certainly her eccentric behavior, her tears and screaming during religious services, did not endear her to all churchmen.[40] She was accused of Lollardy, the heresy associated with John Wycliffe that encouraged laypeople to read and interpret the Bible for themselves and to seek a relationship with God less mediated by the Catholic clergy than the church hierarchy thought appropriate.[41] At Hessle, some shouted at her, "Burn this false heretic!" Others pleaded with her: "Damsel, forsake this life that thou hast, and go and spin and card as other women do, and suffer not so much shame and so much woe."[42] She found enough support—no doubt aided by her high social standing—to save her from harm. In the following selection from her *Book,* Margery details the pact that she made with her husband that enabled her pilgrimages and spiritual practice. She also describes her mystical marriage to Christ, an experience common among medieval women mystics.

THE BOOK OF MARGERY KEMPE*

Then this creature[43] was bidden by Our Lord to go to an anchoress in Norwich, named Dame Jelyan [Julian of Norwich],

---

* From Margery Kempe, *The Book of Margery Kempe (1436): A Modern Version by W. Butler-Bowen* (London: Jonathan Cape, 1936), 72–74, 47–50 (with modernization of the English).

and so she did, and showed her the grace that God put into her soul, of compunction, contrition, sweetness and devotion, compassion with holy meditation and high contemplation, and full many holy speeches and dalliance that Our Lord spoke to her soul; and many wonderful revelations, which she showed to the anchoress to find out if there were any deceit in them, for the anchoress was expert in such things and could give good counsel.

The anchoress, hearing the marvellous goodness of Our Lord, highly thanked God with all her heart for his visitation, counselling this creature to be obedient to the will of Our Lord God and to fulfil with all her might whatever he put into her soul, if it were not against the worship of God, and profit of her fellow Christians, for if it were, then it were not the moving of a good spirit, but rather of an evil spirit. Said she: "The Holy Ghost never moves contrary to charity, for if he did, he would be contrary to his own self for he is all charity. Also he moves a soul to all chasteness, for chaste livers are called the temple of the Holy Ghost, and the Holy Ghost makes a soul stable and steadfast in the right faith and the right belief. And a double person in soul is ever unstable and unsteadfast in all his ways. One who is ever doubting is like the flood of the sea which is moved and born about with the wind, and that person is not likely to receive the gifts of God. Any creature that has these tokens may steadfastly believe that the Holy Ghost dwells in his soul. And much more when God visits a creature with tears of contrition, devotion, and compassion, he may and ought to believe that the Holy Ghost is in his soul. Saint Paul says that the Holy Ghost asks for us with mourning and weeping unspeakable, that is to say, he makes us to ask and pray with mourning and weeping so plenteously that the tears may not be numbered. No evil spirit may give these tokens, for Jerome says that tears torment the devil more than do the pains of hell. God and the devil are ever at odds and they shall never dwell together in one place, and the devil has no power in a person's soul. Holy Writ says that the soul of a rightful person is the seat of God, and so I trust, sister, that you be. I pray God grant you perseverance. Set all your trust in God and fear not the language of the world, for the more despite, shame and reproof that you have in the world, the more is your merit in the sight of God. Patience is necessary to you, for in that you shall keep your soul."

Much was the holy dalliance that the anchoress and this creature had by communing in the love of Our Lord Jesus Christ the many days that they were together.

It befell on a Friday on Midsummer Eve in right hot weather, as this creature was coming from York-ward carrying a bottle with beer in her hand, and her husband a cake in his bosom, that he asked his wife this question:

"Margery, if there came a man with a sword, who would strike off my head unless I should commune naturally with you as I have done before,[44] tell me truly on your conscience—for you say you will not lie—whether you would suffer my head to be smitten off, or whether you would allow me to meddle with you again, as I did at one time?"

"Alas, sir," said she, "why raise this matter, when we have been chaste these eight weeks?"

"For I will know the truth of your heart."

And then she said with great sorrow: "Forsooth, I would rather see you being slain, than that we should turn again to our uncleanness."

And he replied: "You are no good wife. . . ."

[Then she asked]: "I pray you, suffer me to make a vow of chastity at what bishop's hand God wills."

"Nay," he said, "that I will not grant you, for now may I use you without deadly sin, and then I might not do so." Then she said again: "If it be the will of the Holy Ghost to fulfil what I have said, I pray God that you may consent thereto; and if it be not the will of the Holy Ghost, I pray God you never consent to it."

Then they went forth towards Bridlington in right hot weather, the foresaid creature having great sorrow and dread for her chastity. And as they came by a cross, her husband sat down under the cross, calling his wife to him and saying these words unto her: "Margery, grant me my desire, and I shall grant you your desire. My first desire is that we shall still lie together in bed as we have done before; the second, that you shall pay my debts before you go to Jerusalem; and the third, that you shall eat and drink with me on Fridays as you used to do."

"Nay, sir," said she, "to break the Friday, I will never grant you while I live."[45]

"Well," said he, "then I shall meddle with you again."

She prayed him that he would give her leave to say her prayers, and he granted it kindly. Then she knelt down beside a cross in the field and prayed in this manner, with a great abundance of tears:

"Lord God, thou knowest all things. Thou knowest what sorrow I have had to be chaste in my body to thee all these three years, and now might I have my will, and dare not for love of thee. For if I should break that manner of fasting which thou commandest me to keep on the Friday, without meat or drink, I should now have my desire. But, Blessed Lord, thou knowest that I will not contravene thy will, and much now is my sorrow unless I find comfort in thee. Now, Blessed Jesus, make thy will known to me unworthy, that I may follow it thereafter and fulfil it with all my might."

Then Our Lord Jesus Christ with great sweetness spoke to her, commanding her to go again to her husband, and pray him to grant her what she desired: "And he shall have what he desires. For, my dearworthy daughter, this was the cause that I bade thee fast, so that thou shouldst the sooner obtain and get thy desire, and now it is granted to thee. I will no longer that thou fast. Therefore I bid thee in the name of Jesus, eat and drink as thy husband doth." Then this creature thanked Our Lord Jesus Christ for his grace and goodness,

and rose up and went to her husband, saying to him: "Sir, if
it please you, you shall grant me my desire, and you shall
have your desire. Grant me that you will not come into my
bed, and I grant you to requite your debts before I go to
Jerusalem. Make my body free to God so that you never
make challenge to me, by asking any debt of matrimony.
After this day, while you live, I will eat and drink on the Friday at your bidding."

Then said her husband again to her: "As free may your
body be to God as it has been to me."

This creature thanked God, greatly rejoicing that she had
her desire, praying her husband that they should say three
"Our Fathers" in worship of the Trinity for the great grace
he had granted them. And so they did, kneeling under a
cross, and afterwards they ate and drank together in great
gladness of spirit. This was on a Friday on Midsummer's Eve.

7.

∽ Woman as Witch: Witchcraft Persecutions in the Old and New Worlds

One of the most disturbing periods in the history of Western Christianity, particularly with respect to issues of women and sexuality, was the widespread witchcraft persecution of the early modern era. Between 1450 and 1750 in various parts of Europe and European colonies, religious and secular authorities undertook a sustained effort to identify and eliminate practitioners of witchcraft. While scholars debate the extent of witch-hunting in the two hundred years before 1450,[1] from 1450 to 1750 tens (and perhaps hundreds) of thousands were accused and executed for witchcraft.[2]

Until recently, most historians offered only the shallowest acknowledgment of the gendered nature of the witchcraft persecutions,[3] but the vast majority of those charged with witchcraft were women. While there were important regional differences,[4] women appear to have constituted approximately 80 percent of those accused and approximately 85 percent of those executed for witchcraft during the period of the major European witch-hunts.[5] As particularly egregious examples, in 1585 two German villages were left with only one female inhabitant each.[6] The early modern witch craze stands as perhaps the most massive and explicit demonstration of misogyny and fear of women in the history of the European Christianity.

EUROPEAN WITCHCRAFT PERSECUTIONS

During the early medieval period, simple sorcery or natural magic were treated with relative leniency, and Christian theologians and bishops explicitly taught that witchcraft was only illusion, fantasy, or hallucination, a form of pagan superstition.[7] Sorcery was often ignored, and if it was detected, it often brought nothing more than a stiff penance. Indeed, elements of simple sorcery were sometimes incorporated into Christian religious practice, and popular magic and superstitious practices appear to have pervaded many layers of European society.

Historians struggle to account for the dramatic shift from the relatively benign early medieval views of sorcery as misguided illusion to the virulent beliefs that were to sweep Europe concerning the reality of witches and their evil powers. The historian Hugh Trevor-Roper has proposed that the primary causes for this shift are to be found in the major social upheavals of the early modern period, including such factors as the rise of new concerns about various heretical groups and religious orthodoxy, the Black Death, the Hundred Years War, and the later religious wars and social turmoil arising from the Reformation and Counter-Reformation.[8] Surely the early modern era was a period of profound social change throughout the Western world, and Trevor-Roper's argument has exerted an important influence on subsequent historiography.

More recent studies have highlighted further important changing social and political conditions that made the witch craze possible, including broad changes in legal administration and procedure (including the rise of torture as a prominent legal tool), demographic fluctuation, food scarcity, changes in family and kinship patterns, and the development and spread of new capitalist economic systems (which, in turn, increased economic tension and dislocation).[9] Witchcraft accusations and trials could serve important social and psychological functions in a period of such social turmoil.[10] Further, the witchcraft persecutions also vividly reflect the profound tensions that accompanied the extension of centralized social power, control, and acculturation into the countryside by increasingly efficient and centralized nation-states and bureaucratic elites.[11] These new mechanisms of social control required new forms of individual identity and agency in which gender norms were rigidly policed. Not only do the witchcraft persecutions demonstrate an obsessive concern with the regulation of bodies, gender roles, and sexual practices, but they also coincided with increased social and legal concern with other behaviors related to procreation, gender, and sexuality (such as abortion, infanticide, prostitution, and sodomy).[12]

In this confluence of social and economic factors, religious and political concern with nonconformity and heresy increased dramatically at the end of the medieval period, particularly with the rise of various groups that challenged religious orthodoxy and hierarchy (including the Cathars, the Waldensians, and the Lollards, and extending to the Templars and Jews).[13] Scholastic theologians developed elaborate theories of the devil and the devil's kingdom, in which sorcerers were considered to be heretical servants of Satan. In keeping with this heightened concern over heresy, the Vatican authorized new religious orders to teach and promote religious orthodoxy. Between 1227 and 1235, Pope Gregory IX launched a series of papal condemnations of heresy, then a series of commissions of inquisition given most notably to Dominican friars. The inquisition consisted of formal inquests aimed against Jews, Muslims, and other suspected heretics, and in 1252 Pope Innocent IV authorized the use of torture in cases of heresy, a potent means of obtaining confessions. Over time, almost all sorcery and folk magic came to be included under the rubric of heresy.[14]

Despite its reputation, the inquisition appears to have been far less brutal and more concerned with procedural safeguards in its persecution of witchcraft than were the secular and other ecclesiastical authorities.[15] Indeed, after around 1530, the inquisition conducted witch trials only in Italy, Spain, Portugal, and their colonies; elsewhere in Europe, secular or ecclesiastical courts assumed almost exclusive jurisdiction over charges of witchcraft.[16] But the inquisition did provide one ingredient of major significance to the broad witchcraft persecutions: the inquisitors' manuals. These manuals directed investigators concerning the nature of witchcraft and the most effective means of interrogation. Obtaining evidence of witchcraft through the use (or threat) of torture, inquisitors would enter formal reports concerning the phenomenon and thus add to the body of evidence concerning the presence of witches and their evil powers.

In 1484, the Dominican inquisitors Heinrich Institor (Kramer) and Jacob Sprenger obtained a bull from Pope Innocent VIII confirming papal support for the inquisition against witches and authorizing Kramer and Sprenger to combat the problems caused by witchcraft.[17] In 1486–87, Kramer and Sprenger published the *Malleus Maleficarum* (the "Hammer Against Witches"), a handbook for inquisitors to use in witchcraft investigations and trials. The *Malleus* is significant not only because of its compendium of arguments supporting the persecution of witches but also because of its tremendous influence.[18] It appeared in at least twenty-nine editions in its first two hundred years,[19] and through translation and citation, its influence was widespread throughout Europe until the seventeenth century.

The *Malleus* cites a wide array of authorities in its circuitous arguments against witchcraft, including both pre-Christian and early Christian authors (Jerome, Chrysostom, and Origen). But it relies principally on the authority of Aristotle, the Scriptures, Augustine, and Aquinas.[20] In addition, Kramer and Sprenger offer various forms of evidence accumulated through their work as inquisitors.

Among the most striking aspects of the *Malleus* are its preoccupation with sexual functions and its broad and vicious attack on women.[21] The authors argue that women are particularly susceptible to witchcraft because they are light-minded, fickle, feeble in intelligence, quick to waiver in faith, and cursed with sexual desires so insatiable that they lust for intercourse with the devil; they are "by nature" prone to such evils because Eve was originally constructed from a "bent rib." Men are instructed to praise God for preserving them from this terrible curse; the authors claim that God's incarnation as a member of the male sex gives men relative immunity to such evil.

Kramer and Sprenger argue that witches have special powers over sexual and reproductive functions. Moreover, they also assert that witches pose a significant threat to men's potency, though the authors hedge on whether witches actually have the power to undermine male sexual capacity (to the point of removing male genital organs) or whether such problems are merely the result of a bewitching delusion or "glamour." Kramer and Sprenger offer a theological rationale for their overwhelming stress on venereal functions: God permits the devil more power over sexual acts than all other human acts because "the first corruption of sin by which man became the slave of the devil came to us through the act of generation."[22] The devil assumes a feminine form to harvest semen from lustful men, and then, assuming a masculine form, the devil uses the semen to impregnate witches and thus pollute the bodies and souls of both parties.[23] Yet this evil sexuality is bridled in one notable aspect; even demons will not engage in "vices against nature" or acts "wrongfully performed outside the rightful channel."[24]

In sections of the treatise not included in this chapter, Kramer and Sprenger detail the procedures to be followed in witchcraft trials and warn against the wiles that witches will use to escape detection or to deceive judges. Various tortures are appropriate to induce confessions. Thus, despite their acknowledgment in

the *Malleus* that testimony induced by torture is "often fallacious and ineffective,"[25] Kramer and Sprenger propose an attack
on witchcraft that could effectively produce its own evidence.
As the authors assert, "[h]ere we are dealing with actual events;
and it has never yet been known that an innocent person has
been punished on suspicion of witchcraft, and there is no doubt
that God will never permit such a thing to happen."[26]

As the following excerpts will amply demonstrate, the logic
of the *Malleus* is notoriously circular and fallacious.[27] For example, Kramer and Sprenger first argue that women are susceptible to witchcraft because of their general feeblemindedness
and weakness. But practically without pause, they proceed to
argue that women pose a particular threat to men because of
the insidious power and ingenuity of feminine wiles.

It is important to note that Catholics and Protestants shared
in the persecution of witchcraft.[28] Luther and Calvin each declared that witches should be burned as heretics.[29] Henry VIII of
England included a charge of witchcraft against his wife Anne
Boleyn, and James I of England himself wrote a *Daemonologie*
and encouraged new legal measures against witches.[30] Protestants further concurred with Catholics that women were particularly prone to witchcraft,[31] and terror of witchcraft grew in
both Catholic and Protestant regions, reaching its height between 1560 and 1660, an era of intense religious conflict.

MALLEUS MALEFICARUM*

Part 1, Question 6
Concerning Witches who copulate with Devils.
*Why it is that Women are chiefly addicted to Evil Supersti-
tions.*

---

* From Jacob Sprenger and Heinrich Kramer, *Malleus Maleficarum,*
   trans. Montague Summers (London: The Pushkin Press, 1948), 41–48,
   54–55, 117–21.

There is also, concerning witches who copulate with devils, much difficulty in considering the methods by which such abominations are consummated. On the part of the devil: first, of what element the body is made that he assumes; secondly, whether the act is always accompanied by the injection of semen received from another; thirdly, as to time and place, whether he commits this act more frequently at one time than at another; fourthly, whether the act is invisible to any who may be standing by. And on the part of the women, it has to be inquired whether only they who were themselves conceived in this filthy manner are often visited by devils; or secondly, whether it is those who were offered to devils by midwives at the time of their birth; and thirdly, whether the actual venereal delectation of such is of a weaker sort. But we cannot here reply to all these questions, both because we are only engaged in a general study, and because in the second part of this work they are all singly explained by their operations, as will appear in the fourth chapter, where mention is made of each separate method. Therefore let us now chiefly consider women; and first, why this kind of perfidy is found more in so fragile a sex than in men. And our inquiry will first be general, as to the general conditions of women; secondly, particular, as to which sort of women are found to be given to superstition and witchcraft; and thirdly, specifically with regard to midwives, who surpass all others in wickedness.

Why Superstition is chiefly found in Women.

As for the first question, why a greater number of witches is found in the fragile feminine sex than among men; it is indeed a fact that it were idle to contradict, since it is accredited by actual experience, apart from the verbal testimony of credible witnesses. And without in any way detracting from a sex in which God has always taken great glory that His might should be spread abroad, let us say that various men have assigned various reasons for this fact, which nevertheless agree in principle. Wherefore it is good, for the admonition of women, to speak of this matter; and it has often been proved by experience that they are eager to hear of it, so long as it is set forth with discretion.

. . . [S]ince [women] are feebler both in mind and body, it is not surprising that they should come under the spell of witchcraft.

For as regards intellect, or the understanding of spiritual things, they seem to be of a different nature from men; a fact which is vouched for by the logic of the authorities, backed by various examples from the Scriptures. Terence says: Women are intellectually like children. And Lactantius *(Institutiones, 3):* No woman understood philosophy except Temeste. And *Proverbs* 11, as it were describing a woman, says: As a jewel of gold in a swine's snout, so is a fair woman which is without discretion.

But the natural reason is that she is more carnal than a man, as is clear from her many carnal abominations. And it should be noted that there was a defect in the formation of the first woman, since she was formed from a bent rib, that is, a rib of the breast, which is bent as it were in a contrary direction to a man. And since through this defect she is an imperfect animal, she always deceives. For Cato says: When a woman weeps she weaves snares. And again: When a woman weeps, she labours to deceive a man. And this is shown by Samson's wife, who coaxed him to tell her the riddle he had propounded to the Philistines, and told them the answer, and so deceived him. And it is clear in the case of the first woman that she had little faith; for when the serpent asked why they did not eat of every tree in Paradise, she answered: Of every tree, etc.—lest perchance we die. Thereby she showed that she doubted, and had little faith in the word of God. And all this is indicated by the etymology of the word; for *Femina* comes from *Fe* and *Minus,* since she is ever weaker to hold and preserve the faith. And this as regards faith is of her very nature; although both by grace and nature faith never failed in the Blessed Virgin, even at the time of Christ's Passion, when it failed in all men.

Therefore a wicked woman is by her nature quicker to waver in her faith, and consequently quicker to adjure the faith, which is the root of witchcraft. . . .

If we inquire, we find that nearly all the kingdoms of the world have been overthrown by women. Troy, which was a prosperous kingdom, was, for the rape of one woman, Helen, destroyed, and many thousands of Greeks slain. The kingdom of the Jews suffered much misfortune and destruction through the accursed Jezebel, and her daughter Athaliah, queen of Judah, who caused her son's sons to be killed, that on their death she might reign herself; yet each of them was slain. The kingdom of the Romans endured much evil through Cleopatra, Queen of Egypt, that worst of women. And so with others. Therefore it is no wonder if the world now suffers through the malice of women.

And now let us examine the carnal desires of the body itself, whence has arisen unconscionable harm to human life. Justly may we say with Cato of Utica: If the world could be rid of women, we should not be without God in our intercourse. For truly, without the wickedness of women, to say nothing of witchcraft, the world would still remain proof against innumerable dangers. Hear what Valerius said to Rufinus: You do not know that woman is the Chimaera, but it is good that you should know it; for that monster was of three forms; its face was that of a radiant and noble lion, it had the filthy belly of a goat, and it was armed with the virulent tail of a viper. And he means that a woman is beautiful to look upon, contaminating to the touch, and deadly to keep.

Let us consider another property of hers, the voice. For as she is a liar by nature, so in her speech she stings while she delights us. Wherefore her voice is like the song of the Sirens, who with their sweet melody entice the passers-by and kill them. For they kill them by emptying their purses, consuming their strength, and causing them to forsake God. Again Valerius says to Rufinus: When she speaks it is a delight which flavours the sin; the flower of love is a rose, because under its blossom there are hidden many thorns. See *Proverbs* 5:3–4: Her mouth is smoother than oil; that is, her speech is afterwards as bitter as absinthium. (Her throat is smoother than oil. But her end is as bitter as wormwood.)

Let us consider also her gait, posture, and habit, in which is vanity of vanities. There is no man in the world who studies so hard to please the good God as even an ordinary woman studies by her vanities to please men. An example of this is to be found in the life of Pelagia, a worldly woman who was wont to go about Antioch attired and adorned most extravagantly. A holy father, named Nonnus, saw her and began to weep, saying to his companions that never in all his life had he used such diligence to please God; and much more he added to this effect, which is preserved in his orations.

It is this which is lamented in *Ecclesiastes* 7, and which the Church even now laments on account of the great multitude of witches. And I have found a woman more bitter than death, who is the hunter's snare, and her heart is a net, and her hands are bands. He that pleaseth God shall escape from her; but he that is a sinner shall be caught by her. More bitter than death, that is, than the devil: *Apocalypse* 6:8, His name was Death. For though the devil tempted Eve to sin, yet Eve seduced Adam. And as the sin of Eve would not have brought death to our soul and body unless the sin had afterwards passed on to Adam, to which he was tempted by Eve, not by the devil, therefore she is more bitter than death.

More bitter than death, again, because that is natural and destroys only the body; but the sin which rose from woman destroys the soul by depriving it of grace, and delivers the body up to the punishment for sin.

More bitter than death, again, because bodily death is an open and terrible enemy, but woman is a wheedling and secret enemy.

And that she is more perilous than a snare does not speak of the snare of hunters, but of devils. For men are caught not only through their carnal desires, when they see and hear women: for S. Bernard says: Their face is a burning wind, and their voice the hissing of serpents: but they also cast wicked spells on countless men and animals. And when it is said that her heart is a net, it speaks of the inscrutable malice which reigns in their hearts. And her hands are as bands for binding; for when they place their hands on a creature to bewitch it, then with the help of the devil they perform their design.

To conclude. All witchcraft comes from carnal lust, which is in women insatiable. See *Proverbs* 30: There are three things that are never satisfied, yea, a fourth thing which says not, It is enough; that is, the mouth of the womb. Wherefore for the sake of fulfilling their lusts they consort even with devils. More such reasons could be brought forward, but to the understanding it is sufficiently clear that it is no matter for wonder that there are more women than men found infected with the heresy of witchcraft. And in consequence of this, it is better called the heresy of witches than of wizards, since the name is taken from the more powerful party. And blessed be the Highest Who has so far preserved the male sex from so great a crime: for since He was willing to be born and to suffer for us, therefore He has granted to men this privilege.

What sort of Women are found to be above all Others Superstitious and Witches?

As to our second inquiry, what sort of women more than others are found to be superstitious and infected with witchcraft; it must be said, as was shown in the preceding inquiry, that three general vices appear to have special dominion over wicked women, namely, infidelity, ambition, and lust. Therefore they are more than others inclined towards witchcraft, who more than others are given to these vices. Again, since of these three vices the last chiefly predominates, women being insatiable etc., it follows that those among ambitious women are more deeply infected who are more hot to satisfy their filthy lusts; and such are adulteresses, fornicatresses, and the concubines of the Great.

Now there are, as it is said in the Papal Bull, seven methods by which they infect with witchcraft the venereal act and the conception of the womb: First, by inclining the minds of men to inordinate passion; second, by obstructing their generative force; third, by removing the members accommodated to that act; fourth, by changing men into beasts by their magic art; fifth, by destroying the generative force in women; sixth, by procuring abortion; seventh, by offering children to devils, besides other animals and fruits of the earth with which they work much harm. And all these will be considered later; but for the present let us give our minds to the injuries towards men.

And first concerning those who are bewitched into an inordinate love or hatred, this is a matter of a sort that it is difficult to discuss before the general intelligence. Yet it must be granted that it is a fact. For S. Thomas (IV, 34), treating of obstructions caused by witches, shows that God allows the devil greater power against men's venereal acts than against their other actions; and gives this reason, that this is likely to be so, since those women are chiefly apt to be witches who are most disposed to such acts.

For he says that, since the first corruption of sin by which man became the slave of the devil came to us through the act of generation, therefore greater power is allowed by God to the devil in this act than in all others. Also the power of witches is more apparent in serpents, as it is said, than in other animals, because through the means of a serpent the devil tempted woman. For this reason also, as is shown afterwards, although matrimony is a work of God, as being instituted by Him, yet it is sometimes wrecked by the work of the devil: not indeed through main force, since then he might be thought stronger than God, but with the permission of God, by causing some temporary or permanent impediment in the conjugal act.

And touching this we may say what is known by experience; that these women satisfy their filthy lusts not only in themselves, but even in the mighty ones of the age, of whatever state and condition; causing by all sorts of witchcraft the death of their souls through the excessive infatuation of carnal love, in such a way that for no shame or persuasion can they desist from such acts. And through such men, since the witches will not permit any harm to come to them either from themselves or from others once they have them in their power, there arises the great danger of the time, namely, the extermination of the Faith. And in this way do witches every day increase.

And would that this were not true according to experience. But indeed such hatred is aroused by witchcraft between those joined in the sacrament of matrimony, and such freezing up of the generative forces, that men are unable to perform the necessary action for begetting offspring. . . .

Question 8
Whether Witches can hebetate the Powers of Generation or obstruct the Venereal Act.

. . . And as to this, Peter of Palude (III, 34) notes five methods. For he says that the devil, being a spirit, has power over a corporeal creature to cause or prevent a local motion. Therefore he can prevent bodies from approaching each other, either directly or indirectly, by interposing himself in some bodily shape. In this way it happened to the young man who was betrothed to an idol and nevertheless married a young maiden, and was consequently unable to copulate with her. Secondly, he can excite a man to that act, or freeze his desire for it, by the virtue of secret things of which he best knows the power. Thirdly, he can so disturb a man's perception and imagination as to make the woman appear loathsome to him: since he can, as has been said, influence the imagination. Fourthly, he can directly prevent the erection of that member which is adapted to fructification, just as he can prevent a local motion. Fifthly, he can prevent the flow of the vital essence to the members in which lies the motive power; by closing as it were the seminary ducts, so that it does not descend to the generative channels, or falls back from them, or does not project from them, or in any of many ways fails in its function. . . .

Part 2, Question 1, Chapters 6 and 7
How Witches Impede and Prevent the Power of Procreation.

Concerning the method by which they obstruct the procreant function both in men and animals, and in both sexes, the reader may consult that which has been written already on the questions, Whether devils can through witches turn the minds of men to love or hatred. There, after the solutions of the arguments, a specific declaration is made relating to the method by which, with God's permission, they can obstruct the procreant function.

But it must be noted that such obstruction is caused both intrinsically and extrinsically. Intrinsically they cause it in two ways. First, when they directly prevent the erection of the member which is accommodated to fructification. And this need not seem impossible, when it is considered that they are able to vitiate the natural use of any member. Secondly, when they prevent the flow of the vital essences to the members in which resides the motive force, closing up the seminal ducts so that it does not reach the generative vessels, or so that it cannot be ejaculated, or is fruitlessly spilled.

Extrinsically they cause it at times by means of images, or by the eating of herbs; sometimes by other external means, such as cocks' testicles. But it must not be thought that it is by the virtue of these things that a man is made impotent, but by the occult power of devils' illusions witches by this means procure such impotence, namely, that they cause a man to be unable to copulate, or a woman to conceive.

And the reason for this is that God allows them more power over this act, by which the first sin was disseminated, than over other human actions. Similarly they have more power over serpents, which are the most subject to the influence of incantations, than over other animals. Wherefore it has often been found by us and other Inquisitors that they have caused this obstruction by means of serpents or some such things.

For a certain wizard who had been arrested confessed that for many years he had by witchcraft brought sterility upon all the men and animals which inhabited a certain house. Moreover, Nider tells of a wizard named Stadlin who was taken in the diocese of Lausanne, and confessed that in a certain house where a man and his wife were living, he had by his witchcraft successively killed in the woman's womb seven children, so that for many years the woman always miscarried. And that, in the same way, he had caused that all the pregnant cattle and animals of the house were during those years unable to give birth to any live issue. And when he was questioned as to how he had done this, and what manner of charge should be preferred against him, he discovered his crime, saying: I put a serpent under the threshold of the outer door of the house; and if this is removed, fecundity will be restored to the inhabitants. And it was as he said; for though the serpent was not found, having been reduced to dust, the whole piece of ground was removed, and in the same year fecundity was restored to the wife and to all the animals.

Another instance occurred hardly four years ago in Reichshofen. There was a most notorious witch, who could at all times and by a mere touch bewitch women and cause an abortion. Now the wife of a certain nobleman in that place had become pregnant and had engaged a midwife to take care of her, and had been warned by the midwife not to go out of the castle, and above all to be careful not to hold any speech or conversation with that witch. After some weeks, unmindful of that warning, she went out of the castle to visit some women who were met together on some festive occasion; and when she had sat down for a little, the witch came, and, as if for the purpose of saluting her, placed both her hands on her stomach; and suddenly she felt the child moving in pain. Frightened by this, she returned home and told the midwife what had happened. Then the midwife exclaimed: "Alas! you have already lost your child." And so it proved when her time came; for she gave birth, not to an entire abortion, but little by little to separate fragments of its head and feet and hands. And this great affliction was permitted by God to punish her husband, whose duty it was to bring witches to justice and avenge their injuries to the Creator.

And there was in the town of Mersburg in the diocese of Constance a certain young man who was bewitched in such a way that he could never perform the carnal act with any woman except one. And many have heard him tell that he had often wished to refuse that woman, and take flight to other lands; but that hitherto he had been compelled to rise up in the night and to come very quickly back, sometimes over land, and sometimes through the air as if he were flying. . . .

And what, then, is to be thought of those witches who in this way sometimes collect male organs in great numbers, as many as twenty or thirty members together, and put them in a bird's nest, or shut them up in a box, where they move themselves like living members, and eat oats and corn, as has been seen by many and is a matter of common report? It is to be said that it is all done by devil's work and illusion, for the senses of those who see them are deluded in the way we have said. For a certain man tells that, when he had lost his member, he approached a known witch to ask her to restore it to him. She told the afflicted man to climb a tree, and that he might take which he liked out of a nest in which there were several members. And when he tried to take a big one, the witch said: You must not take that one; adding, because it belonged to a parish priest.

All these things are caused by devils through an illusion or glamour, in the manner we have said, by confusing the organ of vision by transmuting the mental images in the imaginative faculty. And it must not be said that these members which are shown are devils in assumed members, just as they sometimes appear to witches and men in assumed aerial bodies, and converse with them. And the reason is that they effect this thing by an easier method, namely, by drawing out an inner mental image from the repository of the memory, and impressing it on the imagination.

THE SALEM WITCHCRAFT TRIALS

The records of the witch trials in Salem, Massachusetts, provide a vivid example of the dynamics of the early modern obsession with witchcraft. When earlier seventeenth-century New England women such as Anne Hutchinson and the Quakers Ann Austin and Mary Fisher were suspected of being witches, their nonconformist religious behavior apparently lay at the root of these suspicions. By the 1690s, however, no link with a suspect religion was necessary in order to bring on the charge of witchcraft. In 1692, the Puritans of Boston and Salem were convinced that the devil was active among them and in league with witches.

One factor distinguishing the Salem witch outbreak from certain others was that the Salem accusers were primarily women, and, for the most part, young women. In late 1691 and early 1692, a group of girls and young women began meeting with Tituba, a West Indian slave of the Reverend Samuel Parris, the spiritual leader of Salem Village (modern Danvers, Massachusetts).[32] Those gathering to learn of voodoo and the occult included nine-year-old Betty Parris and eleven-year-old Abigail Williams (Samuel's daughter and niece, respectively), Elizabeth Hubbard (the seventeen-year-old servant of William Griggs, the village physician), nineteen-year-old Mercy Lewis and twelve-year-old Ann Putnam (the servant and the daughter of one of Salem Village's most prominent families), twenty-year-old Mary Warren, and several others. These girls, and Ann Putnam in particular, were to start the accusations of witchcraft that would result in 185 women and men being accused of witchcraft in Salem, fifty-nine of whom were tried and nineteen of whom were executed.[33]

In January of 1692, Betty Parris began exhibiting odd physical symptoms: hearing strange sounds, adopting contorted body positions, crawling into holes. Abigail Williams soon manifested similar behavior, followed shortly by all the others who attended Tituba's meetings. Those who witnessed the behavior attributed it to witchcraft; in early February, Dr. Griggs concurred. An investigation was set in motion; Reverend Parris and two neighboring ministers sought to root out the demonic influence. Late in February the girls began naming names. Tituba headed the list, followed by two other women of Salem, Sarah Good and Sarah Osborne; all were accused of "pricking and pinching" the bodies of the girls. On the morning of March 1, 1692, all three were brought to the village meetinghouse to be heard.

What happened that day set the stage for the remainder of the witch trials of Salem. The three women were brought before the girls. The girls fell into fits; they complained that Sarah Good's specter was moving among them. Sarah Good denied any such malicious activity, denied that she employed anyone else to do it, denied being in league with the devil, denied heresy, and, in the end, blamed Sarah Osborne, but Osborne too maintained her innocence. Tituba, however, confessed all; not only did she confess to being a witch, she named Good and Osborne as fellow accomplices with Satan.[34] If she had stopped there, the trial might have ended. But Tituba went on to assert that there were six active witches in Massachusetts, led by a white-haired man dressed in black. To find out who these witches were, Tituba was interrogated repeatedly. By the third questioning, the number of alleged witches in Boston and Salem had grown to nine. A week after the questioning began, the three women were in chains and imprisoned in Boston. On May 10, Sarah Osborne, unable to withstand the harsh conditions, died in prison. On July 19, Sarah Good and four other women were hanged on Gallows Hill outside Boston. Tituba, apparently because she was such a good witness, escaped execution.

Over the next few months many women (and a few men) were accused by the group of girls who had originally gathered around the confessed witch, Tituba. Whenever an accused witch was brought to be questioned, the girls obligingly fell into fits and complained that the specters of those accused were tormenting them. And whenever an accused witch confessed, the girls fell silent (satisfied that justice was being done?). Those accused fit no easily discernible pattern. One woman brought before the magistrates was seventy-one-year-old Rebecca Nurse, a respected matriarch of the church in Salem Village. On the same day, five-year-old Dorcas Good was jailed; apparently the devil did not distinguish by age. In May of 1692, George Burroughs, the former minister of Salem Village was arrested. Was he identified as the white-haired, black-garbed ringleader? When Burroughs was executed on August 19, the prominent Puritan Cotton Mather, explaining how a minister might be a witch, claimed "that the Devil has often been transformed into an Angel of Light."[35]

What factors contributed to this outbreak of witch hysteria? On the surface there was little to connect those accused of witchcraft. They were of widely disparate ages. Some were wealthy, upstanding members of the community; others were beggars or tavern keepers.[36] Not all were women. Recent analysis, however, has suggested that many of the accused shared a number of characteristics. Many had been or were currently engaged in disputes with the Putnams, a prominent Salem Village family whose daughter Ann was one of the chief accusers.[37] Moreover, many of those accused belonged to families who were engaged in land or boundary disputes with Salem Village.[38] A third, more sophisticated analysis, suggests that the majority of the women who were accused stood to inherit property, putting them in control of assets beyond the norm for women in that patriarchal society.[39]

Contributing to the persecutions was the method of "justice" that was employed: in the Salem cases the judges appear to have been more interested in maintaining order (that is, in rooting out witchcraft) than in ensuring that justice was done. The fact that "spectral evidence" was allowable complicated the proceedings; if the accusers could claim that they had experienced the "specter" of the accused acting (or having acted) on them, their testimony was generally held as damning evidence. The problem, as many even then could see, was that there was no way of corroborating such evidence. To manufacture a case against someone meant only that the "victim" need claim that the "specter" of the accused was actively tormenting him or her. In November of 1692, the General Court of the colony created a Superior Court to try the remaining witchcraft cases, and here, spectral evidence was not allowed.[40] When such evidence was kept from the courtroom, convictions became rarer and rarer. In May of 1693, the Superior Court sat for the last time, and Governor Phipps then pardoned all those still imprisoned for witchcraft.

The majority of those accused, tried, and executed were women—women who stood to inherit, women who ran taverns, women who did not fit into the orderly Puritanical social system, women who were not the "Daughters of Zion" Cotton Mather wished them to be.

SALEM DOCUMENTS *

Second Version of Sarah Good's Examination of March 1, 1691/92, written down by Ezekiel Cheever. [Sarah Good, the wife of William Good of Salem who is described as a laborer, was brought before the magistrates on the suspicion of witchcraft.]

The examination of Sarah Good before the worshipful assistants John Harthorn [and] Jonathan Curren.

HARTHORN (H): Sarah Good, what evil spirit have you familiarity with?
SARAH GOOD (G): None.
H: Have you made no contract with the devil?
G: (Good answered no.)
H: Why do you hurt these children?
G: I do not hurt them. I scorn it.
H: Who do you employ then to do it?
G: I employ nobody.
H: What creature do you employ then?

---

* The following materials from the Salem witchcraft trials have been adapted from records edited by Richard B. Trask in *"The Devil Hath Been Raised": A Documentary History of the Salem Village Witchcraft Outbreak of March 1692* (West Kennebunk, Maine: Phoenix Publishing, 1992), 5–6, 17, 21, 33. The spelling and punctuation of the records have been modernized.

G: No creature, but I am falsely accused.

H: Why did you go away muttering from Mr. Parris, [from] his house?

G: I did not mutter, but I thanked him for what he gave my child.

H: Have you made no contract with the devil?

G: No.

H: (Harthorn desired the children, all of them, to look upon her and see if this were the person that hurt them, and so they all did look upon her and said this was one of the persons that did torment them. Presently they were all tormented.)

H: Sarah Good, do you not see now what you have done? Why do you not tell us the truth? Why do you thus torment these poor children?

G: I do not torment them.

H: Who do you employ, then?

G: I employ nobody. I scorn it.

H: How did they come to be thus tormented?

G: What do I know? You bring others here and now you charge me with it.

H: Why, who was it?

G: I do not know, but it was someone you brought into the meetinghouse with you.

H: We brought you into the meetinghouse.

G: But you brought in two more.

H: Who was it then that tormented the children?

G: It was Osburn [sic].

H: What is it that you say when you go muttering away from persons' houses?

G: If I must tell, I will tell.

H: Do tell us then.

G: If I must tell, I will tell: it is the commandments; I may say my commandments, I hope.

H: What commandment is it?

G: If I must tell you, I will tell: it is a psalm.

H: What psalm?

G: (After a long time she muttered over some part of a psalm.)

H: Who do you serve?

G: I serve God.

H: What God do you serve?

G: The God that made heaven and earth. (Although she was not willing [to] mention the word "God," her answers were in a very wicked, spiteful manner, reflecting and retorting against the authority with base and abusive words and she was taken in many lies. It was here said that her husband had said that he was afraid she either was a witch or would be one very quickly. The worshipful Mr. Harthorn asked him his reason, why he said so of her, whether he had ever seen anything by her? He [the husband] answered, no, not in this nature, but it was her bad carriage [behavior] to him, and "Indeed," said he, "I may say with tears that she is an enemy to all good. . . .")

Depositions

Elizabeth Hubbard Against Sarah Good

The deposition of Elizabeth Hubbard, age about 17 years, who testified and said that on the 26 February 1691/92, I saw the apparition of Sarah Good, who did most grievously afflict me by pinching and pricking me and so she continued hurting me until the first day of March, being the day of her examination, and then she did also most grievously afflict and torture me also during the time of her examination, and also several times since she has afflicted me and urged me to write in her book. Also on the day of her examination, I saw the apparition of Sarah Good go and hurt and afflict the bodies of Elizabeth Parish, Abigail Williams, and Ann Putnam junior, and I have also seen the apparition of Sarah Good afflicting the body of Sarah Vibber. Also in the night after

Sarah Good's examination, Sarah Good came to me barefoot and barelegged and did most grievously torment me by pricking and pinching me, and I verily believe that Sarah Good has bewitched me. Also that night, Samuel Sibly, who was then attending me, struck Sarah Good on her arm.

[Elizabeth Hubbard also testified against Sarah Osborn [sic] and Tituba, the Indian in the household of Mr. Parish; Ann Putnam, Jr., and Abigail Williams also testified against Sarah Good, Sarah Osborn, and Tituba.]

Samuel Sibly, age about 34 years, testified and said that he was at the house of Doctor Grides that night after Sarah Good was examined. Elizabeth Hubbard said, "There Sarah Good stands upon the table by you with all her naked breast and barefoot, barelegged," and said "O nasty slut, if I had something I would kill her then." I struck her with my staff where she said Sarah Good stood, and Elizabeth Hubbard cried out, "You have hit her right across the back! You have almost killed her!" If anybody was there they may see it.

Ann Putnam, Sr., Against Martha Cory and Rebecca Nurse

The deposition of Ann Putnam, the wife of Thomas Putnam, age about 30 years, who testified and said (that) "on the 18th of March 1691/92, since I was worn out in helping to tend my poor afflicted child and maid, about the middle of the afternoon I lay down on the bed to take a little rest, and immediately I was almost pressed and choked to death; had it not been for the mercy of a gracious God and the help of those that were with me, I could not have lived many moments. Presently I saw the apparition of Martha Cory who tortured me so as I cannot express, [she was] ready to tear me all to pieces, and then departed from me a little while, but before I could recover strength or well take breath, the apparition of Martha Cory fell upon me again with dreadful tortures and hellish temptations to go along with her, and she also brought to me a little red book in her hand and a black pen, urging me vehemently to write in her book. And several times that day she most grievously tortured me, almost ready to kill me. On the 19th March, Martha Cory again appeared to me and also Rebecca Nurse, the wife of Frances Nurse, and they both did torture me a great many times that day with such tortures as no tongue can express, because I would not yield to their hellish temptations. Had I not been upheld by an Almighty arm, I could not have lived [for that] night. The 20th March being Sabbath day, I had a great deal of respite between my fits.

THE END OF THE WITCHCRAFT PERSECUTIONS

Just as perplexing as questions concerning how the witchcraft persecutions arose are questions concerning the shift in social conditions that facilitated their end.[41] Hugh Trevor-Roper suggests that the persecutions finally ended with the spread of new scientific notions of nature in which nature was seen as operating according to regular mechanical laws.[42] Whether because of these new views of nature or because of other social factors such as the consolidation of new forms of social control, greater standardization in criminal procedures, and the stabilization of new gender relations, concern with witchcraft finally subsided among the dominant classes of Europe. The dates of the last executions for witchcraft are as follows: England, 1685; North America, 1692; France, 1745; Germany, 1775; and Poland, 1793.

8.

～ The Protestant Reformations and the Catholic Response

MARTIN LUTHER

The Protestant Reformation, according to historian Roland Bainton, exerted a "greater influence on the family than on the political and economic spheres."[1] Whether or not this influence was especially salutary for women has been hotly debated in recent scholarship. Whatever final assessment we make, Martin Luther's writings on marriage and the family life that he undertook in middle age[2] prepared the way for the Protestant idea of the family for succeeding generations.

It may seem paradoxical that Luther (1483–1546), who stripped marriage of the sacramental status it had been accorded in Catholicism, also revolted against what he considered to be the Catholic church's denigration of marriage and exaltation of celibacy.[3] He openly advocated that monks and nuns should forsake the cloister—just as he had—once they understood that they were living contrary to God's word. When his advice was heeded, Luther found himself in the unaccustomed role of marriage broker for displaced nuns and eventually as the husband of one of them, Katherine von Bora. Luther's protest against the Catholic church, however, was not simply an attempt to correct its ceremonies and practices,[4] but was prompted by his religious conviction that God graciously forgave sinful humans; this belief came to be expressed in Luther's famous doctrine of justification by faith.

The Catholicism of his day, Luther thought, had not sufficiently stressed that God through Christ has accomplished salvation for us. We do not earn favor with God by the performance of religious "works," such as buying letters of indulgence, going on pilgrimages, or offering masses. All humans are, and remain, unworthy sinners who have no righteousness of their own to offer God. Luther thus dismissed the Catholic understanding of merit as a distortion of Christianity's central truth. No monk or nun might presume that he or she was more righteous in the eyes of God than was a layperson; the doctrine of justification by faith was a great leveler of persons. In fact, Luther argued from 1520 on that the practice of taking monastic vows was nonscriptural and destroyed the freedom of a Christian.[5]

LUTHER'S VIEWS ON MARRIAGE AND CELIBACY

The Estate of Marriage was written in 1522 when Luther was still a bachelor, while his *Lectures on Genesis* date from 1535–36, a decade after his marriage. In both treatises, Luther's arguments proceed from his interpretation of the Bible. He claims that God's command is to "reproduce and multiply," not to practice celibacy. Since God has made marriage an ordinance, everyone has the duty to marry except those truly rare persons who have the gift of celibacy or those with bodily defects that would prevent them from performing the sexual act. Antimarital propaganda from both pagan and earlier Christian traditions should be discounted. Luther caps his arguments for marriage by warning that failure to marry early could lead to various evils—fornication, "secret sins" (presumably masturbation), and physical ill health.

Did Luther's new estimate of marriage as an "estate" commanded by God entail a higher position for women? The evidence is contested.[6] Despite Luther's disapproval of the invectives against women and marriage found in earlier writings, his belief that women's real talent lies in childbearing does not strike a progressive note. Much of his thinking on the topic of women appears to be that of traditional Christianity: through Eve's sin, women became subject to men and now serve as a "medicine" or "antidote" for the male when his sexual desires press upon him. Her subjection means that she cannot teach or rule and must continue to be "named" by the man she marries in much the same way as Adam named Eve, along with the animals.[7]

On the other hand, Luther acknowledged that men were dependent on women not just for the bearing of children but in many spheres of life. Without women, he wrote, "the home, cities, economic life and government would virtually disappear."[8] In addition, he admitted that the wife has certain rights to sexual relations and children, rights so essential that if the husband cannot provide her with these, she may, as a last resort, even turn to bigamy.[9] And Luther's depiction of the father engaged in some of the less pleasant aspects of child care—washing diapers, for example—mitigates the impression we elsewhere receive of the patriarchally oriented family. Moreover, on a personal level, Luther's *Table Talk* suggests that he and Katy were a happy and devoted couple. Luther was comforted by Katy and rejoiced to see her pigtails on the pillow next to him.[10]

In the shift from nun to wife, however, many women actually lost personal status, for women in the convent often had considerably more power than they were allowed in the secular world as wives and mothers.[11] When women religious heeded Luther's words and gave their hands in marriage, they relinquished roles as leaders of spiritual life, lost the confirming experience of sisterhood found in monastic communities, and found that the types of work they might perform under a

Protestant regime were greatly narrowed. In the view of the eminent historian Lyndal Roper, the Lutheran Reformation served to bolster the values of civic order and wifely obedience: the "conservative rewriting of the Reformation movement's message around a politics of women's role in marriage and household was the key to its successful implementation and establishment."[12]

For some few women, however, the Protestant Reformation opened up an increased possibility for exercising both a spiritual and a social influence on the world through their new roles as ministers' wives. Thus, for example, Katherine Zell, wife of the reformer Matthew Zell, wrote and spoke in favor of the Reformation cause, despite admonitions from her critics that women's place was to keep silent.[13]

JOHN CALVIN

Luther's movement, to be sure, was only one component of the broader Protestant Reformation. Like Luther, the Genevan reformer John Calvin (1509–64) was opposed to the celibacy practiced within Roman Catholicism. Since human beings are by nature social,[14] Calvin wrote, God could not have stopped his creative activity with the formulation of Adam; indeed, he could not have stopped with that of Eve. Although she was created as a help for Adam and was to be subject to him, God's statement that "it is not good that the man should be alone" (Gen. 2:18) implied for Calvin that there were to be more people than simply the first man and woman. Procreation, therefore, was part of God's plan from the beginning.[15] And within marriage, Calvin saw sex as a good:[16] it curbed lust[17] and provided opportunity for husband and wife to delight in and with each other.[18] Should husband or wife "seek delight" elsewhere (in other words, should they commit adultery), Calvin believed in theory that either spouse (even the wife) could initiate divorce proceedings.[19]

The mutual delight between husband and wife, however, did not mean that Calvin thought that man and woman were equals

of the sight of God:[20] spiritual equality still meant sub-
ation for women in the life here and now.[21] Calvin firmly
eved in good order, which he understood to mean that within
the family, man is superior to woman—both because God so ordained and because "nature" clearly shows it. Men were to
work, to teach, to produce what is most excellent; women were
to help and obey men, to be subject to them.[22] Shunning public
roles, women were to stay at home, keeping house and raising
children.[23]

The limitation placed by Calvin on women's roles extended
to their place in the church as well. Despite their spiritual equality with men, women were denied ordination to the ministry;
they could not preach; they could not serve on the governing
bodies of churches. Yet, at least in theory, women were permitted to speak (as opposed to preach) in church. The Pauline injunction (in 1 Corinthians 14 and 1 Timothy 2) against such
speaking was, according to Calvin, a matter of "indifference"—
that is, it was a local custom rather than an ordinance of God.[24]

THE ANABAPTISTS

Some sixteenth- and early seventeenth-century Christians
thought that the Reformation churches, and not just the
Catholic church, needed to reform themselves still further.
Known as the Radical Reformation, or Anabaptists (so-called
because of their belief in rebaptizing adults who had been previously baptized as infants), these Christian groups took many of
the Reformation ideas to greater lengths than did Lutherans
and Calvinists.[25] As a result of their radical beliefs (which included pacifism, the separation of church and state, and anticlericalism), these groups were frequently victims of harsh
persecution by Catholics and other Protestants whose aim was
to return them to the more established churches. Such persecution was not limited to male Anabaptists; many women were
also tortured and put to death for adhering to their beliefs.[26]

The presence of female martyrs among the Anabaptists points to another area in which the radical reformers differed from the practices of more mainstream believers: the role of women and the place of sexuality.

The Anabaptists took the Bible seriously. In the Bible, women were subject to men; they were equally subordinated to men in Anabaptist circles. Yet with marriage no longer a sacrament and celibacy no longer an option for most people, the Anabaptists, like other Protestants, needed to redefine the relationship between sexuality and the sacred, and some did so by expanding the range of options from traditional marriage to plural marriage or polygamy. For example, one group—the Dreamers—believed that God through an inner voice would call them to leave their spouses and remarry. That same inner voice would then direct them when to engage (or not engage) in intercourse.[27] Better known and documented is the experiment in polygamy found among the Münster Anabaptists. In Münster, where there were many single women as well as married women who had been abandoned by their husbands, polygyny emerged as an acceptable way to extend patriarchal marriage; having multiple husbands, however, was not open to women.[28] In the cases of both the Dreamers and the Münster Anabaptists, the apparent libertinism of marital practice may well have been born of a moral need to deal with the surplus of unattached women.[29]

Like their Reformation counterparts, the Anabaptist churches understood that the Bible prohibited women from taking leadership roles. Moreover, in the writings of Anabaptist men, women were often subjected to the extreme potrayals of prior centuries, as weak and unmanageable, or (alternatively) as chaste and modest.[30] Anabaptist women did, however, play an important role in the spread of the faith. As in the early church and among the Calvinists, Anabaptist women donated money and opened their homes for meetings. Others took a more prominent, active role. For example, a Dutch woman, Elizabeth of Leeuwarden, traveled and worked with the Anabaptist leader nno Simons. When captured, she astounded her interrogators with her knowledge of the Bible and theology.[31]

As we noted earlier, the most dramatic witness to an Anabaptist woman's faith was martyrdom. Here an Anabaptist woman was the equal of a man and was expected to wage the battle against evil with the same weapons as a man: steadfastness of faith and knowledge of the Scriptures. In addition, through martyrdom a woman could exercise her faith in a way that ran counter to cultural norms, for by holding her faith commitment above all else, she might relegate family loyalties to the background. A married woman could "leave" one marriage—the earthly one—for a "marriage" to Christ,[32] but even here her possible roles remained limited: marriage and subordination to an earthly spouse, or "marriage" and subordination to a heavenly spouse, Christ. Being a bride of Christ, however, was the most exalted position an Anabaptist woman could hope for. For example, the Dutch Anabaptist Elizabeth, immediately prior to her own martyrdom, wrote to her infant daughter, Janneken, with this exhortation: "If you follow that which is good, and seek peace, and ensue it, you shall receive the crown of eternal life; this crown I wish you and the crucified, bleeding, naked, despised, rejected and slain Jesus Christ for your bridegroom."[33]

A CATHOLIC NUN'S RESPONSE

We should not imagine, however, that all Catholic women hastened to become Protestants; many nuns resisted the message of Protestantism, remaining loyal to their Catholic belief and religious profession. We are fortunate to possess an account written by one such nun, Jeanne de Jussie, who belonged to the Order of Saint Clare in Geneva when Protestant reform began to take hold in that city during the late 1520s and early 1530s. Her book, *Le Levain du Calvinisme (The Germ of Calvinism)*, written a few years after the events it describes, recounts the strenuous efforts made by Protestant civic leaders to persuade the nuns to convert to Protestantism. She details the stormy scenes that transpired between Protestants and Catholics in the years between 1526 and 1535, when the nuns finally left Geneva to relocate in Catholic France.[34] Sister Jeanne proudly reports that only one nun of her convent defected, a woman who demanded money from the sisters to pay her dowry and enlisted Protestant civic officials to press her case.[35]

One technique the Protestant authorities used in their campaign to "convert" the nuns was to require them to listen to speeches by Protestant ministers and women (sometimes former nuns) who denigrated the virginal profession and advocated marriage. The speeches reported by Sister Jeanne are of considerable interest. The Protestants appeal variously to "nature," to Scripture, and to "experience" as justifications for leaving the nunnery. They accuse the nuns of hypocrisy for claiming to uphold virginity (which is "impossible for nature to keep"[36]) while in actuality preparing succulent food ("good partridges and plump capons") for monks who will bed them down after the sumptuous repast.[37] Appealing to Scripture, the Protestants argue that God opposes virginity and wants men and women to be "two in one flesh."[38] They further claim that Jesus' mother didn't live as a recluse, that women participated in Jesus' ministry ("not wearing a habit as you do"), and that "all the apostles," including Paul, were married.[39] From Sister Jeanne's viewpoint, the Protestants had perverted the "sweet honey" of Scripture into "bitter poison."[40]

Protestant officials also brought former nuns who had married to testify before the Clares. One such woman, Marie d'Entière, tells the nuns:

> Oh, poor creatures! If you knew how good it is to have a handsome husband, how pleasing to God! For a long time I was in this darkness and hypocrisy as you are, but God alone made me know the abuse of my wretched life and through him I gained access to the

veritable light of truth. Know that I live in regret, for in the religious life there is only hypocrisy, mental corruption, and idleness.

Now that Marie has five "beautiful children," she professes that she is living in a way conducive to her health and salvation.[41]

Resisting this Protestant propaganda, the nuns claim that no tortures can make them renounce their religious state; far from living in "diabolic dissoluteness," they have espoused themselves to God, to whom they pledge their faith.[42] The Protestants' attempt to convince the nuns that their lives are corrupt is as futile (Jeanne vividly phrases it) as trying to make butter by beating the sea.[43] Especially do the nuns resist the Protestant claim that they were "forced" into the convent: their profession is one freely chosen.[44] It is rather the Protestants who misuse language, labeling as "conversion" what is truly "perversion."[45]

Although the Protestants prevailed in gaining control of Geneva, they did not succeed in convincing Jeanne and her sisters to become Protestants. On August 29, 1535, the nuns of Saint Clare filed silently out of their convent through a crowd of gaping and hostile spectators to take up residence in Annecy, France.[46] In later years, Jeanne de Jussie's book enjoyed popularity with Catholic audiences, going through five editions.[47] Jeanne and her sisters provide eloquent testimony that not all women of the Reformation era believed the message so ardently preached by Martin Luther and John Calvin.

THE ESTATE OF MARRIAGE *

Jesus. How I dread preaching on the estate of marriage! I am reluctant to do it because I am afraid if I once get really involved in the subject it will make a lot of work for me and for others. The shameful confusion wrought by the accursed

---

* From Martin Luther, *The Estate of Marriage,* in *Luther's Works,* vol. 45, *The Christian in Society* 2, ed. Walter I. Brandt (Philadelphia: Fortress Press, 1962), 17–21, 35–37, 39–41, 43–44, 45–46, 48–49.

papal law has occasioned so much distress, and the lax authority of both the spiritual and the temporal swords has given rise to so many dreadful abuses and false situations, that I would much prefer neither to look into the matter nor to hear of it. But timidity is no help in an emergency; I must proceed. I must try to instruct poor bewildered consciences, and take up the matter boldly. This sermon is divided into three parts.

Part 1. In the first part we shall consider which persons may enter into marriage with one another. In order to proceed aright let us direct our attention to Genesis 1:27, "So God created man ... male and female he created them." From this passage we may be assured that God divided mankind into two classes, namely, male and female, or a he and a she. This was so pleasing to him that he himself called it a good creation (Gen. 1:31). Therefore, each one of us must have the kind of body God has created for us. I cannot make myself a woman, nor can you make yourself a man; we do not have that power. But we are exactly as he created us: I a man and you a woman. Moreover, he wills to have his excellent handiwork honored as his divine creation, and not despised. The man is not to despise or scoff at the woman or her body, nor the woman the man. But each should honor the other's image and body as a divine and good creation that is well-pleasing unto God himself.

In the second place, after God had made man and woman he blessed them and said to them, "Be fruitful and multiply" (Gen. 1:28). From this passage we may be assured that man and woman should and must come together in order to multiply. Now this [ordinance] is just as inflexible as the first, and no more to be despised and made fun of than the other, since God gives it his blessing and does something over and above the act of creation. Hence as it is not within my power not to be a man, so it is not my prerogative to be without a woman. Again, as it is not in your power not to be a woman, so it is not your prerogative to be without a man. For it is not a matter of free choice or decision but a natural and necessary thing, that whatever is a man must have a woman and whatever is a woman must have a man.

For this word which God speaks, "Be fruitful and multiply," is not a command. It is more than a command, namely, a divine ordinance [werck] which it is not our prerogative to hinder or ignore. Rather, it is just as necessary as the fact that I am a man, and more necessary than sleeping and waking, eating and drinking, and emptying the bowels and bladder. It is a nature and disposition just as innate as the organs involved in it. Therefore, just as God does not command anyone to be a man or a woman but creates them the way they have to be, so he does not command them to multiply but creates them so that they have to multiply. And wherever men try to resist this, it remains irresistible nonetheless and goes its way through fornication, adultery, and secret sins, for this is a matter of nature and not of choice.

In the third place, from this ordinance of creation God has himself exempted three categories of men, saying in Matthew 19:12, "There are eunuchs who have been so from birth, and there are eunuchs who have been made eunuchs by men, and there are eunuchs who have made themselves eunuchs for the sake of the kingdom of heaven." Apart from these three groups, let no man presume to be without a spouse. And whoever does not fall within one of these categories should not consider anything except the estate of marriage. Otherwise it is simply impossible for you to remain righteous. For the Word of God which created you and said, "Be fruitful and multiply," abides and rules within you; you can by no means ignore it, or you will be bound to commit heinous sins without end. . . .

From this you can now see the extent of the validity of all cloister vows. No vow of any youth or maiden is valid before God, except that of a person in one of the three categories which God alone has himself excepted. Therefore, priests, monks, and nuns are duty-bound to forsake their vows whenever they find that God's ordinance to produce seed and to multiply is powerful and strong within them. They have no power by any authority, law, command, or vow to hinder this which God has created within them. If they do hinder it, however, you may be sure that they will not remain pure but inevitably besmirch themselves with secret sins or fornication. For they are simply incapable of resisting the word and ordinance of God within them. Matters will take their course as God has ordained.

As to the first category, which Christ calls "eunuchs who have been so from birth," these are the ones whom men call impotent, who are by nature not equipped to produce seed and multiply because they are physically frigid or weak or have some other bodily deficiency which makes them unfit for the estate of marriage. Such cases occur among both men and women. These we need not take into account, for God has himself exempted them and so formed them that the blessing of being able to multiply has not come to them. The injunction, "Be fruitful and multiply," does not apply to them; just as when God creates a person crippled or blind, that person is not obligated to walk or see, because he cannot.

I once wrote down some advice concerning such persons for those who hear confession. It related to those cases where a husband or wife comes and wants to learn what he should do: his spouse is unable to fulfill the conjugal duty, yet he cannot get along without it because he finds that God's ordinance to multiply is still in force within him. Here they have accused me of teaching that when a husband is unable to satisfy his wife's sexual desire she should run to somebody else. Let the topsy-turvy liars spread their lies. The words of Christ and his apostles were turned upside down; should they not also turn my words topsy-turvy? To whose detriment it will be they shall surely find out.

What I said was this: if a woman who is fit for marriage has a husband who is not, and she is unable openly to take unto herself another—and unwilling, too, to do anything dishonorable—since the pope in such a case demands without cause abundant testimony and evidence, she should say to her husband, "Look, my dear husband, you are unable to fulfill your conjugal duty toward me; you have cheated me out of my maidenhood and even imperiled my honor and my soul's salvation; in the sight of God there is no real marriage between us. Grant me the privilege of contracting a secret marriage with your brother or closest relative, and you retain the title of husband so that your property will not fall to strangers. Consent to being betrayed voluntarily by me, as you have betrayed me without my consent."

I stated further that the husband is obligated to consent to such an arrangement and thus to provide for her the conjugal duty and children, and that if he refuses to do so she should secretly flee from him to some other country and there contract a marriage. I gave this advice at a time when I was still timid. However, I should like now to give sounder advice in the matter, and take a firmer grip on the wool of a man who thus makes a fool of his wife. The same principle would apply if the circumstances were reversed, although this happens less frequently in the case of wives than of husbands. It will not do to lead one's fellow-man around by the nose so wantonly in matters of such great import involving his body, goods, honor, and salvation. He has to be told to make it right. . . .

The third category consists of those spiritually rich and exalted persons, bridled by the grace of God, who are equipped for marriage by nature and physical capacity and nevertheless voluntarily remain celibate. These put it this way, "I could marry if I wish, I am capable of it. But it does not attract me. I would rather work on the kingdom of heaven, i.e., the gospel, and beget spiritual children." Such persons are rare, not one in a thousand, for they are a special miracle of God. No one should venture on such a life unless he be especially called by God, like Jeremiah (16:2), or unless he finds God's grace to be so powerful within him that the divine injunction, "Be fruitful and multiply," has no place in him. . . .

Part 3. In the third part, in order that we may say something about the estate of marriage which will be conducive toward the soul's salvation, we shall now consider how to live a Christian and godly life in that estate. . . .

What we would speak most of is the fact that the estate of marriage has universally fallen into such awful disrepute. There are many pagan books which treat of nothing but the depravity of womankind and the unhappiness of the estate of marriage, such that some have thought that even if Wisdom itself were a woman one should not marry. A Roman official was once supposed to encourage young men to take wives (because the country was in need of a large population on account of its incessant wars). Among other things he said to them, "My dear young men, if we could only live without women we would be spared a great deal of annoyance; but since we cannot do without them, take to yourselves wives," etc. He was criticized by some on the ground that his words were ill-considered and would only serve to discourage the young men. Others, on the contrary, said that because Metellus was a brave man he had spoken rightly, for an honorable man should speak the truth without fear or hypocrisy.

So they concluded that woman is a necessary evil, and that no household can be without such an evil. These are the words of blind heathen, who are ignorant of the fact that man and woman are God's creation. They blaspheme his work, as if man and woman just came into being spontaneously! I imagine that if women were to write books they would say exactly the same thing about men. What they have failed to set down in writing, however, they express with their grumbling and complaining whenever they get together.

Every day one encounters parents who forget their former misery because, like the mouse, they have now had their fill. They deter their children from marriage but entice them into priesthood and nunnery, citing the trials and troubles of married life. Thus do they bring their own children home to the devil, as we daily observe; they provide them with ease for the body and hell for the soul.

Since God had to suffer such disdain of his work from the pagans, he therefore also gave them their reward, of which Paul writes in Romans 1:24–28, and allowed them to fall into immorality and a stream of uncleanness until they henceforth carnally abused not women but boys and dumb beasts. Even their women carnally abused themselves and each other. Because they blasphemed the work of God, he gave them up to a base mind, of which the books of the pagans are full, most shamelessly crammed full. . . .

Now observe that when that clever harlot, our natural reason (which the pagans followed in trying to be most clever), takes a look at married life, she turn up her nose and says, "Alas, must I rock the baby, wash its diapers, make its bed, smell its stench, stay up nights with it, take care of it when it cries, heal its rashes and sores, and on top of that care for my wife, provide for her, labor at my trade, take care of this and take care of that, do this and do that, endure this and endure that, and whatever else of bitterness and drudgery married life involves? What, should I make such a prisoner of myself? O you poor, wretched fellow, have you taken a wife? Fie, fie upon such wretchedness and bitterness! It is better to remain free and lead a peaceful, carefree life; I will become a priest or a nun and compel my children to do likewise."

What then does Christian faith say to this? It opens its eyes, looks upon all these insignificant, distasteful, and despised duties in the spirit, and is aware that they are all adorned with divine approval as with the costliest gold and jewels. It says, "O God, because I am certain that thou hast created me as a man and hast from my body begotten this child, I also know for a certainty that it meets with thy perfect pleasure. I confess to thee that I am not worthy to rock the little babe or wash its diapers, or to be entrusted with the care of the child and its mother. How is it that I, without any merit, have come to this distinction of being certain that I am serving thy most precious will? O how gladly will I do so, though the duties should be even more insignificant and despised. Neither frost nor heat, neither drudgery nor labor, will distress or dissuade me, for I am certain that it is thus pleasing in thy sight."

A wife too should regard her duties in the same light, as she suckles the child, rocks and bathes it, and cares for it in other ways; and as she busies herself with other duties and renders help and obedience to her husband. These are truly golden and noble works. This is also how to comfort and encourage a woman in the pangs of childbirth, not by repeating St. Margaret legends and other silly old wives' tales but by speaking thus, "Dear Grete, remember that you are a woman, and that this work of God in you is pleasing to him. Trust joyfully in his will, and let him have his way with you. Work with all your might to bring forth the child. Should it mean your death, then depart happily, for you will die in a noble deed and in subservience to God. If you were not a woman you should now wish to be one for the sake of this very work alone, that you might thus gloriously suffer and even die in the performance of God's work and will. For here you have the word of God, who so created you and implanted within you this extremity." Tell me, is not this indeed, as Solomon says (Prov. 18:22), "to obtain favor from the Lord," even in the midst of such extremity?

Now you tell me, when a father goes ahead and washes diapers or performs some other mean task for his child, and someone ridicules him as an effeminate fool—though that father is acting in the spirit just described and in Christian faith—my dear fellow you tell me, which of the two is most keenly ridiculing the other? God, with all his angels and creatures, is smiling—not because that father is washing diapers, but because he is doing so in Christian faith. Those who sneer at him and see only the task but not the faith are ridiculing God with all his creatures, as the biggest fool on earth. Indeed, they are only ridiculing themselves; with all their cleverness they are nothing but devil's fools.

St. Cyprian, that great and admirable man and holy martyr, wrote that one should kiss the newborn infant, even before it is baptized, in honor of the hands of God here engaged in a brand new deed. What do you suppose he would have said about a baptized infant? There was a true Christian, who correctly recognized and regarded God's work and creature. Therefore, I say that all nuns and monks who lack faith, and who trust in their own chastity and in their order, are not worthy of rocking a baptized child or preparing its pap, even if it were the child of a harlot. This is because their order and manner of life has no word of God as its warrant. They cannot boast that what they do is pleasing in God's sight, as can the woman in childbirth, even if her child is born out of wedlock. . . .

I therefore pass over the good or evil which experience offers, and confine myself to such good as Scripture and truth ascribe to marriage. It is no slight boon that in wedlock fornication and unchastity are checked and eliminated. This in itself is so great a good that it alone should be enough to induce men to marry forthwith, and for many reasons.

The first reason is that fornication destroys not only the soul but also body, property, honor, and family as well. For we see how licentious and wicked life not only brings great disgrace but is also a spendthrift life, more costly than wedlock, and that illicit partners necessarily occasion greater suffering for one another than do married folk. Beyond that it consumes the body, corrupts flesh and blood, nature, and physical constitution. Through such a variety of evil consequences God takes a rigid position, as though he would actually drive people away from fornication and into marriage. However, few are thereby convinced or converted. . . .

The estate of marriage, however, redounds to the benefit not alone of the body, property, honor, and soul of an individual, but also to the benefit of whole cities and countries, in that they remain exempt from the plagues imposed by God. We know only too well that the most terrible plagues [syphilis?] have befallen lands and people because of fornication. This was the sin cited as the reason why the world was drowned in the Deluge (Gen. 6:1–13), and Sodom and Gomorrah were buried in flames (Gen. 19:1–24). Scripture also cites many other plagues, even in the case of holy men such as David (2 Sam. 11–12), Solomon (1 Kings 11:1–13), and Samson (Judg. 16:1–2). We see before our very eyes that God even now sends more new plagues. . . .

Physicians are not amiss when they say: If this natural function is forcibly restrained it necessarily strikes into the flesh and blood and becomes a poison, whence the body becomes unhealthy, enervated, sweaty, and foul-smelling. That which should have issued in fruitfulness and propagation has to be absorbed within the body itself. Unless there is terrific hunger or immense labor or the supreme grace, the body cannot take it; it necessarily becomes unhealthy and sickly. Hence, we see how weak and sickly barren women are. Those who are fruitful, however, are healthier, cleanlier and happier. And even if they bear themselves weary—or ultimately bear themselves out—that does not hurt. Let them bear themselves out. This is the purpose for which they exist. It is better to have a brief life with good health than a long life in ill health.

But the greatest good in married life, that which makes all suffering and labor worth while, is that God grants offspring and commands that they be brought up to worship and serve him. In all the world this is the noblest and most precious work, because to God there can be nothing dearer than the salvation of souls. Now since we are all dutybound to suffer death, if need be, that we might bring a single soul to God, you can see how rich the estate of marriage is in good works. God has entrusted to its bosom souls begotten of its own body, on whom it can lavish all manner of Christian works. Most certainly father and mother are apostles, bishops, and priests to their children, for it is they who make them acquainted with the gospel. In short, there is no greater or nobler authority on earth than that of parents over their children, for this authority is both spiritual and temporal. Whoever teaches the gospel to another is truly his apostle and bishop. Mitre and staff and great estates indeed produce idols, but teaching the gospel produces apostles and bishops. See therefore how good and great is God's work and ordinance!. . .

To sum the matter up: whoever finds himself unsuited to the celibate life should see to it right away that he has something to do and to work at; then let him strike out in God's name and get married. A young man should marry at the age of twenty at the latest, a young woman at fifteen to eighteen; that's when they are still in good health and best suited for marriage. Let God worry about how they and their children are to be fed. God makes children; he will surely also feed them. Should he fail to exalt you and them here on earth, then take satisfaction in the fact that he has granted you a Christian marriage, and know that he will exalt you there; and be thankful to him for his gifts and favors.

With all this extolling of married life, however, I have not meant to ascribe to nature a condition of sinlessness. On the contrary, I say that flesh and blood, corrupted through Adam, is conceived and born in sin, as Psalm 51:5 says. Intercourse is never without sin; but God excuses it by his grace because the estate of marriage is his work, and he preserves in and through the sin all that good which he has implanted and blessed in marriage.

LECTURES ON GENESIS*

Genesis 2:18: *The Lord God also said: It is not good that man is alone; I shall make him a help which should be before him.*

We have the church established by the Word and a distinct form of worship. There was no need of civil government, since nature was unimpaired and without sin. Now also the household is set up. For God makes a husband of lonely Adam and joins him to a wife, who was needed to bring about the increase of the human race. Just as we pointed out above in connection with the creation of man that Adam was created in accordance with a well-considered counsel, so here, too, we perceive that Eve is being created according to a definite plan. Thus here once more Moses points out that man is a unique creature and that he is suited to be a partaker of divinity and of immortality. For man is a more excellent creature than heaven and earth and everything that is in them.

But Moses wanted to point out in a special way that the other part of humanity, the woman, was created by a unique counsel of God in order to show that this sex, too, is suited for the kind of life which Adam was expecting and that this sex was to be useful for procreation. Hence it follows that if the woman had not been deceived by the serpent and had not sinned, she would have been the equal of Adam in all respects. For the punishment, that she is now subjected to the

---

* From Martin Luther, *Lectures on Genesis,* in *Luther's Works,* vol. 1, ed. Jaroslav Pelikan (Saint Louis: Concordia Publishing House, 1958), 115–16, 117–19, 137–38, 202–3, 219.

man, was imposed on her after sin and because of sin, just as the other hardships and dangers were: travail, pain, and countless other vexations. Therefore Eve was not like the woman of today; her state was far better and more excellent, and she was in no respect inferior to Adam, whether you count the qualities of the body or those of the mind. . . .

Today, after our nature has become corrupted by sin, woman is needed not only to secure increase but also for companionship and for protection. The management of the household must have the ministration of the dear ladies. In addition—and this is lamentable—woman is also necessary as an antidote against sin. And so, in the case of the woman, we must think not only of the managing of the household which she does, but also of the medicine which she is. In this respect Paul says (1 Cor. 7:2): "Because of fornication let each one have his own wife." And the Master of the *Sentences* declares learnedly that matrimony was established in Paradise as a duty, but after sin also as an antidote. Therefore we are compelled to make use of this sex in order to avoid sin. It is almost shameful to say this, but nevertheless it is true. For there are very few who marry solely as a matter of duty. . . .

Therefore was this fall not a terrible thing? For truly in all nature there was no activity more excellent and more admirable than procreation. After the proclamation of the name of God it is the most important activity Adam and Eve in the state of innocence could carry on—as free from sin in doing this as they were in praising God. Although this activity, like the other wretched remnants of the first state, continues in nature until now, how horribly marred it has become! In honor husband and wife are joined in public before the congregation; but when they are alone, they come together with a feeling of the utmost shame. I am not speaking now about the hideousness inherent in our flesh, namely, the bestial desire and lust. All these are clear indications of original sin. . . .

... However, it is a great favor that God has preserved woman for us—against our will and wish, as it were—both for procreation and also as a medicine against the sin of fornication. In Paradise woman would have been a help for a duty only. But now she is also, and for the greater part at that, an antidote and a medicine; we can hardly speak of her without a feeling of shame, and surely we cannot make use of her without shame. The reason is sin. In Paradise that union would have taken place without any bashfulness, as an activity created and blessed by God. It would have been accompanied by a noble delight, such as there was at that time in eating and drinking. Now, alas, it is so hideous and frightful a pleasure that physicians compare it with epilepsy or falling sickness. Thus an actual disease is linked with the very activity of procreation. We are in the state of sin and of death; therefore we also undergo this punishment, that we cannot make use of woman without the horrible passion of lust and, so to speak, without epilepsy. ...

Genesis 2:23: *This one will be called Woman, because she has been taken from the man.*

And now, just as through the Holy Spirit Adam had an understanding of past events which he had not seen, and glorified God and praised Him for the creation of his mate, so now he prophesies regarding the future when he says that she must be called "Woman." We are altogether unable to imitate the nicety of the Hebrew language. אִישׁ denotes a man. But he says that Eve must be called אִשָּׁה, as though for "wife" you would say "she-man" from man, a heroic woman who performs manly acts.

Moreover, this designation carries with it a wonderful and pleasing description of marriage, in which, as the jurist also says, the wife shines by reason of her husband's rays. Whatever the husband has, this the wife has and possesses in its entirety. Their partnership involves not only their means but children, food, bed, and dwelling; their purposes, too, are the same. The result is that the husband differs from the wife in no other respect than in sex; otherwise the woman is altogether a man. Whatever the man has in the home and is, this the woman has and is; she differs only in sex and in something that Paul mentions 1 Timothy 2:13, namely, that she is a woman by origin, because the woman came from the man and not the man from the woman.

Also of this fellowship we observe some remnants today, although pitiable ones, if we look back to the first beginning. For if the wife is honorable, virtuous, and pious, she shares in all the cares, endeavors, duties, and functions of her husband. With this end in view she was created in the beginning; and for this reason she is called woman, or, if we were able to say so in Latin, a "she-man." Thus she differs only in sex from the head of the household, inasmuch as she was taken from the flesh of the man. Although this can be said only of Eve, who was created in this manner, nevertheless in Matthew 19:5 Christ applies it to all wives when He says that husband and wife are one flesh. In this way, although your wife has not been made from your bones, nevertheless, because she is your wife, she is the mistress of the house just as you are its master, except that the wife was made subject to the man by the Law which was given after sin. This punishment is similar to the others which dulled those glorious conditions of Paradise of which this text informs us. Moses is not speaking of the wretched life which married people now live but of the innocence in Paradise. There the management would have been equally divided, just as Adam prophesies here that Eve must be called "she-man," or "virago" because she performs similar activities in the home. Now the sweat of the face is imposed upon man, and woman is given the command that she should be under her husband. Yet there remain remnants, like dregs, of the dominion, so that even now the wife can be called "virago" because she has a share in the property. . . .

Genesis 3:16: *But to the woman He said: I will greatly multi-ply your sorrow when you are pregnant. In pain you will bear children, and you will be under your husband's power; and he will rule over you.*

. . . The second part of the curse has to do with cohabita-tion. If Eve had not sinned, she would not only have given birth without pain, but her union with her husband would have been just as honorable as it is honorable today to eat or converse with one's wife at the table. Rearing children would also have been very easy and would have abounded in joy. These benefits have been lost through sin, and there have fol-lowed those familiar evils of pain and work which are con-nected with gestation, birth, and nurturing. Just as a pretty girl, without any inconvenience, nay, even with great plea-sure and some pride, wears on her head a beautiful wreath woven with flowers, so, if she had not sinned, Eve would have carried her child in her womb without any inconve-nience and with great joy. Now there is also added to those sorrows of gestation and birth that Eve has been placed under the power of her husband, she who previously was very free and, as the sharer of all gifts of God, was in no re-spect inferior to her husband.

This punishment, too, springs from original sin; and the woman bears it just as unwillingly as she bears those pains and inconveniences that have been placed upon her flesh. The rule remains with the husband, and the wife is com-pelled to obey him by God's command. He rules the home and the state, wages wars, defends his possessions, tills the soil, builds, plants, etc. The woman, on the other hand, is like a nail driven into the wall. She sits at home, and for this reason Paul, in Titus 2:5, calls her an οἰκουργός. The pagans have depicted Venus as standing on a seashell; for just as the snail carried its house with it, so the wife should stay at home and look after the affairs of the household, as one who has been deprived of the ability of administering those affairs that are outside and that concern the state. She does not go beyond her most personal duties.

If Eve had persisted in the truth, she would not only not have been subjected to the rule of her husband, but she herself would also have been a partner in the rule which is now entirely the concern of males. Women are generally disinclined to put up with this burden, and they naturally seek to gain what they have lost through sin. If they are unable to do more, they at least indicate their impatience by grumbling. However, they cannot perform the functions of men, teach, rule, etc. In procreation and in feeding and nurturing their offspring they are masters. In this way Eve is punished; but, as I said in the beginning, it is a gladsome punishment if you consider the hope of eternal life and the honor of motherhood which have been left her. . . .

Genesis 3:20: *And Adam called the name of his wife Eve, because she was the mother of all the living.*

We heard above that the punishment of being under her husband's power was inflicted on the woman. An indication of that power is given here. It is not God who gives her a name; it is Adam, as the lord of Eve, just as he had previously given names to the animals as creatures put under him. No animal thought out a name for itself; all were assigned their names and received the prestige and honor of a name from their lord Adam. Similarly even today, when a woman marries a man, she loses the name of her family and is called by the name of her husband. It would be unnatural if a husband wanted to be called by his wife's name. This is an indication and a confirmation of the punishment or subjection which the woman incurred through her sin. Likewise, if the husband changes his place of residence, the woman is compelled to follow him as her lord. So manifold are the traces in nature which remind us of sin and of our misfortune. . . .

9.

❧ John Milton: The Puritan Transformation of Marriage

MILTON, PURITANISM, AND MARRIAGE

English Puritanism of the seventeenth century is often credited with shifting earlier notions of marriage into a more companionable and romantic frame. Although the English poet and political polemicist John Milton (1608–74) has sometimes been taken to exemplify this Puritan transformation of marriage, recent scholars have questioned that assessment on two grounds: whether Milton can properly be understood as a Puritan and whether the institution of marriage actually underwent a dramatic change with the development of Puritanism. On the first point, John Halkett argues that Milton is not easily classified as a Puritan on the subject of marriage and divorce, for no Puritan writer claimed that mutual help was the chief purpose of marriage, as Milton did, and Milton's "idiosyncratic" argument in favor of divorce cannot be taken as representative of Puritan thought. On the second point, Halkett notes that Puritan and Anglican teaching on marriage in this era are so similar as to render dubious any specifically "Puritan" traits; indeed, even secular courtesy books lending advice on genteel behavior hold much the same views on marriage as do Protestant religious writers of the period.[1] The debate over Milton's classification as a Puritan, as well as that over whether Puritanism brought significant changes to the understanding of marriage, are part of the broader discussion of whether the institution of marriage changed abruptly from the Middle Ages to the eighteenth century or evolved more gradually.[2]

Milton is best known for his great epic poems *Paradise Lost* and *Paradise Regained*, which he completed toward the end of his life. But in his middle years, he was an active polemicist for social reform, promoting especially freedom of the press and more liberal grounds for divorce. Arthur Barker argues that Milton's general commitment to liberalism—that is, to freedom as the primary social value—led him to promote both of these causes.[3] Other scholars propose, rather, that Milton's views of divorce are only special pleadings for his own interests, since his first marriage began very unhappily.[4] John Halkett speculates that if Milton had argued for the right to divorce on the grounds that his wife deserted him, he probably could have won his case. But he did not, and Halkett concludes that "it is inaccurate to read the tracts as largely personal documents."[5] Rather, Milton's intellectual convictions on the topic stand as primary.

MILTON'S DIVORCE TRACTS

Included in this chapter is an excerpt from Milton's *The Doctrine and Discipline of Divorce,* a treatise he submitted to a synod convened in 1643 by Parliament. It is the first treatise on divorce written in English and is, therefore, more important for how it poses the problems than for how it resolves them. It excited so much controversy that Milton revised and enlarged it, publishing a second edition the following year. Shortly afterward, he also published three more technical treatises on divorce: *The Judgment of Martin Bucer Concerning Divorce,* the *Tetrachordon,* and the *Colasterion.*[6]

Milton's views on marriage and divorce, as he expresses them in *The Doctrine and Discipline of Divorce,* can be summarized as follows. The key to Milton's conception of marriage is that he regards it, first of all, as a spiritual relationship rather than as a sexual relationship. It proceeds "from the mind rather than the body."[7] The chief purpose of this relation, according to Milton, is to provide conversation and companionship, to relieve human loneliness rather than to relieve sexual lust. Hence, Milton believes that marriage was instituted by the Creator before the Fall when God saw that it was not good for man to be alone.

The goal of marriage, according to Milton, is love, a relationship of sharing conducive to happiness and mutual help. But this love presupposes a certain compatibility of persons and temperaments. Where such compatibility is absent, no true marriage can exist, even if there is a sexual relation. In fact, Milton argues that a sexual relation between two incompatible persons makes them even more aware of their separateness and increases the feeling of loneliness, making things worse than if there had been no sex at all. Hence, Milton regards loveless sex as antimarital, for it increases (rather than decreases) the distance between people and their sense of isolation and despair.

Milton concludes by arguing against the entire prior Christian tradition for a new understanding of the biblical law that requires persons to divorce wherever there is "uncleanness" (Deut. 24:1). Milton interprets this uncleanness to mean the "unfitness of mind" that "hinders the solace and perfect society of the married couple, and what hinders that more than the unfitness and defectiveness of an unconjugal mind."[8] According to Milton, this teaching of Scripture is absolute, and not even Christ can revoke it. Divorce, therefore, is not merely allowed to an unhappily married couple; it is commanded to them as a moral obligation. To continue in an unhappy marriage is against the very purpose of marriage itself.

How radical Milton's views of marriage are can also be seen from his judgment regarding adultery. Adultery is usually regarded as the worst offense against marriage, and in the Christian tradition is often the only permissible ground for divorce. But Milton does not regard adultery as the most serious problem. The worst problem, says Milton, is "idolatry," by which he means a rejection of the spiritual companionship, or godly society, which is the main purpose of marriage itself. He says,

> Now whether Idolatry or Adultery be the greatest violation of marriage, if any demand, let him thus consider that among Christian Writers touching matrimony, there be three chief ends thereof agreed on; Godly society, next civil [society], and thirdly, that of the marriage-bed. Of these the first in name to be the highest and most excellent, no baptiz'd man can deny; nor that Idolatry smites directly against this prime end, nor that such as the violated end is, such is the violation: but he who affirms adultery to be the highest breach, affirms the bed to be the highest of marriage, which in truth is a gross and boorish opinion.[9]

In his three other tracts on divorce, as well as in *Paradise Lost*, Milton reconstrues the earlier Christian tradition in notable ways. Arguing from Matthew 5:17 that Jesus came to uphold the Jewish law, not abrogate it, Milton claims that if God permitted divorce to the ancient Hebrews, God certainly permits it to Christians, for God does not change.[10] Milton believed that the early church fathers adopted negative views toward marriage because they so strongly advocated asceticism;[11] in contrast to them, Milton daringly depicts (on the basis of Proverbs 8:22–31) God himself playing in delight with the female wisdom before the creation of the world, thus indicating God's preference for marriage, with its provision for relaxation and "rational delight," over celibacy.[12]

Moreover, Milton completely undoes Augustine's scheme of the "three goods" of marriage (children, sexual fidelity, and the sacramental bond).[13] In Milton's writings, children are almost nowhere alluded to as a "purpose" of marriage,[14] and the containment of lust is held to be an insignificant marital benefit. Interestingly, it is Augustine's third "good" of marriage, the "bond," that Milton finds most usable; citing Protestant reformer Martin Bucer, Milton defines the bond as "the communicating of all duties, both divine and human, each to other, with utmost benevolence and affection."[15] Unlike Augustine, for whom the "bond" meant that no Christian could divorce, Milton argues precisely the opposite: if the purpose of marriage signified by the "bond" is broken or lacking, divorce is appropriate because there *is* no marriage. Moreover, the "two in one flesh" passage so frequently cited by earlier Christian writers to signify the sexual relation of marriage is differently interpreted by Milton: "one flesh" means fitness of mind and disposition.[16]

PARADISE LOST

Milton's epic poem *Paradise Lost* also shows how Milton's understanding of Adam and Eve's relation—which had been paradigmatic for earlier Christian understandings of marriage—differed from that of his predecessors. Recent commentators have stressed that Milton depicts Adam and Eve in sexual relation before the Fall, a relation of "rational delight" that was not linked to procreation. Only *after* the Fall does Milton suggest a more sensual and brutish sexual relation.[17] Milton gives Eve real work to do in tending and keeping the Garden; indeed, her desire to perform her work more efficiently leads her to separate from Adam, the occasion for her encounter with Satan.[18] Eve is not a temptress to Adam, as some earlier Christian writers had imagined, and only after the Fall does Adam complain that the rib from which Eve was made was "crooked."[19] According to Milton, the human race does not fall with Eve's sin but falls when Adam decides he cannot live without Eve and therefore chooses freely and fully to sin. As soon as Eve explains that she has tasted the fatal fruit, Adam determines to join her in sin and death:

> Some cursèd fraud
> Of enemy hath beguiled thee, yet unknown,
> And me with thee hath ruined; for with thee
> Certain my resolution is to die.
>
> . . . I feel
> The link of nature draw me: flesh of flesh,
> Bone of my bone thou art, and from thy state
> Mine never shall be parted, bliss or woe.[20]

Indeed, John Halkett has argued that the poem presents a paradox: Adam "falls" precisely because he loves Eve as Milton thought a husband *should* love his wife; "it is exactly the perfection of his marriage with Eve which acts upon Adam as the greatest incentive to succumb to the temptation to disobey."[21]

OTHER ARGUMENTS IN THE DIVORCE TRACTS

In his divorce tracts, Milton also appeals to the fact that the first few generations of Christian emperors in late antiquity allowed divorce, a fact that Milton hopes will impress upon English kings the need for the reform of British divorce law.[22] Nonetheless, Milton did not wish to rest his case on civil grounds alone. Far from remaining content with a notion of marriage as a civil contract (a view that could have led him to advocate the permissibility of divorce if the contracting parties agreed), Milton appealed to a more spiritual understanding of marriage, often citing the verses in Ephesians 5 that compare husband and wife to Christ and the church.[23] Probably for Milton, the notion of marriage as a contract pure and simple rested too heavily on the notion of the will of the parties. For Milton, "will" is only one aspect of what "makes" a marriage, and in the *Colasterion* he argues explicitly against opponents who counseled unhappy couples to "try harder" rather than to seek divorce. Milton rather believes that marriage rests on a somewhat mysterious compatibility of "soul"; what is essential is a harmony of the man's and woman's "natures"—and over these, the couple may have little control.[24] Compatibility of temperament, which is essential for marriage, cannot be grounded in will alone.

MILTON'S "FEMINISM"?

Is Milton to be understood as a protofeminist for his new views on marriage and divorce?[25] Certainly Milton's understanding of marriage can be regarded as a real advance beyond the traditional viewpoint that made the slaking of male lust and female procreation its primary purposes. Milton's view of marriage is built on the idea of spiritual reciprocity; here men and women are each fully human and complementary of one another. The woman is not placed solely in the role of childbearer and confined to the domestic sphere.

This is, however, to put the best face on the matter, for when we inquire more carefully into what Milton means by the "idolatry" that is a greater violation of marriage than even adultery, we discover his patriarchal attitudes. Idolatry, according to Milton, is loving another Lord rather than one's own Lord, thereby rejecting the proper hierarchy of society. The proper hierarchy of marriage, according to Milton, is that the wife should be subject to her husband, for the two are created "hee for God only, shee for God in him."[26] If the wife disobeys her husband and has a will that is not subject to his, then, in Milton's view, this is a greater wrong to marriage than even adultery. This is the "unconjugal mind" and "uncleanness" for which a man must divorce his wife. Wives, however, are not given the right to divorce on the same grounds as husbands. Although Milton cites passages from ancient Roman law that gave women the right to initiate divorce,[27] these grounds were not in effect in British law at Milton's time; indeed, British law did not permit women to initiate divorce until 1857.[28] Moreover, Milton firmly believed that only males were created "in the image of God,"[29] and in *Paradise Lost,* he does not depict Adam and Eve as equal but as "complementary."[30]

From the feminist viewpoint, Milton is thus a mixture of promising new beginnings that are then immediately compromised by traditional patriarchal prejudices. His view of marriage would lead toward greater equality and freedom, but the combination of Milton's hierarchical viewpoint with his Protestant insistence on the necessity of marriage for everyone drives women into a greater subordination to men. At least in the Catholic spiritual tradition, there is an emphasis on two things that Milton has lost: the notion of a direct relation of married women to God rather than one mediated by their husbands, and the possibility of celibacy as an alternative to marriage. These two factors gave women like Margery Kempe a power with regard to the marriage relation that Milton's wives have lost.[31]

THE DOCTRINE AND DISCIPLINE OF DIVORCE REVISED FOR THE BENEFIT OF BOTH SEXES *

Book I

PREFACE

People are responsible for their own miseries as well as for most of the evils which they attribute to God's activity. Of particular concern is the absurdity of the canonical decrees about divorce. . . .

---

* A modern paraphrase of selections from John Milton's *The Doctrine and Discipline of Divorce Revised for the Benefit of Both Sexes.*

. . . What is more suited to the solace and delight of a person than marriage? Yet the misinterpretation of some Scriptures, especially those Old Testament texts which allow divorce, has often changed the blessing of matrimony into a familiar mutual grief, or at least into a depressing and disconsolate captivity from which there is no refuge or redemption. These misinterpretations run to both extremes: too much freedom to divorce or too great severity against it.

God taught us why he instituted marriage. He expressly implied that its purpose was to be the fitting and happy companionship of man with woman, to comfort and refresh him against the evil of solitary life. The purpose of procreation was not mentioned until later, as a secondary end in dignity even if not in necessity. Yet the practice now is that once two persons have been wedded in church and experienced sexual intercourse, they are obliged forever to live together even though they may have been mistaken in marrying in the first place. Whether because of error, deception, or misadventure, it may turn out that their dispositions, thoughts, or constitutions prevent them from living happily together all their days or being a remedy against loneliness. Yet in such cases, the present law prohibiting divorce forces them, as long as they have any possibility whatsoever for sensual enjoyment, to live together in their unspeakable weariness and to despair of ever having the kind of companionship for which God primarily intended marriage.

What a calamity this is! The writer of Ecclesiastes would sigh out, "What a sore evil is this under the sun!"

The cause of this awful situation is the canon law, whose adherents do not charitably consult the Interpreter and Guide of our faith, but rely instead on the literal interpretation of the text. They are doubtlessly inspired by the Devil to make marriage become so insupportable that some persons do not dare to marry and some others, who do, become weary of it and begin to live licentiously. For many years, in fact, the theologians of the Church despised marriage as almost a defilement of the flesh, forbidding it altogether to priests and seeking to dissuade widows and widowers from remarrying. For example, look at the writings of Tertullian and Jerome. . . .

CHAPTER I

My position proved from the Old Testament. . . .

It is my intention, if at all possible, to remove the canonists' great and sad oppression which has resulted from a literal interpretation of Scripture. That interpretation has not only invaded and disturbed the dearest and most peaceful estate of domestic society, but it has also overburdened, if not overwhelmed, many Christians by leaving them without the Church's helpful pastoral care. My argumentation will involve advocating a position which replies to Scriptural as well as rational objections.

My position is that an indisposition, unfitness for marriage, or a psychological incompatibility which would appear to be unchangeable, is a greater reason for divorce than natural frigidity, for it interferes with the main purpose of marriage, that is, solace and peace. Such grounds for divorce are especially forceful where no children are involved and if there is mutual consent.

This I conclude from the law in Deuteronomy 24:1, "When a man has taken a wife and married her, and it comes to pass that she find no favor in his eyes because he has found some uncleanness in her, let him write her a bill of divorce, give it to her hand, and send her out of his house . . . ." Christ himself teaches that this law shall never be abrogated until the end of the world. . . .

The cause of divorce mentioned in Deuteronomy is "some uncleanness." The Hebrew word means "nakedness of ought" or "lacking what is fitting," which all reputable interpreters understand as referring to the mind as well as to the body. What greater nakedness or unfitness is there than that lack or defect of conjugal mind which hinders the solace and peaceful society of the married couple? My view of divorce is in perfect agreement with that described in the best sense of the law of Moses. Even in the Old Testament, the cause of divorce is a matter of pure charity and is plainly moral; moreover, it is invoked more now than ever before and is, therefore, certainly lawful. If such was God's gracious indulgence under the Old Law, how much more so will it be God's intention under the Covenant of Grace to spare his servants their misery and grief and grant them, instead, remedy and relief. . . .

CHAPTER II

The first reason of this law of divorce is grounded on the primary reason of matrimony: no covenant ever creates obligations that contradict the purpose for which it is made.

Good sense and fairness require that no law or covenant, however solemn, should tend to undermine the very institution it is supposed to preserve. This holds for God's Covenant with man and for covenants between human beings. Hence, the law of marriage should not perpetually bind innocent individuals who have made a mistake in their choice of each other as marriage partners, who have received perpetual sorrow rather than the expected solace. When nothing but a false understanding of God's law keeps partners together, then the force of the law works against God's express purpose for establishing that law. For God's chief end in creating woman to be joined to man is expressed in his own words. It is this expression which tells us what constitutes a true marriage. "It is not good," said God, "for man to be alone. I will create a helpmate for him." The meaning of these words is clear. It is God's intention that a just and happy companionship be the chief and most noble end of marriage. Nothing in these words necessarily indicates sexual union, but rather these words indicate that marriage is to prevent loneliness in a man's mind and spirit. On this point Fagius, Calvin, Pareus, and Rivetus are in total agreement. Indeed it shows both God's blessing and man's excellence that the comfort and satisfaction of the mind is given priority over the sensual satisfaction of the body. To honor this higher purpose is the true sanctity of marriage.

It is thus with all generous married persons. When minds and persons are united, some lack of sexual satisfaction can be borne much more easily. But if the situation is reversed, and there is sexual satisfaction but no mental union, then the delight of the body will quickly become unsavory and contemptible. In such cases the loneliness of man which God had intended marriage to prevent increases in a way much worse than in the loneliest single life.

In single life the absence of a companion trains a man to be self-sufficient or to seek out a mate. But in the situation of the unhappily married man, he is faced continually by his deluded hopes, and has no remedy for them. For men inclined to depression this must be a daily suffering like unto that endured by those condemned to death.

It is unthinkable that by one mistake so noble a creature as man should be imprisoned by marriage in the very loneliness that he sought to escape through marriage. It is evident that if marriage with a given woman not only does not lessen a man's loneliness, but even increases it, and in the increasing leads to a personal dejection and diminishment of family life, then that marriage is not a true marriage.

In such a situation the wronged spouse does the courageous thing in claiming the right to seek true companionship, rather than trying to find compensation in brothels or adultery, or in allowing his vital strength to be drained away by his efforts to cope with such a burden. It was in view of just such a situation that the mercy of the Law of Moses (which commands men to divorce) was practiced.

CHAPTER III

Concerning the ignorance and evil of Canon Law which provides for the right of the body in marriage, but does not provide for the sufferings of the mind and heart.

How preposterous that Canon Law should have been so careful to provide against eventualities of sexual impediment without also providing against impediments in that union of minds and hearts which is so essential to the most sacred end of marriage. If the sensual union of bodies is not possible, then, according to Canon Law, the marriage is not a real one. Yet according to Canon Law the inability to achieve union of minds and hearts in an agreeable companionship is to be endured no matter what the consequences of this suffering may be. Wisdom and love, weighing the intent of God's own institution, would see that an individual imprisoned in loneliness deserves to be freed, even more than does the individual who can not find relief in marriage for his sexual desires.

In the marriage ceremony, we read that we should not enter into marriage just to satisfy our sexual appetites, like brute beasts who are without understanding. But Canon Law is written as though only the satisfaction of the sexual appetite is to be considered, for that Law asserts that if sexual union is impossible, the marriage is annulled. . . .

CHAPTER IV

Marriage, according to the words of our Saviour, is not first the remedy of lust, but rather the fulfillment of conjugal love and companionship.

. . . St. Paul says, "It is better to marry than to burn." Marriage is ordained to remedy man's burning, but exactly what kind of burning? Certainly not the mere bodily impulses toward sensual satisfaction. God does not concern himself principally with such matters. What is this burning then but the desire which God gave to Adam in Paradise before he committed the sin of incontinence. God saw it was not good that man be left alone to experience that burning desire to be united with another, body and soul, in the loving society of wedlock. If this union was so important before the fall when man was perfect in himself, how much more important is it now, after the fall, for man to have an intimate helpmate, a true marriage partner?

A man who has made the mistake of choosing an incompatible spouse, remains more alone than before his marriage and suffers a burning much harder to bear than that of the body's passions. This burning, which cannot be brought under control by physical discipline, is a pure longing for love and companionship, a longing stronger than death itself. This is the true spiritual burning which marriage is ordained to remedy, a burning which cannot be extinguished in those men who have made the choice of an incompatible marriage partner. . . .

CHAPTER IX

Adultery is not the greatest breach of matrimony. There are other violations that are just as important.

In order to determine whether idolatry or adultery be the greatest violation of marriage, let us consider the three chief ends of marriage agreed upon among Christian authors. These ends are: first, spiritual union; second, civil union; and third, the union of the marriage-bed. No baptized man could deny that the first of these ends is the most excellent, nor could he deny that idolatry strikes at the very heart of this primary end.

He who claims that adultery is the greatest breach, claims that the marriage-bed is the greatest good of marriage. And those crude men who believe such a thing, as common as they are, are as far from the light of civility, philosophy, and Scripture as they could possibly be.

It is beyond question that the noblest end of marriage is the help it gives in the pursuit of a holy life. But if the needs of the individual are considered in the light of the three ends of matrimony ordained by God, then the most important is the one that the individual most sought to fulfill through marrying. And a marriage is most broken when it fails to achieve that for which it was undertaken, that is, the attainment of spiritual union, or civil union, or sexual union. That law which recognizes only the last and least noble of those unions is perverse, and as cold as the sexual frigidity of which alone it is mindful.

Now let me return to my first point. There I indicated that incompatibility of minds and hearts is a just cause for divorce. First, because it opposes the purpose of marriage as God instituted it, and keeps marriage from satisfying the pure and spiritual desires that God kindled in man to be the bond of wedlock. Second, that it leads many to enter into adulterous relations, as the heart seeks elsewhere the consolations it had hoped to find at home in marriage. Or else it leads to a man's denying God as he finds himself in a trying situation, bound there by a mistaken notion of God's Law. What is actually binding him is not God, but man's unrighteous ignorance. While such a prohibition against divorce safeguards outward formalities, the inward reality is one in which religious faith dies because a man is compelled to remain married.

CHAPTER XIII

Concerning the ninth reason about marriage. Where genuine relationship is not present, there is no true matrimony. Marriage is to be compared with all the other covenants and vows which can be broken for a good of man. Marriage is the Sacrament of the Papists, and unfit marriage is the Idol of the Protestants.

Ninthly, I suppose everyone would agree that marriage is a human society, and that all genuine relationships must proceed from the mind rather than the body. If the mind cannot find in marriage the companionship that it so reasonably and humanly desires, then marriage is not a human relationship but a contractual formality. In wisdom and fairness such marriages should be dissolved.

But, it is often argued that marriage is more than human since it is the covenant of God (Prov. 2:17). Therefore, man cannot dissolve it. I answer that if marriage be more than human, so much more does it indicate that the most important union is that of souls, rather than bodies. The greatest breach of that covenant is the absence of a union of minds and hearts, not the absence of bodily union, for the body has the least importance in a covenant which is more than human. Thus, the above reason for dissolving the marriage still holds good. . . .

10

∿ Friedrich Schleiermacher and Romantic Theology*

The cultural movement of Romanticism is represented in this volume by the Protestant theologian Friedrich Schleiermacher (1768–1834), who is often called "the father of modern theology." In response to philosophical critiques of the metaphysical foundations of Christianity in the late eighteenth century, Schleiermacher sought to ground religion within the human consciousness in "the feeling of absolute dependence" which he saw as the fundamental human relation to the divine. Schleiermacher elaborated this notion both in his early lectures *On Religion* (1799) and in his later work of systematic theology, *The Christian Faith* (1830). In this way, Schleiermacher sought to transform theology into a teaching about human faith *(Glaubenslehre)* from its traditional definition as a "teaching about God." Schleiermacher thus shifted the paradigm for understanding theology.[1]

---

* The editors acknowledge with gratitude the assistance of Ruth Drucilla Richardson in preparing this introduction. Her translations of the "Credo" and the *Ten Commandments* are used with her permission.

At the turn to the nineteenth century, Schleiermacher was part of a circle of intellectual men and women in Berlin, including his close friends Friedrich Schlegel and Henrietta Herz, who were committed to fostering the theories of Romanticism. Members of this circle engaged in philosophical discussion, translation of the Greek classics, and literary and poetic writing, and were the intellectual avant-garde of their era. It is notable, given the earlier marginalization of Jews in Germany, that most of the women in the group were Jewish.

SCHLEIERMACHER, ROMANTICISM, AND GENDER

An important notion of Romanticism was that the whole of reality is fully present in every living thing. Schleiermacher appropriates the Romantic idea of the whole embodied in each individual in his "Credo":

1. I believe in infinite humanity, which existed before it assumed the cloak of manhood and womanhood.

2. I believe that I live not in order to obey or to seek amusement, but rather to become; and I believe in the power of will and education to bring me close to the infinite again, to deliver me from the chains of miseducation, and to make me independent of the limitations of gender.

3. I believe in inspiration and virtue, in the dignity of art and the excitement of learning, in friendship with men and women, and love of my native country, in past greatness and in future improvement.[2]

In this "Credo," Schleiermacher delineates several significant ideas: that every person is an embodiment of genderless infinite humanity; that gender is a "limitation" that "cloaks" our infinite humanity; that thinking of oneself as a gendered being makes all one's experiences a "miseducation"; that the purpose of life is, through "the power of will and education," to draw "close to the infinite again"; and that "future improvement" in one's life is effected through contact with art, learning, love of country, and especially through friendship between men and women.

Schleiermacher, one of the founders of the University of Berlin and a distinguished professor, advocates scientific scholarly learning as essential to the improvement of every person's life. He insists, nonetheless, that an even more important part of education is "friendship between women and men." Here Schleiermacher stands as an early critic of the patriarchal bias within Western civilization, which emphasizes reason and a predominantly analytical approach to life. To rectify matters, Schleiermacher believes that women should have access to the same "education, art, wisdom, and honor" that men have.[3] But he also insists that men recover capacities for intuition and feeling that they have suppressed in becoming hyperrational. Men must reclaim and develop these sensibilities if they themselves are to overcome the limitations of gender and to develop toward infinite humanity,[4] and this they can do only through friendship with women. The key to friendship, he says, is "conversation," in which friends learn one another's attitudes, viewpoints, problems, and histories. As this occurs, each person's life is multiplied and enlarged by learning how other people feel and think.[5] In this way, one gradually overcomes the "limitations of gender" and develops toward "infinite humanity."

Of all the obstacles that persons must transcend on their way to infinite humanity, however, adulthood is especially important. Schleiermacher wants people to develop not only beyond the limitations created by gender but also beyond those created by aging. In his view, the difference between adults and children is even greater than that between men and women. Like many Romantic thinkers, Schleiermacher believed that children are closer than adults to God, to goodness, and to truth. He claims that Christianity is a "Romantic religion," expressing through the

Christmas festival its belief in "the immediate union of the divine with the being of a child."[6] Just as God became a child, so all adults must seek rebirth into childlikeness, which they can learn only from children. The recovery of our "infinite humanity" requires not simply that we overcome "the limitations of gender" but also that we overcome "the limitations of adulthood." Schleiermacher explores this "double dialectic" of overcoming gender and age difference in his famous text, *Christmas Eve*.

SCHLEIERMACHER'S *CHRISTMAS EVE* DIALOGUE

The literary form of *Christmas Eve* is consistent with its philosophical doctrine: *Christmas Eve* is a conversation that includes several men and women, plus a child and a wise Wanderer. The conversation begins with the child Sophie (her name means Wisdom) playing with Christmas gifts and singing that these must have come from God together with his gift of Jesus. Sophie innocently connects divine grace with her Christmas toys, the family celebration with the biblical story, in a single undifferentiated gestalt.

Sophie's Edenic moment is interrupted by an analytical adult man who tries to make her consider the meaning of Christmas. He asks Sophie whether getting presents has made her sad or has made her happy. Sophie, who has been simply immersed in the Christmas festivities, replies that she is always content with her immediate state in life.

Later in the conversation, the Wanderer Josef (who represents Schleiermacher himself) enters the party and interprets Sophie's feelings. He says, "For my part, today, . . . all forms are rigid, all speech-making too tedious and cold. Itself, unbounded by speech, the subject of Christmas creates in me a speechless joy, and I cannot but laugh and exult like a child."[7] Against the analytical Western philosophical tradition that undergirds patriarchy, Schleiermacher asserts that the child's experience of life in its immediacy and wholeness constitutes the true goal of our existence.

Christmas Eve explores the double dialectic of men and women in conversation (toward the overcoming of gender) and of adults interacting with children (toward the recovery of childlikeness and "new birth"). Sophie and Josef make a pair, representing original and recovered childlikeness (birth and rebirth); the men and women conversationalists represent different types of rational and affective approaches to life. The goal of all life is to regain the "original childlikeness" (Wisdom) that Schleiermacher identifies with "infinite humanity" and our immediate union with the divine. Since, for Schleiermacher, the child is the image of love, the union of infinite humanity with the infinite divine,[8] he opposes dynastic marriages arranged among the aristocracy for political or financial purposes.

Like the later psychologist of religion William James, Schleiermacher sees that some people develop in a manner so gradual that they never revolt against their childhood experiences (the "once-born"). Others seem to mature only by breaking with their childhood roots and, through a crisis, appropriating a new identity (the "twice-born"). In Schleiermacher's view, women stand closer to the "once-born" type than do men and hence retain more of the "original childlikeness" he valued. In his *Pedagogical Writings,* Schleiermacher explains that girls experience a more harmonious development from childhood to adulthood than do boys, who are torn from their families and prepared for a public life in the larger community, a process that necessitates their struggle to regain the virtues of childhood.[9]

SCHLEIERMACHER'S
TEN COMMANDMENTS
[ON SEXUAL LOVE AND MARRIAGE]

In this work,[10] Schleiermacher transposes the first biblical commandment ("You shall have no other Gods before me") to formulate a new love commandment: "You shall have no other lover beside him." While Schleiermacher originally wrote his ten love commandments for women, they can profitably be understood by imagining their application to both women and men.

Schleiermacher's *Ten Commandments* distinguish love from friendship and assert that love—not any material consideration—is the sole proper basis for marriage. Friendship, says Schleiermacher, "originates in the reciprocal completion and confirmation of individuality." But love originates in "a total unification of consciousness which brings forth a new image." Therefore, says Schleiermacher, "procreation is bound up with love rather than with friendship [for sexual] love involves necessarily the merging of two personalities."[11]

Schleiermacher's *Ten Commandments* must be understood in their historical context,[12] in which upper-class children were important for dynastic reasons: estates were protected and transmitted to the next generation through progeny, and financial and political concerns determined the selection of marriage partners among the aristocracy. Against this situation, Schleiermacher asserts that love is the sole valid basis for marriage. But, more startlingly, he claims that a married couple should not conceive children intentionally. This commandment against the "intentional" conception of life has nothing to do with contemporary debates about contraception. Rather, it is Schleiermacher's repudiation of the traditional practice of seeking children for reasons of family line and inheritance. To intend to have children for some human purpose is "idolatry" because the child is the primary "image of God."

Why, then, should people have children? Rejecting the view that children should serve any human purpose, Schleiermacher claims that children are a gift that God bestows upon the love between a man and a woman. Hence, in his fifth commandment, Schleiermacher says, "Honor the individuality and free will of your children so they may prosper and live healthily on the earth"; parents should respect their children's own purposes and not impose adult values on them.

The child who is thus honored can become "a little prophetess" (or "prophet") and, like Sophie, can teach its parents the childlikeness necessary to reclaim "infinite humanity" and to enter the kingdom of God. Children are to be our spiritual teachers; that is God's purpose for their lives.

SCHLEIERMACHER'S "FEMINISM"?

Should Schleiermacher be considered a protofeminist? Only to a certain degree. His views on women's roles remained largely traditional: women should stay at home, raise children, and participate in public life only through their husbands.[13] The innocence that girls should retain was not, in Schleiermacher's view, compatible with scientific and leadership pursuits. As commentator Patricia Guenther-Gleason has put it, although Schleiermacher's "'public' realm may be influenced by feminist values, it would contain no women."[14] Other scholars have nonetheless argued that there are elements in Schleiermacher's theology that might be appropriated by our contemporaries for the development of feminist Christologies.[15]

CHRISTMAS EVE: DIALOGUE
ON THE INCARNATION *

In the meantime Sophie [ten or eleven years old] had been mostly at the piano getting acquainted with her newly acquired treasures. Part of them she did not know, and many of those she knew she wanted to greet at once as her own

---

* From Friedrich Schleiermacher, *Christmas Eve: Dialogue on the Incarnation,* trans. Terrence N. Tice (Richmond: John Knox Press, 1967), 51–56, 85–86.

possessions. At this moment she could be heard singing a chorale from a cantata, her voice carrying with particular clarity the lines:

Who gave his Son that we might ever live,
All things to us with him shall he not give?

upon which there followed the magnificent fugue:

If I possess but thee, I ask no more of earth or heaven.

When she had finished, she closed the keyboard and returned to the drawing room.

"Look there," exclaimed Leonhardt, when he spied her coming—"our little prophetess! Now I shall determine how far she is still under your influence." Stretching out his hand to her, he asked: "Tell me, little one, wouldn't you rather be merry than sad?"

"I do not think I am either at just this moment," she replied.

"What! not merry after receiving so many lovely presents? Ah, the solemn music must have made you feel that way! But you have not quite understood what I meant. What I asked, no doubt unnecessarily, was which of the two you would rather be: merry or sad?"

"Oh, that's hard to say," she responded. "I do not particularly favor one or the other. I always just like to be whatever I am at the moment."

"Now you've got me puzzled all over again, my little sphinx. What do you mean by that?"

"Well," she said, "all I know is that sometimes feelings of gladness and sorrow get strangely mixed up and fight each other; and that makes me uneasy, because I can tell, as Mother has also pointed out, that something is always wrong or out of kilter then, and so I don't like it."

"All right," he asked again, "suppose you have only one feeling or the other, is it all the same to you whether you are merry or sad?"

"Why no! For I just like to be what I am, and what I like to be is not a matter of indifference to me. Oh, Mother," she went on, turning to Ernestine, "please help! He is questioning me in such a strange way, and I don't understand at all what he is getting at. Let him ask the grownups, for they will certainly know better how to answer him."

"Actually," said Ernestine, "I don't think you will get much further with her, Leonhardt. She isn't at all accustomed to sorting out her experiences."

Ernst was smiling at him broadly. "But don't let this one attempt scare you off," he comforted. "Catechising is nonetheless a fine art, of which one can make as good use in the courts as elsewhere. And one always learns something from it, unless of course one has started off on the wrong track!"

"But isn't she going to have any feeling about this?" Leonhardt asked of Ernestine, ignoring Ernst's jesting. "I mean, doesn't she know whether she would prefer a glad state of mind to a sad one?"

"Who knows?" she rejoined. "What do you think, Sophie?"

"I really don't know, Mother. I can be satisfied in one attitude or the other, and at present I feel extraordinarily fine without being in either one. Only he makes me uneasy with his questions, because I can't make out what all I am supposed to pull together to answer them." Thereupon she softly kissed her mother's hand and retreated to the far end of the room, now dark but for the lingering glow of a few lamps, to seek the company of her Christmas presents.

"Well, this she has clearly shown us," uttered Karoline only half aloud: "what that childlike attitude is without which one cannot enter into the kingdom of God. It is simply to accept each mood and feeling for itself and to desire only to have them pure and whole."

"True," spoke Eduard, "except that she is no longer just a child, but a young girl; and therefore this is not altogether the attitude of a child."

Karoline looked over at him and went on: "What you say is true enough, but only from our point of view. Think of the complaints one hears from both young and old, even in these special days of childlike celebration, that they can no longer enjoy themselves so much as when they were children. I would just say that these surely do not arise from people who have had such a happy childhood. Only yesterday I was saying that my capacity for lively enjoyment is as great as ever it was, in fact greater. The people who heard this were astonished! And I could only marvel that they were."

"Yes," joked Leonhardt, "and the poor child herself will often be thought silly by such ogres as these, even when she has done nothing more than react with childlike joy over something requiring girlish dignity! But let it pass, my fine child, for these gainsayers are so deprived that nature has assigned them a second childhood at life's end, so that when they have reached this goal they may take one last consoling draught from the cup of joy, to close their long, doleful, dreary years."

"Surely this is more serious and tragic than funny," countered Ernst. "For me, at least, scarcely anything makes me shudder more than the vision you have just stirred up. How horrible that the great body of mankind should become unaware of the beautiful growth of a human life, and tormented with boredom, simply because they have to leave the first objects of childish delight behind but never nourish the capacity for gaining higher things! I do not know whether to say they even look upon life, or are even in attendance, for even this would seem too much for their utter incapacity to bear. And so their life would go on, until at last, out of nothing, a second childhood is born. But such a childhood is as much related to the first as a contrary old dwarf is to a lovely and winsome child, or as the wavering flicker of a dying flame is to the embracing splendor and dancing form of one newly lit."

"One thing leads me to enter an objection," spoke up Agnes. "Is it really true that our first objects of delight as children have to be dropped behind before we can attain to higher things? May there not be a way of attaining these without letting the first go? Does life begin, then, with a sheer illusion, in which there is no truth at all, nothing enduring? I wonder how I am to understand this. Think of the man who has achieved a mature awareness of himself and the world and who has found God. Obviously this does not happen without struggle and conflict. Do his joys, then, depend upon destroying not only what is evil in his life but also what is innocent and faultless? For this is how we always designate what is childlike—or, if you prefer, even what is childish. Or must time already have killed off, by I don't know what poison, the pristine joys of life? And must the transition out of the one state into the other pass, in every instance, through a 'nothing'?"

"One might indeed call it a nothing," added Ernestine thoughtfully. "And yet it seems that men, in contrast to women, tend to lead an odd, wild sort of life between childhood and their better days, a life passionate and perplexed. They will admit this themselves—one might almost say the best men will admit it most of all. On the one hand, the period looks like a continuation of childhood, whose delights also have their own impetuous and disruptive character. On the other hand, the period takes the form of a restless striving, an indecisive, ever-changing grasping and letting go which we women are simply unable to understand. In our sex, the two tendencies also fuse, but less perceptibly. The course of our entire life already lies indicated in our childhood play, except that as we grow older the higher meaning of this and that gradually becomes clear. Even when, in our own way, we come to an understanding of God and of the world, we tend to express our sublimest, tenderest feelings over and over again in those same precious trifles and with that same gentle demeanor which put us on friendly terms with the world in our childhood days."

"Thus," said Eduard, "we see that in the development of their spiritual nature, although it must be the same in both, men and women have their different ways—to the end that here too they may become one by sharing knowledge of each other. It may well be true, and it seems clearly so to me, that the contrast between the spontaneous and the reflective emerges more strongly in us men. And during the period of transition it reveals itself in that restless striving, that passionate conflict with the world and within oneself you referred to. But within the calm, graceful nature of women comes to light the continuity and inner unity of the two, the spontaneous and the reflective. With you, holy earnestness and blithesome play are effortlessly united."

"But then," Leonhardt jocularly countered, "we men, oddly enough, would be more Christian than the women! For Christianity is always speaking of a conversion, a change of heart, a new life whereby the old man is driven out. And of this, if what we have just heard is true, you women—leaving out a few Magdalenes—would have no need whatsoever."

"But Christ himself," rejoined Karoline, "was not converted. For this very reason he has always been the patron and protector of women; and whereas you men have only contended about him, we have loved and honored him. Or consider: what can you say against the notion that we have at last applied the correct interpretation to the old proverb that we women go right on being children while you men must first be turned about to become so again?"

"And to bring this matter close to home," added Eduard: "what is the celebration of Jesus' infancy but the distinct acknowledgment of the immediate union of the divine with the being of a child, by virtue of which no conversion is further needed? And remember the view Agnes has expressed on behalf of all women. She said, in effect, that from the point of birth on they already presupposed and seek for the divine presence in their children, even as the church presupposes and seeks for it in Christ."

"Yes, this very festival," said Friederike, "is the most direct proof, and the best, that our situation really is as Ernestine has described it."

"How so?" asked Leonhardt.

"Because here," she replied, "one can examine the nature of our joy in small yet neither forgotten nor unrecognizable sections of our life story, to see whether this joy has undergone any number of sudden changes. One scarcely need put the question to our conscience, for the matter speaks for itself. It is obvious enough that on the whole women and girls are the soul of these little celebrations. They fuss the most over them, but are also the most purely receptive and get the most heightened enjoyment. If these were left only to you men, they would soon go under. Through us alone do they become ongoing traditions.

"But couldn't we have religious joy for its own sake alone?" she inquired. "And wouldn't that be so if we had only made a new discovery of it later on? So one may ask. For us, however, everything fits together now just as it did in our earlier years. Already in our childhood we attributed special significance to these gifts, for example. They meant more to us than the same gifts at other times. Then, of course, it was only a dark, mysterious presentiment of what has since gradually become clearer. Yet we always most prefer it to appear in much the same shape as before. We will not let the accustomed symbol go. In fact, given the exactness with which the precious little moments of life stick in our memory, I think one could trace out, step by step, just how the higher awareness has emerged in us."

[The women now tell stories that focus on the image of the Mother and the Christchild, but develop its archetypal meaning as a symbol of spiritual growth and rebirth. After these stories, the four men present discourses on "The Meaning of Christmas." Each man presents a different theoretical viewpoint: skeptical, historical, aesthetic, philosophical. The fourth man to speak is Eduard, who picks up the Marian theme by stressing the Johannine teaching that the Word was made flesh. What this means, says Eduard, is that we must see the divine in the finite and fleshly; we must see, as Mary did, the Christ in the child. Finally, Josef (i.e., Schleiermacher himself) joins the party and mediates between the "stories" of the women and the "discourses" of the men by extolling the speechlessness of the child, who experiences things in true immediacy. Josef's words provide the rationale and vindication of Sophie's attitudes that appear at the beginning of our selection. In Sophie, there is an immediacy of "the feeling of absolute dependence" that is Schleiermacher's definition of religion.]

Josef had come in while he was talking and, although he had very quietly entered and taken a seat, Eduard had noticed him. "By no means," he replied when Eduard addressed him. "You shall certainly be the last. I have not come to deliver a speech but to enjoy myself with you; and I must quite honestly say that it seems to me odd, almost folly even, that you should be carrying on with such exercises, however nicely you may have done them. Aha! but I already get the drift. Your evil principle is among you again: this Leonhardt, this contriving, reflective, dialectical, super-intellectual man. No doubt you have been addressing yourselves to him; for your own selves you would surely not have needed such goings on and wouldn't have fallen into them. Yet they couldn't have been to any avail with him! And the poor women must have had to go along with it. Now just think what lovely music they could have sung for you, in which all the piety of your discourse could have dwelt far more profoundly. Or think how charmingly they might have conversed with you, out of hearts full of

love and joy. Such would have eased and refreshed you differently, and better too, than you could possibly have been affected by these celebratory addresses of yours!

"For my part, today I am of no use for such things at all.
For me, all forms are too rigid, all speech-making too tedious and cold. Itself unbounded by speech, the subject of
Christmas claims, indeed creates in me a speechless joy, and
I cannot but laugh and exult like a child. Today all men
are children to me, and are all the dearer on that account.
The solemn wrinkles are for once smoothed away, the years
and cares do not stand written on the brow. Eyes sparkle and
dance again, the sign of a beautiful and serene existence
within. To my good fortune, I too have become just like a
child again. As a child stifles his childish pain, suppressing
his sighs and holding back his tears, when something is done
to arouse his childish joy, so it is with me today. The long,
deep, irrepressible pain in my life is soothed as never before.
I feel at home, as if born anew into the better world, in
which pain and grieving have no meaning and no room any
more. I look upon all things with a gladsome eye, even what
has most deeply wounded me. As Christ had no bride but
the church, no children but his friends, no household but the
temple and the world, and yet his heart was full of heavenly
love and joy, so I too seem to be born to endeavor after such
a life.

"And so I have roamed about the whole evening, everywhere taking part most heartily in every little happening
and amusement I have come across. I have laughed, and I
have loved it all. It was one long affectionate kiss which
I have given to the world, and now my enjoyment with you
shall be the last impress of my lips. For you know that you
are the dearest of all to me.

"Come, then, and above all bring the child if she is not yet
asleep, and let me see your glories, and let us be glad and
sing something religious and joyful!"

THE TEN COMMANDMENTS
[ON SEXUAL LOVE AND MARRIAGE]*

1. You shall have no other lover besides him, but you shall be capable of being a friend without playing in the various hues of love and without coquetry or idolizing.

2. You shall not make any ideal for yourself, either an angel in heaven or a hero out of a poem or a novel or of one you have dreamed up or created in your imagination, but you shall love a man as he is. For Nature, your mistress, is a strict Goddess, who visits the wild imaginings of girls upon women into the third or fourth decade of their feelings.

3. You shall not profane even the smallest of the sanctuaries of love, for she will lose her tender feelings who profanes her goodness and gives herself up for presents and gifts, or for the sake of peace and quietness in motherhood.

4. Remember the Sabbath day of your heart by celebrating it, and if any detain you, then free yourself or perish.

5. Honor the individuality and free will of your children so they may prosper and live healthily on earth.

6. You shall not conceive life intentionally.

7. You shall not contract a marriage that is fated to be broken.

8. You shall not desire to be loved where you do not love.

9. You shall not bear false witness towards men; [but] you shall not conceal their barbarism through word or deed.

10. You shall desire for yourself the same education, art, wisdom, and honor that men can attain.

---

* From Friedrich Schleiermacher, "Idee zu einen Katechismus der Vernunft für edle Frauen," *Athenaeum* 1, no. 2 (1798): 109–11; reprint ed., Darmstadt: Wissenschaftliche Buchgesellschaft, 1983, 285–87 (here translated by Ruth Drucilla Richardson).

II.

ᴗ Communitarian Movements in America: Shakers, the Oneida Community, and Mormons

Nineteenth-century America abounded in utopian societies; as many as five hundred such communities may have flourished in this period.[1] While the three religious movements examined in this chapter may all be seen as prefiguring a new world order, they represent very different approaches. The Shakers and the Oneida Community can be labeled communitarian; the Mormons do not fit this designation so well, but their unusual views of marriage and family marked an important alternative to the monogamous arrangements favored by most nineteenth-century American Christians (as well as by laws throughout the United States).

THE SHAKERS

Shakerism presents an interesting case for our consideration. Although popular opinion designates Ann Lee (1736–84) as the

Shakers' founder, some early Shakers did not stress Ann Lee as the female Messiah; only in writings dated from 1808 on was she proclaimed to the larger world as the female Savior.[2] Born into poverty in Manchester, England, in 1736, Ann Lee was an illiterate working woman whose four children all died. Convinced that the death of her children stemmed from God's condemnation of her sexual desire, Lee was prompted to adopt an ascetic life. Around 1770, Lee had a vision of the sin in the Garden of Eden that centered on the sexual union of Adam and Eve. In place of "carnal marriage," Ann Lee believed that she had experienced a spiritual marriage to Christ.[3] She urged her followers to adopt this true kind of marriage, not the sexual marriages of "the world."

Settling a community near Albany, New York, in the late 1770s, the Shakers undertook missionizing expeditions around New England. They welcomed new members to their ranks: a group that eschews procreation must find its base of adherents from conversion. The Shakers also gained members from educational activities and the care of orphans. They became known for the singing and dancing that accompanied their worship, as well as for the economic productivity of their communities.

Recent historians of Shakerism argue that its characteristic organizational structure (communities with separate houses for men and for women) and its theology appear to have developed only in the second and third generations of the movement.[4] The historiographical problem thus signaled is similar to the one facing scholars of the New Testament: how to reconstruct the "original kerygma" from pronouncements that later tradition *ascribed* to the founder.[5] Scholars now believe that the distinctive Shaker pattern of communal living received its impetus a few years after Ann Lee's death in 1784.[6] Likewise, Shaker theology was elaborated beginning in the first decade of the nineteenth century, stimulated by the ignorance and antagonism of "outsiders" to the movement as well as by the need for instructional materials to use in missionizing.[7] Although women apparently played little part in formulating Shaker theology, there were several notable women leaders (particularly Lucy Wright) who did much to increase women's visibility in the movement and to raise Ann Lee to a position of special prominence.[8] Of special significance is Rebecca Cox Jackson (1795–1871), a free black woman from Philadelphia who converted from Methodism to Shakerism; we receive some impression of her powerful preaching from her writings, edited and published more than a century after her death.[9] By the turn of the twentieth century, the United Society of Believers in Christ's Second Appearing (the official name of the Shakers) had been so "feminized" that about 75 percent of its membership was female, and the predominance of women in the movement has continued ever since.[10] The feminization of the Shaker movement by about 1900 represents an extreme case of the large female membership of numerous American religious organizations in this era.

The major work of early Shaker theology, Calvin Green and Seth Y. Wells's *A Summary View of the Millennial Church,* was published first in 1823 and explicates themes that came to be the hallmark of Shaker teaching. Green and Wells explain the theological (and practical) consequences of Ann Lee's vision that "the lustful gratifications of the flesh" were the "source and foundation of human corruption": "no soul could follow Christ in the regeneration, while living in the works of natural generation, or in any of the gratifications of lust."[11] Although they denied the standard Christian doctrine of the "inherited" transmission of original sin from Adam and Eve, Shakers believed that sexual activity rendered people sinful; it was only through ascetic self-denial that humans could find salvation.[12] Mainstream Christians were to be faulted for attempting to sanction the sexual act under the guise of a legal ceremony (marriage) and for calling such marriage a "divine institution."[13] For Shakers, the claim that "this heathen *Venus,* this adorable goddess of lust" was an ordinance of God verged on blasphemy.[14] Green and Wells were nonetheless careful to state that they did not oppose the practice of marriage for those still bound to "the world": Luke 20:34 teaches that in contrast to those who commit themselves to Christ, the children of "*this age*" marry.[15]

According to developed Shaker teaching, the Second Coming of Jesus had occurred in the person of Ann Lee. Green and Wells argue that indeed it was necessary, if women were to be saved as well as men, that Christ appear in the form of a woman.[16] Believing that God is both male and female, Shakers could see in Ann Lee "the image and likeness of the Eternal Mother."[17] Ann Lee is thus understood as completing and enlarging the teaching that had originally been given by Jesus.

Whether or not the Shakers should be deemed protofeminists has been debated by commentators on the movement. Lawrence Foster writes that although the belief in a male/female God and the practice of celibacy freed Shaker women from customary domestic roles, nonetheless labor within the community was organized along traditional lines, with different "spheres" of work for men and for women.[18] Moreover, the imagery of Ann Lee as Christ's "bride" tended to reinforce the theme of marriage and female subordination—even when marriage in "the world" was not practiced by Shakers.[19] Shaker women themselves, however, could justify their missionary activity and their speaking out at meetings on the grounds that biblical injunctions interpreted by mainstream Christians to subject women to their husbands and to silence them in church did not apply to the unmarried who lived in sexual purity.[20] And the Shaker system of separate houses for men and for women in itself necessitated the development of leadership roles for Shaker women.

MOTHER ANN LEE AND THE SHAKERS

In the early part of the year 1781, a large assembly of the Believers were gathered at Watervliet. . . . Mother [Ann Lee] was at that time, under great sufferings of soul. She came forth with a very powerful gift of God and reproved the people for their hardness of heart, and unbelief in the Second Appearance of Christ. "Especially ye men and brethren, I upbraid you for your unbelief and hardness of heart," said she. She spake of the unbelieving Jews, in Christ's first appearance, and, added she, "Even his own disciples, after he arose from the dead, though he had often told them that he should rise, the third day, believed it not." "They would not believe that he had risen because he appeared, first, to a woman! So great was their unbelief that the words of Mary seemed to them like idle tales! His appearing first, to a woman, showed that his Second Appearing would be in a woman." So great was the manifestation of the power of God in Mother at this time, that many were unable to abide in her presence, her words were like flames of fire, and her voice like peals of thunder. . . . [Reported by] Eunice Goodrich.

∾

. . . Samuel Fitch believed the gospel, being at Watervliet, and having received a great manifestation of light and understanding, he said to Mother Ann, "Christ is called the Second Adam, and thou art the Second Eve." She answered, "Flesh and blood has not revealed it unto thee, Samuel; but God has" [cf. Matt. 16:16–17]. [Reported by] Samuel Fitch.

∾

Morell Baker, Senr., visited the Church at Watervliet in 1784. . . . [H]e said to her, "Thou art the Bride, the Lamb's wife!" She answered, "Thou hast rightly said, for so I am. Christ is my husband. I now see many souls who have left the body, and have come to hear the gospel! I now hear the hosts of heaven singing praises to God." [Reported by] Morell Baker, Senr.

∾

The same year ... Mother Ann appeared clothed in majesty, and her visage was exceedingly glorious. She spake with great power, saying, "I am married to the Lord Jesus Christ! He is my head and my husband, and I have no other! I have walked hand in hand with him in Heaven! I have seen the Patriarchs, Prophets and Apostles; I have conversed with them, and I know them. ..." [Reported by] David Slosson.*

Ann Lee, seventeen hundred and seventy years after Jesus, began her practical era.... As her birth is chronicled in the midst of a modern civilization, which exceeded that of the times of Origen, Luther, and Calvin, so is her religious development, *more than their's, startling, and important* to mankind. The reasons are: 1st. Because she was a woman. 2d. Because she was an inspired woman. 3d. Because she enlarged the scope of religious experience. 4th. Because she unfolded a principle, an IDEA which no man, not even Jesus, had announced, or, perhaps, surmised!

Abraham, Isaac, Jesus, Paul, and other inspired persons, were illuminated, on many integral principles, but never sufficiently to perceive the plenitude of woman's nature, and the equality of her destiny. They had a God of almighty force; of infinite intelligence; of inconstant temper; of love for the lovely; of hate for the hateful; with a heaven for his friends; with a hell for his enemies (Jesus was excepted in this). But, in the outreaching of these minds toward a comprehension and presentation of their God, you will detect a one-sided dependence, confessed; a short sighted obligation and re-

---

* From *Testimonies of the Life, Character, Revelations and Doctrines of Mother Ann Lee* (Albany, N.Y.: Weed, Parsons, and Company, Printers, 1888), 161–66.

sponsibility, and a semi-civilized acknowledgment of the Divine personality and character. It was all *manish!* God was a "Male" God, and woman was supplemental. Paul, therefore, *permitted* the women "to speak," in meeting, with *certain insulting restrictions and by-laws affixed*. The Jews kept women in the back ground, if not in the tented kitchen; and nowhere does their God disapprobate the custom! . . .

Ann Lee's crime was, *she was a woman, with a claim upon mankind by Heaven's inspiration*. Her sin, was unpardonable! Gracious Heavens! A *woman* inspired?! What a blemish on the masculine fraternity!" "God of *masculine* quantities infinite. The eternally isolated 'male' of the Prophets and Apostles, down with this ambitious Venus in religion! Scare her fanatical followers, and confound the people who listen at her meetings!" "But she would not 'down' at their bidding! The (Male) God of the churches lived as complacently and essentially in this (Female) incarnation, as in the expanded universe. . . . Ann Lee demonstrated the IDEA, the impersonal principle . . . that, qualitatively and quantitatively, the celestial stream set just as *surely* through *woman's* soul, as through man's fertilizing, and equalizing the sexual hemispheres as they flow. She broke down the partition wall which custom had built between the *woman* spirit and its celestial Fountain Source. . . .

"But it is the central *Principle,* the IDEA of Ann Lee, for which we now reverently inquire. That principle in brief is this: God is DUAL—Male and Female—FATHER AND MOTHER! Hindoo teachers obtained a golden glimpse of this impersonal truth. Forming and destroying principles—male and female energies and laws were perceived and taught by early inhabitants. But not one person, from god Brahma to President Buchanan has done what Ann Lee did, for this world-revolutionizing IDEA! She centrifugated it in a thousand different forms of expression. It took wings in her spirit. Better than the Virgin Mary's sainted position in the ethical temple, is the simple announcement that *God is as much woman as man*—a oneness, composed of two individual equal halves—love and wisdom, absolute, and balanced eternally."*

෴

... [W]hen the foundation of man's redemption was laid by the work of Christ's first appearing, the way began also to be prepared for his second appearing, to make a final end of sin, and to bring in everlasting righteousness. For, although the foundation was laid, yet there could be no complete redemption from sin, until the revelation of Christ, for its final destruction, should be made where sin first took its seat.

As sin first took its seat in the woman, and thence entered the human race, and as Christ in taking upon him the nature of fallen man, in Jesus, to purify and redeem him, made his first appearing in the line of the male only; therefore the mystery of iniquity or MAN OF SIN was not fully revealed, nor the mystery of God finished, in Christ's first appearing.

And therefore, it was also necessary, that Christ should make his second appearing in the line of the female, and that in one who was conceived in sin, and lost in the fulness of man's fall; because in the woman the root of sin was first planted, and its final destruction must begin where its foundation was first laid, and from whence it first entered the human race.

Therefore, in the fulness of time, according to the unchangeable purpose of God, that same Spirit and word of power, which created man at the beginning—which spake by all the Prophets—which dwelt in the man Jesus—which was given to the Apostles and true witnesses as the holy Spirit and word of promise, which groaned in them, waiting for the day

---

* From Andrew Jackson Davis, "Ann Lee," in Giles B. Avery, *Sketches of Shakers and Shakerism* (Albany, N.Y.: Weed, Parsons, and Company, Printers, 1884), 27–30.

of redemption—and which was spoken of in the language of prophecy, as "a woman travailing with child, and pained to be delivered" [cf. Rev. 12:2], was revealed in a WOMAN.

And that *woman*, in whom was manifested that Spirit and word of power, who was anointed and chosen of God, to reveal the mystery of iniquity, to stand as the first in her order, to accomplish the purpose of God, in the restoration of that which was lost by the transgression of the first woman, and to finish the work of man's final redemption, was ANN LEE.

As a chosen vessel, appointed by Divine wisdom, she, by her faithful obedience to that same anointing, became the temple of the Holy Spirit, and the second heir with Jesus, in the covenant and promise of eternal life. And by her sufferings and travail for a lost world, and her union and subjection to Christ Jesus, her Lord and Head, she became the *first born of many sisters,* and the true MOTHER *of all living* in the new creation. . . .

And in this covenant, both male and female, as brethren and sisters in the family of Christ, jointly united by the bond of love, find each their correspondent relation to the first cause of their existence, through the joint parentage of their redemption.

Then the man who was called JESUS, and the woman who was called ANN, are verily the two first visible foundation pillars of the Church of Christ—the two anointed ones—the two first *heirs* of promise, between whom the covenant of eternal life is established—the first *Father* and *Mother* of all the children of regeneration—the two first visible Parents in the work of redemption—and in whom was revealed the invisible joint Parentage in the new creation, for the increase of that seed through which "all the families of the earth shall be blessed" [cf. Gen. 12:3]. . . .

As it is not possible that there can be any offspring or increase in the human family, without a natural mother, so neither is it possible that there can be any offspring, or any increase in the family of Christ, without a spiritual Mother. . . . Not the existence of *male and female* in the man alone, but all creation, in both the animal and vegetable kingdoms, the fishes that swim in the seas, the birds that fly in the air, yea, the very herbs and flowers of the field, all demonstrate and establish this fact, namely: That all living creation is supported and advanced through the *female order*. And that therefore the female is the crowning *glory*, and perfects the creative works of God. . . .

It is believed and acknowledged likewise, that Christ the second Adam is, and must be, the *Father* of all who are born again—of all the children of the second or spiritual birth; but how can these be born again, without a *Mother?* Can a father *beget* and also *conceive*, and *bear*, and bring forth children? There can be no such thing, either in heaven or on earth. . . . To no individual person, nor to any personages whatever, from the beginning to the end of time, can these prophetic figures be applied; save only to Christ, the quickening Spirit, and to their first born Son and Daughter, the *Lord Jesus* and *Mother Ann*, who of God are blessed forevermore—yea, *forever and ever.* *

∽

Some people suppose the opposite sexes among the Shakers never commune together; this is simply preposterous! While Shakers live, absolutely, pure virgin lives, no people in the world enjoy such a range of freedom, in the social sense, between the sexes; but it is required to be free from all that would tend to fleshly affections and actions. The power thus to live, in virgin purity and innocence, is found in the conviction that a spotless, virgin, angelic life is the order of the kingdom of Christ, and is higher, better, happier than a sensual,

* From Benjamin S. Youngs and Calvin Green, *Testimony of Christ's Second Appearing, etc.,* 4th ed. (Albany, N.Y.: Van Benthuysen, Printer, 1856), 383–84, 513–15.

worldly life. Add to this, protective by-laws, which all are in honor bound to keep, thus: "One brother and one sister not allowed to work together, walk out, or ride out together alone." "Males and females not allowed to touch each other unnecessarily, nor to hold secret correspondence." "Males and females not allowed to room together." Shakers are anti-Mormon, anti-Oneidian, and anti-Nicholaitan, in faith and practice, as becomes the true followers of Christ. They do not condemn marriage, nor orderly generation, *as worldly institution,* but claim these have no place in Christ's kingdom; therefore, *relegate them to the world, where alone they belong.* In contradistinction, nevertheless, to monastics, Shakers have no cloisters or nunneries to seclude and abnormalize the sexes, in their social and spiritual relations, to dry up the fountain of *pure* life-giving magnetism—true brotherly and sisterly love and *angelic* affection between the sexes.*

∾

THE NEW SONG

Lo, Christ again hath come! The Prophet's purpose
Now begins to dawn! Christ, our God reveals—
A dual Spirit—Father—Mother—God!
Thus, *all the signs declare.* First, tables two
Mosaic Law proclaimed: then cherubs two,
The Mercy seat adorn! . . .
. . . All nations to embrace,
May all their courts now open, their doors ajar
Now stand, and let the Queen of glory in.
The Dual Christ upon the cloud now sits
Sickle in hand, to thrust, and reap the world!
The clusters of earth's vine to gather home,
To garner of Our Father—Mother—God. . . .**

---

* From Giles B. Avery, *Sketches of Shakers and Shakerism,* 12.
** From Giles B. Avery, *Sketches of Shakers and Shakerism,* 24.

∾

MOTHER

(1)
Let names and sects and parties
Accost my ears no more,
My ever blessed Mother,
Forever I'll adore:
Appointed by kind heaven,
My Saviour to reveal,
Her doctrine is confirmed
With an eternal seal.

(2)
She was the Lords anointed,
To show the root of sin;
And in its full destruction,
Her gospel did begin:
She strip'd a carnal nature,
Of all its deep disguise,
And laid it plain and naked,
Before the sinner's eyes.

(3)
"Sunk in your base corruptions,
Ye wicked and unclean!
You read your sealed Bibles,
But know not what they mean:
Confess your filthy actions,
And put your lusts away,
And live the life of JESUS:
This is the only way.". . .

(6)
At Manchester, in England,
This blessed fire began,
And like a flame in stubble,
From house to house it ran:

A few at first receiv'd it,
And did their lusts forsake;
And soon their inward power
Brought on a mighty shake. . . .
(14)
How much are they deceived,
Who think that Mother's dead!
She lives among her offspring,
Who just begin to spread;
And in her outward order,
There's one supplies her room,
And still the name of Mother,
Is like a sweet perfume.*

THE ONEIDA COMMUNITY

One of America's most famous communitarian societies, the Oneida Community in upstate New York, was founded by John Humphrey Noyes (1811–86) and remained in operation from 1849 until 1881. At its height, Oneida counted over three hundred persons in its membership.[21]

Noyes, who had studied theology at Andover Theological Seminary and Yale Theological School, adopted the belief of some revivalists of his day that Christianity was a religion of "perfectionism": Christians no longer were held captive by sin but were members of the kingdom of God, which was in the process of establishment. Noyes, however, developed conclusions from this view that were not acceptable to the religious establishment—nor to "respectable" people in general—of the midnineteenth century. In the kingdom, Noyes thought, all men

---

* From Edward D. Andrews, *The Gift to Be Simple: Songs, Dances and Rituals of the American Shakers* (New York: Dover Publications, 1940, 1962), 47–49, 51; there are sixteen stanzas to "Mother."

and women would give their affection freely to fellow believers; no longer would they limit their loving to the traditional marriage relation, which Noyes once described as "the odious obligation of one party and the sensual recklessness of the other."[22]

In contrast to the Shaker conviction that sexual abstinence was necessary among those dedicated to God, Noyes formulated his idea of "complex marriage," in which all believers would be married to each other and "brotherly love" would abound. Since the world at large did not appear sufficiently advanced to renounce the exclusive ties of monogamy, Noyes endeavored to experiment with his plan at the Oneida commune. "Complex marriage" was practiced at Oneida until 1879, shortly before the breakup of the community. It is clear from Noyes's writings that he thought the arrangement was one way of implementing the biblical decrees regarding love for one's fellow humans in the kingdom of God.

Sexual union, Noyes believed, was the chief means of demonstrating one's love for others.[23] The "amative" function of sex was the one he thought to be the most important, the one that raised humans above the level of the beasts; the procreative function, on the other hand, needed careful regulation. The latter was accomplished by the practice of "male continence," intercourse without ejaculation.[24] Noyes thought that engaging in the sex act without taking precautions of the sort he recommended to prevent the conception of unwanted children was a great evil. That "male continence" must have had considerable success is demonstrated by the fact that only thirty children were born to the community in the first twenty years of its existence.[25] The rigors of pregnancy and the raising of numerous children put a blight on the lives of women, Noyes thought, and did not necessarily contribute to "amativeness" between the sexes. The method of "amative" sexual relations was taught in the Oneida Community by the initiation of the younger members by older ones—not merely younger women by older men, but also younger men by older women, who thus assumed roles traditionally considered "male" by serving as sexual initiators.[26] (The fundamental distinction in the Oneida group was not between male and female but between the more spiritual and the less spiritual membership.) Needless to say, these practices were not viewed with much favor by the law, and periodically Noyes found himself in difficulties with the authorities, charged with adultery or statutory rape.

Noyes's concern for women's lives was shown not just in his desire that women be relieved from excessive childbearing and time-consuming childrearing activities;[27] he wished them to *enjoy* sexual relations. Moreover, he encouraged them to engage in a variety of daily occupations, including some usually considered to be masculine pursuits, such as hoeing corn.[28] Noyes looked forward to the day when men and women would share their labors, with the result, he thought, that work would be much more appealing.[29] In preparation for that new order of life, Noyes encouraged the women to dress in a comfortable, free fashion (some wore a trouser costume) and to cut their hair short.[30] Nonetheless, Noyes's belief in the superiority of the masculine to the feminine, his program of selective breeding, and his criticisms of the women's rights movement rather qualify his designation as a "feminist."[31]

The Oneida women do not seem to have embraced the ideals of the suffrage movement; in fact, they were rather critical of Elizabeth Cady Stanton, Susan B. Anthony, and their associates. The Oneida females disliked the view that men and women could be considered as independent of one another, or even worse, as competitors.[32] One woman wrote in the Oneida newsletter, the *Circular,* "The grand right I ask for women is to love the men and be loved by them. That I imagine would adjust all other claims. It is but a cold, dismal right, in my opinion, to be allowed to vote, or to acquire and hold property. . . . I would rather be tyrannized over by him, than to be *independent* of him, and I would rather have no *rights* than to be separate."[33] The intention behind such a statement, of course, is to reject

American individualism and the belief that relations between the sexes could be justly worked out within that framework, as was advocated by the suffrage leaders. Perhaps the females in the Oneida Community felt that they had already achieved sexual equality and did not have to concern themselves with the plight of women who remained in a society that had not comprehended the new communal order of life open to Christians. Within the Oneida commune itself, however, the revolutionary view of "amativeness" pointed the way toward new modes of sexual relationships for the future, if not toward feminist ideals.

BIBLE COMMUNISM *

Proposition 5. In the kingdom of heaven, the institution of marriage which assigns the exclusive possession of one woman to one man, does not exist (Matt. 22:23–30). "In the resurrection they neither marry nor are given in marriage."

Note: Christ, in the passage referred to, does not exclude the sexual distinction, or sexual intercourse, from the heavenly state, but only the world's method of assigning the sexes to each other, which alone creates the difficulty presented in the question of the Sadducees. Their question evidently referred only to the matter of *ownership*. Seven men had been married to one woman, and dying successively, the question was, whose she should be in the resurrection. Suppose the question had been asked, in reference to Slavery instead of marriage, thus: A man owning a slave dies and leaves him to his brother, he dying, bequeaths him to the next brother, and so seven of them in succession own this slave; now whose slave shall he be in the resurrection? This, evidently, is the amount of the Sadducees' question, and Christ's answer is as

---

* From Oneida Community, *Bible Communism* (Philadelphia: Porcupine Press, 1972; original printing by the Office of the *Circular*, Brooklyn, 1853), 26–27, 31–33, 40–41, 42, 45–48, 49–53.

though he had said that in the resurrection there are neither slaves nor slaveholders. It is nullification of the idea of marriage ownership. Can any thing more be made of it? To assume from this passage a nullification of the sexual relation, as the Shakers and others do, is as absurd as it would be to assume that because there is no slavery, there is therefore no serving one another in the resurrection; whereas the gospel teaches that there is more serving one another there than in the world. The constitutional distinctions and offices of the sexes belong to their original paradisaical state; and there is no proof in the Bible or in reason, that they are ever to be abolished, but abundance of proof to the contrary (1 Cor. 11:3–11). The saying of Paul that in Christ "there is neither Jew nor Greek, *neither male nor female,*" etc., simply means that the unity of life which all the members of Christ have in him, overrides all individual distinctions. In the same sense as that in which the apostle excludes distinctions of *sexes,* he also virtually excludes distinction of persons; for he adds, "Ye are all *one* in Christ Jesus." Yet the several members of Christ, in perfect consistency with their spiritual unity, remain distinct persons; and so the sexes, though one in their innermost life, as members of Christ, yet retain their constitutional distinctions.

Proposition 6. In the kingdom of heaven, the intimate union of life and interests, which in the world is limited to pairs, extends through the whole body of believers; i.e., *complex* marriage takes the place of simple (John 17:21). Christ prayed that *all* believers might be one, *even as* he and the Father are one. His unity with the Father is defined in the words *"All mine are thine, and all thine are mine"* (v. 10). This perfect community of interests, then will be the condition of *all,* when his prayer is answered. The universal unity of the members of Christ, is described in the same terms that are used to describe marriage-unity. Compare 1 Cor. 12:12–27 with Gen. 2:24. See also 1 Cor. 6:15–17, and Eph. 5:30–32. . . .

Proposition 9. The abolishment of sexual exclusiveness is involved in the love-relation required between all believers by the express injunction of Christ and the apostles, and by the whole tenor of the New Testament. "The new commandment is, that we love one another," and that, not by pairs, as in the world, but *en masse*. We are required to love one another *fervently* (1 Pet. 1:22), or, as the original might be rendered, *burningly*. The fashion of the world forbids a man and woman who are otherwise appropriated, to love one another burningly—to flow into each other's hearts. But if they obey Christ they must do this; and whoever would allow them to do this, and yet would forbid them (on any other ground than that of present expediency) to express their unity of hearts by bodily unity, would "strain at a gnat and swallow a camel;" for unity of hearts is as much more important than the bodily expression of it, as a camel is bigger than a gnat. . . .

Proposition 10. The abolishment of worldly restrictions on sexual intercourse, is involved in the anti-legality of the gospel. It is incompatible with the state of perfected freedom towards which Paul's gospel of 'grace without law' leads, that man should be allowed and required to *love* in all directions, and yet be forbidden to *express* love in its most natural and beautiful form, except in one direction. In fact, Paul says with direct reference to sexual intercourse—"All things are *lawful* for me, but all things are not expedient;" "all things are lawful for me, but I will not be brought under the power of any" (1 Cor. 6:12); thus placing the restrictions which were necessary in the transition period on the basis, not of law, but of expediency and the demands of spiritual freedom, and leaving it fairly to be inferred that in the final state, when hostile surroundings and powers of bondage cease, all restrictions also will cease. . . .

Note: . . . In a perfect state of things, where corrupting attractions have no place, and all susceptibilities are duly subordinated and trained, the denying exercise of the will ceases, and attraction reigns without limitation. In such a state, what is the difference between the love of man towards man, and that of man towards woman? Attraction being the essence of love in both cases, the difference lies in this, that man and woman are so adapted to each other by the differences of their natures, that attraction can attain a more perfect union between them than between man and man, or between woman and woman. . . . [L]ove between man and man can only advance to something like plain contact; while love between man and woman can advance to interlocked contact. In other words, love between the different sexes, is peculiar, not in its essential nature, but because they are so constructed with reference to each other, both spiritually and physically, (for the body is an index of the life), that more intimate unity, and of course more intense happiness in love, is possible between them than between persons of the same sex. . . .

Proposition 16. The restoration of true relations between the sexes, is a matter second in importance only to the reconciliation of man to God. The distinction of male and female is that which makes man the image of God, i.e. the image of the Father and the Son (Gen. 1:27). The relation of male and female was the first social relation (Gen. 2:22). It is therefore the root of all other social relations. The derangement of this relation was the first result of the original breach with God (Gen. 3:7; cf. 2:25). Adam and Eve were, at the beginning, in open, fearless, spiritual fellowship, first with God, and secondly, with each other. Their transgression produced two corresponding alienations, viz., first, an alienation from God, indicated by their fear of meeting him, and their hiding themselves among the trees of the garden; and, secondly, an alienation from each other, indicated by their shame at their nakedness, and their hiding themselves from each other by clothing. These were the two great manifestations of original sin—the only manifestations presented to notice in the inspired record of the apostasy. The first thing then to be done, in an attempt to redeem man and reorganize society, is to bring about reconciliation with God; and the second thing is to bring about a true union of the sexes. In other words, religion is the first subject of interest, and sexual mortality the second, in the great enterprise of establishing the kingdom of God on earth. . . .

Proposition 17. Dividing the sexual relation into two branches, the amative and propagative, the amative or love-relation is first in importance, as it is in the order of nature. God made woman because "he saw it was *not good for man to be alone*" (Gen. 2:18); i.e. for social, not primarily for propagative purposes. Eve was called Adam's "help-meet." In the whole of the specific account of the creation of woman, she is regarded as his companion, and her maternal office is not brought into view (Gen. 2:18–25). Amativeness was necessarily the first social affection developed in the garden of Eden. The second commandment of the eternal law of love—"thou shalt love thy neighbor as thyself"—had amativeness for its first channel; for Eve was at first Adam's only neighbor. Propagation, and the affections connected with it, did not commence their operation during the period of innocence. After the fall, God said to the woman, "I will greatly multiply thy sorrow and thy conception" from which it is to be inferred that in the original state, conception would have been comparatively infrequent. . . .

Proposition 19. The propagative part of the sexual relation is in its nature the *expensive* department. (1) While amativeness keeps the capital stock of life circulating between two, propagation introduces a third partner. (2) The propagative act, i.e. the emission of the seed, is a drain on the life of man, and when habitual, produces disease. (3) The infirmities and vital expenses of woman during the long period of pregnancy, waste her constitution. (4) The awful agonies of child-birth heavily tax the life of woman. (5) The cares of the nursing period bear heavily on woman. (6) The cares of both parents, through the period of the childhood of their offspring, are many and burdensome. (7) The labor of man is greatly increased by the necessity of providing for children. A portion of these expenses would undoubtedly have been curtailed, if human nature had remained in its original integrity, and will be, when it is restored. But it is still self-evident, that the birth of children, viewed either as a vital or a mechanical operation, is in its nature expensive; and the fact that multiplied conception was imposed as a curse, indicates that it was so regarded by the Creator. . . .

Note 3: The grand problem which must be solved before redemption can be carried forward to immortality, is this:— *How can the benefits of amativeness be secured and increased, and the expenses of propagation be reduced to such limits as life can afford?* The human mind has labored much on this problem. Shakerism is an attempt to solve it. Ann Lee's attention, however, was confined to the latter half of it—the reduction of expenses; (of which her own sufferings in child-birth gave her a strong sense;) and for the sake of stopping propagation she prohibited the union of the sexes—thus shutting off the profitable as well as the expensive part of the sexual relation. This is cutting the knot—not untying it. Robert Dale Owen's *Moral Physiology* is another attempted solution of the grand problem. He insists that sexual intercourse is of some value by itself, and not merely as a bait to propagation. He proposes therefore to limit propagation, and retain the privilege of sexual intercourse, by the practice of withdrawing previous to the emission of the seed, after Onan's fashion (Gen. 38:9). This method, it will be observed, is unnatural, and even more wasteful of life, so far as the man is concerned, than ordinary practice; since it gives more freedom to desire, by shutting off the propagative consequences. The same may be said of various French methods. The system of producing abortions, is a still more unnatural and destructive method of limiting propagation, without stopping sexual intercourse. A satisfactory solution of the grand problem, must propose a method that can be shown to be natural, healthy for both sexes, favorable to amativeness, and effectual in its control of propagation. Such a solution will be found in what follows. . . .

Proposition 20. The amative and propagative functions of the sexual organs are distinct from each other, and may be separated practically. They are confounded in the world, both in the theories of physiologists and in universal practice. The amative function is regarded merely as a bait to the propagative, and is merged in it. The sexual organs are called "organs of reproduction," or "organs of generation," but not organs of love or organs of union. But if amativeness is, as we have seen, the first and noblest of the social affections, and if the propagative part of the sexual relation was originally secondary, and became paramount by the subversion of order in the fall, we are bound to raise the amative office of the sexual organs into a distinct and paramount function. It is held in the world, that the sexual organs have two distinct functions, viz., the urinary and the propagative. We affirm that they have *three*—the urinary, the propagative, and the amative, i.e., they are conductors, first of the urine, secondly of the semen, and thirdly of the social magnetism. And the amative is as distinct from the propagative, as the propagative is from the urinary. In fact, strictly speaking, the organs of propagation are *physiologically* distinct from the organs of union in both sexes. The testicles are the organs of reproduction in the male, and the uterus in the female. These are distinct from the organs of union. The sexual conjunction of male and female, no more necessarily involves the discharge of the semen than of the urine. The discharge of the semen, instead of being the main act of sexual intercourse, properly so called, is really the sequel and termination of it. Sexual intercourse, pure and simple, is the conjunction of the organs of union, and the interchange of magnetic influences, or conversation of spirits, through the medium of that conjunction. The communication from the seminal vessels to the uterus, which constitutes the propagative act, is distinct from, subsequent to, and not necessarily connected with, this intercourse. (On the one hand, the seminal discharge can be voluntarily withheld in sexual connection; and on the other, it can be produced without sexual connection, as it is in masturbation. This latter fact demonstrates that the discharge of the semen and the pleasure connected with it, is not essentially social, since it can be produced in solitude; it is a personal and not a dual affair. This, indeed, is evident from a physiological analysis of it. The pleasure of the act is not produced by contact and interchange of life with the female, but by the action of the seminal fluid on certain internal nerves of the male organ. The appetite and that which satisfies it, are both within the man, and of course the pleasure is personal, and may be obtained without sexual intercourse.) We insist then that the amative function—that which consists in a simple union of persons, making "of twain one flesh," and giving a medium of magnetic and spiritual interchange—is a distinct and independent function, as superior to the reproductive as we have shown amativeness to be to propagation. . . .

Note 3: Here is a method of controlling propagation, that is natural, healthy, favorable to amativeness, and effectual. First, It is *natural.* The useless expenditure of seed certainly is not natural. God cannot have designed that men should sow seed by the way-side, where they do not expect it to grow, or in the same field where seed has already been sown, and is growing; and yet such is the practice of men in ordinary sexual intercourse. They sow seed habitually where they do not *wish* it to grow. This is wasteful of life, and cannot be natural. So far the Shakers and Grahamites are right. Yet it is equally manifest that the natural instinct of our nature demands frequent congress of the sexes, not for propagative, but for social and spiritual purposes. It results from these opposite indications, that simple congress of the sexes, *without the propagative crisis,* is the order of nature for the gratification of ordinary amative instincts; and that the act of propagation should be reserved for its legitimate occasions, when conception is intended. The idea that sexual intercourse, pure and simple, is impossible or difficult, and therefore not natural, is contradicted by the experience of many. Abstinence from masturbation is impossible or difficult, where habit has made it a second nature; and yet no one will say that habitual masturbation is natural. So abstinence from the propagative part of sexual intercourse may seem impracticable to depraved natures, and yet be perfectly natural and easy to persons properly trained to chastity. Our method simply proposes the subordination of the flesh to the spirit, teaching men to seek principally the elevated spiritual pleasures of sexual intercourse, and to be content with them in their general intercourse with women, restricting the more sensual part to its proper occasions. This is certainly natural and easy to spiritual men, however difficult it may be to the sensual.

Secondly, this method is *healthy.* In the first place, it secures woman from the curses of involuntary and undesirable procreation; and secondly, it stops the drain of life on the part of man. This cannot be said of Owen's system, or any other method that merely prevents the *propagative effects* of the emission of the seed, and not the emission itself.

Thirdly, this method is *favorable* to amativeness. Owen can only say of his method that it does not *much diminish* the pleasure of sexual intercourse; but we can say of ours, that it *vastly increases* that pleasure. Ordinary sexual intercourse (in which the amative and propagative functions are confounded) is a momentary affair, terminating in exhaustion and disgust. If it begins in the spirit, it soon ends in the flesh; i.e., the amative, which is spiritual, is drowned in the propagative, which is sensual. The exhaustion which follows, naturally breeds self-reproach and shame, and this leads to dislike and concealment of the sexual organs, which contract disagreeable associations from the fact that they are the instruments of pernicious excess. This undoubtedly is the philosophy of the origin of shame after the fall. Adam and Eve first sunk the spiritual in the sensual, in eating the forbidden fruit; and then, having lost the true balance of their natures, they sunk the spiritual in the sensual in their intercourse with each other, by pushing prematurely beyond the amative to the propagative, and so became ashamed, and began to look with an evil eye on the instruments of their folly. On the same principle we may account for the process of "cooling off" which takes place between lovers after marriage, and often ends in indifference and disgust. Exhaustion and self-reproach make the eye evil not only toward the instruments of excess, but toward the person who tempts to it. In contrast with all this, lovers who use their sexual organs simply as the servants of their spiritual natures, abstaining from the propagative act, except when procreation is intended, may enjoy the highest bliss of sexual fellowship for any length of time, and from day to day, without satiety or exhaustion; and thus marriage life may become permanently sweeter than courtship, or even the honey-moon.

Fourthly, this method of controlling propagation is *effectual*. The habit of making sexual intercourse a quiet affair, like conversation, restricting the action of the organs to such limits as are necessary to the avoidance of the sensual crisis, can easily be established, and then there is no risk of conception without intention.

Note 4: Ordinary sexual intercourse, i.e., the performance of the propagative act, without the intention of procreation, is properly to be classed with masturbation. The habit in the former case is less liable to become besotted and ruinous, than in the latter, simply because a woman is less convenient than the ordinary means of masturbation. It must be admitted, also, that the amative affection favorably modifies the sensual act to a greater extent in sexual commerce than in masturbation. But this is perhaps counterbalanced by the cruelty of forcing or risking undesired conception, which attends sexual commerce, and does not attend masturbation.

Note 5: Our theory, separating the amative from the propagative, not only relieves us of involuntary and undesirable procreation, but opens the way for *scientific* propagation. We are not opposed, after the Shaker fashion, or even after Owen's fashion, to the increase of population. We believe that the order to "multiply" attached to the race in its original integrity, and that propagation, rightly conducted, and kept within such limits as life can fairly afford, is the next blessing to sexual love. But we are opposed to *involuntary* procreation. A very large proportion of all children born under the present system, are begotten contrary to the wishes of both parents, and lie nine months in their mother's womb under their mother's curse, or a feeling little better than a curse. Such children cannot be well organized. We are opposed to *excessive,* and of course oppressive procreation, which is almost universal. We are opposed to *random* procreation, which is unavoidable in the marriage system. But we are in favor of *intelligent, well-ordered* procreation. The physiologists say that the race cannot be raised from ruin till propagation is made a matter of science; but they point out no way of making it so. True, propagation is controlled and reduced to a science in the case of valuable domestic brutes; but marriage and fashion forbid any such system among human beings. We believe the time will come when involuntary and random propagation will cease, and when scientific combination will be applied to human generation as freely and successfully as it is to that of other animals. The way will be open for this, when amativeness can have its proper gratification without drawing after it procreation, as a necessary sequence. And at all events, we believe that good sense and benevolence will *very soon* sanction and enforce the rule, that women shall bear children only when they choose. They have the principal burdens of breeding to bear, and they, rather than men, should have their choice of time and circumstances, at least till science takes charge of the business.

Note 6: The political economist will perhaps find in our discovery some help for the solution of the famous "population question." Carey, and other American writers on political economy, seem to have exploded the old Malthusian doctrine that population necessarily outruns subsistence; but there is still a difficulty in the theoretical prospect of the world in regard to population, which they do not touch. Admitting that the best soils are yet in reserve, and that with the progress of intelligence, means of subsistence may for the present increase faster than population; it is nevertheless certain that the actual area of the earth is a limited thing, and it is therefore certain that if its population goes on doubling, as we are told, once in twenty-five years, a time must come at last when there will not be standing-room! Whether such a catastrophe is worth considering and providing for or not, we may be certain, that man, when he has grown wise enough to be worthy of his commission as Lord of nature, will be able to determine for himself what shall be the population of the earth, instead of leaving it to be determined by the laws that govern the blind passions of brutes.

Note 7: The separation of the amative from the propagative, places amative sexual intercourse on the same footing with other ordinary forms of intercourse, such as conversation, kissing, shaking hands, embracing, etc. So long as the amative and propagative are confounded, sexual intercourse carries with it physical consequences which necessarily take it out of the category of mere social acts. If a man under the cover of a mere social call upon a woman, should leave in her apartments a child for her to breed and provide for, he would do a mean wrong. The call might be made without previous negotiation or agreement, but the sequel of the call—the leaving of the child—is a matter so serious that it is to be treated as a business affair, and not be done without good reason and agreement of the parties. But the man who under the cover of social intercourse, commits the propagative act, leaves his child with the woman in a meaner and more oppressive way, than if he should leave it full born in her apartments; for he imposes upon her not only the task of breeding and providing for it, but the sorrows and pains of pregnancy and child-birth. It is right that law, or at least public opinion, should frown on such proceedings even more than it does; and it is not to be wondered at that women, to a considerable extent, look upon ordinary sexual intercourse with more dread than pleasure, regarding it as a stab at their life, rather than a joyful act of fellowship. But separate the amative from the propagative—let the act of fellowship stand by itself—and sexual intercourse becomes a purely social affair, the same in kind with other modes of kindly interchange, differing only by its superior intensity and beauty. Thus the most popular, if not the most serious objection to free love and sexual intercourse, is removed. The difficulty so often urged, of knowing to whom children belong in complex-marriage, will have no place in a community trained to keep the amative distinct from the propagative. Thus also the only plausible objection to amative intercourse between near relatives, founded on the supposed law of nature that "breeding in and in" deteriorates offspring (which law however was not recognized in Adam's family) is removed; since science may dictate in this case as in all others, in regard to propagation, and yet amativeness may be free.

Note 7 [sic]: In society trained in these principles, as propagation will become a science, so amative intercourse will have place among the "fine arts." Indeed it will take rank above music, painting, sculpture, &c.; for it combines the charms and benefits of them all. There is as much room for cultivation of taste and skill in this department as in any.

Note 8: The practice which we propose will advance civilization and refinement at railroad speed. The self-control, retention of life, and ascent out of sensualism, which must result from making freedom of love a bounty on the chastening of physical indulgence, will at once raise the race to new vigor and beauty, moral and physical. And the refining effects of sexual love (which are recognized more or less in the world) will be increased a thousandfold, when sexual intercourse becomes a method of ordinary conversation, and each is married to all.

THE MORMONS

Mormon approaches to issues of women and the family differed greatly from those of both the Shakers and the Oneida Community. Officially named the Church of Jesus Christ of Latter-Day Saints, the movement was founded by Joseph Smith in upstate New York. In the 1820s, Smith came to believe that God had instructed him in visions to restore the true church. Smith also claimed that he had been given new scriptures, which were published in 1830 as the *Book of Mormon*. Often prodded by persecution at the hands of "Gentile" (that is, non-Mormon) Americans, Smith's followers pursued a progressively westward path across America, many of them moving to Ohio, Illinois, Missouri, and finally, under the leadership of Brigham Young, settling in Utah at midcentury.

Although Joseph Smith received his original revelation in the 1820s, plural marriage (polygamy) developed as a Mormon practice only in the early 1840s and was not announced to the larger world until 1852. Appealing to the plural marriages of the Old Testament patriarchs (Abraham, Isaac, and Jacob), Mormon teachers argued that polygamy better aided believers to carry out the commandment to "reproduce and multiply"

(Gen. 1:28) and to fulfill the promise given by God to Abraham that his descendants would be as numerous as the stars in the heavens (Gen. 15:5). Since the millennium that was soon to come would involve a "restoration of all things" (Acts 4:21), polygamy as practiced in the Old Testament should also be reinstituted. In practical terms, polygamy allowed for the growth of a much larger kinship network (with its attendant loyalties) than did conventional marriage.[34]

Along with the practice of plural marriage went a teaching that Mormon marriages given the "seal" of blessing by the group's Elders would continue into eternity—whereas secular marriages were not eternal and in fact could be ended with relative ease in the Mormon community.[35] Salvation was to be achieved through such celestial marriages, which enabled men to progress toward "godhood." Mormon men could imagine themselves as replicating the practices of the Old Testament patriarchs and could speculate that they and their large progeny might be called to settle the new worlds with which visionary Mormons believed the universe abounds.[36]

Women were not necessarily as enthusiastic about the arrangement of plural marriage as were some Mormon men. Joseph Smith's wife Emma was a staunch opponent of polygamy, declaring that the teaching came "straight from hell."[37] At the Mormon community in Nauvoo, Illinois, Mormon men shut down the Female Relief Society when they came to believe that some women were using the group as a rallying place to oppose plural marriage.[38] Nonetheless, many Mormon women came to accept the practice, since male leaders told them that it was essential for their own and their husbands' salvation.[39] Some Mormon women argued that polygamy had several benefits: it ensured that all women might find "good" husbands, restrained men's sexual passions, and produced healthy children.[40] Only in the very late nineteenth and early twentieth centuries, under pressure from government officials who viewed the practice as illegal, did most Mormons abandon plural marriage,[41] a practice called by Lawrence Foster "the largest, best-organized, and most controversial venture in radically restructuring marriage and family life in nineteenth-century America."[42]

Somewhat ironically, Mormonism—which non-Mormons thought degraded women—can even in some respects be viewed as protofeminist: Utah was among the first American territories to permit women to vote; Mormon women generally supported the wider suffrage movement of the nineteenth century; and many Mormon women who entered plural marriages engaged in income-producing labor to help support their families.[43] Unlike the Oneida Community, which disbanded, or the Shakers, whose ranks have now dwindled to a handful of the faithful, only the Mormons made a "successful transition from a persecuted subculture to a mainstream movement in America," albeit at the price of officially abandoning the system of plural marriage.[44]

The following selection is from a discourse entitled "Celestial Marriage," delivered by the Mormon Elder Orson Pratt in the Tabernacle in Salt Lake City on August 29, 1852.

CELESTIAL MARRIAGE *

The Lord ordained marriage between male and female as a law through which spirits should come here and take tabernacles, and enter into the second state of existence. The Lord Himself solemnized the first marriage pertaining to this globe, and pertaining to flesh and bones here upon this earth. I do not say pertaining to mortality; for when the first marriage was celebrated, no mortality was there. The first marriage that we have any account of, was between two immortal beings— old father Adam and old mother Eve; they were immortal beings; death had no dominion, no power over them; they

---

* From Brigham Young, *Journal of Discourses,* reported by G. D. Watt (Liverpool: F. D. and S. W. Richards, 1854), I: 58–62, passim. Reprint: Gartner Printing & Litho Co., Los Angeles, 1956, I: 58–62.

were capable of enduring for ever and ever, in their organization. Had they fulfilled the law, and kept within certain conditions and bounds, their tabernacles would never have been seized by death; death entered entirely by sin, and sin alone. This marriage was celebrated between two immortal beings. For how long? Until death? No. That was entirely out of the question; there could have been no such thing in the ceremony.

What would you consider, my hearers, if a marriage was to be celebrated between two beings not subject to death? Would you consider them joined together for a certain number of years, and that then all their covenants were to cease for ever, and the marriage contract be dissolved? Would it look reasonable and consistent? No. Every heart would say that the work of God is perfect in and of itself, and inasmuch as sin had not brought imperfection upon the globe, what God joined together could not be dissolved, and destroyed, and torn asunder by any power beneath the celestial world, consequently it was eternal; the ordinance of union was eternal; the sealing of the great Jehovah upon Adam and Eve was eternal in its nature, and was never instituted for the purpose of being overthrown and brought to an end. It is known that the "Mormons" are a peculiar people about marriage; we believe in marrying, not only for time, but for all eternity. This is a curious idea, says one, to be married for all eternity. It is not curious at all; for when we come to examine the Scriptures, we find that the very first example set for the whole human family, as a pattern instituted for us to follow, was not instituted until death, for death had no dominion at that time; but it was an eternal blessing pronounced upon our first parents. I have not time to explain further the marriage of Adam and Eve, but will pass on to their posterity. . . .

And if Adam and Eve were married for all eternity, the ceremony was an everlasting ordinance, that they twain should be one flesh for ever. If you and I should ever be accounted worthy to be restored back from our fallen and degraded condition to the privileges enjoyed before the fall, should we not have an everlasting marriage seal, as it was with our first progenitors? If we had no other reasons in all the Bible, this would be sufficient to settle the case at once in the mind of every reflecting man and woman, that inasmuch as the fall of man has taken away any privileges in regard to the union of male and female, these privileges must be restored in the redemption of man, or else it is not complete.

What is the object of this union? is the next question. We are told the object of it; it is clearly expressed; for, says the Lord unto the male and female, I command you to multiply and replenish the earth. And, inasmuch as we have proved that the marriage ordinance was eternal in its nature, previous to the fall, if we are restored back to what was lost by the fall, we are restored for the purpose of carrying out the commandment given before the fall, namely, to multiply and replenish the earth. Does it say, continue to multiply for a few years, and then the marriage contract must cease, and there shall be no further opportunity of carrying out this command, but it shall have an end? No, there is nothing specified of this kind; but the fall has brought in disunion through death; it is not a part of the original plan; consequently, when male and female are restored from the fall, by virtue of the everlasting and eternal covenant of marriage, they will continue to increase and multiply to all ages of eternity, to raise up beings after their own order, and in their own likeness and image, germs of intelligence, that are destined, in their times and seasons, to become not only sons of God, but Gods themselves.

This accounts for the many worlds we heard Elder Grant speaking about yesterday afternoon. The peopling of worlds, or an endless increase, even of one family, would require an endless increase of worlds; and if one family were to be united in the eternal covenant of marriage, to fulfil that great commandment, to multiply his species, and propagate them, and if there be no end to the increase of his posterity, it would call for an endless increase of new worlds. And if one family calls for this, what would innumerable millions of families call for? They would call for as many worlds as have already been discovered by the telescope; yea, the number must be multiplied to infinity in order that there may be room for the inheritance of the sons and daughters of the Gods. . . .

How did Abraham manage to get a foundation laid for this mighty kingdom? Was he to accomplish it all through one wife? No. Sarah gave a certain woman to him whose name was Hagar, and by her a seed was to be raised up unto him. Is this all? No. We read of his wife Keturah, and also of a plurality of wives and concubines, which he had, from whom he raised up many sons. Here then, was a foundation laid for the fulfilment of the great and grand promise concerning the multiplicity of his seed. It would have been rather a slow process, if Abraham had been confined to one wife, like some of those narrow, contracted nations of modern Christianity.

I think there is only about one-fifth of the population of the globe, that believe in the one-wife system; the other four-fifths believe in the doctrine of a plurality of wives. They have had it handed down from time immemorial, and are not half so narrow and contracted in their minds as some of the nations of Europe and America, who have done away with the promises, and deprived themselves of the blessings of Abraham, Isaac, and Jacob. The nations do not know anything about the blessings of Abraham; and even those who have only one wife, cannot get rid of their covetousness, and get their little hearts large enough to share their property with a numerous family; they are so penurious, and so narrow and contracted in their feelings, that they take every possible care not to have their families large; they do not know what is in the future, nor what blessings they are depriving themselves of, because of the traditions of their fathers; they do not know that a man's posterity, in the eternal worlds, are to constitute his glory, his kingdom, and dominion.

Here, then, we perceive, just from this one principle, reasoning from the blessings of Abraham alone, the necessity—if we would partake of the blessings of Abraham, Isaac, and Jacob—of doing their works; and he that will not do the works of Abraham, and walk in his footsteps, will be deprived of his blessings.

Again, let us look at Sarah's peculiar position in regard to Abraham. She understood the whole matter; she knew that, unless seed was raised up to Abraham, he would come short of his glory; and she understood the promise of the Lord, and longed for Abraham to have seed. And when she saw that she was old, and fearing that she should not have the privilege of raising up seed, she gave to Abraham, Hagar. Would Gentile Christendom do such things now-a-days? O no; they would consider it enough to send a man to an endless hell of fire and brimstone. Why? Because tradition has instilled this in their minds as a dreadful, awful thing.

It matters not to them how corrupt they are in female prostitution, if they are lawfully married to only one wife; but it would be considered an awful thing by them to raise up a posterity from more than one wife; this would be wrong indeed; but to go into a brothel, and there debauch themselves in the lowest haunts of degradation all the days of their lives, they consider only a trifling thing; nay, they can even license such institutions in Christian nations, and it all passes off very well.

That is tradition; and their posterity have been fostered and brought up in the footsteps of wickedness. This is death, as it stalks abroad among the great and popular cities of Europe and America.

Do you find such haunts of prostitution, degradation, and misery here, in the cities of the mountains? No. Were such things in our midst, we should feel indignant enough to see that such persons be blotted out of the page of existence. These would be the feelings of this community.

12

∾ Movements for Religious and Social Reform in Nineteenth- and Twentieth-Century America

As we saw in the prior chapter on communitarian movements, the nineteenth century witnessed significant social change—and conflict—in the United States. Women were founders and leaders of many of the most significant movements for social and religious reform throughout the nineteenth and early twentieth centuries. In this chapter we will consider some of the notable women of this period.

SARAH GRIMKÉ

Sarah Moore Grimké (1792–1873) was an important member of the Quaker opposition to slavery. Her *Letters on the Equality of the Sexes and the Condition of Women* (1837–38) grew out of her experiences as a public speaker in support of abolition. Written a decade before the Seneca Falls Convention of 1848 (the event usually acknowledged as the formal beginning of the nineteenth-century women's movement), Grimké's letters are a significant early expression of feminism in America.[1] The letters were addressed to Mary Parker, president of the Boston Female Anti-Slavery Society, who had suggested to Grimké that she set down her thoughts on the topic of women in a form suitable for publication.[2]

The route by which Sarah Grimké entered the movement for women's rights was an indirect one. She and her younger sister Angelina, daughters of a South Carolina slaveholder, early in life developed an intense aversion to slavery. On reaching adulthood, they moved to Philadelphia where they joined the Quaker sect, and in early 1835 the Grimké sisters became active in the antislavery campaign.[3] As Gerda Lerner points out, it is notable that many of the early women publicly involved in the abolition movement were Quakers, members of a movement that allowed women to speak freely in mixed assemblies.[4]

Because of their firsthand experience of slavery and their passion against it, the Grimkés quickly became prominent abolitionist speakers, first speaking to women's circles in private homes, but soon addressing "promiscuous" audiences of men and women in churches and halls. During the sisters' tour of New England in 1837, the Massachusetts General Association of Congregationalist Ministers became alarmed at the spectacle of women publicly addressing audiences that included men and championing controversial causes such as abolition and the rights of women as full and equal moral beings.[5] The ministers issued a pastoral letter relying heavily on arguments derived from the Bible to outline the deleterious effects of women assuming the place of public reformers and moral leaders (roles traditionally reserved for men). In Sarah Grimké's Letter 3, excerpted in this chapter, she refers to passages from the Congregationalist ministers' rebuke and delivers a strong feminist response.[6]

It was not only the traditional clergy who opposed the sisters' activities, however. Some fellow abolitionists expressed

anxiety over the Grimkés' writing and lecturing on the condition of women. Both John Greenleaf Whittier and Theodore
Weld (who married Angelina in 1838) were concerned that if
the sisters became embroiled in feminist causes, the campaign
against slavery might suffer. Whittier wrote them in 1837, "Is it
not forgetting the great and dreadful wrongs of the slave in a
selfish crusade against some paltry grievance of our own?"[7]
Weld took a humanist line: if the public could be convinced of
the importance of human rights in general and be sufficiently
aroused to the horrors of slavery to rectify that injustice, then it
would be "an easy matter to take millions of females from their
knees and set them on their feet, or in other words transform
them from *babies* into *women*."[8] A practical compromise was
reached; the sisters would no longer address women's rights in
their lectures, but Sarah would complete and publish the articles she was writing, the *Letters on the Equality of the Sexes*.[9]

After completing the 1837 lecture tour and the *Letters*,
Sarah apparently gave up her public advocacy of women's issues and devoted herself to the Weld household. In 1838, the sisters were disowned by the Quakers after a number of conflicts,
including Angelina's marriage to the Presbyterian Theodore
Weld, Sarah's frustration at being denied the role of minister,
and other disputes with Quaker leaders (particularly over the
leaders' racial prejudice and reluctance to endorse the sisters'
public efforts against slavery).[10] Much later Sarah reappeared,
walking about the countryside at the age of seventy-nine, selling
copies of John Stuart Mill's feminist tract, *The Subjection of
Women*.[11]

As a Christian (if nonconformist), Sarah Grimké clearly
wished to uphold the Bible as an ethical guide. She sometimes
labeled passages that did not bend easily to her feminist interpretation "mistranslations"; at other points she argued that
men had "misinterpreted" the meaning of particular verses. She
asserted that if Scripture were properly understood, it would be
seen largely to support the equality of women.[12] Her attempt to

read the Bible in a spiritual and reformist manner was a bold one, not only because of the novelty of her feminist stance but also because she was writing at a time when Americans had little exposure to the "higher criticism" of the Bible.[13]

Despite her lack of formal theological education, Sarah Grimké was sensitive to the nuances of Scripture. Her defense of the equality of men and women on the basis of the opening chapters of Genesis is a strong one. She argued that women's "worship" of men was, from a Christian standpoint, idolatrous. Phrases from her work have found their way into the rhetoric of American feminism, especially her famous declaration, "I ask no favors for my sex. I surrender not our claim to equality. All I ask of our brethren is, that they will take their feet from off our necks, and permit us to stand upright on that ground which God designed us to occupy."[14]

LETTER 3 *

Haverhill, 7th Mo. 1837.

Dear friend,

When I last addressed thee, I had not seen the Pastoral Letter of the General Association. It has since fallen into my hands, and I must digress from my intention of exhibiting the condition of women in different parts of the world, in order to make some remarks on this extraordinary document. I am persuaded that when the minds of men and women become emancipated from the thraldom of superstition and "traditions of men," the sentiments contained in the Pastoral Letter will be recurred to with as much astonishment as the opinions of Cotton Mather and other distinguished men of his day, on the subject of witchcraft; nor will it be deemed less

---

* From Sarah Grimké, Letter 3 of *Letters on the Equality of the Sexes and the Condition of Women* (New York: Burt Franklin, 1970 [1838]), 14–21.

wonderful, that a body of divines should gravely assemble and endeavor to prove that woman has no right to "open her mouth for the dumb," than it now is that judges should have sat on the trials of witches, and solemnly condemned nineteen persons and one dog to death for witchcraft.

But to the letter. It says, "We invite your attention to the dangers which at present seem to threaten the FEMALE CHARACTER with wide-spread and permanent injury." I rejoice that they have called the attention of my sex to this subject, because I believe if woman investigates it, she will soon discover that danger is impending, though from a totally different source from that which the Association apprehends,—danger from those who, having long held the reins of *usurped* authority, are unwilling to permit us to fill that sphere which God created us to move in, and who have entered into league to crush the immortal mind of woman. I rejoice, because I am persuaded that the rights of woman, like the rights of slaves, need only be examined to be understood and asserted, even by some of those, who are now endeavoring to smother the irrepressible desire for mental and spiritual freedom which glows in the breast of many, who hardly dare to speak their sentiments.

"The appropriate duties and influence of women are clearly stated in the New Testament. Those duties are unobtrusive and private, but the sources of *mighty power*. When the mild, *dependent,* softening influence of woman upon the sternness of man's opinions is fully exercised, society feels the effects of it in a thousand ways." No one can desire more earnestly than I do, that woman may move exactly in the sphere which her Creator has assigned her; and I believe her having been displaced from that sphere has introduced confusion into the world. It is, therefore, of vast importance to herself and to all the rational creation, that she should ascertain what are her duties and her privileges as a responsible and immortal being. The New Testament has been referred to, and I am willing to abide by its decisions, but must enter my protest against the false translation of some passages by the MEN who did that work, and against the perverted interpretation by MEN who undertook to write commentaries thereon. I am inclined to think, when we are admitted to the honor of studying Greek and Hebrew, we shall produce some various readings of the Bible a little different from those we now have.

The Lord Jesus defines the duties of his followers in his Sermon on the Mount. He lays down grand principles by which they should be governed, without any reference to sex or condition: —"Ye are the light of the world. A city that is set on a hill cannot be hid. Neither do men light a candle and put it under a bushel, but on a candlestick, and it giveth light unto all that are in the house. Let your light so shine before men, that they may see your good works, and glorify your Father which is in Heaven." I follow him through all his precepts, and find him giving the same directions to women as to men, never even referring to the distinction now so strenuously insisted upon between masculine and feminine virtues: this is one of the anti-christian "traditions of men" which are taught instead of the "commandments of God." Men and women were CREATED EQUAL; they are both moral and accountable beings, and whatever is *right* for man to do, is *right* for woman.

But the influence of woman, says the Association, is to be private and unobtrusive; her light is not to shine before man like that of her brethren; but she is passively to let the lords of the creation, as they call themselves, put the bushel over it, lest peradventure it might appear that the world has been benefitted by the rays of *her* candle. So that her quenched light, according to their judgment, will be of more use than if it were set on the candlestick. "Her influence is the source of mighty power." This has ever been the flattering language of man since he laid aside the whip as a means to keep woman in subjection. He spares her body; but the war he has waged against her mind, her heart, and her soul, has been no less destructive to her as a moral being. How monstrous, how anti-christian, is the doctrine that woman is to be dependent on man! Where, in all the sacred Scriptures, is this taught? Alas! she has too well learned the lesson, which MAN has labored to teach her. She has surrendered her dearest RIGHTS, and been satisfied with the privileges which man has assumed to grant her; she has been amused with the show of power, whilst man has absorbed all the reality into himself. He has adorned the creature whom God gave him as a companion, with baubles and gewgaws, turned her attention to personal attractions, offered incense to her vanity, and made her the instrument of his selfish gratification, a plaything to please his eye and amuse his hours of leisure. "Rule by obedience and by submission sway," or in other words, study to be a hypocrite, pretend to submit, but gain your point, has been the code of household morality which woman has been taught. The poet has sung, in sickly strains, the loveliness of woman's dependence upon man, and now we find it re-echoed by those who profess to teach the religion of the Bible. God says, "Cease ye from man whose breath is in his nostrils, for wherein is he to be accounted of?" Man says, depend upon me. God says, "HE will teach us of his ways." Man says, believe it not, I am to be your teacher. This doctrine of dependence upon man is utterly at variance with the doctrine of the Bible. In that book I find nothing like the softness of woman, nor the sternness of man: both are equally commanded to bring forth the fruits of the Spirit, love meekness, gentleness, &c.

But we are told, "the power of woman is in her dependence, flowing from a consciousness of that weakness which God has given her for her protection." If physical weakness is alluded to, I cheerfully concede the superiority; if brute force is what my brethren are claiming, I am willing to let

them have all the honor they desire; but if they mean to intimate, that mental or moral weakness belongs to woman,
more than to man, I utterly disclaim the charge. Our powers
of mind have been crushed, as far as man could do it, our
sense of morality has been impaired by his interpretation of
our duties; but no where does God say that he made any distinction between us, as moral and intelligent beings.

"We appreciate," say the Association, "the *unostentatious*
prayers and efforts of woman in advancing the cause of religion at home and abroad, in leading religious inquiries TO
THE PASTOR for instruction." Several points here demand
attention. If public prayers and public efforts are necessarily
ostentatious, then "Anna the prophetess (or preacher) who
departed not from the temple, but served God with fastings
and prayers night and day," "and spake of Christ to all them
that looked for redemption in Israel," was ostentatious in
her efforts. Then, the apostle Paul encourages women to be
ostentatious in their efforts to spread the gospel, when he
gives them directions how they should appear, when engaged
in praying, or preaching in the public assemblies. Then, the
whole association of Congregational ministers are ostentatious, in the efforts they are making in preaching and praying to convert souls.

But women may be permitted to lead religious inquirers to
the PASTORS for instruction. Now this is assuming that all
pastors are better qualified to give instruction than woman.
This I utterly deny. I have suffered too keenly from the teaching of man, to lead any one to him for instruction. The Lord
Jesus says, —"Come unto me and learn of me." He points
his followers to no man; and when woman is made the favored instrument of rousing a sinner to his lost and helpless
condition, she has no right to substitute any teacher for
Christ; all she has to do is, to turn the contrite inquirer to the
"Lamb of God which taketh away the sins of the world."
More souls have probably been lost by going down to Egypt

for help, and by trusting in man in the early stages of religious experience, than by any other error. Instead of the petition being offered to God,—"Lead me in thy truth, and TEACH me, for thou art the God of my salvation,"—instead of relying on the precious promises—"What man is he that feareth the Lord? Him shall HE TEACH in the way that he shall choose"—"I will instruct thee and TEACH thee in the way which thou shalt go; I will guide thee with mine eye," the young convert is directed to go to man, as if he were in the place of God, and his instructions essential to an advancement in the path of righteousness. That woman can have but a poor conception of the privilege of being taught of God, what he alone can teach, who would turn the "religious inquirer aside" from the fountain of living waters, where he might slake his thirst for spiritual instruction, to those broken cisterns which can hold no water, and therefore cannot satisfy the panting spirit. The business of men and women, who are ORDAINED OF GOD to preach the unsearchable riches of Christ to a lost and perishing world, is to lead souls to Christ, and not to Pastors for instruction.

The General Association say, that "when woman assumes the place and tone of man as a public reformer, our care and protection of her seem unnecessary; we put ourselves in self-defence against her, and her character becomes unnatural." Here again the unscriptural notion is held up, that there is a distinction between the duties of men and women as moral beings; that what is virtue in man, is vice in woman; and women who dare to obey the command of Jehovah, "Cry aloud, spare not, lift up thy voice like a trumpet, and show my people their transgression," are threatened with having the protection of the brethren withdrawn. If this is all they do, we shall not even know the time when our chastisement is inflicted; our trust is in the Lord Jehovah, and in him is everlasting strength. The motto of woman, when she is engaged in the great work of public reformation should be, —"the

Lord is my light and my salvation; of whom shall I fear? The Lord is the strength of my life; of whom shall I be afraid?" She must feel, if she feels rightly, that she is fulfilling one of the important duties laid upon her as an accountable being, and that her character, instead of being "unnatural," is in exact accordance with the will of Him to whom, and to no other, she is responsible for the talents and the gifts confided to her. As to the pretty simile, introduced into the "Pastoral Letter," "If the vine whose strength and beauty is to lean upon the trellis work, and half conceal its clusters, thinks to assume the independence and the overshadowing nature of the elm," etc., I shall only remark that it might well suit the poet's fancy, who sings of sparkling eyes and coral lips, and knights in armor clad; but it seems to me utterly inconsistent with the dignity of a Christian body, to endeavor to draw such an anti-scriptural distinction between men and women. Ah! how many of my sex feel in the dominion, thus unrighteously exercised over them, under the gentle appellation of *protection,* that what they have leaned upon has proved a broken reed at best, and oft a spear.

Thine in the bonds of womanhood,

Sarah M. Grimké

ELIZABETH CADY STANTON

The generally affirmative estimation of the Bible by Sarah Grimké contrasts sharply with the more critical estimation by Elizabeth Cady Stanton (1815–1902), the central thinker of the nineteenth-century women's movement. *The Woman's Bible,* which was inspired and in large part written by Stanton, is one of the most remarkable products of nineteenth-century American feminism. *The Woman's Bible* offers commentaries on passages from the Hebrew Bible and the New Testament pertaining to women.

Not all the women who collaborated with Stanton in the 1890s to produce *The Woman's Bible* shared her radical views on religion. Although Stanton was not an atheist (she believed in a "Supreme Intelligence" that governed the world by natural law), she had no use for the doctrines and ethical teachings of the Christian churches of her time. In fact, she argued that organized religion had been a greater barrier to the freedom of women than disenfranchisement.[15]

The seeds of Elizabeth Cady Stanton's nonconformity and irreverent attitudes were apparently sown in her youth. In her famous autobiography she recounts that she was a rebellious child who received a boy's education and was bitterly disappointed when she was not allowed, because of her sex, to attend Union College with her male friends.[16] Shortly after her marriage to the abolitionist Henry B. Stanton, she attended the 1840 World Anti-Slavery Convention in London. The women in the American delegation were not permitted to sit with the men on the floor of the conference. The ministers present were among the most vociferous defenders of male privilege. As Stanton later recounted, "The clergymen seemed to have God and his angels especially in their care and keeping, and were in agony lest the women should do or say something to shock the heavenly hosts."[17] Stanton's attitude toward these "narrow-minded bigots, pretending to be teachers and leaders of men"[18] and the church they represented did not mellow with the years. She gave the ecclesiastical establishment absolutely no credit for the movement toward women's freedom; women, she said, could rather thank religion for emphasizing their "inferiority and subjection."[19] In retrospect, her viewpoint appears to have been excessive, for many ministers did lend their support—and the support of the Christian religion—to the suffrage cause.[20]

In the latter part of the nineteenth century, the American women's movement divided over the scope of its platform. Some thought that feminists should focus exclusively on winning the vote; others wished to expand the debate to include a whole spectrum of concerns relating to women.[21] Stanton always promoted the wider platform: women's domestic situations, marriage and divorce laws, the conditions of working women.[22] Yet despite her broad vision, following the Civil War (particularly in the bitter fight over granting the franchise to African-American men), Stanton invoked viciously racist and anti-immigrant arguments in support of her feminist agenda—an agenda directed, it sadly appears, largely toward the benefit of white women.[23]

Freedom for women meant, in Stanton's view, more than obtaining the vote; women must be able to exercise their God-given right to determine their own "spheres of activity."[24] But for women to regulate their own lives, they first had to be freed from the internalized forms of oppression that kept them subdued. It was to help women free themselves from this internalized oppression that Stanton sought, toward the end of her long and active career in the suffrage movement, to organize a group of colleagues who could write commentaries on biblical passages relating to women.[25] Stanton believed that the Bible, a primary source of Western values and worldview, not only contributed to the social suppression of women but also constituted a powerful form of internal bondage for women.[26] Her first attempt to enlist associates to work on the project failed, in 1886, from lack of cooperation.[27] But she persisted, and two volumes of *The Woman's Bible* were published in 1895 and 1898.

Although *The Woman's Bible* was an instant best-seller, it also proved quite controversial.[28] In 1896, the National American Woman Suffrage Association voted to disclaim any official connection with *The Woman's Bible*.[29] This decision demonstrates the degree to which American feminism was becoming socially respectable. Women of more conventional values than Stanton now made up the core of the movement, and they were not happy to be associated with her biting criticism of Judaism and Christianity.[30]

Elizabeth Cady Stanton, from whose pen all of the following passages came, argued her case in a variety of ways. When it fit her purpose, she praised the biblical authors, such as the author of Genesis 1, for writing in a manner that suggested the equality of the sexes. At other points, she argued that the text is hopelessly warped by the patriarchal biases of its fallible male authors. Nor did she shrink from reinterpreting the biblical stories to derive a feminist moral. Thus Jephthah's nameless daughter, if the women's movement could have reached her, might have declared to her father, "Self-development is a higher duty than self-sacrifice." And, Stanton asserted, Matthew's parable of the wise and foolish virgins is in actuality a lesson in "the cultivation of courage and self-reliance" for females.

Contemporary feminism builds on Stanton's belief that women's oppression cannot be overcome without liberation from restrictive and repressive social authority, including those forms of authority that are internalized.[31] The fact that today we see *The Woman's Bible* as a pioneering attack on the patriarchal construction of women's consciousness is a vindication of Stanton's efforts.

THE WOMAN'S BIBLE*

The Old Testament

Genesis 1:26, 27, 28:

. . . Here is the sacred historian's first account of the advent of woman; a simultaneous creation of both sexes, in the image of God. It is evident from the language that there was consultation in the Godhead, and that the masculine and feminine elements were equally represented. Scott in his commentaries says, "this consultation of the Gods is the origin of the doctrine of the trinity." But instead of three male

---

* From Elizabeth Cady Stanton, *The Woman's Bible,* Parts 1, 2, and Appendix (New York: Arno Press, 1972 [1895–98]), part 1, 14–16; part 2, 24–26, 113, 123–26, 214.

personages, as generally represented, a Heavenly Father, Mother, and Son would seem more rational.

The first step in the elevation of woman to her true position, as an equal factor in human progress, is the cultivation of the religious sentiment in regard to her dignity and equality, the recognition by the rising generation of an ideal Heavenly Mother, to whom their prayers should be addressed, as well as to a Father.

If language has any meaning, we have in these texts a plain declaration of the existence of the feminine element in the Godhead, equal in power and glory with the masculine. The Heavenly Mother and Father! "God created man in his *own image, male and female.*" Thus Scripture, as well as science and philosophy, declares the eternity and equality of sex. . . .

The above texts plainly show the simultaneous creation of man and woman, and their equal importance in the development of the race. All those theories based on the assumption that man was prior in the creation have no foundation in Scripture.

As to woman's subjection, on which both the canon and the civil law delight to dwell, it is important to note that equal dominion is given to woman over every living thing, but not one word is said giving man dominion over woman.

Here is the first title deed to this green earth giving alike to the sons and daughters of God. No lesson of woman's subjection can be fairly drawn from the first chapter of the Old Testament.

Judges 11:30–37:

A woman's vow, as we have already seen, could be disallowed at the pleasure of any male relative; but a man's was considered sacred even though it involved the violation of the sixth commandment, the violation of the individual rights of another human being. These loving fathers in the

Old Testament, like Jephthah and Abraham, thought to make themselves specially pleasing to the Lord by sacrificing their children to Him as burnt offerings. If the ethics of their moral code had permitted suicide, they might with some show of justice have offered themselves, if they thought that the first-born kid would not do; but what right had they to offer up their sons and daughters in return for supposed favors from the Lord?

The submission of Isaac and Jephthah's daughter to this violation of their most sacred rights is truly pathetic. But, like all oppressed classes, they were ignorant of the fact that they had any natural, inalienable rights. We have such a type of womanhood even in our day. If any man had asked Jephthah's daughter if she would not like to have the Jewish law on vows so amended that she might disallow her father's vow, and thus secure to herself the right of life, she would no doubt have said, "No; I have all the rights I want," just as a class of New York women said in 1895, when it was proposed to amend the constitution of the State in their favor.

The only favor which Jephthah's daughter asks, is that she may have two months of solitude on the mountain tops to bewail the fact that she will die childless. Motherhood among the Jewish women was considered the highest honor and glory ever vouchsafed to mortals. So she was permitted for a brief period to enjoy her freedom, accompanied by young Jewish maidens who had hoped to dance at her wedding.

Commentators differ as to the probable fate of Jephthah's daughter. Some think that she was merely sequestered in some religious retreat, others that the Lord spoke to Jephthah as He did to Abraham forbidding the sacrifice. We might attribute this helpless condition of woman to the benighted state of those times if we did not see the trail of the serpent through our civil laws and church discipline.

This Jewish maiden is known in history only as Jephthah's daughter—she belongs to the no-name series. The father owns her absolutely, having her life even at his disposal. We often hear people laud the beautiful submission and the self-sacrifice of this nameless maiden. To me it is pitiful and painful. I would that this page of history were gilded with a dignified whole-souled rebellion. I would have had the daughter receive the father's confession with a stern rebuke, saying: "I will not consent to such a sacrifice. Your vow must be disallowed. You may sacrifice your own life as you please, but you have no right over mine. I am on the threshold of life, the joys of youth and of middle age are all before me. You are in the sunset; you have had your blessings and your triumphs; but mine are yet to come. Life is to me full of hope and of happiness. Better that you die than I, if the God whom you worship is pleased with the sacrifice of human life. I consider that God has made me the arbiter of my own fate and all my possibilities. My first duty is to develop all the powers given to me and to make the most of myself and my own life. Self-development is a higher duty than self-sacrifice. I demand the immediate abolition of the Jewish law on vows. Not with my consent can you fulfill yours." This would have been a position worthy of a brave woman.

The New Testament

"Great is Truth, and might above all things." 1 Esdras 4:41.

Does the New Testament bring promises of new dignity and of larger liberties for woman? When thinking women make any criticisms on their degraded position in the Bible, Christians point to her exaltation in the New Testament, as if, under their religion, woman really does occupy a higher position than under the Jewish dispensation. While there are grand types of women presented under both religions, there is no difference in the general estimate of the sex. In fact, her inferior position is more clearly and emphatically set forth by the Apostles than by the Prophets and the Patriarchs. There are no such specific directions for woman's subordination in the Pentateuch as in the Epistles.

We are told that the whole sex was highly honored in Mary being the mother of Jesus. Surely a wise and virtuous son is more indebted to his mother than she is to him, and is honored only by reflecting her superior characteristics. Why the founders of the Christian religion did not improvise an earthly Father as well as an earthly Mother does not clearly appear. The questionable position of Joseph is unsatisfactory. As Mary belonged to the Jewish aristocracy, she should have had a husband of the same rank. If a Heavenly Father was necessary, why not a Heavenly Mother? If an earthly Mother was admirable, why not an earthly Father? The Jewish idea that Jesus was born according to natural law is more rational than is the Christian record of the immaculate conception by the Holy Ghost, the third person of the Trinity. These Biblical mysteries and inconsistencies are a great strain on the credulity of the ordinary mind.

Matthew 25:1–12:

In this chapter we have the duty of self-development impressively and repeatedly urged in the form of parables, addressed alike to man and to woman. The sin of neglecting and of burying one's talents, capacities, and powers, and the penalties which such a course involve, are here strikingly portrayed. . . .

. . . It [this parable] fairly describes the two classes which help to make up society in general. The one who, like the foolish virgins, have never learned the first important duty of cultivating their own individual powers, using the talents given to them, and keeping their own lamps trimmed and burning. The idea of being a helpmeet to somebody else has been so sedulously drilled into most women that an individual life, aim, purpose and ambition are never taken into consideration. They oftimes do so much in other directions that they neglect the most vital duties to themselves.

We may find in this simple parable a lesson for the cultivation of courage and of self-reliance. These virgins are summoned to the discharge of an important duty at midnight, alone, in darkness, and in solitude. No chivalrous gentleman is there to run for oil and to trim their lamps. They must depend on themselves, unsupported, and pay the penalty of their own improvidence and unwisdom. Perhaps in that bridal procession might have been seen fathers, brothers, friends, for whose service and amusement the foolish virgins had wasted many precious hours, when they should have been trimming their own lamps and keeping oil in their vessels.

And now, with music, banners, lanterns, torches, guns, and rockets fired at intervals, come the bride and the groom, with their attendants and friends numbering thousands, brilliant in jewels, gold and silver, magnificently mounted on richly caparisoned horses—for nothing can be more brilliant than were those nuptial solemnities of Eastern nations. As this spectacle, grand beyond description, sweeps by, imagine the foolish virgins pushed aside, in the shadow of some tall edifice, with dark, empty lamps in their hands, unnoticed and unknown. And while the castle walls resound with music and merriment, and the lights from every window stream out far into the darkness, no kind friends gather round them to sympathize in their humiliation, nor to cheer their loneliness. It matters little that women may be ignorant, dependent, unprepared for trial and for temptation. Alone they must meet the terrible emergencies of life, to be sustained and protected amid danger and death by their own courage, skill, and self-reliance, or perish.

Woman's devotion to the comfort, the education, the success of men in general, and to their plans and projects, is in a great measure due to her self-abnegation and self-sacrifice having been so long and so sweetly lauded by poets, philosophers and priests as the acme of human goodness and glory.

Now, to my mind, there is nothing commendable in the action of young women who go about begging funds to educate young men for the ministry, while they and the majority of their sex are too poor to educate themselves, and if able, are still denied admittance into some of the leading institutions of learning throughout our land. It is not commendable for women to get up fairs and donation parties for churches in which the gifted of their sex may neither pray, preach, share in the offices and honors, nor have a voice in the business affairs, creeds and discipline, and from whose altars come forth the Biblical interpretations in favor of woman's subjection.

It is not commendable for the women of this Republic to expend much enthusiasm on political parties as now organized, nor in national celebrations, for they have as yet no lot or part in the great experiment of self-government.

In their ignorance, women sacrifice themselves to educate the men of their households, and to make of themselves ladders by which their husbands, brothers and sons climb up into the kingdom of knowledge, while they themselves are shut out from all intellectual companionship, even with those they love best; such are indeed like the foolish virgins. They have not kept their own lamps trimmed and burning; they have no oil in their vessels, no resources in themselves; they bring no light to their households nor to the circle in which they move; and when the bridegroom cometh, when the philosopher, the scientist, the saint, the scholar, the great and the learned, all come together to celebrate the marriage feast of science and religion, the foolish virgins, though present, are practically shut out; for what know they of the grand themes which inspire each tongue and kindle every thought? Even the brothers and the sons whom they have educated, now rise to heights which they cannot reach, span distances which they cannot comprehend.

The solitude of ignorance, oh, who can measure its misery! The wise virgins are they who keep their lamps trimmed, who burn oil in their vessels for their own use, who have improved every advantage for their education, secured a healthy, happy, complete development, and entered all the profitable avenues of labor, for self-support, so that when the opportunities and the responsibilities of life come, they may be fitted fully to enjoy the one and ably to discharge the other.

These are the women who to-day are close upon the heels of man in the whole realm of thought, in art, in science, in literature, and in government. With telescopic vision they explore the starry firmament, and bring back the history of the planetary world. With chart and compass they pilot ships across the mighty deep, and with skilful fingers send electric messages around the world. In galleries of art, the grandeur of nature and the greatness of humanity are immortalized by them on canvas, and by their inspired touch, dull blocks of marble are transformed into angels of light. In music they speak again the language of Mendelssohn, of Beethoven, of Chopin, of Schumann, and are worthy interpreters of their great souls. The poetry and the novels of the century are theirs; they, too, have touched the keynote of reform in religion, in politics and in social life. They fill the editors' and the professors' chairs, plead at the bar of justice, walk the wards of the hospital, and speak from the pulpit and the platform.

Such is the widespread preparation for the marriage feast of science and religion; such is the type of womanhood which the bridegroom of an enlightened public sentiment welcomes to-day; and such is the triumph of the wise virgins over the folly, the ignorance and the degradation of the past as in grand procession they enter the temple of knowledge, and *the door is no longer shut.*

Appendix

... The real difficulty in woman's case is that the whole foundation of the Christian religion rests on her temptation and man's fall, hence the necessity of a Redeemer and a plan of salvation. As the chief cause of this dire calamity, woman's degradation and subordination were made a necessity. If however, we accept the Darwinian theory, that the race has been a gradual growth from the lower to a higher form of life, and that the story of the fall is a myth, we can exonerate the snake, emancipate the woman, and reconstruct a more rational religion for the nineteenth century, and thus escape all the perplexities of the Jewish mythology as of no more importance than those of the Greek, Persian and Egyptian.

WOMEN AS RELIGIOUS LEADERS

An important aspect of nineteenth- and early twentieth-century American history is the explosion of religious movements founded and led by women. To be sure, there had been notable women involved with early American religious life—Anne Hutchinson (1591–1643), the religious reformer banished from the Massachusetts Bay Colony to Rhode Island in 1637, stands as a prominent example[32]—but nineteenth-century developments are especially remarkable. Some scholars have called attention to the "feminization" of American Protestantism in this period,[33] including both the growing numbers of women in religious groups and a "softening," sentimentalizing trend in theology—even though, to be sure, men continued to dominate clerical leadership. Thus we find women active in a wide spectrum of religious activities, from revivalism[34] and the reestablishment of the deaconess movement to social welfare and reform work.[35] Women were especially prominent in the mission field; according to historian Barbara Welter, by 1893 a full 60 percent of American Protestant missionaries were women.[36]

Although many of these women retained ties to mainstream Protestantism, their effective leadership, it has been argued, often depended largely on their being "outside the mainstream," where the divine could be construed differently and traditional clergy roles could either be deemphasized or abandoned.[37] This principle is amply illustrated by the presence of women preachers in African-American churches: here, among the most dispossessed of nineteenth-century American society, the appeal to the inspiration of the Holy Spirit could take precedence over more restrictive notions of clerical ordination.[38]

Jarena Lee

A notable example of nineteenth-century African-American woman preachers is Jarena Lee, who in 1836 published a vivid account of her life, religious experience, and visions. Four or five years after her "sanctification," Lee reports, she heard a voice instructing her, "Go preach the Gospel!" Although a minister whom she consulted informed her that the Methodists (that is, members of the African Methodist Episcopal Church) did not permit women to preach, Jarena Lee reasoned otherwise:

> . . . it should be remembered that nothing is impossible with God. And why should it be thought impossible, heterodox, or improper for a woman to preach? seeing the Saviour died for the woman as well as for the man.
>
> If the man may preach, because the Saviour died for him, why not the woman? seeing he died for her also. Is he not a whole Saviour, instead of a half one? as those who hold it wrong for a woman to preach, would seem to make it appear.
>
> Did not Mary *first* preach the risen Saviour, and is not the doctrine of the resurrection the very climax of Christianity—hangs not all our hope on this, as argued by St. Paul? Then did not Mary, a woman, preach the gospel? for she preached the resurrection of the crucified Son of God.
>
> But some will say that Mary did not expound the Scripture, therefore, she did not preach, in the proper sense of the term. To this I reply, it may be that the term *preach* in those primitive times, did not mean exactly what it is now *made* to mean; perhaps it was a great deal more simple then, than it is now—if it were not, the

unlearned fishermen could not have preached the gospel at all, as they had no learning. . . .

. . . If then, to preach the gospel, by the gift of heaven, comes by inspiration solely, is God straitened; must he take the man exclusively? May he not, did he not, and can he not inspire a female to preach the simple story of the birth, life, death, and resurrection of our Lord, and accompany it too with power to the sinner's heart. As for me, I am fully persuaded that the Lord called me to labor according to what I have received, in his vineyard. If he has not, how could he consistently bear testimony in favor of my poor labors, in awakening and converting sinners?

. . . I firmly believe that I have sown seed, in the name of the Lord, which shall appear with its increase at the great day of accounts, when Christ shall come to make up his jewels.[39]

With the passage of years, as she gained the approval of her bishop, Jarena Lee moved from "exhortation" to full preaching, powerfully affecting many of those who heard her, both African-American and white, in her travels. Her own explanation of her success was that "by the instrumentality of a poor coloured woman, the Lord poured forth his spirit among the people."[40] In the face of opposition to her preaching, Jarena Lee raised the argument that "if an ass reproved Balaam, and a barn-door fowl reproved Peter, why should not a woman reprove sin?"[41] Acknowledging the questionable link here between women and animals, Jarena Lee quoted with approval the response of a former slave-woman: "'May be a speaking women is like an ass—but I can tell you one thing, the ass seen the angel when Balaam didn't.'"[42] Jarena Lee states at the conclusion of her journal that just as the blind have heightened sense perceptions, "so it may be with such as I am, who has never had more than three months schooling; and wishing to know much of the way and law of God, have therefore watched the more closely, the operations of the Spirit, and have in consequence been led thereby."[43]

Phoebe Palmer, Ellen Harmon White, Mary Baker Eddy, and Aimee Semple McPherson

Among other prominent women founders and leaders of religious movements in this period were Phoebe Palmer, Ellen Harmon White, Mary Baker Eddy, and Aimee Semple McPherson. Again, it is probably no accident that the movements they stimulated stand outside "mainstream" Protestantism. Characteristic of these women is the notion that the Holy Spirit, or spiritual principles, empower women such as themselves to speak and to lead. Especially in groups loosely lumped under the umbrella term "the Holiness movement," we find women appealing to their experiences of the Spirit's call to preach the message of Christian perfectionism. In contrast to the few mainstream denominations that grudgingly, if at all, began to accept women into the ministry in this period, Holiness denominations, such as the Church of the Nazarene and the Pilgrim Holiness Church, had relatively large complements of female ministers from early in their history.[44]

Phoebe Palmer (1807–74) was an important leader in the Holiness movement in America. Her book, *Promise of the Father,* first published in 1859, argues its case for women preachers from the biblical promise that in the Last Days there would be an outpouring of the Spirit on women as well as on men.[45] Since, according to Palmer, "preaching" meant "explaining the teachings, or enforcing the commands, of Christ and his apostles," biblical injunctions taken by mainstream denominations to oppose women preaching did not apply.[46] Anyone, female as well as male, who had "an experimental knowledge of the grace of Christ, as the Saviour of sinners" is free to proclaim the good news of our renewed natures.[47]

Yet, like several other women religious leaders of her time and beyond, Palmer did not particularly advocate women's rights. She believed that the sexes have their "separate spheres" as regards their position in the material world.[48] According to

Palmer, the Bible tells us that Adam was created first and that woman was not to usurp his authority: this is the law for women today as it was for the world's beginning.[49] It is only under the extraordinary circumstances of the Last Days—in which Palmer thought she was living—that the Spirit gives women the right to preach.[50] Thus Palmer set herself apart from the claims of feminists such as Sarah Grimké and Elizabeth Cady Stanton.

The notion that the end of the world was coming soon and that spiritual gifts (such as visions and prophecies) accompanied it was also characteristic of the message of Ellen Harmon White (1827–1915). White was important in helping the Adventist movement adjust to the failed expectation of Jesus' Second Coming, which many millennialists had believed would occur in 1843. In one of her visions, White experienced Jesus carrying her to the heavenly Jerusalem, where she learned that keeping the Sabbath was to be in effect forever, not just for Old Testament times[51]—a view that has since characterized the religious practice of Seventh-Day Adventists.

Mary Baker Eddy (1821–1910) was the founder of the Christian Science movement. Like the Shakers, Baker Eddy's vision of God incorporated the female dimension as well as the male. Thus she spoke of the "Father/Mother God." The Christian Scientist understanding of spiritual power differed from that of the Holiness groups by stressing the powers of the human mind. A central theme of Christian Science detailed in Mary Baker Eddy's 1875 book, *Science and Health with Key to the Scriptures,* is the overcoming of the limitations of materiality by mind. She served as leader of the movement in an authoritative (some would say authoritarian) way until her death. Yet despite her critique of mainstream Christianity and its leaders (not to speak of medical practitioners) and her exaltation of a female religious principle,[52] Baker Eddy did not pursue her activities through the women's suffrage movement. A recent commentator, Susan Hill Lindley, concludes that "women's rights were, for her, a subordinate interest."[53] For example, despite the fact that she thought that marriage had no place in the final kingdom of God, she held conventional views of marital chastity and of the different "spheres" appropriate to the two sexes.[54]

Finally, Aimee Semple McPherson (1890–1944), perhaps the most noted woman evangelist of the twentieth century, was the founder of the International Church of the Four-Square Gospel, which by the 1990s counted churches in seventy-four countries and claimed 1,700,000 members.[55] Believing that Jesus is the same "yesterday, today, and forever," Semple McPherson developed a ministry of healing and of recovering what she believed to be "Bible Christianity, with emphasis on the plenary inspiration of Scripture, the Second Coming of Jesus, and a call to holiness."[56] The movement's religious conservatism is underscored in Semple McPherson's opposition to evolutionary theory (she sided with William Jennings Bryan in his famous debate with Clarence Darrow).[57]

Thousands across America flocked to hear this itinerant evangelist preach and to witness her perform healings. In 1923, her Angelus Temple was dedicated in Los Angeles; the auditorium's 5,300-seat capacity indicates the strength of her following.[58] Aimee Semple McPherson's popularity stemmed in part from her sense of "religious theater"—her ability to use such secular extravaganzas as the Tournament of Roses parade and the newly developed medium of radio to advance her cause.[59] Speaking to middle-class audiences (those "below," she thought, could be left to the kind auspices of the Salvation Army),[60] she, like some of her preaching predecessors, believed that when God called, you did not resist God's will—even if you were a woman.[61] According to one of Semple McPherson's recent commentators, Edith Blumhofer, she broadened the base of Pentecostalism by linking Pentecostal concerns to a wider stream of popular piety in America.[62]

WOMEN'S ORDINATION IN
MAINLINE DENOMINATIONS

Women in mainline Protestant denominations have had a much harder struggle winning the right to preach. The ordination of Antoinette Brown (later Blackwell) as a Congregationalist minister in 1853 is usually cited as the first such event.[63] Many denominations refused to ordain women well into the twentieth century: it was not until after 1950 that two branches of the Presbyterian church, the Methodists, some branches of the Lutherans, and the Episcopalians granted women the right to be ordained. The 1970s was a particularly active decade, with the number of women ministers rising in some denominations by about 60 percent in just a few years. This rapid expansion of women's ordination was spurred on by the women's movement, which was finding a strong voice in the wider culture. So many women wished to prepare for the ministry that some more liberal seminaries found that the majority of their students were female. Older arguments that the Bible prohibited women ministers were defeated in many denominations, as was the appeal by conservatives to an unvarying "tradition" that opposed women's ordination.[64] Instead, a more progressive generation appealed to notable women depicted in the Bible (such as Deborah in Judges 4–5 and Phoebe in Romans 16) and to verses such as Galatians 3:28 ("there is no male and female, for you are all one in Christ Jesus") to justify their claim to more visible leadership roles within Christian churches.

The argument against women priests from church tradition has been employed most notably by the Vatican. The 1977 *Vatican Declaration on the Ordination of Women (Inter Insigniores)*, for example, claims that excluding women from the priesthood has been part of the constant tradition from the time of Jesus and the apostles. This exclusion, it is alleged, did not result from the backwardness of the times or from any discrimination on the part of early Christianity's leaders but stems directly from God's dispensation. Among the subsidiary arguments here employed by the Vatican is that the priest offering the Eucharist acts "in the person of Christ" and must stand as an easily recognizable "sign" by his "natural resemblance" to Christ, a resemblance that appears to center exclusively on the priest's maleness. Women simply do not have a "vocation" (a "call") to the priesthood, the document concludes—and if they imagine otherwise, they should be told that they feel a "purely subjective attraction" rather than a genuine "vocation," which requires authentication by the church.[65]

Although some of the more vulnerable arguments in the 1977 declaration have been set aside in recent discussions, Pope John Paul II in the 1994 Apostolic Letter *Ordinatio Sacerdotalis* (*Priestly Ordination*) reaffirmed the traditional Catholic stand against women's ordination. In a telling inversion of the argument used by the Protestant women evangelists to legitimate their calling, the Pope reiterated that Christ chose those whom he desired to be apostles—and he chose twelve men. Far from being a mere matter of church discipline (which could presumably be changed), the ordination of women, according to the Pope, cannot be countenanced, for the church has no authority to do so—and "this judgment is to be definitively held by all the Church's faithful."[66] Thus although most Protestant denominations now ordain women, Catholicism remains a bulwark against the practice. Given the ever-declining numbers of celibate male priests to serve Catholics, we find it interesting to speculate on whether the Vatican will come to endorse the marriage of male priests rather than concede the ordination of females—or whether some other strategy will be found to increase the supply of Catholic priests worldwide.

13.

∼ Twentieth-Century Sexual Issues: Contraception, Abortion, and Homosexuality

As previous chapters have suggested, theologians and church leaders of the patristic and medieval periods thought that the only permissible sexual activity was heterosexual and, ideally, intended for procreation. For them, contraception and abortion constituted a continuum of evil actions, since both practices encouraged sexual intercourse without the conception and birth of children. In Augustine's famous words that were repeated by ecclesiastical writers throughout the Middle Ages,

> Sometimes, indeed, this lustful cruelty, or, if you please, cruel lust, resorts to such extravagant methods as to use poisonous drugs to secure barrenness; or else, if unsuccessful in this, to destroy the conceived seed by some means previous to birth, preferring that its offspring should rather perish than receive vitality; or if it was advancing to life within the womb, should be slain before it was born. Well, if both parties alike are so flagitious, they are not husband and wife; and if such were their character from the beginning, they have not come together by wedlock but by debauchery.[1]

Although in later centuries Catholic moralists such as Thomas Sanchez (1550–1610) argued that abortion might be considered morally permissible if the prospective mother acted with the intent to save her own life (for example, if she thought the fetus were dangerously "attacking" her, or if as an unmarried girl she feared that her family would kill her if they learned she was pregnant), the general sentiment of Catholic writers held that abortion was tantamount to homicide, especially after the point of the fetus's "ensoulment." With the growing acceptance from the seventeenth century onward of the belief that the fetus received its soul at the moment of conception—not after a month or two of gestation—Catholic views against abortion at *any* stage of pregnancy hardened. And new knowledge regarding the biology of conception, as this field became known in the nineteenth century, served only to bolster the church's absolute prohibition of abortion.[2]

In the course of the twentieth century, some Catholic theologians and numerous laypeople have moved away from the earlier view that contraception and abortion are comparable sexual evils and have come to see contraception as far less morally problematic than abortion. To understand the process through which this change has occurred, we must consider the social and other factors that have prompted the Catholic church's official pronouncements cited in the next section and Catholic progressives' criticism of those pronouncements.

CONTRACEPTION

The Vatican since the time of Leo XIII (1878–1903) has attempted to bring the Catholic church more into dialogue with the society of its time than Leo's predecessors saw fit. Many social changes had taken place in various parts of the world by the late nineteenth century concerning women and their roles. In some countries, such as England and America, the suffrage movement had made great strides. Thousands of females had joined the workforce outside the home; they were spending part of their lives in a "man's world," with all the attendant privileges and responsibilities, not the least of which was earning their own income. In addition, various developments in contraception had taken place that gave women (and men) greater control over their reproductive faculties than had been possible earlier.[3] As the 1920s dawned, the movement toward sexual freedom for women, accompanied by a revolution in female dress, brought a new consciousness and style of life to many young women in the West.

For traditional Catholicism, these developments were unsettling. From Leo XIII to Pius XI (whose papacy ended in 1939), popes repudiated the Marxist critique of traditional marriage as a bourgeois institution. They expressed uneasiness at women's entrance into the world of professions and politics with the accompanying desertion of the home as the center of their lives, and appeared scandalized by the lack of modesty in female dress.[4] In America, the birth control movement, spearheaded by Margaret Sanger, met with opposition from the Catholic hierarchy; the Catholic archbishop of New York attempted to shut down her speech in Town Hall in November 1921.[5] But the decisive shock to Catholic thinking came in the summer of 1930, when Anglican bishops meeting at Lambeth Palace issued a statement sanctioning the use of birth control for members of the Church of England. This pronouncement was a blow to Catholics who felt that the Anglican communion was the Protestant denomination closest to their own. In response, Pius XI thought the time was at hand for a firm clarification of Catholic views on marriage.

Casti Connubii (*On Chaste Marriage*), Pius's famous encyclical[6] issued on December 31, 1930, which we excerpt in this chapter, is structured around Augustine's analysis of the threefold "goods" of marriage. With respect to the first purpose of marriage identified by Augustine, offspring, Pius discussed the issues of birth control (forbidden as "against nature" and "intrinsically vicious"), abortion ("the direct murder of the innocent"), and sterilization. The second of Augustine's "goods," conjugal fidelity, was taken by Pius to exclude any kind of extramarital sexual experimentation. And the "sacramental bond" was interpreted by the Pope, as it was by Augustine, to mean the prohibition of divorce except in very rare cases. Thus the church of the 1930s portrayed itself as retaining the same ideals of sexual morality upheld by the bishop of Hippo over 1,500 years before.

The encyclical also presents a clear notion of the position of women. Although Pius was aware that contemporary society permitted women increased civil and legal rights, he wished women to use these rights in such a way that the traditional idea of the female role, especially the function of wife and mother, was not overturned. Women are reminded that despite the rights now granted to them, they are to be in "ready subjection" to the chief of the family, the husband. Husbands and children are to be the center of their existence. Activities in the larger world outside the home are sanctioned only insofar as they do not interfere with the calling of motherhood and do not injure the modesty and fragility of the "female temperament." Pius saw the feminist movement as offering women a false freedom, and he condemned it. He asserted that the liberty offered women under the feminist banner is "debasing" to the female character. Catholics are also warned against enthusiastically espousing the relaxation of the divorce laws; greater freedom of divorce is seen not only as damaging the family structure but also as lowering the position of women, leaving them helpless and undefended in a ruthless male world. And in a section not included in the following passages from the encyclical, the state is called on to aid the church by forbidding abortion and sterilization and by helping to ensure youthful modesty.

The views of *Casti Connubii* set the tone for Catholic attitudes in the years that followed. Various Vatican pronouncements clarified and developed the themes of the encyclical. Starting in the mid-1940s, Pope Pius XII delivered a number of speeches on women's roles in which he stressed the spiritual equality of men and women and acknowledged the new social role of women, but upheld, in addition, the more traditional attitudes toward family life.[7] Perhaps the most important of Pius XII's statements is *The Apostolate of the Midwife,* issued in 1951 amid the devastation and poverty of postwar Europe, which, although it championed the church's stand against abortion and contraception in general, did permit the use of the "rhythm method" of birth control (which takes account of a woman's infertile periods) in some circumstances.[8]

In light of the rapid development and improvement of methods of contraception, many lay Catholics were hopeful when Pope Paul VI, in response to discussions concerning marriage and sexuality that took place at the Second Vatican Council (1962–65),[9] set up a special commission to study the problem of contraception. Catholics throughout the world thought that perhaps there would be a change in viewpoint on the issue of contraception. Although the Majority Report of the Pope's commission recommended a relaxation of the church's strict attitude in view of newer understandings of "human nature," the personal values present in the marriage relationship, and the changed place of women in society, this view did not meet with the Vatican's approval.[10] In response to the commission, Pope Paul VI issued the encyclical *Humanae Vitae (Of Human Life)* in 1968.

In *Humanae Vitae* the Pope acknowledges the changed circumstances of twentieth-century life, especially in Western nations, but he disagrees with Catholic progressives that married couples should be free to choose the number of children they might have and the spacing of those children through the use of contraceptives; natural law as well as Christian revelation stood against this concession. The writers of the Majority Report, the Pope argues, did not sufficiently emphasize that our worldly circumstances constitute only a small part of a larger "supernatural and eternal vocation" that would be imperiled by Catholics' modification, or defiance, of traditional church teaching. Against the attempt by liberal Catholics to level the hierarchical assessment that children stood as the first and foremost purpose of marriage, the Pope reaffirms the traditional notion of "hierarchy of values" in marriage, which leaves little room for the convenience and wishes of the couple. Since each and every "marriage act [that is, sexual intercourse] must remain open to the transmission of life," couples should not imagine that they are *sometimes* permitted to use contraceptives just because they plan to have children, or more children, in the future. "*Never* do evil so that good may follow therefrom" is the moral dictum that, according to the Pope, rules out contraceptive practices for *every* sex act. Even "natural" methods of regulating fertility (the rhythm method) are to be used *only* if there are "serious motives to space out births."[11]

In March 1995, Pope John Paul II renewed the teachings of *Humanae Vitae* in a lengthy and important new encyclical, *Evangelium Vitae* (*The Gospel of Life*), in which he addresses the violence and materialism of modern life. In this encyclical, the Pope places the controversies concerning contraception and abortion in the context of a broad range of issues, including euthanasia and assisted suicide, the use of human embryos for medical research, capital punishment, warfare, and the unjust distribution of the world's resources. All of these phenomena are, for the Pope, signs of the sinister modern "culture of death" that threatens human dignity and freedom. On the basis of a natural law that he sees as being available to believer and nonbeliever alike, John Paul II advocates an alternative "culture of life" which respects all human life from conception to the moment of natural death.

In this regard, the Pope affirms prior teachings concerning "the negative values inherent in the 'contraceptive mentality.'" Recognizing that from a moral point of view, contraception and abortion are different evils (one attacking "the full truth of the sexual act," the other destroying human life), *Evangelium Vitae* nonetheless affirms that the two issues are "often closely connected, as fruits of the same tree." Indeed, this link is vividly demonstrated by recent technological developments that make the boundary between contraceptives and abortifacients increasingly vague. In only the slightest modification of *Humanae Vitae*'s teachings on contraception, John Paul II implies that natural methods of regulating fertility might be permitted to a married couple "indefinitely" if chosen "for serious reasons and in respect of the moral law."[12]

The restrictiveness of *Humanae Vitae* prompted a sharp response from Catholic laity and the more liberally minded clergy alike, and it precipitated a crisis of confidence that the church continues to face.[13] Despite the Vatican's emphatic opposition to contraception, the church's position has been disregarded by the majority of Catholic couples in America, who by all accounts use contraceptive techniques at rates comparable to their non-Catholic counterparts.

ON CHRISTIAN MARRIAGE:
ENCYCLICAL LETTER CASTI CONNUBII
(December 31, 1930)*

(10) Now when We come to explain, Venerable Brethren, what are the blessings that God has attached to true matrimony, and how great they are, there occur to Us the words of that illustrious Doctor of the Church whom We commemorated recently in Our encyclical *Ad Salutem* on the occasion of the fifteenth centenary of his death: "These," says St. Augustine, "are all the blessings of matrimony on account of which matrimony itself is a blessing: offspring, conjugal faith and the sacrament." And how under these three heads is contained a splendid summary of the whole doctrine of

---

* From Pius XI, *Casti Connubii* (*On Christian Marriage*), in *The Church and the Reconstruction of the Modern World: The Social Encyclicals of Pius XI*, ed. T. P. McLaughlin (Garden City, N.Y.: Doubleday, Image Books, 1957), 121–22, 123–24, 126–27, 135–39, 142–43, 149–50 (footnotes deleted).

Christian marriage, the holy Doctor himself expressly declares when he said: "By conjugal faith it is provided that there should be no carnal intercourse outside the marriage bond with another man or woman; with regard to offspring, that children should be begotten of love, tenderly cared for and educated in a religious atmosphere; finally, in its sacramental aspect that the marriage bond should not be broken and that a husband or wife, if separated, should not be joined to another even for the sake of offspring. This we regard as the law of marriage by which the fruitfulness of nature is adorned and the evil of incontinence is restrained."

(11) Thus amongst the blessings of marriage, the child holds the first place. And indeed the Creator of the human race Himself, Who in His goodness wished to use men as His helpers in the propagation of life, taught this when, instituting marriage in Paradise, He said to our first parents, and through them to all future spouses: "Increase and multiply, and fill the earth" (Gen. 1:28). As St. Augustine admirably deduces from the words of the holy Apostle St. Paul to Timothy when he says: "The Apostle himself is therefore a witness that marriage is for the sake of generation: 'I wish,' he says, 'young girls to marry' (1 Tim. 5:14). And, as if someone said to him, 'Why?' he immediately adds: 'To bear children, to be mothers of families.'". . .

(13) But Christian parents must also understand that they are destined not only to propagate and preserve the human race on earth, indeed not only to educate any kind of worshipers of the true God, but children who are to become members of the Church of Christ, to raise up fellow citizens of the saints, and members of God's household, that the worshipers of God and Our Saviour may daily increase. . . .

(17) Since, however, we have spoken fully elsewhere on the Christian education of youth, let Us sum it all up by quoting once more the words of St. Augustine: "As regards the offspring, it is provided that they should be begotten

lovingly and educated religiously,"—and this is also expressed succinctly in the Code of Canon Law—"The primary end of marriage is the procreation and the education of children.". . .

(26) Domestic society being confirmed, therefore, by this bond of love, there should flourish in it that "order of love," as St. Augustine calls it. This order includes both the primacy of the husband with regard to the wife and children, the ready subjection of the wife and her willing obedience, which the Apostle commends in these words: "Let women be subject to their husbands as to the Lord, because the husband is the head of the wife, as Christ is the head of the church" (Eph. 5: 22, 23).

(27) This subjection, however, does not deny or take away the liberty which fully belongs to the woman both in view of her dignity as a human person, and in view of her most noble office as wife and mother and companion; nor does it bid her obey her husband's every request if not in harmony with right reason or with the dignity due to a wife; nor, in fine, does it imply that the wife should be put on a level with those persons who in law are called minors, to whom it is not customary to allow free exercise of their rights on account of their lack of mature judgment, or of their ignorance of human affairs. But it forbids that exaggerated liberty which cares not for the good of the family; it forbids that in this body which is the family, the heart be separated from the head to the great detriment of the whole body and the proximate danger of ruin. For if the man is the head, the woman is the heart, and as he occupies the chief place in ruling, so she may and ought to claim herself the chief place in love.

(28) Again, this subjection of wife to husband in its degree and manner may vary according to the different conditions of persons, place and time. In fact, if the husband neglect his duty, it falls to the wife to take his place in directing the family. But the structure of the family and its fundamental law,

established and confirmed by God, must always and everywhere be maintained intact. . . .

(53) And now, Venerable Brethren, We shall explain in detail the evils opposed to each of the benefits of matrimony. First consideration is due to the offspring, which many have the boldness to call the disagreeable burden of matrimony and which they say is to be carefully avoided by married people, not through virtuous continence (which Christian law permits in matrimony when both parties consent), but by frustrating the marriage act. Some justify this criminal abuse on the ground that they are weary of children and wish to gratify their desires without their consequent burden. Others say that they cannot on the one hand remain continent nor on the other can they have children because of the difficulties, whether on the part of the mother or on the part of family circumstances.

(54) But no reason, however grave, may be put forward by which anything intrinsically against nature may become conformable to nature and morally good. Since, therefore, the conjugal act is destined primarily by nature for the begetting of children, those who in exercising it deliberately frustrate its natural power and purpose sin against nature and commit a deed which is shameful and intrinsically vicious.

(55) Small wonder, therefore, if Holy Writ bears witness that the Divine Majesty regards with greatest detestation this horrible crime and at times has punished it with death. As St. Augustine notes: "Intercourse even with one's legitimate wife is unlawful and wicked where the conception of the offspring is prevented. Onan, the son of Juda, did this and the Lord killed him for it."

(56) Since, therefore, openly departing from the uninterrupted Christian tradition, some recently have judged it possible solemnly to declare another doctrine regarding this question, the Catholic Church, to whom God has entrusted the teaching and defense of the integrity and purity of

morals, standing erect in the midst of the moral ruin which surrounds her, in order that she may preserve the chastity of the nuptial union from being defiled by this foul stain, raises her voice in token of her divine ambassadorship and through Our mouth proclaims anew: any use whatsoever of matrimony exercised in such a way that the act is deliberately frustrated in its natural power to generate life is an offense against the law of God and of nature, and those who indulge in such are branded with the guilt of a grave sin. . . .

(58) As regards the evil use of matrimony, to pass over the arguments which are shameful, not infrequently others that are false and exaggerated are put forward. Holy Mother Church very well understands and clearly appreciates all that is said regarding the health of the mother and the danger to her life. And who would not grieve to think of these things? Who is not filled with the greatest admiration when he sees a mother risking her life with heroic fortitude, that she may preserve the life of the offspring which she has conceived? God alone, all bountiful and all merciful as He is, can reward her for the fulfillment of the office allotted to her by nature, and will assuredly repay her in a measure full to overflowing.

(59) Holy Church knows well that not infrequently one of the parties is sinned against rather than sinning, when for a grave cause he or she reluctantly allows the perversion of the right order. In such a case there is no sin, provided that, mindful of the law of charity, he or she does not neglect to seek to dissuade and to deter the partner from sin. Nor are those considered as acting against nature who in the married state use their right in the proper manner, although on account of natural reasons either of time or of certain defects, new life cannot be brought forth. For in matrimony as well as in the use of the matrimonial rights there are also secondary ends, such as mutual aid, the cultivating of mutual love, and the quieting of concupiscence which husband and

wife are not forbidden to consider so long as they are subordinated to the primary end and so long as the intrinsic nature of the act is preserved.

(60) We are deeply moved by the sufferings of those parents who, in extreme want, experience great difficulty in rearing their children.

(61) However, they should take care lest the calamitous state of their external affairs should be the occasion for a much more calamitous error. No difficulty can arise that justifies the putting aside of the law of God which forbids all acts intrinsically evil. There are no possible circumstances in which husband and wife cannot, strengthened by the grace of God, fulfill faithfully their duties and preserve in wedlock their chastity unspotted. . . .

(63) But another very grave crime is to be noted, Venerable Brethren, which regards the taking of the life of the offspring hidden in the mother's womb. Some wish it to be allowed and left to the will of the father or the mother; others say it is unlawful unless there are weighty reasons which they call by the name of medical, social, or eugenic "indication." Because this matter falls under the penal laws of the State by which the destruction of the offspring begotten but unborn is forbidden, these people demand that the "indication," which in one form or another they defend, be recognized as such by the public law and in no way penalized. There are those, moreover, who ask that the public authorities provide aid for these death-dealing operations, a thing which, sad to say, everyone knows is of very frequent occurrence in some places.

(64) As to the medical and therapeutic "indication" to which, using their own words, We have made reference, Venerable Brethren, however much We may pity the mother whose health and even life is gravely imperiled in the performance of the duty allotted to her by nature, nevertheless what could ever be a sufficient reason for excusing in any

way the direct murder of the innocent? This is precisely what we are dealing with here. Whether inflicted upon the mother or upon the child, it is against the precept of God and the law of nature: "Thou shalt not kill" (Ex. 20:13). The life of each is equally sacred, and no one has the power, not even the public authority, to destroy it. It is of no use to appeal to the right of taking away life, for here it is a question of the innocent, whereas that right has regard only to the guilty; nor is there here question of defense by bloodshed against an unjust aggressor (for who would call an innocent child an unjust aggressor?); again there is no question here of what is called the "law of extreme necessity" which could never extend to the direct killing of the innocent. . . .

(65) All of which agrees with the stern words of the Bishop of Hippo in denouncing those wicked parents who seek to remain childless, and, failing in this, are not ashamed to put their offspring to death: "Sometimes this lustful cruelty or cruel lust goes so far as to seek to procure sterilizing poisons, and if this fails, the foetus conceived in the womb is in one way or another smothered or evacuated, in the desire to destroy the offspring before it has life, or if it already lives in the womb, to kill it before it is born. If both man and woman are party to such practices they are not spouses at all; and if from the first they have carried on thus they have come together not for honest wedlock, but for impure gratification; if both are not party to these deeds, I make bold to say that either the one makes herself a mistress of the husband, or the other simply the paramour of his wife.". . .

(74) The same false teachers who try to dim the luster of conjugal faith and purity do not scruple to do away with the honorable and trusting obedience which the woman owes to the man. Many of them even go further and assert that such a subjection of one party to the other is unworthy of human dignity, that the rights of husband and wife are equal; wherefore, they boldly proclaim, the emancipation of women has

been or ought to be effected. This emancipation, in their opinion, must be threefold, in the ruling of the domestic society, in the administration of family affairs and in the rearing of the children. It must be social, economic, physiological:—physiological, that is to say, the woman is to be freed at her own good pleasure from the burdensome duties properly belonging to a wife as companion and mother (We have already said that this is not an emancipation but a crime); social, inasmuch as the wife being freed from the care of children and family, should, to the neglect of these, be able to follow her own bent and devote herself to business and even public affairs; finally economic, whereby the woman even without the knowledge and against the will of her husband may be at liberty to conduct and administer her own affairs, giving her attention chiefly to these rather than to children, husband and family.

(75) This, however, is not the true emancipation of woman, nor that rational and exalted liberty which belongs to the noble office of a Christian woman and wife; it is rather the debasing of the womanly character and the dignity of motherhood, and indeed of the whole family, as a result of which the husband suffers the loss of his wife, the children of their mother, and the home and the whole family of an ever watchful guardian. More than this, this false liberty and unnatural equality with the husband is to the detriment of the woman herself, for if the woman descends from her truly regal throne to which she has been raised within the walls of the home by means of the Gospel, she will soon be reduced to the old state of slavery (if not in appearance, certainly in reality) and become as amongst the pagans the mere instrument of man.

(76) This equality of rights, which is so much exaggerated and distorted, must indeed be recognized in those rights which belong to the dignity of the human soul and which are proper to the marriage contract and inseparably bound up with wedlock. In such things undoubtedly both parties enjoy

the same rights and are bound by the same obligations; in other things there must be a certain inequality and due accommodation, which is demanded by the good of the family and the right ordering and unity and stability of home life.

(77) As, however, the social and economic conditions of the married woman must in some way be altered on account of the changes in social intercourse, it is part of the office of the public authority to adapt the civil rights of the wife to modern needs and requirements, keeping in view what the natural disposition and temperament of the female sex, good morality, and the welfare of the family demand, and provided always that the essential order of the domestic society remain intact, founded as it is on something higher than human authority and wisdom, namely on the authority and wisdom of God, and so not changeable by laws or at the pleasure of private individuals. . . .

(89) If, therefore, the Church has not erred and does not err in teaching this, and consequently it is certain that the bond of marriage cannot be loosed even on account of the sin of adultery, it is evident that all the other weaker excuses that can be and are usually brought forward are of no value whatsoever. . . .

(90) To revert again to the expressions of Our predecessor, it is hardly necessary to point out what an amount of good is involved in the absolute indissolubility of wedlock and what a train of evils follows upon divorce. Whenever the marriage bond remains intact, then we find marriage contracted with a sense of safety and security, while, when separations are considered and the dangers of divorce are present, the marriage contract itself becomes insecure, or at least gives ground for anxiety and surprises. On the one hand we see a wonderful strengthening of good will and cooperation in the daily life of husband and wife, while, on the other, both of these are miserably weakened by the presence of a facility for divorce. Here we have at a very opportune moment a source of help by which both parties are enabled to preserve their

purity and loyalty; there we find harmful inducements to un-faithfulness. On this side we find the birth of children and their tuition and upbringing effectively promoted, many av-enues of discord closed amongst families and relations, and the beginnings of rivalry and jealousy easily suppressed; on that, very great obstacles to the birth and rearing of children and their education, and many occasions of quarrels, and seeds of jealousy sown everywhere. Finally, but especially, the dignity and position of women in civil and domestic soci-ety are integrally restored by the former; while by the latter they are shamefully lowered and the danger is incurred "of their being considered outcasts, slaves of the lust of men."

ABORTION

While abortion is only a secondary concern in *Casti Connubii*, Pius XI there categorically rejects abortion despite whatever medical, social, or eugenic arguments might be posed. Even in the case of a pregnant woman whose life is threatened by carry-ing the fetus to term, abortion is not to be permitted; she is to be reminded of "the duty allotted to her by nature," which could never sanction "the direct murder of the innocent." At-tempts by progressives to justify abortion by analogizing it to capital punishment or "just war"—practices of which the church has approved—are rebuffed in *Casti Connubii*, for, ac-cording to Pius XI, the fetus can never be compared to a guilty criminal or to an "unjust aggressor" whose attack might permit "retaliation."[14] Likewise, in *Humanae Vitae*, Paul VI declares abortion to be "absolutely excluded as a licit means of regulat-ing birth," even for "therapeutic reasons."[15]

In *Evangelium Vitae*, John Paul II emphatically affirms the Vatican's position on abortion.[16] Invoking his full papal authority (though not infallibility), the Pope declares that direct abortion "willed as an end or as a means, always constitutes a grave moral disorder, since it is the deliberate killing of an innocent human being." Thus, even abortion undertaken to protect the health of the mother is still a "deliberate and direct killing." John Paul II states that blame for abortion must be shared by legislators who approve permissive abortion laws and even international institutions that promote abortion. Arguing that the natural law is itself "the obligatory point of reference for civil law," the Pope asserts that civil laws authorizing abortion are "completely lacking in authentic juridical validity" and fail to constitute "true, morally binding civil law." Thus, there is "a grave and clear obligation to oppose them by conscientious objection."

One particularly interesting aspect of *Evangelium Vitae*'s pronouncements on abortion is the Pope's acknowledgment that the Bible never speaks directly about abortion. The reason for this omission, he states, is that "the mere possibility of harming, attacking or actually denying life in these circumstances is completely foreign to the religious and cultural way of thinking of the people of God."[17] Thus, the biblical silence itself is made to speak in support of the Vatican's position.

Such antiabortion sentiments remain common to partisans of the "pro-life" movement, both Catholic and Protestant. Juxtaposed to such arguments, we here excerpt a statement by the Protestant feminist Beverly Wildung Harrison, professor of Christian ethics at Union Theological Seminary in New York. Against the ecclesiastical prohibition of abortion, Harrison argues that there is a need for a theology of "pro-choice," a theology that points up the misogynistic substructure of earlier church teaching. Such a theology of pro-choice, she ventures, would emphasize the health and welfare of females *already* born and would reject the claim that procreative superabundance is a sign of God's blessing. She calls on pro-choice Christians not to let their opponents claim a monopoly on religious and moral language about abortion. For Harrison, "moral" should be defined as "that which makes for the self-respect and well-being of human persons and their environment." She also instructs her readers that abortion has not been a topic of vast concern throughout the long history of Christian ethics; indeed, the debate has escalated significantly since 1973, when the Supreme Court issued its decision in *Roe v. Wade* legalizing abortion (with important restrictions) throughout the United States. Harrison's feminist approach to Christian morality stands in marked contrast to those of earlier male theologians we have considered. As she asserts, "enforced pregnancy would be viewed as a morally reprehensible violation of bodily integrity if women were recognized as fully human moral agents."[18]

THEOLOGY OF PRO-CHOICE: A FEMINIST PERSPECTIVE*

Much discussion of abortion betrays the heavy hand of misogyny or the hatred of women. We all have a responsibility to recognize this bias—sometimes subtle—when ancient negative attitudes toward women intrude into the abortion debate. It is morally incumbent on us to convert the Christian position to a teaching more respectful of women's concrete history and experience.

My professional peers who are my opponents on this question feel they own the Christian tradition in this matter and recognize no need to rethink their positions in the light of this claim. As a feminist, I cannot sit in silence when women's right to shape the use of our own procreative power is denied. Women's competence as moral decision-makers is once again challenged by the State, even before the moral basis of women's right to procreative choice has been fully elaborated and recognized. Those who deny women control of procreative power claim that they do so in defense of moral sensibility, in the name of the sanctity of human

---

* From Beverly Wildung Harrison, "Theology of Pro-choice: A Feminist Perspective," in *Abortion: The Moral Issues,* ed. Edward Batchelor Jr. (New York: Pilgrim Press, 1982), 210–15, 219–20, 222–23.

life. We have a long way to go before the sanctity of human life will include genuine regard and concern for every female already born, and no social policy discussion that obscures this fact deserves to be called moral.

Although some Protestants wrongly claim scriptural warrant for antiabortion teaching, it is, in fact, the assumptions about women and sexuality imbedded in ancient natural-law reasoning that have shaped abortion teaching in Christianity.[19] Unfortunately, all major strands of natural-law reflection have been every bit as awful as Protestant Biblicism on any matter involving human sexuality, including discussion of women's nature and women's divine vocation in relation to procreative power.

As a result, Protestants who oppose procreative choice[20] either tend to follow official Catholic moral theology on these matters or ground their positions in Biblicist anti-intellectualism, claiming that God's word requires no justification other than their claim that it (God's word) says what it says. Against such irrationalism, no rational objections have a chance. But when Protestant fundamentalists give clear reasons why they believe abortion is evil, they, too, invariably revert to traditional natural-law assumptions about women, sex, and procreation. Therefore, it is from the claims of traditional Catholic natural-law thinking on the subject of sexuality, procreation, and women's power of rational choice that misogyny stems and to which direct objection must be registered.

A treatment of any moral problem is inadequate if it fails to analyze the morality of a given act in a way that represents the concrete experience of the agent who faces a decision with respect to this act. Misogyny in Christian discussions of abortion is evidenced clearly in that the abortion decision is never treated in the way it arises as part of the female agent's life process. The decision at issue when the dilemma of choice arises for women is whether or not to be pregnant. In most discussions of the morality of abortion it is treated as an abstract act,[21] rather than as a possible way we deal with a pregnancy, which, frequently, is the result of circumstances beyond the woman's control. In any pregnancy a woman's life is deeply, irrevocably affected. Those who uphold the unexceptional immorality of abortion are probably wise to obscure the fact that an unwanted pregnancy always involves a life-shaping consequence for a woman, because suppressing the identity of the moral agent and the reality of her dilemma greatly reduces the ability to recognize the moral complexity of abortion. When the question of abortion arises it is usually because a woman finds herself facing an *unwanted* pregnancy. Consider the actual circumstances that may precipitate this. One is the situation in which a woman did not intend to be sexually active or did not enter into a sexual act voluntarily. Since women are frequently victims of sexual violence, numerous cases of this type arise because of rape, incest, or forced marital coitus. Many morally sensitive opponents of abortion concede that in such cases abortion *may* be morally justifiable. I insist that in such cases it is a moral *good,* because it is not rational to treat a newly fertilized ovum as though it had the same value as the existent, pregnant, female person, and because it is morally wrong to make the victim of sexual violence suffer the further agonies of unwanted pregnancy and childbearing against her will. Enforced pregnancy would be viewed as a morally reprehensible violation of bodily integrity if women were recognized as fully human moral agents.

Another more frequent case results when a woman— or usually a young girl—participates in heterosexual activity without clear knowledge of how pregnancy occurs and without intention to conceive a child. A girl who became pregnant in this manner would, by traditional natural-law morality, be held to be in a state of invincible ignorance and therefore not morally culpable. One scholarly Roman

Catholic nun I met argued—quite appropriately, I believe—that her Church should not consider the abortions of young Catholic girls as morally culpable because the Church overly protected them, which contributed to their lack of understanding procreation or to their inability to cope with the sexual pressures girls experience in contemporary society.

A related type of pregnancy happens when a woman runs risks by not using contraceptives, perhaps because taking precaution in romantic affairs is not perceived as ladylike or requires her to be too unspontaneous about sex. However, when pregnancies occur because women are skirting the edges of responsibility and running risks out of immaturity, is enforced motherhood a desirable solution? Such pregnancies could be minimized only by challenging precisely those childish myths of female socialization embedded in natural-law teaching about female sexuality.

In likelihood, most decisions about abortion arise because mature women who are sexually active with men and who understand the risk of pregnancy nevertheless experience contraceptive failure. Misogynist schizophrenia in this matter is exhibited in that many believe women have more responsibility than men to practice contraception, and that family planning is always a moral good, but even so rule out abortion altogether. Such a split consciousness ignores the fact no inexorable biological line exists between prevention of conception and abortion.[22] More important, such reasoning ignores the genuine risks involved in female contraceptive methods. Some women are at higher risk than others in terms of using the most reliable means of birth control. Furthermore, the reason we do not have more concern for safer contraceptive methods for men and women is that matters relating to women's health and well-being are never urgent in this society. Moreover, many contraceptive failures are due to the irresponsibility of the producers of contraceptives rather than to bad luck.[23] Given these facts, should a woman who actively attempts to avoid pregnancy be punished for contraceptive failure when it occurs?

Misogyny in Theological Argument

In the history of Christian theology, a central metaphor for understanding life, including human life, is as a gift of God. Creation itself has always been seen primarily under this metaphor. It follows that in this creational cojntext procreation itself took on special significance as the central image for divine blessing, the more so within patriarchal societies where it is the male's power that is enhanced by this divine gift. To this day males tend to romanticize procreation as *the* central metaphor for divine blessing.

Throughout history, however, women's power of procreation stands in definite tension with male social control. In fact, what we feminists call patriarchy, i.e., patterned or institutionalized legitimations of male superiority, derives from the need of men, through male-dominated political institutions, such as tribes, states, and religious systems, to control women's power to procreate the species. One with critical consciousness should begin by assuming, then, that many of these efforts at social control of procreation—including some church teaching on contraception and abortion—were part of this institutional system. The perpetuation of patriarchal control itself depended on wresting the power of procreation from women and shaping women's lives accordingly. Natural-law teaching about women's nature is itself part of this system of control.

In the past four centuries the entire Christian story has had to undergo dramatic accommodation to new and emergent world conditions and to the scientific revolution. As the older theological metaphors for creation encountered the rising power of science, a new self-understanding including our human capacity to affect nature had to be incorporated into Christian theology or its central theological story would have become obscurantist. Human agency had to be introjected into a dialectical understanding of creation.

The range of human freedom to shape and enhance creation is now celebrated theologically, but only up to the point of changes in our understanding of what is natural for women. Here a barrier has been drawn that declares, No Radical Freedom! The only difference between mainline Protestant and Roman Catholic theologians on these matters is on the point of contraception, which Protestants more readily accept. However, Protestants like Karl Barth and Helmut Thielicke exhibit a subtle shift of mood when they turn to discussing issues regarding women. They exhibit the typical Protestant pattern; they have accepted contraception or family planning as part of the new freedom, granted by God, but both draw back from the idea that abortion could be morally acceptable. In the *Ethics of Sex*, Thielicke offers a romantic, ecstatic celebration of family planning on one page and a total denunciation of abortion as unthinkable on the next.[24] Most Christian *theological* opinion draws the line between contraception and abortion, whereas the *official* Catholic teaching still anathematizes contraception.

The problem, then, is that Christian theology celebrates the power of human freedom to shape and determine the quality of human life except when the issue of procreative choice arises. Abortion is anathema, and widespread sterilization abuse is hardly mentioned! The power of *man* to shape creation radically is never rejected. When one stops to consider the awesome power over nature that males take for granted and celebrate, including the power to alter the conditions of human life in myriad ways, the suspicion dawns that the near hysteria that prevails about the immorality of women's right to choose abortion derives its forces from misogyny rather than from any passion for the sacredness of human life. The refusal of male theologians to incorporate the full range of human power to shape creation into their theological world view when this power relates to the quality of women's lives and women's freedom and women's role as full moral agents, is an index of the continuing misogyny in Christian tradition.

By contrast, a feminist theological approach recognizes that *nothing* is more urgent, in light of the changing circumstances of human beings on planet Earth, than to recognize that the entire natural-historical context of human procreative power has shifted.[25] We desperately need a desacralization of our *biological* power to reproduce,[26] and at the same time a real concern for human dignity and the social conditions for personhood and the values of human relationship.[27] And note that desacralization does not mean complete devaluation of the worth of procreation. It means we must shift away from the notion that the central metaphors for divine blessing are expressed at the biological level to the recognition that our social relations bear the image of what is most holy. The best statement I know on this point comes from Marie Augusta Neal, a Roman Catholic feminist who is also a distinguished sociologist of religion:

As long as the central human need called for was continued motivation to propagate the race, it was essential that religious symbols idealize that process above all others. Given the vicissitudes of life in a hostile environment, women had to be encouraged to bear children and men to support them; childbearing was central to the struggle for existence. Today, however, the size of the base population, together with knowledge already accumulated about artificial insemination, sperm banking, cloning, make more certain a peopled world.

The more serious human problems now are who will live, who will die and who will decide.[28]

Misogynist Moral Factors in the Debate

The greatest *strategic* problem of pro-choice advocates is the wide-spread assumption that pro-lifers have a monopoly on the moral factors that ought to enter into decisions about abortion. Moral legitimacy seems to adhere to *their* position in part because traditionalists have an array of religiomoral terminology at their command that the sometimes more secular proponents of choice lack. But those who would displace women's power of choice by the power of the State and/or the medical profession do not deserve the aura of moral sanctity. We must do our homework if we are to dispel this myth of moral superiority. A major way in which Christian moral theologians and moral philosophers contribute to this monopoly of moral sanctity is by equating fetal or prenatal life with human personhood in a simplistic way, and by failing to acknowledge changes regarding this issue in the history of Christianity.

We need to remember that even in Roman Catholic teaching the definition of the status of fetal life has shifted over time and that the status of prenatal life involves a moral judgment, not a scientific one. The question is properly posed this way: What status are we morally wise to predicate to prenatal human life, given that the fetus is not yet a fully existent human being? Those constrained under Catholic teaching have been required for the past ninety years to believe a human being exists from conception, when the ovum and sperm merge.[29] This answer from *one* tradition has had far wider impact on our culture than most people recognize. Other Christians come from traditions that do not offer (and could not offer, given their conception of the structure of the church as moral community) a definitive answer to this question.

∽

Even so, some contemporary Protestant medical ethicists, fascinated by the recent discoveries in genetics—deoxyribonucleic acid (DNA), for example—have all but sacralized the moment in which the genetic code is implanted as the moment of humanization, which leaves them close to the traditional

Roman position. Protestant male theologians have long let their enthrallment with science lead to a sacralization of specific exciting scientific discoveries, usually to the detriment of theological and moral clarity. (*Moral* here is defined as that which makes for the self-respect and well-being of human persons and their environment.)

∾

Two other concerns related to our efforts to make a strong moral case for women's right to procreative choice need to be touched on.

The first has to do with the problems our Christian tradition creates for any attempt to make clear why women's right to control our bodies is an urgent and substantive moral claim. One of Christianity's greatest weaknesses is its spiritualizing neglect of respect for the physical body and physical well-being. Tragically, women, more than men, are expected in Christian teaching never to take their own well-being as a moral consideration. I want to stress, then, that we have no moral tradition in Christianity which starts with body-space, or body-right, as a basic condition of moral relations. Hence, many Christian ethicists simply do not get the point when we speak of women's right to bodily integrity. They seem to think such talk is a disguise for women to plead self-indulgence.

We must articulate our view that body-right is a basic moral claim and also remind our hearers that there is no analogy among other human activities to women's procreative power. Pregnancy is a unique human experience. In any social relation, body-space must be respected or nothing deeply human or moral can be created. The social institutions most similar to compulsory pregnancy in their moral violations of body-space are chattel slavery or peonage. These institutions distort the moral relations of the community and deform this community over time. (Witness racism in the United States.) Coercion of women, through enforced sterilization or enforced pregnancy legitimates unjust power in the intimate human relationships, and cuts to the heart of our capacity for moral social relations. As we should recognize, given our violence-prone society, people learn violence at home and at an early age when women's lives are violated!

∾

A final point that needs to be mentioned is the need, as we work politically for a pro-choice social policy, to avoid the use of morally objectionable arguments to mobilize support for our side of the issue. One can get a lot of political mileage in U.S. society by using covert racist and classist appeals ("abortion lowers the cost of welfare roles or reduces illegitimacy," or "paying for abortions saves the taxpayers money in the long run"). Sometimes it is argued that good politics is more important than good morality and that one should use whatever arguments work to gain political support. I do not believe these crassly utilitarian[30] arguments turn out, in the long run, to be good politics—for they are costly to our sense of polis and of community. But even if they were effective in the short run, I am doubly sure that on the issue of the right to choose abortion, good morality doth a good political struggle make. I believe, deeply, that moral right is on the side of the struggle for the freedom and self-respect of women, especially poor and nonwhite women, and on the side of developing social policy which assures that every child born can be certain to be a wanted child. Issues of justice are those that deserve the deepest moral caretaking as we develop a political strategy.

HOMOSEXUALITY

On the issue of same-sex sexual relations, official Christian teachings have tended, until quite recently, to be uniformly negative. Patristic theologians alluded darkly to "acts against nature" that could not result in conception (homosexual practice here shares the same faults as masturbation, contraception, and abortion) and railed against pederasty, a common form of same-sex relation in ancient Greece.[31] In the Middle Ages, Thomas Aquinas adopted the earlier definition of "unnatural" sexual acts as those from which human generation cannot follow. In an interesting (but unsettling) discussion of various kinds of "unnatural" sexual practices, Thomas concludes that same-sex sexual relations are worse than heterosexual rape and incest, which, in his view, are more closely aligned with the "natural."[32]

Within official Catholic teaching, homosexual acts continue to be sharply condemned. Thus the 1975 *Declaration on Certain Questions Concerning Sexual Ethics,* issued by the Sacred Congregation for the Doctrine of the Faith and approved by Paul VI, proclaims that such acts "lack an essential and indispensable finality" (that is, they cannot result in conception) and hence are "intrinsically disordered."[33] The 1986 Vatican declaration on *The Pastoral Care of Homosexual Persons,* although it has been hailed as an advance over the 1975 declaration in its concern for the spiritual and emotional well-being of those whose acts it nonetheless condemns,[34] continues to argue that since it "is only in the marital relationship that the use of the sexual faculty can be morally good," anyone "engaging in homosexual behavior therefore acts immorally" and in opposition to "the Creator's sexual design." As a form of "moral disorder," homosexual activity hinders a person from finding "fulfillment and humanness." Rejecting political and cultural pressures—called "the trend of the moment"—to modify its stance, the Vatican here pronounces that all support, including the use of church property, is to be denied to those who oppose the church's position, a move designed to disallow Catholic gay and lesbian groups, such as Dignity, from access to meeting places in church buildings. Although *The Pastoral Care of Homosexual Persons* finds it "deplorable that homosexual persons have been and are the object of violent malice in speech or in action," it rejects any claim that homosexuals are "compelled" to their activities; the only appropriate path for those who feel that they are "innately" homosexual is chastity, sacrificial self-dedication to God's will.[35]

To be sure, many conservative Protestant groups in the United States, such as the Southern Baptists, currently echo the Vatican's stand against homosexual activity. The arguments of Protestant conservatives tend to differ from those of their Catholic counterparts, however, in appealing less to natural law and more to specific texts of the Bible, such as the condemnations of male same-sex activity in Leviticus 18:22 and 20:13. Likewise, Protestant conservatives construe such New Testament passages as Romans 1:26–27 to mean that Christian commitment and homosexual activity are mutually incompatible. Karl Barth, hailed by some as the most significant Protestant theologian of the twentieth century, appealed to Romans 1:26–27 to justify his overwhelmingly negative assessment of homosexuality. Describing homosexuality as "the physical, psychological and social sickness, the phenomenon of perversion, decadence and decay," Barth argued that homosexuality showed "man's" refusal "to admit the validity of the divine command" that males and females were meant to be in sexual relation with each other. It is God's command, Barth asserts, "that as a man he can only be genuinely human with woman, or as woman with man."[36]

Other Protestant denominations, church leaders, and theologians have taken quite a different stand on the issue of homosexuality. Particularly since the 1950s, a growing number of Christian theologians and ethicists, both Catholic and Protestant, have come to reexamine traditional theological attitudes toward same-sex relationships and behavior.[37] As early as 1969, the United Church of Christ published *The Same Sex,* which has been called "the first church-related collection of essays on homosexuality that allowed gay and lesbian Christians to speak for themselves."[38] Beginning in the 1970s, a variety of Protestant denominations, from the United Presbyterians U.S.A. to the Lutheran Church in America, from the Episcopalians to the United Methodists, have examined the issue, particularly with respect to the standards for the ordination of ministers.[39]

Notable as an example of progressive arguments on this issue is a report issued by a study committee of the Episcopal Diocese of Michigan in 1973. This statement called on Episcopalians to reflect on their church's mission "to bear witness to the all embracing love of God," wryly noting that "we have no evidence that this love does not include homosexuals." This document's authors asked their denomination to open all ministries to homosexuals and to speak out against civil discrimination against them. In a sharp rebuke to Episcopalians who chose to overlook the sexual misbehavior of heterosexual candidates for priesthood, the authors of the Michigan statement affirm that an "oppressive or destructive use of sexuality within personal relationships, whatever the sexual preference or orientation, should give reason to doubt the candidate's fitness for office."[40] Yet despite such sentiments, by 1991 the furthest that the General Convention of the Episcopal Church had proceeded with such an agenda was to continue to study the issue, meanwhile reaffirming that "physical sexual experience is appropriate only within the lifelong monogamous" marital union prescribed in the *Book of Common Prayer.*[41]

Similarly, the General Assembly Committee on Human Sexuality of the Presbyterian Church U.S.A. in 1991 called on its denomination to ordain without regard to sexual orientation (with a special provision that celibacy not be made a condition for homosexual ministers) and to work actively for the repeal of all laws discriminating against homosexuals (including laws criminalizing "private acts between consenting adults").[42] The Presbyterian Church U.S.A. as a whole, however, rejected this resolution.

Still another document, prepared by the Division for Church and Society of the Evangelical Lutheran Church in America and published in October 1993, entitled "The Church and Human Sexuality: A Lutheran Perspective," takes the issue of gay and lesbian Lutherans as an occasion to reflect on the biblical command to "love our neighbor." One acceptable interpretation of this command's application, according to the document's authors, is for Lutherans to show compassion toward and understanding of homosexuals, even for those who will not keep to "lifelong abstinence." But the interpretation preferred by the study authors is actively to affirm openly gay and lesbian persons "and their mutually loving, just, committed relationships of fidelity." Prohibiting relationships of homosexual love is declared to be incompatible "with the love of God we know through Jesus Christ, who challenged religious rules that hindered love for the neighbor."[43] Yet despite progressive reports proposed by various denominational study committees, it is notable that no mainstream Protestant denomination as a whole has yet implemented such progressive recommendations.

The views in these recent study documents reflect changing attitudes toward homosexuality among many Christians. As lesbians and gays have become more socially visible in recent decades, new analyses have emerged in the social sciences and in medicine, cultural theory, and theology to challenge traditional opposition to homosexual behavior. In conjunction with the advent of modern feminism, with recent lesbian, gay, and AIDS activism, and with the proliferation of various forms of liberation theology, a number of contemporary lesbian and gay theologians challenge the exclusion of homosexual believers from equal status within Christian communities.[44] As reflected in the denominational study documents just discussed, many of these theologians seek to reinterpret or recontextualize the scriptural texts traditionally invoked to condemn same-sex behavior,[45] while others challenge traditional notions of normative theological anthropology to argue that lesbian and gay sexuality is morally good.[46] Lesbian liberationist theologies often stress the systemic links between heterosexism and the more general cultural oppression of women and their bodies. These lesbian theologies commonly invoke the theological value of human embodiment, touch and pleasure, the spiritual power of friendship and erotic love, and the recovered histories of intimate relations among Christian women.[47]

We include here two selections from Carter Heyward. One of the most prominent contemporary lesbian theologians, Heyward was ordained as an Episcopal priest in 1974 and is currently professor of theology at the Episcopal Divinity School in Cambridge, Massachusetts. In the first excerpt, Heyward offers a radical broadside against the misuse of natural law and individualistic psychological theory in heterosexist Christian theology.[48] She argues that the demands of feminists and homosexuals for affirmation threaten the essence of liberal Christianity by exposing its hollow individualism and fundamental inability to address systemically unequal power relations. Liberal Christian theology has been shaped, she asserts, by a sexist and heterosexist "normative dualism" in which human bodies and sexuality (and, in particular, the female) have been devalued as "material" and thus subsidiary to the spiritualized, disembodied, and archetypically male mind. In the second excerpt, Heyward continues her attack on heterosexist, patriarchal religion by valorizing the erotic power of openly lesbian women as creative, liberating, mutually empowering, and sacred.

Even progressive statements such as Heyward's, however, are critiqued by a new wave of theological theorists who believe that the church (along with the broader society) has unthinkingly accepted the notion of a "sexual identity" that stands as a "given" and is taken as "an absolutely fundamental status-determinative reality about subjects."[49] Thus, for example, Mary McClintock Fulkerson has argued that poststructuralist critiques of "identity" may give us new ways to understand the principle of Galatians 3:28 that in Christ there is "no male and female." Since Christianity, McClintock Fulkerson argues, does not ask us to accept a notion of "sexed identity" as an essential "fact," and since strong evidence presented by historians and theoreticians of sexuality suggests that identity and desire are historically constructed, Christians might rather profess that there are no restricting "conditions on access to the gospel." Christianity might refuse "to require gendered identity just as it refuses to require circumcision." In this view, moral distinctions based on a believer's gender could be seen as a form of idolatry, the imposition of a human construction in place of divine truth. Thus, although "identity politics" will continue to contribute much to progressive political action, McClintock Fulkerson worries that under its rubric "the heterosexual" will continue to be seen as "the real," with "the homosexual" remaining subordinate or secondary.[50]

As Heyward's excerpts and McClintock Fulkerson's challenge indicate, gay and lesbian liberation theology is a burgeoning and diverse field. Debates over the most effective strategies for the incorporation of homosexual believers within the Christian community will continue.

A SACRED CONTEMPT: HETEROSEXIST THEOLOGY*

Heterosexist theology is constructed on the assumption that male domination of female lives is compatible with the will of God. The rightness of compulsory heterosexuality is predicated on the belief that in a natural order, heterosexuality alone is good. Any deviation from it is sinful. Basing contemporary moral theory on medieval concepts of natural law necessitates projecting an image or fantasy of "good order" onto human social relations—thereby denying altogether the role of human agency in determining moral good.[51] We play no part in creating sexual morality.

While belief in natural law may not strike us as necessarily heterosexist, in a sexist situation like the praxis of the

---

* From Carter Heyward, "A Sacred Contempt: Heterosexist Theology," in *Touching Our Strength* (San Francisco: Harper & Row, Publishers, 1989), 61–63, 67–71.

church, the assumption of a natural order is infused with the corollary presuppositions about gender and sexuality.[52] In this social praxis, historical and contemporary, the image of heterosexual marriage emerges as the prototype for the Right—that is, the Natural and Moral—Relation not only between male and female, but also between Christ and his church. Compulsory heterosexuality safeguards this divinely willed Right Relation. To coerce heterosexual bonding is simply to affirm what is natural. And what is natural reflects the good order of the cosmos, thereby revealing the divine purpose. The Be-ing of God involves being heterosexual.

The church often draws on individualistic psychology for support in upholding the sanctity of compulsory heterosexual relations. Church bodies often commission psychiatrists to make clinical judgments of individual candidates for the ordained ministry. More often than not, the person's health is understood by the ecclesiastical authority (and often by the psychiatrist) as synonymous with being heterosexual and married (or open to marriage)—or, at least, with the candidate's willingness to abstain from sexual activity outside marriage. On this basis, church authorities frequently will deny that they are against homosexuality per se, but rather will insist that they are opposed to all sexual activity outside of marriage, heterosexual as well as homosexual. To the rejoinder that *homosexual* marriages are not permitted in church, the typical response is bewilderment, as if the very notion were unintelligible to christian sensibilities of what is both natural and moral.[53]

It should not be surprising that the church would consecrate psychology as its Great High Priest. Psychology, for the most part, remains the most highly individualistic of the modern sciences, and liberals have strong investment in the interior life and yearnings of individuals as the locus of sin and grace, problems and transformation.[54] Moreover, what is psychologically "normal" provides the content for the theologian's understanding of what is natural and moral. What specifically is lacking in most psychology, as in most theology, is a critical analysis of the ways in which unjust power relations between men and women shape the lens through which we view the natural/moral order. Liberal proponents of natural law fail to enter into serious engagement with those whose lives are marginalized by its truth-claims.

Liberal christianity is morally bankrupt in relation to women and homosexuals. The liberal church damages us because, as a theo-political ideology, liberalism not only is set against collective advocacy as a primary mode of christian witness; it is also contemptuous of the particular claims of feminists and openly gaymen and lesbians.

∾

The traditional God/Father's anthropomorphic antagonism toward women and wanton sexual behavior is well documented in christian history. Unlike this God, the liberal God of self-consciousness, human potential, therapy, and science controls women and homosexual people not because he is hostile to us (God forbid!), but rather because he is neutral in relation to us.

Liberal morality is generated in an individualistic realm, in which the subject determines right from wrong. As Friedrich Schleiermacher wrote,

> But in the sinful nature the bad exists only correlatively with the good, and no moment is occupied exclusively by sin. . . . Insofar as the consciousness of our sin is a true element of our being, *and sin therefore a reality,* it is ordained by God as that which makes redemption necessary. [My italics.][55]

Not only are good and evil, grace and sin, necessary correlates in the work of redemption in liberal protestantism, but the reality of sin is predicated upon our noticing it! We are first and finally moral monads, accountable to the pangs of our own God-*consciousness,* not to be a God whose justice may be calling us to account *regardless* of how we may feel about it or what we may think.

Among liberals, one simply holds one opinion while someone else holds another. No judgment is passed. What may be at stake morally goes unnoticed when there is no understanding of how our power relations shape our opinions. Liberal priests, therapists, and others fail to recognize fully the significance of the power they hold over others. They do not see the demonic character of unequal power relations nor do they see the sacred character of mutual power relations.

Liberals do not understand the term *power relations* as denoting the dynamic context in which our lives constantly are being shaped by, and are shaping, one another's. From a liberal perspective, *power* is either a social force or established authority that belongs to someone or it is a personal charisma anyone can receive. In a liberal worldview, power is not understood as pertaining to how we live in the ongoing tensions between creativity and destruction, life-enhancing and death-dealing dynamics, solidarity and alienation, healing and abuse, which affect us all.

To believe that we can discern our own ethics, choose from many options, and act on the basis of individual "conscience" is to admit defeat in the struggle against the structures of our alienation. It is to give *explicit* assent to the immoral proposition that whether one rapes or not, pays taxes or not, drops the bomb or not, are decisions that only the responsible individual or individuals can make. It is furthermore to give implicit assent to the dualistic assumption that such matters, in historical fact, are none of God's business. In the realm of God, the opinions of a Jesse Helms and a Jesse Jackson are of equal consequence—none at all. For the liberal deity has turned over to us the realm of human affairs. What we do, each of us, about racism, sexism, heterosexism, or any other human problem is our business.

To their peril, many women as well as homosexual christians draw upon the moral neutrality of christian liberalism in arguing for their right to live and let live.[56] This is a self-defeating argument, for the problems of injustice cannot be solved by appeals to "freedom" and "differences of opinion" as value-free "rights."[57] From a moral perspective, freedom is not value free. It is the power of personal agency in the context of *just* social relations in which the positive value of all persons has been established as a given.

Of course, it would seem logical that, pleading for neutrality and freedom in matters of morality, liberal christians should have no reason to believe that God cares whether people are feminists, lesbians, or gaymen. It would seem truer to its own ethical heritage if the liberal church were to say to its members who do not conform to traditional gender roles or sexual practices: "God doesn't care whether you are gay or straight, or whether you are a feminist or an adherent to traditional gender roles. God wants you to be true to yourself and faithful in relation to God and God's people." But this is not what most liberal churches have said.

In one sense, the implications of theological liberalism for gaymen, lesbians, and feminists are identical with those for all women, racial/ethnic minority peoples, the poor, and others whose oppression should be of more immediate moral concern to church leaders than the "spiritual" pilgrimages of individuals.

There is another sense, however, in which gender and sexual injustice occupy a special place at the hallowed table of christian fellowship. Sexism and heterosexism receive a particular "blessing" from the liberal philosophical tradition's *trivialization* of the female gender and human sexuality as embodied, material, "lower" phenomena. The "normative dualism" of christian liberalism has been shaped by sexism and sealed in heterosexism.[58]

I need not elaborate here examples from the works of christian fathers who have located creative spiritual power in the hypothetically disembodied male mind.[59] Thus today, while the material concerns of *men* of color and poor *men* can be subsumed *idealistically* into the liberal vision of a non-racist, nonclassist world, women and openly homosexual people *embody and represent* the specific material phenomena that, in christian idealism, came early to its full expression in the contributions of Augustine.

From the standpoint of christian idealism, to press seriously for women's liberation or for the affirmation of gay and lesbian sexual activity is to fly in the face of the idealistic tradition, in which femaleness and sexual activity are, *de facto*, ungodly and thus singularly undeserving of the justice that constitutes the liberal vision of the divinely ordained world.[60] Thus does liberal christianity embody its own contradiction between its ideal of one, inclusive world and its sacred contempt for femaleness and sexual passion.[61]

While many liberal churches appear to have attended to the problem of sexism, they fail utterly to take heterosexism seriously and thus actually fail to do justice to women's lives, whether lesbian, heterosexual, bisexual, genitally active, genitally inactive, or celibate.

The liberal churches have always displayed some measure of tolerance toward those women and homosexual people whose *public* presence has been strictly in conformity with patriarchal social relations.[62] Passive, self-effacing women, and men and women who have kept their homosexual activities closeted from public knowledge, have been well received, on the whole, throughout christian history. Such women and men have comprised a large part of the church. Women and homosexual people pose no practical problem to the church unless we *publicly challenge* the church's sexism and heterosexism.

This is exactly what is happening today. Many feminists, gaymen, and lesbians have begun to come out of our concealment and put ourselves visibly on the ecclesial line as representative of those women and men who, throughout christian history and the ecumenical church today, have seen that the liberal christian emperor has no clothes—no sense of the misogynist, erotophobic, and oppressive character of his realm.

Thus it is true that, from the standpoint of advanced patriarchal capitalist social relations, the liberal deity has begun to incorporate, superficially, the "rights" of women and of racial/ethnic minorities and the poor into his divine agenda as *idealistic* moral claims that need not disrupt the harmony of life as it is meant to be lived in the realm of God. However, the feminist and gay/lesbian demand (not request) that women and homosexual persons be affirmed (not tolerated) poses a challenge not only to the good ordering of liberal social relations, but also a threat to the essence of liberal religion. For the liberal deity is, above all, a noncontroversial gentleman—the antithesis of much that is embodied by feminists and by openly gaymen and lesbians who dare to challenge the moral deficit of liberal christianity. At stake, finally, from a feminist liberation perspective, are not the bodies of witches and faggots, but the nature and destiny of God.

COMING OUT AND
RELATIONAL EMPOWERMENT*

Erotic as Sacred Power

Openly lesbian women are dangerous to heterosexist patriarchy because, whether or not it is our intention, our visibility signals an erotic energy that has gotten out of control—out of men's control. Historically, we have learned that this erotic power is not good—for us, for others, for the world or

---

* From Carter Heyward, "Coming Out and Relational Empowerment," in *No Easy Peace: Liberating Anglicanism—A Collection of Essays in Memory of William John Wolf*, eds. Carter Heyward and Sue Phillips (Lanham, Md.: University Press of America, 1992), 192–94.

for God. Operating on the basis of an interpretive principle of suspicion in relation to heterosexist patriarchal religious and social teachings, feminist liberation theologians in Christianity and Judaism have begun to suspect that our erotic power—this object of such massive fear among ruling class men, from generation to generation—is, in fact, our most creative, liberating power—that is to say, our sacred power, that which many of us call our God or Goddess. And she is indeed dangerous to a culture of alienation and abuse because she signals a better way. She sparks our vision, stirs our imagination and evokes our yearning for liberation. In the image of old wise women, dark and sensual, she calls us forth and invites us to share her life, which is our own, in right, mutual relation. From a theological perspective, coming out as lesbians—icons of erotic power—is not only a significant psychological process. It is also a spiritual journey, a movement of profoundly moral meaning and value, in which we struggle, more and more publicly, to embrace our sisters, our friends and ourselves as bearers of sacred power. Let me say a bit more about eros as sacred power.

Christian theology, which has shaped the prevailing relational norms of European and American cultures, traditionally has held that eros (sexual love) and philia ("brotherly" love, or friendship), are, at best, merely derivative from agape (God's love for us, and ours for God and our neighbor— "neighbor" being interpreted usually as those who are hardest to love: humankind in general, our enemies, those who aren't like us . . .). The moral distinctions among the three forms of love has been fastened in the classical Christian dualisms between spiritual and material reality and between self and other and, moreover, in the assumption that it is more difficult— therefore, better—to express God's (spiritual) love of enemies and strangers than to love our friends and sexual partners.

These distinctions represent a radical misapprehension of love. They fail to reflect, as godly and sacred, the embodied human experience of love among friends and sexual partners because they are steeped in the assumption that erotic power—or, in patriarchal, androcentric culture, women's power—is dangerous and bad and therefore always in need of spiritual justification.

To this, feminist liberation theologians say "No." To the contrary, the erotic is our most fully embodied experience of the love of God. It is the source of our capacity for transcendence, or the "crossing over" among ourselves, making connections between and among ourselves. The erotic is the divine Spirit's yearning, through us, toward mutually empowering relation which becomes our most fully embodied experience of God as love.

And how do we know this? We know this by living life, by experiencing the power in mutuality. We know this by having learned to trust our own voices, not in isolation, but in relation to the voices of those whose lives we have learned to trust—prophets, poets, people in our past and present, known personally to us or only by reputation, those whose ways of being in the world, and in history, draw us more fully into mutual connection with one another.

Mutuality is not a matter simply of give and take. It is not, Margaret Huff notes, mere reciprocity.[63] Nor is it equality. Mutuality is not a static place to be. It is movement into a way of being in a relation in which both or all parties are empowered with one another to be more fully themselves: mutually, we come to life.

In the context of mutually empowering relationship, we come to realize that our shared experience of our power in mutual relations is sacred: that by which we are called forth more fully into becoming who we are—whole persons, whose integrity is formed in our connection with one another. And our shared power, this sacred resource of creation and liberation, is powerfully erotic.

14

∽ Feminist Liberation Theologies

The efforts by proponents of abolition and suffrage, discussed in Chapter 12, to remake American society met with limited success. Following the Civil War, the Fifteenth Amendment to the United States Constitution (ratified in 1870) extended the franchise to African-American men. It was fifty years later in 1920 when the suffrage movement finally obtained the ratification of the Nineteenth Amendment, giving women the right to vote. Yet despite these hard-won victories, the profound social changes in American life envisioned by these social reformers were thwarted by an array of factors in the late nineteenth and early twentieth centuries.[1]

Deeply embedded racism undercut the promise of the Civil War amendments and led to renewed oppression of African-Americans and other racial minorities. Many women who joined the suffrage campaign in its closing stages concentrated their efforts solely on winning the vote, to the neglect of the social, economic, and political changes that would be required before fuller social equality could be attained.[2] Although the early twentieth century saw many significant advances in the economic and political lives of American women, organized feminism faded as a significant political force during the middle decades of the century, particularly during the social retrenchment that followed World War II.

Just as the nineteenth-century feminist movement had emerged in conjunction with the abolition movement, so it was in conjunction with the civil rights movement of the 1950s and the radical politics of the 1960s that feminism gained new life in the United States. Many young Americans were politicized by the civil rights, student, and antiwar movements, and female activists came to recognize the sexism that existed even in these progressive factions. By the mid-1960s, radical women were gathering for discussion and analysis of their situations. A new grassroots feminist movement took shape throughout the United States.

This second-wave feminist movement soon incorporated itself into a wide range of organizations, from the reformist National Organization for Women to numerous more radical groups. Many spheres of American life were challenged by women who saw themselves as carrying forward the unfinished aims of nineteenth-century feminism. These women demanded that laws be changed to eliminate gender discrimination in education and employment. They sought a greater range of options for women in all aspects of their lives, and they demanded the right to control their reproductive functions and to express their varied sexualities.

This second-wave feminism led to fundamental changes in many aspects of American life. Legal, educational, and political institutions have been dramatically transformed in recent decades. Yet profound forms of gender oppression remain ingrained in American life, and recent years have seen a disturbing and systematic backlash against the gains of women. In response to such persistent gender inequality, a new wave of feminism is emerging that seeks still more radical analyses of the sex-class system. Prominent among the themes of contemporary feminism are analyses of interlocking systems of oppression (including gender, race, class, and sexuality), broader vistas of gender and queer theory, and reinvigorated focus on the social construction of identity and agency.

Throughout recent decades, the deepening awareness of the centrality of gender to social and political life has contributed to an extended feminist analysis—and critique—of religion. Both within the academy and from other groups of believers, feminist voices challenge the Christian tradition with renewed vigor. The argument for extending the feminist critique to Christianity was cogently stated in 1972 by Elizabeth Farians:

> The basic argument for women's rights is justice. The hardness of the line is most evident in relation to the church. The church itself, i.e., its doctrine, practice and law, cannot be excepted. Justice does not admit of exception. If something is due, it is due. If women have rights, they have rights in the church the same as anywhere else.[3]

Acting on this understanding, women have undertaken a two-pronged response with respect to Christianity. On the one hand, they have challenged the practices of churches that force them into subordinate roles and exclude them from the shaping of polity and doctrine. As discussed in Chapter 12, the movement for women's ordination—and steps to ensure full equality within the church once ordination is attained—have been central objectives of women within the modern church.

But feminists have also undertaken an extended critique of the values and ideals of Christianity, past and present. Here again the church has been found to be lacking. Despite the traditional Christian acknowledgment that God is beyond gender, the church has characteristically depicted God as masculine, and the Bible has been interpreted as prescribing the subordination of women. Even in ethical debates involving issues most directly affecting women (such as contraception and abortion), theologians have rarely taken into account women's experience and attitudes. Thus Mary McClintock Fulkerson outlines three major convictions upon which much feminist theology is based: "(1) the central character of women's experience as source and criterion; (2) the need for a critical hermeneutics of suspicion in relation to scripture and tradition, and (3) the centrality of oppression-liberation categories."[4]

Feminist theology forms a major component of the broader liberation theology movement.[5] Liberation theology traces its genealogy both to long-standing traditions of salvation and liberation within Protestant, Catholic, and Orthodox theology and to traditions of Christian social action.[6] The liberation theology movement has taken particular impetus from the religious reforms instituted by the Second Vatican Council (1962–65) and global political changes of recent decades, particularly in former colonial territories. Emerging with great force in Latin America, liberation theology movements have spread to Christian communities throughout the world, particularly Asia and Africa. Liberation theologians stress solidarity with the socially oppressed and offer strong critiques of collective, structural sin.[7]

In pursuing liberationist analyses of issues such as sexism, racism, classism, and ecological destruction, feminist liberation theologians have underscored the church's collusion with an array of oppressive social, political, and economic structures. Such theologians seek to reformulate the principles of Christianity in a manner that heightens the capacity for human liberation and faithfulness. Here we offer four American examples of a tremendously prolific and diverse theological movement now active throughout the world.

MARY DALY

One of the most prominent feminist critics of Christianity is Mary Daly, professor of theology at Boston College, who first caught public attention in 1968 with her book *The Church and the Second Sex*.[8] In that work, Daly denounced the sexist attitudes and practices of Christianity, particularly Roman Catholicism, but remained optimistic that the church would correct its past injustice toward women. Her position soon shifted to a more negative assessment of traditional Christianity and its willingness to undergo self-correction. In her subsequent work, Daly presents a radical feminist challenge to Christianity.

In her influential book of 1973, *Beyond God the Father: Toward a Philosophy of Women's Liberation,* Daly pursues with rigorous precision the classical outline of Christian systematic theology; she explores notions of God, creation, Fall, Christ and redemption, ethics, the church, and eschatology. But the content that Daly gives these doctrines contrasts sharply with their meanings in traditional Christian orthodoxy. Daly explains that her methodology "involves a castrating of language and images that reflect and perpetuate the structure of a sexist world."[9] Thus, Daly proclaims that the death of God the Father is necessary for the liberation of women; the Supreme Phallus, as she puts it, must be cut away.[10] Her point is not just the one made by earlier thinkers who affirmed the nonsexual nature of God; rather, she proceeds from the insight that as long as God is perceived as male, "the male is God."[11]

Daly offers comparably radical interpretations of creation and the Fall. In opposition to traditional notions that see humanity as abusing its freedom in a Fall into sin, Daly prescribes a new Fall into freedom, in which we exorcise the evil traditionally associated with womankind and cease the affirmation of male values.[12] From the "original sin of sexism," we cannot find liberation through a male symbol, the God-Man.[13] We must rather redeem ourselves by repudiating the "myth of feminine evil" and by refusing to affirm the "structures and ideologies of patriarchy."[14] Daly views this healing process as a "movement toward androgynous being," in which both men and women will strive for the "completeness of human being."[15]

In numerous subsequent works, Daly has continued to expound her radical critique of patriarchal religion and to pursue her spiritual quest.[16] We here excerpt a sermon Daly gave at

Harvard Memorial Church in 1971. As she points out, it was the first time a woman had ever preached at a Sunday service in that church in its 336-year history. At the conclusion of the service, an "exodus" was staged in which those committed to the search for a new community favorable to women exited from "the land of the fathers." The theme of the sermon—the women's movement as an exodus—demonstrates how ancient religious themes can be appropriated in the context of twentieth-century feminism.

THE WOMEN'S MOVEMENT: AN EXODUS COMMUNITY*

Sisters and other esteemed members of the congregation:

There are many ways of refusing to see a problem—such as the problem of the oppression of women by society in general and religion in particular. One way is to make it appear trivial. For example, one hears: "Are you on that subject of *women* again when there are so many *important* problems—like war, racism, pollution of the environment." One would think, to hear this, that there is no connection between sexism and the rape of the Third World, the rape of the Blacks, or the rape of land and water. Another way of refusing to see the problem of the oppression of women is to particularize it. For instance, one hears: "Oh, that's a Catholic problem. The Catholic church is so medieval." One would imagine, to listen to this, that there is no patriarchy around *here*. Another method of refusing to see is to spiritualize, that is, to refuse to look at concrete oppressive facts. There is a significant precedent for this in Christian history: Paul wrote that "in Christ there is neither male nor female," but was not exactly concerned about social equality for

---

* From Mary Daly, "The Women's Movement: An Exodus Community," *Religious Education* 67 (Sept./Oct. 1972): 327–33.

women. The repetition of that famous line from Paul by would-be pacifiers of women invites the response that even if "in Christ there is neither male nor female," everywhere else there damn well is. Finally, some people, especially academics, attempt to make the problem disappear by universalizing it. One frequently hears: "But isn't the *real* problem *human* liberation?" The difficulty with this is that the words spoken may be "true," but when used to avoid the issue of sexism they are radically untruthful.

There *is* a problem. It is this: There exists a world-wide phenomenon of sexual caste, which is to be found not only in Saudi Arabia but also in Sweden. This planetary sexual caste system involves birth-ascribed, hierarchically ordered groups whose members have unequal access to goods, services, prestige, and physical and mental well-being. This exploitative system is masked by sex role segregation. Thus it is possible for a woman with a Ph.D. to fail to recognize any inequity in church regulations which forbid her to serve Mass while permitting a seven year old retarded boy to do so. Sexual caste is masked also by women's duality of status, for women have a derivative status stemming from relationships with men, which serves to hide our infrahuman condition *as women*. Finally, it is masked by ideologies and institutions that alienate women from our true selves, deluding us with false identifications, sapping our energies, deflecting our anger and our hope.

It is easy, then, to fail to see the problem of sexual caste. Moreover, patriarchal religion has made it more difficult to see through the injustices of the system by legitimating and reinforcing it. The long history of legitimation of sexism by religion is too well known to require detailed repetition here. I need not recite those infamous Pauline passages on women. I need not allude to the misogynism of the church Fathers—for example, Tertullian, who informed women in general: "You are the devil's gateway," or Augustine, who opined that women are not made to the image of God. I can omit reference to Thomas Aquinas and his numerous commentators and disciples who defined women as misbegotten males. I can overlook Martin Luther's remark that God created Adam lord over all living creatures but Eve spoiled it all. I can pass over the fact that John Knox composed a "First Blast of the Trumpet against the Monstrous Regiment of Women." All of this, after all, is past history.

Perhaps, however, we should take just a cursory glance at more recent history. Pope Pius XII more or less summarized official ecclesiastical views on women when he wrote that "the mother who complains because a new child presses against her bosom seeking nourishment at her breast is foolish, ignorant of herself, and unhappy." In another address he remarked that "she loves it the more, the more pain it has cost her." It may be objected, however, that in the year 1970 the official Catholic position leaped into the twentieth century, for in that year chaste lay women (c-h-a-s-t-e) willing to take vows of chastity were offered special consecration in what was called the answer to the modern world's obsession with sex. . . . The question unasked was: Just *whose* obsession is this?

Meanwhile on the Protestant front things have not really been that different. Theologian Karl Barth proclaimed that woman is ontologically subordinate to man as her "head." Dietrich Bonhoeffer in his famous *Letters and Papers from Prison,* in which he had proclaimed the attack of Christianity upon the adulthood of the world to be pointless, ignoble, and unchristian—in this very same volume—insists that women should be subject to their husbands.

Theology which is overtly and explicitly oppressive to women is by no means a thing of the past. Exclusively masculine symbolism for God, for the notion of divine "incarnation" in human nature, and for the human relationship to God reinforces sexual hierarchy. Tremendous damage is

WOMEN AND RELIGION

done, particularly in ethics, when theologians construct one-dimensional arguments that fail to take women's experience into account. This is evident in biased ethical arguments concerning abortion—for example, those of some well-known professors at this university. To summarize briefly the situation: The entire conceptual apparatus of theology, developed under the conditions of patriarchy, has been the product of males and serves the interests of sexist society.

To a large extent in recent times the role of the church in supporting the sexual caste system has been assumed by psychoanalysis. Feminists have pointed out that it is by no accident that Freudian theory emerged as the first wave of feminism was cresting. This was part of the counterrevolution, the male backlash. Psychoanalysis has its own creeds, priesthood, spiritual counseling, its rules, anathemas, and jargon. Its power of psychological intimidation is enormous. Millions who might smile at being labeled "heretic" or "sinful" for refusing to conform to the norms of sexist society can be cowed and kept in line by the labels "sick," "neurotic," or "unfeminine." This Mother Church of contemporary secular patriarchal religions has sent its missionaries everywhere, not excluding the traditional churches themselves.

It isn't "prudent" for women to see all of this. Seeing means that everything changes: the old identifications and the old securities are gone. Therefore the ethic that is emerging in the women's movement is not an ethic of prudence but one whose dominant theme is existential courage. This is the courage to *see* and to *be* in the face of the nameless anxieties that surface when a woman begins to see through the masks of sexist society and to confront the horrifying fact of her own alienation from her authentic self.

The courage to be and to see that is emerging in the women's revolution expresses itself in sisterhood—an event which is new under the sun. The so-called "sisterhoods" of patriarchy were and are in fact mini-brotherhoods, serving

314

male interests and ideals. The ladies' auxiliaries of political parties, college sororities, religious orders of nuns—all have served the purposes of sexist society. In contrast to these, the new sisterhood is the bonding of women for liberation from sex role socialization. The very word itself *says* liberation and revolution.

There is no reason to think that sisterhood is easy. Women suffer from a duality of consciousness, as do the members of all oppressed groups. That is, we have internalized the image that males have created of "the woman," and this is in constant conflict with our authentically striving selves. One of the side effects of this duality is a kind of paralysis of the will. This is sometimes experienced as fear of ridicule, or of being considered abnormal, or—more basically—simply of being rejected, unwanted, unloved. Other effects of this dual consciousness are self-depreciation and emotional dependence. All of this is expressed in feminine anti-feminism—the direction by women of our self-hatred toward each other. Each of us has internalized the "male chauvinist pig." It exists inside our heads and it is a devil that must be exorcised and exterminated.

How can we do this? For women, the first salvific moment comes when we realize the fact of our exploitation and oppression. But—and this is an important "but"—unless the insight gives birth to externalized action it will die. This externalized action, or *praxis*, authenticates insight and creates situations out of which new knowledge can grow. It must relate to the building of a new community, to the bonding of women in sisterhood.

Sisterhood is both revolutionary and revelatory. By refusing—together—to be objects, we can break down the credibility of sex stereotyping and bring about a genuine psychic revolution. By the same token, sisterhood is revelation. The plausibility of patriarchal religion is weakening. Nietzsche, the prophet, asked: "What are these churches now if they are

not the tombs and sepulchres of God?" Nietzsche's misogynism did not permit him to see that the God who had to die
was the patriarchal tyrant. Women who are "getting it together" are beginning to see that as long as God is imaged
exclusively as male, then the male can feel justified in playing
God. The breakdown of the idols of patriarchal religion,
then, is consequent upon women's new consciousness. Out
of our courage to be in the face of the absence of these
idols—in the face of the experience of non-being—can
emerge a new sense of transcendence, that is, a new and
more genuine religious consciousness. This means that a
transvaluation of values can take place. Faith, instead of
being blind acceptance of doctrines handed down by authority, can be a state of ultimate concern that goes beyond big-
otry. Hope, instead of being reduced to passive expectation
of a reward for following rules allegedly set down by the Father and his surrogates, can be a communal creation of the
future. Love, instead of being abject acceptance of exploitation, can become clean and free, secure in the knowledge
that the most loving thing we can do in an oppressive situation is to work against the structures that destroy both the
exploited and the exploiter. The transvaluation of values that
is implied in the revolution of sisterhood touches the very
meaning of human life itself. It may be the key to turning our
species away from its course of destroying life on this planet.

Sisterhood, then, is in a very real sense an anti-church. In
creating a counter-world to the society endorsed by patriarchal religion women are at war with sexist religion *as sexist*.
This is true whether we concern ourselves directly with religion or not. Women whose consciousness has been raised are
spiritual exiles whose sense of transcendence is seeking alternative expressions to those available in institutional religion.

Sisterhood is also functioning as church, proclaiming dimensions of truth which organized religion fails to proclaim.
It is a space set apart, in which we can be ourselves, free
of the mendacious contortions of mind, will, and feeling

demanded of us "out there." It is a charismatic community, in which we experience prophecy and healing. It is a community with a mission to challenge the distortions in sexually unbalanced society, to be a counter-force to the prevailing sense of reality by building up a new sense of reality. Finally, sisterhood is an *exodus community* that goes away from the land of our fathers—leaving that behind because of the promise in women that is still unfulfilled. It is an exodus community that, perhaps for the first time in history, is putting our own cause—the liberation of women—*first*. It is a positive refusal to be co-opted any more—a positive refusal based on the prophetic insight that the sisterhood of women opens out to universal horizons, pointing outward to the sisterhood of man.

Sisters:

The sisterhood of man cannot happen without a real exodus. We have to go out from the land of our fathers into an unknown place. We can this morning demonstrate our exodus from sexist religion—a break which for many of us has already taken place spiritually. We can give physical expression to our exodus community, to the fact that we must go away.

We cannot really belong to institutional religion as it exists. It isn't good enough to be token preachers. It isn't good enough to have our energies drained and co-opted. Singing sexist hymns, praying to a male god breaks our spirit, makes us less than human. The crushing weight of this tradition, of this power structure, tells us that *we do not even exist*.

The women's movement is an exodus community. Its basis is not merely in the promise given to our fathers thousands of years ago. Rather its source is in the unfulfilled promise of our mothers' lives, whose history was never recorded. Its source is in the promise of our sisters whose voices have been robbed from them, and in our own promise, our latent creativity. We can affirm now our promise and our exodus as we walk into a future that will be our *own* future.

Sisters—and brothers, if there are any here: Our time has come. We will take our own place in the sun. We will leave behind the centuries of silence and darkness. Let us affirm our faith in ourselves and our will to transcendence by rising and walking out together.

ROSEMARY RADFORD RUETHER

Rosemary Radford Ruether is a Roman Catholic theologian teaching at Garrett-Evangelical Theological Seminary and Northwestern University. A prolific and widely influential author, Ruether has written extensively on feminist theology, feminist liturgies, and ecofeminism.[17] Ruether seeks to interrogate and reformulate Christian traditions in a manner conducive to the full humanity of women.

The following excerpts are from Ruether's 1983 book, *Sexism and God-Talk: Toward a Feminist Theology*. In this book, Ruether invokes a critical principle for feminist theology that provides her with new theological methodology, sources, and norms. In an assertion echoed by other prominent feminist scholars of religion such as Elisabeth Schüssler Fiorenza,[18] Ruether argues that any aspect of tradition or Scripture that diminishes the full humanity of women is not redemptive and cannot be seen to reflect an authentic relation to the divine. Further, Ruether asserts that since the Christian tradition itself has failed to affirm the principle of the full humanity of women, Christian resources alone are insufficient for feminist theology. Ruther also turns to marginal or heretical Christian traditions, non-Christian Near East and Greco-Roman religion and philosophy, and the resources of "critical post-Christian world views."[19] Armed with these varied resources and her critical feminist methodology, Ruether applies her prophetic-liberating principle to the Christian tradition and Scripture.[20]

Ruether proceeds in *Sexism and God-Talk* to explore various aspects of the Christian tradition, including creation, Chris-

tology, and notions of evil and salvation. In the selections excerpted here, Ruether challenges traditional Christian doctrines
of God and Christology and points toward new Christian images and understandings of God/ess and new vistas of feminist
Christology.[21]

SEXISM AND GOD-TALK *

The critical principle of feminist theology is the promotion
of the full humanity of women. Whatever denies, diminishes,
or distorts the full humanity of women is, therefore, ap-
praised as not redemptive. Theologically speaking, whatever
diminishes or denies the full humanity of women must be
presumed not to reflect the divine or an authentic relation to
the divine, or to reflect the authentic nature of things, or to
be the message or work of an authentic redeemer or a community of redemption.

This negative principle also implies the positive principle:
what does promote the full humanity of women is of the
Holy, it does reflect true relation to the divine, it is the true
nature of things, the authentic message of redemption and
the mission of redemptive community. But the meaning of
this positive principle—namely, the full humanity of women—
is not fully known. It has not existed in history. What we
have known is the negative principle of the denigration and
marginalization of women's humanity. Still, the humanity of
women, although diminished, has not been destroyed. It has
constantly affirmed itself, often in only limited and subversive ways, and it has been the touchstone against which we
test and criticize all that diminishes us. In the process we experience our larger potential that allows us to begin to imagine a world without sexism.

---

* From Rosemary Radford Ruether, *Sexism and God-Talk: Toward a
Feminist Theology* (Boston: Beacon Press, 1983), 18–19, 31–32,
68–72, 135–38.

This principle is hardly new. In fact, the correlation of original, authentic human nature (*imago dei*/Christ) and diminished, fallen humanity provided the basic structure of classical Christian theology. The uniqueness of feminist theology is not the critical principle, full humanity, but the fact that women claim this principle for themselves. Women name themselves as subjects of authentic and full humanity. . . .

༈

Feminist theology is not asserting unprecedented ideas; rather it is rediscovering the prophetic context and content of Biblical faith itself when it defines the prophetic-liberating tradition as norm. On one level, this means that feminist theology, along with other liberation theologies, strips off the ideological mystifications that have developed in the traditions of Biblical interpretation and that have concealed the liberating content. The prophetic advocacy of the poor and the oppressed and the denunciation of unjust social hierarchies and their religious justifications leap into clear focus as one assumes a stance of social justice rather than of collaboration with unjust powers. The entire Biblical message becomes radically transformed in meaning and purpose when the full implications of the Church's social advocacy for the oppressed are grasped today. Such a reevaluation of Scripture is clearly seen in the Biblical reflection taking place in Basic Christian Communities in Latin America today.

On another level, feminism goes beyond the letter of the prophetic message to apply the prophetic-liberating principle *to women*. Feminist theology makes explicit what was overlooked in male advocacy of the poor and oppressed: that liberation must start with the oppressed of the oppressed, namely, *women* of the oppressed. This means that the critique of hierarchy must become explicitly a critique of patriarchy. All the liberating prophetic visions must be deepened and transformed to include what was not included: women. . . .

∾

... If all language for God/ess is analogy, if taking a particular human image literally is idolatry, then male language for the divine must lose its privileged place. If God/ess is not the creator and validator of the existing hierarchical social order, but rather the one who liberates us from it, who opens up a new community of equals, then language about God/ess drawn from kingship and hierarchical power must lose its privileged place. Images of God/ess must include female roles and experience. Images of God/ess must be drawn from the activities of peasants and working people, people at the bottom of society. Most of all, images of God/ess must be transformative, pointing us back to our authentic potential and forward to new redeemed possibilities. God/ess-language cannot validate roles of men or women in stereotypic ways that justify male dominance and female subordination. Adding an image of God/ess as loving, nurturing mother, mediating the power of the strong, sovereign father, is insufficient.

Feminists must question the overreliance of Christianity, especially modern bourgeois Christianity, on the model of God/ess as parent. Obviously any symbol of God/ess as parent should include mother as well as father. Mary Baker Eddy's inclusive term, *Mother-Father God,* already did this one hundred years ago. Mother-Father God has the virtue of concreteness, evoking both parental images rather than moving to an abstraction (Parent), which loses effective resonance. Mother and father image God/ess as creator, as the source of our being. They point back from our own historical existence to those upon whom our existence depends. Parents are a symbol of roots, the sense of being grounded in the universe in those who have gone before, who underlie our own existence.

But the parent model for the divine has negative resonance as well. It suggests a kind of permanent parent-child relationship to God. God becomes a neurotic parent who does not want us to grow up. To become autonomous and responsible for our own lives is the gravest sin against God. Patriarchal theology uses the parent image for God to prolong spiritual infantilism as virtue and to make autonomy and assertion of free will a sin. Parenting in patriarchal society also becomes the way of enculturating us to the stereotypic male and female roles. The family becomes the nucleus and model of patriarchal relations in society. To that extent parenting language for God reinforces patriarchal power rather than liberating us from it. We need to start with language for the Divine as redeemer, as liberator, as one who fosters full personhood and, in that context, speak of God/ess as creator, as source of being.

∾

. . . Once the mythology about Jesus as Messiah or divine *Logos,* with its traditional masculine imagery, is stripped off, the Jesus of the synoptic Gospels can be recognized as a figure remarkably compatible with feminism. This is not to say, in an anachronistic sense, that "Jesus was a feminist," but rather that the criticism of religious and social hierarchy characteristic of the early portrait of Jesus is remarkably parallel to feminist criticism.

Fundamentally, Jesus renews the prophetic vision whereby the Word of God does not validate the existing social and religious hierarchy but speaks on behalf of the marginalized and despised groups of society. Jesus proclaims an iconoclastic reversal of the system of religious status: The last shall be first and the first last. The leaders of the religious establishment are blind guides and hypocrites. The outcasts of society—prostitutes, publicans, Samaritans—are able to hear the message of the prophet. This reversal of social order doesn't just turn hierarchy upside down, it aims at a new reality in which hierarchy and dominance are overcome as principles of social relations. . . .

Jesus as liberator calls for a renunciation, a dissolution, of the web of status relationships by which societies have defined privilege and deprivation. He protests against the identification of this system with the favor or disfavor of God. His ability to speak as liberator does not reside in his maleness but in the fact that he has renounced this system of domination and seeks to embody in his person the new humanity of service and mutual empowerment. He speaks to and is responded to by low-caste women because they represent the bottom of this status network and have the least stake in its perpetuation.

Theologically speaking, then, we might say that the maleness of Jesus has no ultimate significance. It has social symbolic significance in the framework of societies of patriarchal privilege. In this sense Jesus as the Christ, the representative of liberated humanity and the liberating Word of God, manifests the *kenosis of patriarchy,* the announcement of the new humanity through a lifestyle that discards hierarchical caste privilege and speaks on behalf of the lowly. In a similar way, the femaleness of the social and religiously outcast who respond to him has social symbolic significance as a witness against the same idolatrous system of patriarchal privilege. This system is unmasked and shown to have no connection with favor with God. Jesus, the homeless Jewish prophet, and the marginalized women and men who respond to him represent the overthrow of the present world system and the sign of a dawning new age in which God's will is done on earth. . . .

Christ, as redemptive person and Word of God, is not to be encapsulated "once-for-all" in the historical Jesus. The Christian community continues Christ's identity. As vine and branches Christic personhood continues in our sisters and brothers. In the language of early Christian prophetism, we can encounter Christ *in the form of our sister.* Christ, the liberated humanity, is not confined to a static perfection of one person two thousand years ago. Rather, redemptive humanity goes ahead of us, calling us to yet incompleted dimensions of human liberation.

JACQUELYN GRANT

Jacquelyn Grant, who teaches at the Interdenominational Theological Center in Atlanta, is an eloquent representative of the application of liberationist themes by American women of color.[22] Critical of the deeply imbedded layers of racism that have pervaded white feminism, many African-American women have adopted the term "womanist" to identify a distinctive African-American response to issues of sex and race oppression. Alice Walker has defined "womanist" in part as follows: "From the colloquial expression of mothers to daughters, 'You're acting womanish,' i.e., like a woman. Usually referring to outrageous, audacious, courageous or *willful* behavior."[23] As Barbara Smith points out, the use of the term womanist not only distinguishes women of color from a too-facile assimilation into the cause of white women but also signals important traditions of empowerment and agency among women of color.[24] Grant explains that "womanist just means *being* and *acting* out who you are."[25]

African-American women liberationist theologians identify themselves and their work as womanist in order to underscore the profound differences between white women and women of color. These differences affect both the objectives and methodology of theology. Womanist theology thus underscores the importance of social location and power relations in the formulation of theological critique and strategy.[26]

In Grant's *White Women's Christ and Black Women's Jesus*, she explores white feminist Christology and offers a womanist response. She begins with an analysis of the compound oppressive structures of race, gender, and class that shape the lives of African-American women. As she states, "the daily struggles of poor Black women must serve as the gauge for the verification of the claims of womanist theology."[27] From this perspective, womanist theology can engage in an internal critique of the

Bible and an active reappropriation of the traditions of Jesus to find "Christ in the community of Black women."[28]

WHITE WOMEN'S CHRIST AND
BLACK WOMEN'S JESUS*

Because it is important to distinguish Black and White women's experiences, it is also important to note these differences in theological and Christological reflection. To accent the difference between Black and White women's perspective in theology, I maintain that Black women scholars should follow Alice Walker by describing our theological activity as "womanist theology." The term "womanist" refers to Black women's experiences. It accents, as Walker says, our being responsible, in charge, outrageous, courageous and audacious enough to demand the right to think theologically and to do it independently of both White and Black men and White women.

Black women must do theology out of their tridimensional experience of racism/sexism/classism. To ignore any aspect of this experience is to deny the holistic and integrated reality of Black womanhood. When Black women say that God is on the side of the oppressed, we mean that God is in solidarity with the struggles of those on the under side of humanity. . . .

༄

Theological investigation into the experiences of Christian Black women reveals that Black women considered the Bible to be a major source for religious validation in their lives. Though Black women's relationship with God preceded their introduction to the Bible, this Bible gave some content to their God-consciousness.[29] The source for Black women's

---

* From Jacquelyn Grant, *White Women's Christ and Black Women's Jesus: Feminist Christology and Womanist Response* (Atlanta: Scholars Press, 1989), 209, 211–12, 215–20.

understanding of God has been twofold: first, God's revelation directly to them, and secondly, God's revelation as witnessed in the Bible and as read and heard in the context of their experience. The understanding of God as creator, sustainer, comforter, and liberator took on life as they agonized over their pain, and celebrated the hope that as God delivered the Israelites, they would be delivered as well. The God of the Old and New Testament became real in the consciousness of oppressed Black women. Though they were politically impotent, they were able to appropriate certain themes of the Bible which spoke to their reality. For example, Jarena Lee, a nineteenth century Black woman preacher in the African Methodist Episcopal Church constantly emphasized the theme "Life and Liberty" in her sermons which were always biblically based. This interplay of scripture and experience was exercised by many other Black women. An ex-slave woman revealed that when her experience negated certain oppressive interpretations of the Bible given by White preachers, she, through engaging the biblical message for herself rejected them. Consequently, she also dismissed White preachers who distorted the message in order to maintain slavery. . . .

The Bible must be read and interpreted in the light of Black women's own experience of oppression and God's revelation within that context. Womanists must, like Sojourner [Truth], "compare the teachings of the Bible with the witness" in them.[30]

To do Womanist Theology, then, we must read and hear the Bible and engage it within the context of our own experience. This is the only way that it can make sense to people who are oppressed. Black women of the past did not hesitate in doing this and we must do no less. . . .

In the experiences of Black people, Jesus was "all things."[31] Chief among these however, was the belief in Jesus as the divine co-sufferer, who empowers them in situations of oppression. For Christian Black women in the past, Jesus was their central frame of reference. They identified with Jesus because they believed that Jesus identified with them. As Jesus was persecuted and made to suffer undeservedly, so were they. His suffering culminated in the crucifixion. Their crucifixion included rape, and babies being sold. But Jesus' suffering was not the suffering of a mere human, for Jesus was understood to be God incarnate. As Harold Carter observed of Black prayers in general, there was no difference made between the persons of the trinity, Jesus, God, or the Holy Spirit. "All of these proper names for God were used interchangeably in prayer language. Thus, Jesus was the one who speaks the world into creation. He was the power behind the Church. . . ."[32]

More than anyone, Black theologians have captured the essence of the significance of Jesus in the lives of Black people which to an extent includes Black women. They all hold that the Jesus of history is important for understanding who he was and his significance for us today. By and large they have affirmed that this Jesus is the Christ, that is, God incarnate. They have argued that in the light of our experience, Jesus meant freedom.[33] They have maintained that Jesus means freedom from the sociopsychological, psychocultural, economic and political oppression of Black people. In other words, Jesus is a political messiah.[34] "To free (humans) from bondage was Jesus' own definition of his ministry."[35] This meant that as Jesus identified with the lowly of his day, he now identifies with the lowly of this day, who in the American context are Black people. The identification is so real that Jesus Christ in fact becomes Black. It is important to note that Jesus' blackness is not a result of ideological distortion of a few Black thinkers, but a result of careful Christological investigation. [James] Cone examines the sources of Christology and concludes that Jesus is Black because "Jesus was a Jew." He explains:

> It is on the basis of the soteriological meaning of the particularity of his Jewishness that theology must affirm the christological significance of Jesus' present blackness. He *is* black because he was a Jew. The affirmation of the Black Christ can be understood when the significance of his past Jewishness is related dialectically to the significance of his present blackness. On the one hand, the Jewishness of Jesus located him in the context of the Exodus, thereby connecting his appearance in Palestine with God's liberation of oppressed Israelites from Egypt. Unless Jesus were truly from Jewish ancestry, it would make little theological sense to say that he is the fulfillment of God's covenant with Israel. But on the other hand, the blackness of Jesus brings out the soteriological meaning of his Jewishness for our contemporary situation when Jesus' person is understood in the context of the cross and resurrection are Yahweh's fulfillment of his original intention for Israel. . . .[36]

The condition of Black people today reflects the cross of Jesus. Yet the resurrection brings the hope that liberation from oppression is immanent. The resurrected Black Christ signifies this hope. . . .

﹌

To locate the Christ in Black people is a radical and necessary step, but an understanding of Black women's reality challenges us to go further. Christ among the least must also mean Christ in the community of Black women. . . .

﹌

Although I have argued that the White feminist analysis of theology and Christology is inadequate for salvific efficacy with respect to Black women, I do contend that it is not to-tally irrelevant to Black women's needs. I believe that Black women should take seriously the feminist analysis, but they should not allow themselves to be coopted on behalf of the agendas of White women, for as I have argued, they are often racist unintentionally or by intention.

The first challenge therefore, is to Black women. Feminists have identified some problems associated with language and symbolism of the church, theology, and Christology. They have been able to show that exclusive masculine language and imagery are contributing factors undergirding the op-pression of women.

In addressing the present day, womanists must investigate the relationship between the oppression of women and the-ological symbolism. Even though Black women have been able to transcend some of the oppressive tendencies of White male (and Black male) articulated theologies, careful study reveals that some traditional symbols are inadequate for us today. The Christ understood as the stranger, the out-cast, the hungry, the weak, the poor, makes the traditional male Christ (Black and White) less significant. Even our sis-ters, the womanist of the past though they exemplified no problems with the symbols themselves, they had some suspi-cions about the effects of a male image of the divine, for they did challenge the oppressive and distorted use of it in the church's theology. In so doing, they were able to move from a traditional oppressive Christology, with respect to women, to an egalitarian Christology. This kind of equali-tarian Christology was operative in Jarena Lee's argument for the right of women to preach. She argued ". . . the Sav-iour died for the woman as well as for the man."[37] The cru-cifixion was for universal salvation, not just for male salvation or, as we may extend the argument to include, not just for White salvation. Because of this Christ came and died, no less for the woman as for the man, no less for Blacks as for Whites. . . .

If Jesus Christ were a Savior of men then it is true the maleness of Christ would be paramount.[38] But if Christ is a Saviour of all, then it is the humanity—the wholeness—of Christ which is significant. . . .

. . . the significance of Christ is not his maleness, but his humanity. The most significant events of Jesus Christ were the life and ministry, the crucifixion, and the resurrection. The significance of these events, in one sense, is that in them the absolute becomes concrete. God becomes concrete not only in the man Jesus, for he was crucified, but in the lives of those who will accept the challenges of the risen Saviour the Christ.

For [Jarena] Lee, this meant that women could preach; for Sojourner [Truth], it meant that women could possibly save the world; for me, it means today, this Christ, found in the experiences of Black women, is a Black woman. The commitment that to struggle not only with symptoms (church structures, structures of society), as Black women have done, but with causes (those beliefs which produce and re-inforce structures) yield deeper theological and christological questions having to do with images and symbolism. Christ challenges us to ask new questions demanded by the context in which we find ourselves.

ADA MARÍA ISASI-DÍAZ

Just as womanist theologians underscore the power of naming by asserting a distinctive and specific identity, so also Ada María Isasi-Díaz, a theologian at Drew University, passionately stresses the desire of Hispanic women in the United States to demarcate their particular social locations and identities with a distinctive name, a name "that will call us together, that will help us to understand our oppression, that will identify the specificity of our struggle without separating us from our communities."[39] In her essay "*Mujeristas:* A Name of Our Own," Isasi-Díaz proposes the name *mujerista,* "one who struggles to liberate herself, who is consecrated to God as proclaimer of the hope of her people."[40] *Mujeristas,* she states, are "anointed by God as servants, prophets, and witnesses of redemption."[41]

Acknowledging the profound indebtedness of all liberation theologians to the pioneering work of Gustavo Gutiérrez, Isasi-Díaz proceeds in this essay to paint the outlines of *mujerista* theology. Her stress on the communal nature of this theological enterprise and her reflections on how Scripture can be unlocked for liberatory purposes echo themes prominent in the work of other Hispanic liberation theologians.[42]

MUJERISTAS: *A NAME OF OUR OWN**

To name oneself is one of the most powerful acts any human person can do. A name is not just a word by which one is identified. A name also provides the conceptual framework, the mental constructs, that are used in thinking, understanding, and relating to a person. For many years now, Hispanic women in the United States—who struggle against ethnic prejudice, sexism, and, in many cases, classism—have been at a loss as to what to call ourselves. The majority of Hispanic women have simply called themselves *cubanas, chicanas,* or *puertorriquenas,* and most probably will continue to do so. Some of us have called ourselves *feministas hispanas.* Though *feministas hispanas* has been an appellation riddled with difficulties, we have felt the need for a name that would indicate primarily the struggle against sexism that is part of our daily

---

* From Ada María Isasi-Díaz, "*Mujeristas*: A Name of Our Own," in *Yearning to Breathe Free: Liberation Theologies in the United States,* eds. Mar Peter-Raoul, Linda Rennie Forcey, and Robert Frederick Hunter, Jr. (Maryknoll, N.Y.: Orbis Books, 1990), 121–25, 128.

bread while also helping us identify one another in the trenches as we fight for our survival within Hispanic communities and U.S. society at large. But using *feministas hispanas* has meant giving long explanations of what such a phrase does not mean.[43]

Feministas hispanas have been consistently marginalized in the Anglo-feminist community because of our critique of its ethnic/racial prejudice and lack of class analysis. At the same time, when we have insisted on calling ourselves *feministas*, we have been rejected by many in the Hispanic community because they consider feminism a preoccupation of Anglo women. Yet Hispanic women widely agree with an analysis of sexism as an evil within our communities, an evil that plays into the hands of the dominant forces of society and helps to repress and exploit us in such a way that we constitute the largest number of those at the lowest economic stratum. Likewise, Hispanic women widely agree that, though we make up the vast majority of those who participate actively in the Hispanic churches, we do the work but do not participate in deciding what work is to be done; we do the praying but our understanding of the God to whom we pray is ignored. . . .

At the same time that we name ourselves *mujeristas,* we want to rename our theological enterprise. What we called up to now Hispanic women's liberation theology will henceforth be called *mujerista* theology. *Mujerista* theology, a concept which is beginning to be articulated, is part of the daily voice of *mujeristas,* for Christianity is an intrinsic element of Hispanic culture. *Mujerista* theology articulates religious understandings of Hispanic women. It always uses a liberative lens, which requires placing oneself radically at the core of our own struggling pueblo. *Mujerista* theology brings together elements of feminist theology, Latin American liberation theology, and cultural theology—three perspectives that intertwine to form a whole. These three perspectives critique and challenge each other; they inform each other, giving birth to new elements of a new reality.

Like other liberation theologies, *mujerista* theology is indebted to the generative theological work of Gustavo Gutiérrez. This essay, which is a further development of the articulation of *mujerista* theology that I have already published,[44] deals with two *mujerista* understandings that engage specific themes of Gutiérrez's theological writings. Here I further develop the *mujerista* position that the real theologian is the community and not exclusively those of us with academic training. I will demonstrate that this is firmly rooted in the epistemological privilege of those who are oppressed and in the fact that all liberation theologies are about "doing theology," which cannot be done but as a member of a community. Secondly, after suggesting a nonoppressive way of using the Bible, I will propose the story of Shiphrah and Puah at the beginning of the Book of Exodus as a biblical interpretive key to the *mujerista* struggle. A third theme this article deals with has not been explicitly addressed by Gutiérrez but is a must for *mujerista* theology because of the twofold and at times threefold oppression Hispanic women suffer. It is the issue of power. . . .

Mujeristas are increasingly aware of how false and evil is any attempt to separate action from reflection. The physical participation of Hispanic women in programs and action is often sought, but they are seldom asked to be involved in deciding or designing content. Hispanic women are seldom invited to reflect on the reasons and motivations for their actions. But *mujeristas* will always insist on the need to be actively involved in the reflective moment of praxis. Without reflection there is no critical awareness, no conscientization and, therefore, no possibility of self-definition and liberation.

One of the most pervasive themes of *mujerista* theology is the preferential option for the poor and oppressed. This preferential option is based on the epistemological privilege of the poor because they can see and understand what the rich and privileged cannot. It is not that the poor and oppressed are morally superior or that they can see better. No, their epistemological privilege is based on the fact that, because their point of view is not distorted by power and riches, they can see differently: "The point of view of the poor, ... pierced by suffering and attracted by hope, allows them, in their struggles, to conceive another reality. Because the poor suffer the weight of alienation, they can conceive a different project of hope and provide dynamism to a new way of organizing human life for all."[45]

The epistemological privilege of the poor should be operative in a very special way in the theological enterprise. It is the understandings of the divine and the way of grappling with questions of ultimate meaning in the daily lives of grass-roots Hispanic women which constitute *mujerista* theology. Theological reflection cannot be separated from theological action in the doing of theology. Therefore *mujerista* theology is a praxis which consists of two interlinked moments: action and reflection. *Mujerista* theology is a doing theology, which does not place reflection and articulation above action. Neither does *mujerista* theology see the theological enterprise as a second moment following the praxis, for all action, at the moment that it is taking place, has a reflective quality. Because *mujerista* theology is a praxis, it is, therefore, the community as a whole that engages in the theological enterprise.

∽

For *mujeristas* the primary role of the Bible is to influence the "horizon or ultimate way in which the Christian looks at reality."[46] This biblical influence yields mainly an ethical model of relationality and responsibility that is/can be/should be operative in the struggle for liberation. The way liberation theologies have used the Bible up to now, however, will not effectively contribute to building a model of relationality and responsibility. Most liberation theologies' use of the Bible is limited to a "simple learning."[47] What liberation theologies have promoted are "certain exemplary themes such as exodus, prophetic criticism of society, ... Jesus' confrontation with authorities,"[48] Jesus as a member of a marginated group—the Galileans—[49] and so forth. Or liberation theologies have also reworded biblical stories using popular terminology in order to make them relevant to different situations of struggle in the world today.[50]

Instead, the Bible should be used to promote a critical consciousness, to trigger suspicion, which is the starting point of the process of conscientization. The Bible should be used to learn how to learn—"to involve the people in an unending process of acquiring new ... information that multiplies the previous store of information."[51] This new information becomes a source that can be consulted "in order to solve new problems the people have not faced before."[52] The Bible must not be directly applied to a problem—it does not offer a solution to any given problem. Instead the Bible must become a resource for learning what questions to ask in order to deal appropriately with the problem at hand.

This way of using the Bible liberates the Bible—frees it from becoming a mere guidebook about the correct thing to do. The Bible cannot be the only tool, nor is it always the main tool, which *mujeristas* use to reflect on who we are, on our "attitudes, dispositions, goals, values, norms, and decisions."[53] The Bible should always be seen as only *one* of the traditions through which the community can remember its past, its roots, the source of its values, customs, and practices. Any and all sources that help "to nurture and reform the community's self-identity as well as the personal character of its members"[54] must be seriously engaged by *mujeristas*. Furthermore, the Bible as well as any other text to which the community of Hispanic women gives authority should be used only as an integral part of a process that helps Hispanic women to be self-determining. This way of using the Bible makes it clear that each person has to decide how she is to participate in the struggle for liberation.

⁓

For us *mujeristas* power is the ability to enable all persons to become the most they themselves can be. It must be clearly understood that in the Hispanic culture persons can become fully themselves only in relation to the community and not as isolated individuals who look out only for themselves. Our understanding of power demands that we work incessantly to create the political, economic, and social conditions needed for the self-realization of all persons. It also requires establishing relational structures and operational modes in all spheres of life which facilitate and promote the self-realization of all persons. Finally, our understanding of power requires promotion of the creativity of all persons so they can contribute efficaciously to the common good.[55] *Mujerista* theology struggles to bring up the question of power in every single moment of the doing of theology. Furthermore, *mujerista* theology challenges all liberation theologies to place the question of power at the heart of their theological enterprise. The focus might be different but the questions about power must always be asked. For example, what do we mean when we say that God is all-powerful? Is our God an enabling God or a controlling God made to the image and likeness of the males who control the society in which we live? If power as understood today in our society is good, then it should be shared by all. Then why has Mary been portrayed exclusively as a submissive woman and why is this submissive Mary proposed as the main example for Roman Catholic women? What would reinventing power mean for the "power of orders" so very central to the present understanding of priesthood in the Roman Catholic church? What would priestly ministry entail if power is understood as enablement and fostering creativity instead of control and domination? What happens to our ethics and morality if we raise the question of power when making decisions? In conclusion, how do our theological discourse and the structures of our churches bless and sanctify the understanding of power as control and domination?

The struggle for liberation of Hispanic women is being carried out in many different ways by many different *mujeristas* all around the United States. *Mujerista* theology is one of the voices of such a struggle—a struggle which is life for us because we have learned from our grandmothers and mothers that *la vida es la lucha*.

∿ Notes

INTRODUCTION

1. D. S. Bailey, *Sexual Relation in Christian Thought* (New York: Harper & Row, 1959), 6.
2. Adrienne Rich, *Of Woman Born: Motherhood as Experience and Institution* (New York: Norton, 1976), 57, cited in Judith M. Bennett, "Feminism and History," *Gender and History* 1 (1989): 260.
3. Bennett, "Feminism and History," 261.
4. Bennett, "Feminism and History," 263.
5. Bernadette J. Brooten, "Early Christian Women and Their Cultural Context: Issues of Method in Historical Reflection," in *Feminist Perspectives on Biblical Scholarship,* ed. by Adela Yarbro Collins (Chico, Calif.: Scholars Press, 1985), 66. Borrowing a term from Mary Daly, Brooten thus argues that feminist investigators of the early Christian past are engaged in exploring "prehistory" (p. 67).
6. For an affirmation, see the essays of Elizabeth A. Clark in her *Jerome, Chrysostom, and Friends* (New York/Toronto: Edwin Mellen Press, 1979) and *Ascetic Piety and Women's Faith* (Lewiston, N.Y.: Edwin Mellen Press, 1986); for questions, see Elizabeth Castelli, "Virginity and Its Meaning for Women's Sexuality in Early Christianity," *Journal of Feminist Studies in Religion* 2 (1986): 61–88.
7. See Lyndal Roper, *The Holy Household: Women and Morals in Reformation Augsburg* (Oxford/New York: Oxford University Press, 1991); *Oedipus and the Devil: Witchcraft, Sexuality, and Religion in Early Modern Europe* (New York: Routledge, 1994).
8. See, for example, Elizabeth A. Clark, "Ideology, History, and the Construction of 'Woman' in Late Ancient Christianity," *Journal of Early Christian Studies* 2 (1994): 155–84.
9. Tertullian, *On the Dress of Women* 1.1.2.

1. THE NEW TESTAMENT AND CHRISTIAN ORIGINS

1. For an early discussion of the topic, see Leonard Swidler, "Jesus Was a Feminist," *Catholic World* 212 (Jan. 1971): 177–83. A sharp critique of the anti-Jewish bias of Swidler's essay is made by Judith Plaskow, "Blaming Jews for Inventing Patriarchy," *Lilith* 7 (1980): 11–12.

2. See, for example, Elisabeth Schüssler Fiorenza, *Bread Not Stone: The Challenge of Feminist Biblical Interpretation* (Boston: Beacon Press, 1984), 142, which borrows themes especially from Hayden White.

3. For an explanation of the problems of androcentric interpretation, see Elisabeth Schüssler Fiorenza, *In Memory of Her: A Feminist Theological Reconstruction of Christian Origins* (New York: Crossroad, 1983), 41–53.

4. Bernadette J. Brooten, "Early Christian Women and Their Cultural Context: Issues of Method in Historical Reconstruction," in *Feminist Perspectives on Biblical Scholarship*, ed. by Adela Yarbro Collins (Chico, Calif.: Scholars Press, 1985), 65–68, 80.

5. See Chapters Six and Seven in *The Postmodern Bible*, ed. The Bible and Culture Collective (New Haven/London: Yale University Press, 1995); and (for a slightly later period) Elizabeth A. Clark, "Ideology, History, and the Construction of 'Woman' in Late Ancient Christianity," *Journal of Early Christian Studies* 2 (1994): 155–84.

6. The classic statement of early Christianity as a Jewish renewal movement is made by Gerd Theissen in *The Sociology of Early Palestinian Christianity*, trans. by John Bowden (Philadelphia: Fortress Press, 1978 [German original, 1977]); for feminist implications, see Schüssler Fiorenza, *In Memory of Her*, chap. 4; and Ross Shepard Kraemer, *Her Share of the Blessings: Women's Religions Among Pagans, Jews, and Christians in the Greco-Roman World* (New York/Oxford: Oxford University Press, 1992), 133, 138.

7. See Schüssler Fiorenza, *In Memory of Her*, 109; for some interesting slightly later manifestations of this principle, see Susanna Elm, *"Virgins of God": The Making of Asceticism in Late Antiquity* (Oxford: Clarendon Press, 1994), esp. p. 166.

8. For example, Schüssler Fiorenza, *In Memory of Her*, chap. 5.

9. See, for example, Antoinette Clark Wire, *The Corinthian Women Prophets: A Reconstruction Through Paul's Rhetoric* (Minneapolis: Fortress Press, 1990), 182 ("In Corinth, Paul is the wary one . . . "); Dale B. Martin, *The Corinthian Body* (New Haven: Yale University Press, 1995), esp. chaps. 8 and 9.

10. Brooten, "Early Christian Women," 81.

11. The Greek text of this verse reads (in translation) "neither Jew nor Greek, neither slave nor free, no male and female." The change of wording in the last phrase indicates that Paul was calling to mind the words of Genesis 1:27, that God had created mankind as "male and female." English translations of the verse do not usually bring out this distinction. Since "male and female" are words from Genesis 1:27 introducing God's command for and blessing on marriage, Paul's use of the phrase *could* be taken as an exhortation that patriarchal marriage be overcome: see Schüssler Fiorenza, *In Memory of Her*, 211.

12. See, for example, Dennis Ronald MacDonald, *There Is No Male and Female: The Fate of a Dominical Saying in Paul and Gnosticism* (Philadelphia: Fortress Press, 1987), esp. p. 130.

13. Biblical translators usually render this word as "deaconess," although there is no reason, based on the Greek text, why she should not rather be called a "deacon." The word conveys the notion of "serving."

14. For a recent (though probably overly optimistic) assessment of women's leadership roles in early Christianity, see Karen Jo Torjesen, *When Women Were Priests: Women's Leadership in the Early Church and the Scandal of their Subordination in the Rise of Christianity* (San Francisco: HarperSanFrancisco, 1993).

15. For an early stage of the debate, see Robin Scroggs, "Paul and the Eschatological Woman," *Journal of the American Academy of Religion* 41 (1972): 283–303; also, a more popular version of the same argument, Scroggs, "Paul: Chauvinist or Liberationist?" *The Christian Century* 89 (March 15, 1972): 307–9; answered by Elaine H. Pagels, "Paul and Women: A Response to Recent Discussion," *Journal of the American Academy of Religion* 42 (1974): 538–49.

16. The passage in 1 Corinthians 11 has been extensively discussed—with variant interpretations—by such New Testament scholars as J. Murphy-O'Connor, "Sex and Logic in 1 Corinthians 11:2–16," *Catholic Biblical Quarterly* 42 (1980): 482–500; Schüssler Fiorenza, *In Memory of Her,* 226–30; Wire, *The Corinthian Women Prophets,* chap. 6; Martin, *The Corinthian Body,* chap. 9; MacDonald, *There Is No Male and Female,* 72–111.

17. See, for example, Scroggs, "Paul and the Eschatological Woman," 284; Schüssler Fiorenza, *In Memory of Her,* 230–33 (with many footnotes to the scholarly discussion of the topic). Wire, *The Corinthian Women Prophets,* 149–58, 229–32, provides a learned discussion of problems besetting the Pauline text and its transmission.

18. See especially Bernadette J. Brooten, "Paul's Views on the Nature of Women and Female Homoeroticism," in *Immaculate and Powerful: The Female in Sacred Image and Social Reality,* eds. Clarissa W. Atkinson, Constance H. Buchanan, and Margaret R. Miles (Boston: Beacon Press, 1985), 61–87; and Dale B. Martin, "Heterosexism and the Interpretation of Romans 1:18–32," *Biblical Interpretation* 3 (1995): 332–55.

19. New Testament texts such as 1 Timothy 5:14 and Titus 2:4–5 provide ammunition for this argument. For a study of how these interpretations deviated from Paul's position, see William O. Walker Jr., "The 'Theology of Woman's Place' and the 'Paulinist' Tradition," *Semeia* 28 (1983): 101–12.

20. See the major discussions of such writers as David L. Balch, *Let Wives Be Submissive: The Domestic Code in 1 Peter* (Chico, Calif.: Scholars Press, 1981); John H. Elliott, *A Home for the Homeless: A Sociological Exegesis of 1 Peter—Its Situation and Strategy* (Philadelphia: Fortress Press, 1981); James E. Crouch, *The Origins and Intention of the Colossian Haustafel* (Göttingen: Vandenhoeck and Ruprecht, 1972); Schüssler Fiorenza, *In Memory of Her,* chap. 7 (she claims that "Western misogynism has its root in the rules for the household as the model of the state," p. 257).

21. See the excellent discussion by Jouette M. Bassler, "The Widows' Tale: A Fresh Look at 1 Tim. 5:3–16," *Journal of Biblical Literature* 103 (1984): 23–41. Since there are admission requirements and duties listed for these women, "widows" are clearly an organized group, not merely "women whose husbands have died." "Widows" as a group are attested in many second- and third-century ecclesiastical writings.

22. Constance F. Parvey, "The Theology and Leadership of Women in the New Testament," in *Religion and Sexism: Images of Woman in the Jewish and Christian Traditions,* ed. Rosemary R. Ruether (New York: Simon & Schuster, 1974), 146.

23. "The Protevangelium of James," in Edgar Hennecke and W. Schneemelcher, eds., *New Testament Apocrypha* (Philadelphia: Westminster Press, 1963), 1: 385.

24. The "immaculate conception" does not mean that Mary's mother was also a virgin; rather, the conception took place in the usual manner, but God intervened so that original sin would not be passed to the fetus.

25. For a feminist discussion of Mary's contested role in Christianity, see Mary Daly, *Beyond God the Father: Toward a Philosophy of Women's Liberation* (Boston: Beacon Press, 1973), 81–92.

26. See Chapter Three.

27. See Stevan L. Davies, *The Revolt of the Widows: The Social World of the Apocryphal Acts* (Carbondale: Southern Illinois University Press, 1980); Virginia Burrus, *Chastity as Autonomy: Women in the Stories of Apocryphal Acts* (Lewiston/Queenston: Edwin Mellen Press, 1987).

28. An English translation of the Acts of Paul and Thecla (as well as of other Apocryphal Acts) can be found in Hennecke and Schneemelcher's *New Testament Apocrypha* II: 353–64.

29. Tertullian, *On Baptism* 1.17. See also Stevan L. Davies, "Women, Tertullian, and the *Acts of Paul,*" *Semeia* 38 (1986): 139–43; this issue of *Semeia* is dedicated completely to material pertaining to the Apocryphal Acts.

30. Dennis Ronald MacDonald, *The Legend and the Apostle: The Battle for Paul in Story and Canon* (Philadelphia: Westminster Press, 1983). MacDonald thus writes, ". . . the Pastorals did not develop linearly from Paul's ministry but dialectically; that is, they were written to oppose another strand of Pauline tradition whose legends depicted him as a social radical" (p. 97). For a brief description of the two trajectories emanating from Paul's writings, see Brooten, "Early Christian Women," 85–87.

2. CLEMENT OF ALEXANDRIA AND THE GNOSTICS: WOMEN, SEXUALITY, AND MARRIAGE IN ORTHODOXY AND HETERODOXY

1. We put quotation marks around this word advisedly. What the church later considered "orthodox" teaching was, in the second century, still a matter of opinion.

2. Hans Jonas, *The Gnostic Religion,* 2nd ed. (Boston: Beacon Press, 1963), 32. Jonas's book provides a number of the most important primary source documents from the Gnostic sects as well as lucid commentary by one of the foremost scholars of Gnosticism.

3. "On Marriage" is part of a larger work by Clement, the *Stromateis,* usually translated as *Miscellanies,* which suggests the rather rambling, unsystematic character of Clement's musings on various aspects of Christian life and thought. Clement worked in the closing years of the second century and the opening ones of the third, largely in Alexandria, where church tradition tells us he was associated with a Christian catechetical school. One of the reasons for the enduring interest in Clement's writing is that he attempted to link the best of classical learning and culture with the Christian tradition, in order to demonstrate that Christianity could appeal to the more educated classes within Greco-Roman society rather than only to the rabble, as some of his contemporaries affirmed.

4. The documents are collected and translated in James M. Robinson, ed., *The Nag Hammadi Library,* 2nd ed. (San Francisco: Harper & Row, 1981). For a dramatic account describing the discovery of the texts, see Elaine Pagels, *The Gnostic Gospels* (New York: Random House, 1979), introduction.

5. W. E. G. Floyd, in *Clement of Alexandria's Treatment of the Problem of Evil* (Oxford: Oxford University Press, 1971), notes that "Clement of Alexandria's speculation on the problem of evil is in large measure dictated by his antignostic polemic" (p. 91).

6. See Jonas, *The Gnostic Religion,* chap. 11.

7. Henry Chadwick, "The Domestication of Gnosis," in *The Rediscovery of Gnosticism,* ed. Bentley Layton (Leiden: E. J. Brill, 1980), 1: 3–16.

8. A trait especially associated with the Gospel of Philip. At the beginning of *Stromateis* 3, Clement acknowledges that the Valentinians approve of marriage.

9. Floyd, *Clement,* 28.

10. See excerpt from Clement below. A similar argument about Jesus being married was developed by William Phipps, *Was Jesus Married? The Distortion of Sexuality in the Christian Tradition* (New York: Harper & Row, 1970).

11. For a discussion of the "middle way" of passion, *metriopatheia,* see Salvatore R. C. Lilla, *Clement of Alexandria: A Study in Christian Platonism and Gnosticism* (Oxford: Oxford University Press, 1971), 103–4.

12. John Ferguson, in *Clement of Alexandria* (New York: Twayne Publishers, 1974), disagrees with commentators who argue that Clement would have liked people to desist from sexual relations altogether: "Clement's ideal is not to feel sexual desire, and let sexual union be determined wholly by will" (p. 131).

13. Irenaeus, *Against Heretics* 1.1.

14. Irenaeus, *Against Heretics* 1.1–7.

15. In Robert M. Grant, *Gnosticism: A Sourcebook of Heretical Writings from the Early Christian Period* (New York: Harper & Bros., 1961), 70.

16. See Chapters 6 and 11.

17. Tertullian, *On the Prescription of Heretics,* 41.

18. Montanism was a prophetic Christian movement that arose in mid-second century Asia Minor (present-day Turkey). Montanists believed that the end of the world was soon to come and that the kingdom of God would be established in their midst. The group's leader, Montanus, was accompanied by two female prophetesses; followers believed (to the horror of "mainstream" Christians) that the Holy Spirit spoke directly through them.

19. As explained by Henri-Charles Puech, the gospel is probably a compilation of two originally separate parts. E. Hennecke and W. Schneemelcher, eds., *New Testament Apocrypha* (Philadelphia: Westminster Press, 1963), 1: 344.

20. As Elaine Pagels points out in *The Gnostic Gospels* (pp. 64–65), Peter is depicted as warring against women in Gnostic literature; perhaps he is representative of attitudes among the orthodox? In view of her suggestion, we find it interesting to recall that in Paul's version of the people witnessing the resurrected Jesus (1 Cor. 15), Peter has usurped the place given to Mary Magdalene and the other women in the Gospels.

3. JEROME: THE EXALTATION OF CHRISTIAN VIRGINITY

1. See J. N. D. Kelly, *Jerome: His Life, Writings, and Controversies* (New York: Harper & Row, 1976). For a shorter account, see Pierre de Labriolle, *History and Literature of Christianity from Tertullian to Boethius,* trans. Herbert Wilson (New York: Barnes and Noble, 1968), 333–86.

2. Kelly, *Jerome,* 48, discusses the difficulty of pinpointing the period that Jerome spent in the desert.

3. *Letter* 48.20.

4. See the selections that follow.

5. For Jerome's borrowing from the classical antifeminist tradition, see David Wiesen, *Saint Jerome as a Satirist: A Study in Christian Latin Thought and Letters* (Ithaca: Cornell University Press, 1964), chap. 4; and Harold Hagendahl, *Latin Fathers and the Classics: A Study in the Apologists, Jerome, and Other Christian Writers* (Göteborg: Universitet Press, 1958), 147–61. Kelly, in *Jerome,* doubts that Jerome really was familiar with Juvenal (p. 12).

6. Wiesen, *Saint Jerome,* 119.

7. Wiesen, *Saint Jerome,* 160, n. 160.

8. For a discussion of these women, see chap. 10 of Kelly, *Jerome,* and Elizabeth A. Clark, *Jerome, Chrysostom, and Friends: Essays and Translations* (New York: Edwin Mellen Press, 1979), 35–106.

9. Jerome was one of the few early Christian fathers who learned Hebrew. His motives for doing so appear to have been mixed: not only did he have a scholarly desire to master the language of the Old Testament, he also believed that the study of Hebrew would help calm his sex drive (*Letter* 125.12).

10. Kelly, *Jerome,* offers this explanation: "Strongly sexed but also, because of his convictions, strongly repressed as well, his nature craved for female society, and found deep satisfactions in it when it could be had without doing violence to his principles" (p. 91). Also see Clark, *Jerome, Chrysostom, and Friends,* 35–106.

11. See the analysis in Patrica Cox Miller, "The Blazing Body: Ascetic Desire in Jerome's Letter to Eustochium," *Journal of Early Christian Studies* 1 (1993): 21–45.

12. Here Jerome was referring to the *agapetae* or *subintroductae.* They were women who had devoted themselves to celibacy but nonetheless lived with monks. Although the couples claimed that they remained chaste, the church was scandalized by the practice. Jerome was one of the church fathers who refused to believe that the relationships were innocent. He wrote *Letter* 117 to a mother

and daughter who each had been living under such arrangements, urging them to seek roommates of the same sex.

13. *Letter* 48. See Kate Cooper, *The Virgin and the Bride: Idealized Womanhood in Late Antiquity* (Cambridge, Mass.: Harvard University Press, 1996).

14. *Letter* 48.3.

15. For an attempt to defend Jerome against charges of misogyny in *Against Jovinian,* see Gerard Campbell, "Saint Jerome's Attitude Toward Marriage and Women," *The American Ecclesiastical Review* 143 (1960): 310–20, 384–94.

16. *Against Helvidius,* 16–17. For a discussion of the Helvidius-Jerome dispute, see David G. Hunter, "Helvidius, Jovinian, and the Virginity of Mary in Late Fourth-Century Rome," *Journal of Early Christian Studies* 1 (1993): 47–71.

17. *Against Helvidius,* 21.

18. Hans von Campenhausen, *The Virgin Birth in the Theology of the Ancient Church* (Napierville, Ill.: Alec R. Allenson, 1964).

19. For further material on Mary, see Chapter 6.

4. AUGUSTINE: SINFULNESS AND SEXUALITY

1. *Confessions* 4.2. Augustine was born in North Africa in 354 and received his early education there before journeying to Rome and Milan. In the latter city, under the influence of Ambrose's powerful preaching, he resolved to take the step of baptism. After this initiatory rite, he returned to North Africa and became associated with the church at Hippo where soon he was raised to the bishopric. He remained in Hippo until his death in 430. The standard biography remains that of Peter Brown, *Augustine of Hippo* (Berkeley/Los Angeles: University of California Press, 1967).

2. *Confessions* 8.8 and 11. See Kenneth Burke, *The Rhetoric of Religion: Studies in Logology* (Boston: Beacon Press, 1961), 86 and 114f., for an interesting discussion of how Augustine changed his "loves." Augustine's ambivalence about his sexual life is revealed in his famous prayer, "Grant me chastity and continence—but not yet" (*Confessions* 8.7).

3. *Confessions* 6.15.

4. *Confessions* 9.9.

5. *Confessions* 9.9.

6. For discussions of Manichaeanism, see Geo Widengren, *Mani and Manichaeism* (London: Weidenfeld and Nicolson, 1965), and Samuel N. C. Lieu, *Manichaeism in the Later Roman Empire and Medieval China* (Tübingen: J. C. B. Mohr [P. Siebeck], 1992).

7. John T. Noonan Jr., *Contraception: A History of Its Treatment by the Catholic Theologians and Canonists,* enlarged ed. (Cambridge, Mass./London: Harvard University Press, 1986), 119. Augustine's views on Manichaean sexual practices can be found in *On the Morals of the Manicheans* 18.65 and *Against Faustus* 22.30.

8. *Confessions* 6.14.

9. For a discussion of Pelagius and his views, see John Ferguson, *Pelagius: A Historical and Theological Study* (Cambridge: W. Heffer, 1956) or Robert Evans,

Pelagius: Inquiries and Reappraisals (London: A. & C. Black, 1968). Pelagius, a British visitor to Rome at the end of the fourth century, was shocked by the moral laxity of the Christians he observed in the imperial city. In 412 he arrived in North Africa where he took up a fierce literary debate with Augustine on the topics of God's grace and humans' free will. Councils in the following years made a variety of pronouncements regarding the "correct" opinion; in 529 the Council of Orange accepted in essence the Augustinian position regarding the ravages of original sin but stressed the sacrament of baptism as the means for alleviating its dire results.

10. Selections from Pelagius's writings can be found in Henry Bettenson, ed., *Documents of the Christian Church,* 2nd ed. (Oxford: Oxford University Press, 1967), 52–54; also see B. R. Rees, *The Letters of Pelagius and His Followers* (Woodbridge: Boydell Press, 1991); and Theodore De Bruyn, ed., *Pelagius: Commentary on Saint Paul's Epistle to the Romans* (Oxford: Oxford University Press, 1993).

11. *The City of God* 22.30.

12. Noonan, *Contraception,* 132.

13. *Retractions* 2.22. For the debate between Jerome and Jovinian, see Chapter 3.

14. As revealed, for example, in his *Treatise on the Sermon on the Mount* 1.15.41: the good Christian is to love woman insofar as she is a human being, a creature of God, but he is to hate what in her belongs to being a female, which Augustine associates with sexual intercourse. Thus the Christian husband is enjoined to love his wife as he would an enemy, for the human potential in her, not for what is distinctive to her sexual nature.

15. Earlier in his career, Augustine had considered other options regarding the sex life of Adam and Eve in Eden. See *On the Good of Marriage,* 2.

16. Rosemary R. Ruether, "Misogynism and Virginal Feminism in the Fathers of the Church," in *Religion and Sexism: Images of Woman in the Jewish and Christian Tradition,* ed. Rosemary R. Ruether (New York: Simon & Schuster, 1974), 162.

17. Elizabeth A. Clark, "Theory and Practice in Late Ancient Asceticism: Jerome, Chrysostom, and Augustine," *Journal of Feminist Studies in Religion* 5 (1989): 25–46.

18. Noonan, *Contraception,* 135–39.

19. See the selection that follows.

5. THOMAS AQUINAS AND THE SCHOLASTIC WOMAN

1. Feminists raise the same issue with regard to modern theologians. Mary Daly, for example, notes that Paul Tillich laid the basis for a nonsexist theology in his notion of God as "the Ground of Being." See Daly, *Beyond God the Father: Toward a Philosophy of Women's Liberation* (Boston: Beacon Press, 1973), chap. 1.

2. *ST* 1.92.4 ad 2. The patristic speculation that Eve was created through the mediation of angels rather than directly by God was one means of according her a lower status than Adam. Citations from the *Summa Theologica* will be abbreviated as *ST* throughout. This reference, for example, indicates that the material can be found in part 1, question 92, article 4, reply to objection 2. Where no

concluding number is given, the citation is from the "I answer that" section of the article. For an extensive discussion of Aquinas's views on women and their Augustinian and Aristotelian precedents, see Kari Elisabeth Børresen, *Subordination and Equivalence: The Nature and Role of Woman in Augustine and Thomas Aquinas,* trans. Charles H. Talbot (Washington, D.C.: University Press of America, 1981 [French original: 1968]), pt. 2.

3. Aristotle, for Thomas, was "the Philosopher." Thomas wished to make known to Latin Christendom Aristotle's physical and metaphysical writings, which had not been available to Christian thinkers of the early Middle Ages. Thomas did not follow Aristotle blindly, nor did he necessarily try to "make a Christian" of him. As F. C. Copleston has written, "he was not concerned with patching together Aristotle as Aristotle with Christian theology. If he adopted and adapted a number of Aristotelian theories, this was not because he thought them 'useful,' but because he believed them to be true." *Aquinas* (Baltimore: Penguin Books, 1955), 63.

4. Eleanor Commo McLaughlin, "Equality of Soul, Inequality of Sexes: Women in Medieval Theology," in *Religion and Sexism: Images of Woman in the Jewish and Christian Traditions,* ed. Rosemary R. Ruether. (New York: Simon & Schuster, 1974), 256.

5. *On the Generation of Animals* 2.3 and 4.2.

6. Aristotle's theory of female defectiveness, feminists point out, finds its modern counterpart in the Freudian theory that girls see themselves as "castrated."

7. *ST* 1.92.1 ad 1.

8. *ST* 1.99.2 ad 2 and ad 3. The attempt to decide the sex of the child will soon be a possibility through developments in biogenetic engineering. Feminists may worry, however, that our society would choose to produce more males than females, contrary to Thomas's expectations.

9. *ST* 1.92.1 ad 1.

10. *ST* 1.99.2.

11. Copleston, *Aquinas,* 89.

12. *On the Generation of Animals* 1.20. See John T. Noonan Jr., *Contraception: A History of Its Treatment by the Catholic Theologians and Canonists,* enlarged ed. (Cambridge, Mass./London: Harvard University Press, 1986), 89.

13. *On the Generation of Animals* 2.3.

14. *ST* 2–2.26.10 ad 1.

15. *ST* 2–2.26.10 ad 1.

16. *ST* 2–2.156.1 ad 1.

17. *ST* 1.92.1.

18. *ST* 3 Supplement, 64.5. (The idea is also found in Aristotle, *On the Generation of Animals* 1.20.) Thomas also believed that the "fit" position for sexual intercourse was for the woman to be below the man: *Commentary on the Sentences* 4.31; *ST* 2–2.154.11.

19. *ST* 2–2.165.2 ad 1; *ST* 2–2.163.4. According to Thomas, Eve believed the serpent's malicious words accusing God of jealousy, while Adam did not.

20. *ST* 1.92.1 ad 2.

21. *ST* 1.92.1.

22. Note how Thomas, in the excerpt below, downplays the clerical status of women in early Christianity.
23. *ST* 3 Supplement, 39.1.
24. *ST* 3 Supplement, 39.1 ad 1.
25. *ST* 1.92.2.
26. *ST* 1.92.3.
27. *ST* 1.92.2.
28. *ST* 1.98.1 and 2.
29. *ST* 1.98.2 ad 4.
30. *ST* 1.98.2.
31. *ST* 1.98.2 ad 3. In his earlier *Commentary on the Sentences* (of Peter Lombard) (4.31.1.1), Aquinas even ventures that God put pleasure in the sex act as an inducement to its performance. Thomas's view that the sex act would have been different in the Garden of Eden represents his adoption of Augustinian teaching rather than that of his teacher Albert the Great, who held that the "nature" of the sexual act couldn't change because of original sin. See the discussion in James A. Brundage, *Law, Sex, and Christian Society in Medieval Europe* (Chicago/London: University of Chicago Press, 1987), 421. For a discussion of the view that the sexual "appetite" itself is not a perversion of human nature, see John Giles Milhaven, "Thomas Aquinas on Sexual Pleasure," *Journal of Religious Ethics* 5 (1977): 159–60. For a defense of Thomas as an advocate of pleasure if rightly ordered, see Cornelius Williams, "The Hedonism of Aquinas," *The Thomist* 38 (1974): 257–90, esp. 281–83.
32. Noonan, *Contraception,* 288.
33. *ST* 3 Supplement, 49.6.
34. *ST* 3 Supplement, 49.6 ad 4.
35. See Chapter Eleven.
36. *ST* 1–2.91.2.
37. See Copleston, *Aquinas,* 214, for a discussion of this point regarding natural law. For a longer exploration of Thomas's idea of the natural law, see Walter Farrell, O.P., *The Natural Moral Law According to St. Thomas and Suarez* (Ditchling: St. Dominic's Press, 1930).
38. *ST* 1–2.94.2. Nevertheless, some ambivalence remains in Aquinas's thought, no doubt the sediment of earlier discussions: is not "natural" to be defined by what "animals do"? See Noonan, *Contraception,* 240–41. Among the items that Thomas thought were "contrary to nature" are concubinage, fornication, and polygyny (although Thomas concedes that the latter is not "contrary to nature" in a certain sense, for a man can have more children—the first "end" of marriage—with several wives than with one): see discussion and references in Brundage, *Law,* 445, 459, 478.
39. The Catholic church's condoning of the "rhythm" method of contraception is predicated on a person's ability to control his or her sexual behavior through reason and will.
40. For articles critical of the Vatican's interpretation of natural law and contraception, see Daniel Callahan, ed., *The Catholic Case for Contraception* (New York: Macmillan Company, 1969).

6. WOMEN RELIGIOUS OF THE MIDDLE AGES

1. This trend seems to cross geographical boundaries in the Middle Ages. For Italy, see Diane Owen Hughes, "Invisible Madonnas? The Historiographical Tradition and the Women of Medieval Italy," in *Women in Medieval History and Historiography*, ed. Susan Mosher Stuard (Philadelphia: University of Pennsylvania Press, 1987), esp. pp. 34–36, 47–50; for France, Susan Mosher Stuard, "Fashion's Captives: Medieval Women in French Historiography," in *Women in Medieval History*, esp. pp. 59–61, 66–67; for Germany, Martha Howell (with S. Wemple and D. Kaiser), "A Documented Presence: Medieval Women in Germanic Historiography," in *Women in Medieval History*, esp. pp. 101–11, 124.

2. Susan Mosher Stuard, "A New Dimension? North American Scholars Contribute Their Perspective," in *Women in Medieval History*, 94.

3. Barbara A. Hannawalt, "Golden Ages for the History of Medieval English Women," in *Women in Medieval History*, 17.

4. See the summary discussion in Brenda M. Bolton, "Mulieres sanctae," in *Women in Medieval Society*, 146–48 (Bolton's essay originally appeared in *Studies in Church History*, vol. 10, ed. Derek Baker [London: Basil Blackwell, 1973], 77–85).

5. Penelope D. Johnson, *Equal in Monastic Profession: Religious Women in Medieval France* (Chicago/London: University of Chicago Press, 1991), 232–33.

6. Suzanne Fonay Wemple, *Women in Frankish Society: Marriage and the Cloister, 500–900* (Philadelphia: University of Pennsylvania Press, 1981), 154–55, 160, 167–68, 187–88, 194, 195.

7. Sharon K. Elkins, *Holy Women of Twelfth-Century England* (Chapel Hill/London: University of North Carolina Press, 1988), xiii, 161.

8. Johnson, *Equal in Monastic Profession*, 102, 141, 188, 219–20, 225–26, 266.

9. Jane Tibbetts Schulenburg, "Strict Active Enclosure and Its Effects on the Female Monastic Experience (ca. 500–1100)," in *Distant Echoes: Medieval Religious Women*, vol. 1, eds. John A. Nichols and Lillian Thomas Shank (Kalamazoo: Cistercian Publishers, 1984), esp. pp. 52–54, 70. For an interesting discussion of one such "double monastery," see the essay by Penny Shine Gold, "Male/Female Cooperation: The Example of Fontevrault," in *Distant Echoes*, 151–68.

10. Jane Tibbetts Schulenburg, "Women's Monastic Communities, 500–1000: Patterns of Expansion and Decline," in *Sisters and Workers in the Middle Ages*, eds. Judith M. Bennett et al. (Chicago/London: University of Chicago Press, 1989), esp. pp. 213—14.

11. Sally Thompson, "The Problem of the Cistercian Nuns in the Twelfth and Early Thirteenth Centuries," in *Medieval Women*, ed. Derek Baker (Oxford: Basil Blackwell, 1978), 227–52.

12. Howell, "A Documented Presence," 120, citing statistics from Herbert Grundmann, *Religiöse Bewegungen im Mittelalter*, 3rd ed. (Darmstadt: Wissenschaftliche Buchgesellschaft, 1970).

13. Patricia J. F. Rosof, "The Anchoress in the Twelfth and Thirteenth Centuries," in *Peaceweavers: Medieval Women Religious,* vol. 2, eds. Lillian T. Shank and John A. Nichols (Kalamazoo: Cistercian Studies, 1987), 124, 126. In many nunneries, women were expected to bring their dowries, a fact that limited the number of women eligible for monastic life by class (p. 129). Also see Elkins, *Holy Women,* xiii.

14. Elkins, *Holy Women,* 78–81, 88.

15. From Merovingian Gaul to the High Middle Ages, wealth was usually a prerequisite for women wishing to enter nunneries. For examples, see Jo Ann McNamara, "A Legacy of Miracles: Hagiography and Nunneries in Merovingian Gaul," in *Women of the Medieval World: Essays in Honor of John H. Mundy,* eds. Julius Kirshner and Suzanne F. Wemple (Oxford/New York: Basil Blackwell, 1985), 41; Dennis Devlin, "Feminine Lay Piety in the High Middle Ages: The Beguines," in *Distant Echoes,* 183.

16. Rosof, "The Anchoress," esp. pp. 126–32. Also see Ann K. Warren, "The Nun as Anchoress: England 1100–1500," in *Distant Echoes,* 197–212.

17. Christopher J. Holdsworth, "Christina of Markyate," in *Medieval Women,* 185–204 (citation at p. 187); also see Elkins, *Holy Women,* 27–28, and Elizabeth Alvilda Petroff, *Body and Soul: Essays on Medieval Women and Mysticism* (New York/Oxford: Oxford University Press, 1994), 9–10, 140–46; Eleanor McLaughlin, "Women, Power, and the Pursuit of Holiness in Medieval Christianity," in *Women of Spirit: Female Leadership in the Jewish and Christian Traditions,* eds. Rosemary Ruether and Eleanor McLaughlin (New York: Simon and Schuster, 1979), 108–15. The text of Christina's *Life* is now conveniently available in *Medieval Women's Visionary Literature,* ed. Elizabeth Alvilda Petroff (New York/Oxford: Oxford University Press, 1986), 144–50.

18. Devlin, "Feminine Lay Piety," 183–84, 191; Howell, "A Documented Presence," 120.

19. Devlin, "Feminine Lay Piety," 192–93. Also see Petroff, *Body,* chap. 3; François Vandenbroucke, "New Milieux, New Problems," in J. Leclercq, F. Vandenbroucke, and L. Bouyer, *The Spirituality of the Middle Ages* (New York: Seabury Press, 1982), 353–57. See Ernest W. McDonnell, *The Beguines and Beghards in Medieval Culture* (New York: Octagon, 1969 [1953]), for an account of the Beguines that emphasizes both religious and socioeconomic factors.

20. Howell, "A Documented Presence," 120.

21. Lioba's *Life* is conveniently translated in Petroff, *Medieval Women's Visionary Literature,* 106–14.

22. See Rudolph M. Bell, *Holy Anorexia* (Chicago/London: University of Chicago Press, 1985).

23. Women's fasting practices have been extensively examined by Caroline Walker Bynum, *Holy Feast, Holy Fast: The Religious Significance of Food to Medieval Women* (Berkeley: University of California Press, 1987); Bynum, "Fast, Feast, and Flesh: The Religious Significance of Food to Medieval Women," *Representations* 11 (1985): 1–25.

24. See especially Laurie A. Finke, "Mystical Bodies and the Dialogics of Vision," in *Maps of Flesh and Light: The Religious Experience of Medieval Women Mystics,* ed. Ulricke Wiethaus (Syracuse: Syracuse University Press, 1993), 42; and Ellen Ross's essay in the same volume (pp. 45–59), "'She Wept and Cried Right Loud for Sorrow and for Pain': Suffering, the Spiritual Journey, and Women's Experience in Late Medieval Mysticism."

25. Finke, "Mystical Bodies," 32–35.

26. Some of these writings are now conveniently translated in the Classics of Western Spirituality series published by Paulist Press.

27. Barbara Newman, "Divine Power Made Perfect in Weakness: Saint Hildegard on the Frail Sex," in *Peaceweavers,* 104. Newman here argues that Hildegard's scientific understanding of bodily humors and temperaments differed considerably from that of standard scientific writers. See also Newman's longer work, *Sister of Wisdom: St. Hildegard's Theology of the Feminine* (Berkeley: University of California Press, 1987).

28. Peter Dronke, *Women Writers of the Middle Ages: A Critical Study of Texts from Perpetua (+203) to Marguerite Porete (+1310)* (Cambridge: Cambridge University Press, 1984), 144.

29. See Theresa Coletti, "Purity and Danger: The Paradox of Mary's Body and the En-gendering of the Infancy Narrative in the English Mystery Cycles," in *Feminist Approaches to the Body in Medieval Literature,* eds. Linda Lomperis and Sarah Stanbury (Philadelphia: University of Pennsylvania Press, 1993), 65–95.

30. Caroline Walker Bynum, *Jesus as Mother: Studies in the Spirituality of the High Middle Ages* (Berkeley: University of California Press, 1982). Such men's devotion to Mary, however, did not preclude their expression of misogyny.

31. The "Hail Mary" prayer is, in English, "Hail, Mary, full of grace, the Lord is with thee, blessed art thou among women. Blessed is the fruit of thy womb, Jesus. Holy Mary, Mother of God, pray for us sinners now and at the hour of our death. Amen." Several of its phrases are taken from Luke 1, in which the angel Gabriel announces to Mary her pregnancy, and Elizabeth, soon to be the mother of John the Baptist, greets the pregnant Mary.

32. A convenient summary of the history of devotion to Mary can be found in the *New Catholic Encyclopedia* (New York: McGraw Hill, 1967), IX: 365–69.

33. Birgitta of Sweden, *Revelations,* Book Seven, 1–17, in *In Her Words: Women's Writings in the History of Christian Thought,* ed. Amy Oden (Nashville: Abingdon Press, 1994), 178–80.

34. For an informative introduction to Angela's life and teaching, along with an English translation of her writings, see Angela of Foligno, *Complete Works,* trans. Paul Lachance, preface by Romana Guarnieri (New York/Mahwah: Paulist Press, 1993).

35. For helpful comments on Angela's piety, see Bynum, *Holy Feast, Holy Fast,* esp. pp. 140–48, 246–48. Also see Elizabeth Alvilda Petroff, "Writing the Body: Male and Female in the Writings of Marguerite d'Oingt, Angela of Foligno, and Umiltà of Faenza," in Petroff's *Body and Soul,* 204–24.

36. Angela's "companion" was probably a woman named Masazuola, about whom almost nothing is known.

37. "Brother scribe" is Angela's confessor, scribe, and advisor, the Franciscan Brother Arnaldo.

38. For further discussion of Julian and her theology, see the essays in *Peaceweavers* by Ritamary Bradley ("Julian on Prayer," 291–304) and Charles Cummings ("The Motherhood of God According to Julian of Norwich," 305–14).

39. Among the interesting recent studies of Margery and her *Book,* see Clarissa W. Atkinson, *Mystic and Pilgrim: The Book and the World of Margery Kempe* (Ithaca/London: Cornell University Press, 1983); Sarah Beckwith, "A Very Material Mysticism: The Medieval Mysticism of Margery Kempe," in *Medieval Literature: Criticism, Ideology, and History,* ed. David Aers (Brighton: Harvester Press, 1986), 34–57; Wendy Harding, "Body into Text: The *Book of Margery Kempe,*" in *Feminist Approaches to the Body,* 166–87; Karma Lochrie, *Margery Kempe and the Translations of the Flesh* (Philadelphia: University of Pennsylvania Press, 1991); Janel M. Mueller, "Autobiography of a New 'Creature': Female Spirituality, Selfhood, and Authorship in the *Book of Margery Kempe,*" in *Women in the Middle Ages and the Renaissance: Literary and Historical Perspectives,* ed. Mary Beth Rose (Syracuse: Syracuse University Press, 1986), 155–71; Anthony Goodman, "The Piety of John Brunham's Daughter, of Lynn," in *Medieval Women,* 347–58.

40. This aspect of Margery's behavior is discussed by Ross, "'She Wept and Cried Right Loud,'" 45–59.

41. For a discussion of women in the Lollard movement, see Margaret Aston, "Lollard Women Priests?," *Journal of Ecclesiastical History* 31 (1980): 441–61.

42. Margery Kempe, *The Book of Margery Kempe (1436): A Modern Version by W. Butler-Bowden* (London: Jonathan Cape, 1936), 1: 53 (p. 194).

43. "This creature" is Margery's usual, humble way of referring to herself.

44. In other words, by means of sexual intercourse.

45. In a previous communication with Jesus, he had put Margery under strict obedience to observe a meatless fast on Fridays.

7. WOMAN AS WITCH: WITCHCRAFT PERSECUTIONS IN THE OLD AND NEW WORLDS

1. See Hugh Trevor-Roper, *The European Witch-Craze of the Sixteenth and Seventeenth Centuries* (Harmondsworth, England: Penguin Books, 1969), 24–28; and Joseph Klaits, *Servants of Satan: The Age of the Witch Hunts* (Bloomington: Indiana University Press, 1985), 48.

2. For an overview of debates among historians concerning the number of victims of the witchcraft persecutions, see Anne Llewellyn Barstow, *Witchcraze: A New History of the European Witch Hunts* (San Francisco: HarperSanFrancisco/Pandora, 1994), 20–23; and Brian Levack, *The Witch-hunt in Early Modern Europe* (London: Longman, 1987), 19–22. Estimates range from relatively conservative views (120,000 charged, 60,000 executed) to unsubstantiated estimates of many millions executed. For an overview of the diffusion of the witch persecutions from their origins in northern Italy through central Europe to its peripheries, see Bengt Ankarloo and Gustav Henningsen, eds., *Early Modern European Witchcraft: Centres and Peripheries* (Oxford: Clarendon Press, 1990).

3. See in this regard Barstow, *Witchcraze,* 2–10.

4. In regions on the European periphery, such as Iceland, Finland, and Estonia, the majority of those associated with witchcraft were men. See Ankarloo and Henningsen, *Early Modern European Witchcraft,* 13.

5. Barstow, *Witchcraze,* 23–25.

6. Trevor-Roper, *The European Witch-Craze,* 76.

7. Indeed, Charlemagne had decreed the death penalty for anyone who burned supposed witches. Trevor-Roper, *The European Witch-Craze,* 12–14; see also Ioan P. Couliano, *Eros and Magic in the Renaissance,* trans. Margaret Cook (Chicago: University of Chicago Press, 1987), 152–53; and Julio Caro Baroja, "Witchcraft and Catholic Theology," in *Early Modern European Witchcraft,* 19–43.

8. Trevor-Roper, *The European Witch-Craze,* 24–39, 112–22.

9. See, for example, Ankarloo and Henningsen, *Early Modern European Witchcraft,* 9–15, and the works cited therein; and see Nachman Ben-Yehuda, "Problems Inherent in Socio-Historical Approaches to the European Witch Craze," *Journal for the Scientific Study of Religion* 20 (1981): 326–38.

10. Alan Macfarlane, *Witchcraft in Tudor and Stuart England* (New York: Harper & Row, 1970); Keith Thomas, *Religion and the Decline of Magic* (New York: Scribners, 1971); and Lyndal Roper, *Oedipus and the Devil: Witchcraft, Sexuality, and Religion in Early Modern Europe* (New York: Routledge, 1994).

11. The period of the witchcraft persecutions appears to coincide with the period of the final Christianization of Europe. See Robert Muchembled, "Satanic Myths and Cultural Reality," in *Early Modern European Witchcraft,* 139–60.

12. See E. William Monter, *Witchcraft in France and Switzerland: The Borderlands During the Reformation* (Ithaca, N.Y.: Cornell University Press, 1976), 118–24, 136–41; Christina Larner, *Enemies of God: The Witch-hunt in Scotland* (London: Chatto & Windus, 1981), 51; Barstow, *Witchcraze,* 4, 41; and Roper, *Oedipus and the Devil,* 22–26, 47, 137–38, 149, 171–98.

13. See Christopher Baxter, "Jean Bodin's *De la Démonomanie des Sorciers*: The Logic of Persecution," in *The Damned Art: Essays in the Literature of Witchcraft,* ed. Sydney Anglo (London: Routledge & Kegan Paul, 1977), 81.

14. See Henry Kamen, "Notes on Witchcraft, Sexuality, and the Inquisition," in *The Spanish Inquisition and the Inquisitorial Mind,* ed. Angel Alcalá (Boulder: Social Science Monographs, 1987), 237–47.

15. See John Tedeschi, "Inquisitorial Law and the Witch," in *Early Modern European Witchcraft,* 83–118; Kamen, "Notes on Witchcraft," 237–47; and Barstow, *Witchcraze,* 49.

16. See Ankarloo and Henningsen, *Early Modern European Witchcraft,* 5.

17. See "The Bull of Innocent VIII," in *Malleus Maleficarum,* trans. Montague Summers (London: Pushkin Press, 1948), xix–xxi; and Couliano, *Eros and Magic,* 184–91.

18. See Sydney Anglo, "Evident Authority and Authoritative Evidence: The *Malleus Maleficarum,*" in *The Damned Art,* 14.

19. See Anglo, "Evident Authority," 14–15; Barstow, *Witchcraze,* 171, 196 n. 16.

20. Anglo, "Evident Authority," 18.

21. The link between women and witchcraft has, of course, deep roots in Greek and Latin culture. See Julio Caro Baroja, "Witchcraft and Catholic Theology," 22–23. On the view of women in the *Malleus,* see Eliane Camerlynck, "Féminité et sorcellerie chez les théoriciens de la démonologie à la fin du Moyen Age: Etude du *Malleus Maleficarum,*" *Renaissance and Reformation/Renaissance et Réforme* 7 (new series) (February 1983): 13–25.

22. *Malleus Maleficarum,* 48.

23. *Malleus Maleficarum,* 21–28.

24. *Malleus Maleficarum,* 30.

25. *Malleus Maleficarum,* 243.

26. *Malleus Maleficarum,* 136.

27. See Anglo, "Evident Authority," 20–24.

28. See Stuart Clark, "Protestant Demonology: Sin, Superstition, and Society (c. 1520–c. 1630)," in *Early Modern European Witchcraft,* 45–81; and Robert Scribner, "Witchcraft and Judgement in Reformation Germany," *History Today* 40 (April 1990): 12–19.

29. Trevor-Roper, *The European Witch-Craze,* 64–65.

30. See Stuart Clark, "King James's *Daemonologie:* Witchcraft and Kingship," in *The Damned Art,* 174–77; Christina Larner, *Witchcraft and Religion: The Politics of Popular Belief* (Oxford: Basil Blackwell, 1984), 3–22; and Retha M. Warnicke, "Sexual Heresy at the Court of Henry VIII," *The Historical Journal* 30 (1987): 247–68.

31. Roper, *Oedipus and the Devil,* 192.

32. The Reverend Mr. Parris had dropped out of Harvard and had tried his hand (and failed) as a trader in Barbados. He returned to Salem Village as minister to a community that had had difficulty in deciding on a spiritual leader. Tituba was acquired (along with her husband, John) by Mr. Parris in Barbados.

33. In addition, two women (including Sarah Osborne) died in prison and one man died from torture. Of the accused, 141 (76 percent) were women; of those tried, fifty-two (88 percent) were women; of those convicted, twenty-six (84 percent) were women, and of those executed, fourteen (74 percent) were women. Carol F. Karlsen, *Devil in the Shape of a Woman: Witchcraft in Colonial New England* (New York: Vintage Books, 1987), 51.

34. It is possible that if Tituba and the girls had not accused others, the entire craze might have been averted. It is possible that Tituba was confused (her English was not very good); it is also possible that the whippings she had received at the hands of her master, the Rev. Mr. Parris, had convinced her that her only salvation was in telling her tormentors what they wanted to hear. That seemed to work in subsequent cases; it was primarily those who *denied* that they were witches who were executed.

35. Quoted in David C. Brown, *A Guide to the Salem Witchcraft Hysteria of 1692* (Pittsburgh: D. C. Brown, 1984), 95. Mather alludes to Paul's words in 2 Corinthians 11:14–15 (referring to the "false apostles" who are damaging Paul's mission and authority): "Even Satan disguises himself as an angel of light. So it is not strange if his servants also disguise themselves as servants of righteousness."

36. Bridget Bishop ran an alehouse in Salem Town and had, prior to 1692, been examined as a witch (1680). Tavern keepers were suspect because their products might do damage to a man (ale or cider might lead to a drunken stupor; cheese had green mold and might poison). She was examined on April 19 with Mary Warren and Giles Corey, tried on June 2, and, on June 10, was the first witch to be executed.

37. Sarah Osborne, for example, was handling land in trust for her children but was supervised by John Putnam and his brother Thomas (Ann's father), with whom Osborne came into conflict. The Putnams associated Rebecca Nurse and her sisters with the deaths of a number of children, including their own; the women's family had been long engaged in a land dispute with the Putnams. George Burroughs, during his tenure as minister in Salem Village, had angered the Putnams.

38. Borders between townships, and therefore land ownership of the lands contained therein, was very uncertain. Salem Village, Salem Town, and Topsfield (not to mention the individual landowners involved) all laid claim to various landholdings. *All* of those accused of witchcraft between February 29 and April 21, 1692, were members of families who held contested lands. Martha and Giles Corey, for example, owned one hundred acres of very valuable land along the Ipswich River. Selma R. Williams and Pamela Williams Adelman, *Riding the Nightmare: Women and Witchcraft from the Old World to Colonial Salem* (New York: HarperPerennial, 1978), 149, 165, 171ff.

39. Carol Karlsen examines the inheritance laws in effect in the late seventeenth century, relates them to the various women accused of witchcraft, and concludes, "However varied their backgrounds and economic positions, as women without brothers or women without sons, they stood in the way of the orderly transmission of property from one generation of males to another" (Karlsen, *Devil in the Shape of a Woman,* 116). Karlsen's analysis simply adds another layer of complexity to the "land dispute" theory; Martha Corey, for example, stood to inherit valuable land from her eighty-one-year-old husband.

40. Spectral evidence had been controversial for months. Many notable New England clergymen spoke out against it as open to abuse, including Increase Mather, Cotton Mather's father. Cotton Mather, on the other hand, argued that spectral evidence should be admissible; he was absolutely certain of a diabolical plot.

41. Ankarloo and Henningsen, *Early Modern European Witchcraft,* 3.

42. Trevor-Roper, *The European Witch-Craze,* 97–111.

8. THE PROTESTANT REFORMATIONS AND THE CATHOLIC RESPONSE

1. Roland Bainton, *Women of the Reformation in Germany and Italy* (Minneapolis: Augsburg Press, 1971), 9.

2. And for rather dubious reasons: that it would please his father, spite his enemies and the devil, and convince people that he had practiced what he preached. See *Letters* 154, 157, and 158 in *Luther's Works,* vol. 49 (vol. 2 of *Letters*), ed. and trans. Gottfried G. Krodel (Philadelphia: Fortress Press, 1972), 111, 117, 123.

3. The puzzle is resolved by noting Luther's concept of a sacrament—and why marriage does not qualify. See *The Babylonian Captivity of the Church,* in

Luther's Works, vol. 36, ed. and trans. A. R. Wentz (Philadelphia: Fortress Press, 1959), 92–106.

4. The Catholic church undertook its own reformation in the sixteenth century, particularly through its implementation of the decrees of the Council of Trent (1545–63).

5. See *The Babylonian Captivity of the Church,* 80–81, 102–3.

6. For a statement of the conflicts, see Merry Wiesner, "Luther and Women: The Death of Two Marys," in *Disciplines of Faith: Studies in Religion, Politics, and Patriarchy,* eds. Jim Obelkevich, Lyndal Roper, and Raphael Samuel (London: Routledge & Kegan Paul, 1987), 295–97.

7. For a study of Luther's treatment of Eve, see Kristen E. Kvam, *Luther, Eve, and Theological Anthropology: Reassessing the Reformer's Response to the "Frauenfrage,"* Ph.D. dissertation, Emory University, 1992.

8. *Table Talk* 1658, in *Luther's Works,* vol. 54, ed. and trans. Theodore G. Tappert (Philadelphia: Fortress Press, 1967), 160–61.

9. Luther's allowance for bigamy in difficult marital cases led to problems for the Protestant cause when one of the German Protestant princes, Philip of Hesse, undertook a bigamous marriage, contrary to imperial law, with Luther's blessing. The result was the division of the Schmalkaldic League (the Protestant military league) when the Emperor Charles V applied sanctions to Philip.

10. *Table Talk* 505, 89; 3178A, 191.

11. See, for example, Wiesner, "Luther and Women," 303–4; Thomas A. Brady Jr., "'You Hate Us Priests': Anticlericalism, Communalism, and the Control of Women at Strasbourg in the Age of the Reformation," in *Anticlericalism in Late Medieval and Early Modern Europe,* eds. Peter A. Dykema and Heiko A. Oberman (Leiden/New York/Köln: E. J. Brill, 1993), 191–92, 205; Lyndal Roper, *The Holy Household: Women and Morals in Reformation Augsburg* (Oxford: Oxford University Press, 1989), 1–5, 203, 237.

12. Roper, *Holy Household,* 5; also see 3, 15, 31, 47, 55.

13. A discussion of her life and work can be found in Roland H. Bainton, *Women of the Reformation in Germany and Italy* (Boston: Beacon Press, 1971), 55–76.

14. Calvin, *Institutes of the Christian Religion* 2.8.43; 4.13.3.

15. Calvin, *Commentary on Genesis* 1 (English trans.: *Commentaries on the First Book of Moses Called Genesis,* ed. and trans. John King [Grand Rapids: Eerdman's, 1948], 1: 128–30).

16. Calvin, *Commentary on* 1 *Corinthians* 7:6 (*Ioannis Calvinis Opera* 49 = *Corpus Reformatorum* 77, eds. W. Baum, E. Cunitz, E. Reuss [Brunswick, 1892]), 405–6. (English trans. in *Calvin's Commentaries: The First Epistle of Paul the Apostle to the Corinthians,* trans. John W. Fraser, eds. David W. Torrance and Thomas F. Torrance [Edinburgh: Oliver and Boyd, 1960], 140–42.) Calvin cites Augustine's treatise *On the Good of Marriage.*

17. Calvin, *Institutes of the Christian Religion* 2.8.43.

18. Calvin, *Sermon 137 on Deuteronomy* 24:5 (*Ioannis Calvinis Opera* 28 = *Corpus Reformatorum* 56 [1885]), 156–57. Calvin comments on verses from the Mosaic law that command the newly married man not to go out with the army or

pursue (foreign?) business, but to stay home for his first year of marriage "to be happy with his wife whom he has taken."

19. See "The Marriage Ordinances of Geneva," in *The Register of the Company of Pastors of Geneva in the Time of Calvin,* ed. and trans. P. E. Hughes (Grand Rapids: William B. Eerdmanns, 1966), 77–78. In practice, it appears that couples were encouraged to stay married.

20. Calvin, *Commentary on 1 Corinthians* 11:7 (*Ioannis Calvinis Opera* 49 = *Corpus Reformatorum* 77 [1872], 476); also see Jane Dempsey Douglass, *Women, Freedom, and Calvin* (Philadelphia: Westminster Press, 1985), 51.

21. Douglass, *Women,* 79.

22. Calvin, *Sermon 12 on 1 Corinthians* 11:4–10 (*Ioannis Calvinis Opera* 49 = *Corpus Reformatorum* 77 [1892]), 723–24, 730.

23. Calvin, *Sermon 16 on 2 Samuel* 6:3 (*Supplementa Calviniana: Sermons inédits. Predigten über das 2. Buch Samuelis,* ed. Hanns Rückert [Neukirchen, 1961], 138).

24. Calvin, *Institutes of the Christian Religion* 4.10.27–32. Douglass (*Women,* 106, 46) takes this concession to mean Calvin believed the custom could be changed. John L. Thompson, on the other hand, thinks Douglass's reading of Calvin is too optimistic: Calvin does not offer women much "beyond eschatological hope"; God makes exceptions for women's leadership only in dismal times when men need to be shamed by women's activity. See Thompson's "*Creata Ad Imaginem Dei, Licet Secundo Gradu:* Woman as the Image of God According to John Calvin," *Harvard Theological Review* 81 (1988): 136.

25. Not all of the radical reformers were Anabaptists, although most were. Groups identified as Anabaptists were found throughout Europe, but chiefly in Switzerland, Germany, and the Netherlands. Their modern representatives include the pacifist (and sometimes separatist) Amish and Mennonites. Anabaptists believed that infant baptism counted as "no baptism," since no personal decision can be made by an infant.

26. One of our chief sources for the martyrs of Anabaptists is the *Martyr's Mirror,* a seventeenth-century Mennonite collection of martyr stories. Of the over nine hundred martyrs whose stories are told, almost one-third (278) concern women.

27. In this example, intercourse was a spiritual act when commanded by an inner voice. The belief also led to reciprocal spouse exchange, mostly among small groups of believers. See Lyndal Roper, "Sexual Utopianism in the German Reformation," *Journal of Ecclesiastical History* 41 (1991): 399–402.

28. Roper, "Sexual Utopianism," 405–7.

29. Roper, "Sexual Utopianism," 407.

30. See, for example, Conrad Grebel's description of his mother (in Harold S. Bender, *Conrad Grebel, c. 1498–1526* [Scottsdale: Herald Press, 1950], 4); Balthasar Hubmeier's blame of Eve for the Fall in his 1527 treatise *On Free Will;* and the Hutterite *Account of Our Religion, Doctrine and Faith* by Peter Riedemann (1506–1556). The writings of Menno Simons (1496–1561) recall the chaste and controlled woman of the Pastoral Epistles.

31. See the account of her trial in Thieleman Jan van Braght, *The Bloody Theatre or Martyrs' Mirror of the Defenceless Christians,* trans. Joseph F. Sohm (Scottdale, Penn.: Mennonite Publishing House, 1951), 481–82; see also p. 546.

32. While Anabaptist women did receive the right to divorce, for the most part the traditional patterns were maintained: women did not divorce their husbands. Lucille M. Marr, "Anabaptist Women of the North: Peers in the Faith, Subordinates in Marriage," *Mennonite Quarterly Review* 61 (1987): 352.

33. "Elizabeth, a Dutch Anabaptist Martyr: A Letter (1573)," in *The Protestant Reformation,* ed. Hans Hillerbrand (New York: Harper & Row, 1968), 152.

34. Jeanne de Jussie, *Le Levain du Calvinisme ou commencement de l'heresie de Geneve* (Geneva: Jules-Guillaume Fick, 1865), 13–14, 20.

35. Jeanne de Jussie, *Le Levain du Calvinisme,* 36, 165–66.

36. Jeanne de Jussie, *Le Levain du Calvinisme,* 172.

37. Jeanne de Jussie, *Le Levain du Calvinisme,* 116–17.

38. Jeanne de Jussie, *Le Levain du Calvinisme,* 117, 173–74, 186.

39. Jeanne de Jussie, *Le Levain du Calvinisme,* 172, 185–86.

40. Jeanne de Jussie, *Le Levain du Calvinisme,* 186.

41. Jeanne de Jussie, *Le Levain du Calvinisme,* 173–74.

42. Jeanne de Jussie, *Le Levain du Calvinisme,* 177, 174.

43. Jeanne de Jussie, *Le Levain du Calvinisme,* 44.

44. Jeanne de Jussie, *Le Levain du Calvinisme,* 172, 179, 182, 185.

45. Jeanne de Jussie, *Le Levain du Calvinisme,* 186.

46. Jeanne de Jussie, *Le Levain du Calvinisme,* 198–209, (20).

47. Jeanne de Jussie, *Le Levain du Calvinisme* (5).

9. JOHN MILTON: THE PURITAN TRANSFORMATION OF MARRIAGE

1. John Halkett, *Milton and the Idea of Matrimony: A Study of the Divorce Tracts and Paradise Lost, Yale Studies in English* 173 (New Haven/London: Yale University Press, 1970), viii, 5, 24, 30, 42, 47.

2. See the discussion in Chapters 6 and 8. The view that Puritanism transformed marriage into a "romantic" institution is primarily associated with the work of William and Malleville Haller; see, for example, "The Puritan Art of Love," *Huntington Library Quarterly* 5 (1942): 235–72, and W. Haller, "Hail Wedded Love," *English Literary History* 13 (1946): 79–97.

3. Arthur Barker, *Milton and the Puritan Dilemma, 1641–1660* (Toronto: University of Toronto, 1942).

4. For example, V. Norskov Olsen, *The New Testament Logia on Divorce* (Tübingen: J. C. B. Mohr, 1971), 129ff.

5. Halkett, *Milton,* 3.

6. The *Tetrachordon* (1645) is a scholarly treatise seeking to harmonize Old and New Testament texts on marriage; the *Colasterion* (1645) is a reply to an anonymous attack on *The Doctrine and Discipline of Divorce. The Judgment of Martin Bucer Concerning Divorce* is an English version of the sixteenth-century Protestant reformer Martin Bucer's views on divorce, which was originally published during the reign of Edward VI (1547–53). The urge to change divorce laws was short-lived, as was the seventeenth-century attempt to make marriage a strictly civil affair: on the latter, see George E. Howard, *A History of Matrimonial Institutions* (Chicago: University of Chicago Press/London: T. Fisher Unwin,

1904), 1: 408, 432–33. A useful overview of Milton's teaching on marriage and divorce is provided by James Turner Johnson, *A Society Ordained by God: English Puritan Marriage Doctrine in the First Half of the Seventeenth Century* (Nashville/New York: Abingdon Press, 1970), chap. 4.

7. John Milton, *The Doctrine and Discipline of Divorce* 1: 13 in Milton, *Complete Prose Works,* ed. Don M. Wolfe, 8 vols. (New Haven/London: Yale University Press, 1953–82), II: 275. All references to Milton's divorce tracts are cited from this volume. Questioning whether Milton really understood the male-female relation as "mental" are David Aers and Bob Hodge, "'Rational Burning': Milton on Sex and Marriage," *Milton Studies* 13 (Pittsburgh: University of Pittsburgh, 1979): 3–33.

8. Milton, *The Doctrine and Discipline of Divorce* 1: 1 (Wolfe, II: 244).

9. Milton, *The Doctrine and Discipline of Divorce* 1: 9 (Wolfe, II: 268–69).

10. Milton, *The Judgment of Martin Bucer Concerning Divorce* 27, 28, 36 (Wolfe, II: 455, 456, 462).

11. Milton, *The Judgment of Martin Bucer* 22 (Wolfe, II: 447–48); *Tetrachordon* (on Gen. 2:18) (Wolfe, II: 596).

12. Milton, *Tetrachordon* (on Gen. 2:18) (Wolfe, II: 596–97); *Paradise Lost* 8.389–92.

13. See Chapter 4 for Augustine's discussion.

14. See Halkett, *Milton,* 27. When Milton interprets Paul's words in 1 Corinthians 7:14 (that if a Christian partner stays with an "unbelieving" spouse, the children will be "holy"), he uses the verse to argue that children cannot be "holy" if they are brought into unhappy households.

15. Milton cites Bucer in *The Judgment of Martin Bucer* 38 (Wolfe, II: 465). Like some earlier thinkers such as Augustine, Milton can cite the example of Joseph and Mary as a support for his view of marriage: their relation shows that it is neither sexual intercourse nor children that make a marriage, but a "bond" between the two people.

16. Milton, *Tetrachordon* (on Gen. 2:24) (Wolfe, II: 605).

17. Halkett, *Milton,* 128–29; Diane Kelsey McColley, *Milton's Eve* (Urbana/Chicago/London: University of Illinois Press, 1983), 1.

18. Especially emphasized by McColley, *Milton's Eve,* 1, 110, 123, 166.

19. McColley, *Milton's Eve,* 3; Milton, *Paradise Lost* 10.884–88.

20. Milton, *Paradise Lost* 9.904–7, 914–16.

21. Halkett, *Milton,* 122.

22. Milton, citing Bucer in *The Judgment of Martin Bucer* 37, 40 (Wolfe, II: 44, 51); *Tetrachordon* (Wolfe, II: 99, 214).

23. Milton, *Tetrachordon* (on Deut. 24:1–2; 1 Cor. 7:10f.) (Wolfe, II: 621–22, 682).

24. Halkett, *Milton,* 30, 56.

25. Some early entries to the discussion are Marcia Landy, "Kinship and the Role of Women in *Paradise Lost,*" *Milton Studies* 4 (Pittsburgh: University of Pittsburgh Press, 1972): 3–18; and Barbara K. Lewalski, "Milton on Women—Yet Once More," *Milton Studies* 6 (Pittsburgh: University of Pittsburgh Press, 1975): 3–20. Joseph Wittreich (*Feminist Milton* [Ithaca/London: Cornell University Press,

1987], 44–82) provides evidence that female readers in the eighteenth and early nineteenth centuries *did* find Milton a support for women's rights arguments.

26. Milton, *Paradise Lost* 4.295–99. The words can, however, be read as representing the viewpoint of Satan.

27. Milton, *Tetrachordon* (on Deut. 24:1–2) (Wolfe, 11: 626); also citing Bucer in *The Judgment of Martin Bucer* 37, 40 (Wolfe, 11: 462–63, 467–70); also see Halkett, *Milton,* 52, 90.

28. On Milton's failure to allow women to initiate divorce, see Janet E. Halley, "Female Autonomy in Milton's Sexual Poetics," in *Milton and the Idea of Women,* ed. Julia M. Walker (Urbana/Chicago: University of Illinois Press, 1988), 243–44.

29. Milton, *Tetrachordon* (on Gen. 1:27) (Wolfe 11: 589).

30. See Halkett, *Milton,* 103; McColley, *Milton's Eve,* 22.

31. See the section on Margery Kempe in Chapter 6. On Milton negating the direct relation between women and God, see Maureen Quilligan, *Milton's Spenser: The Politics of Reading* (Ithaca: Cornell University Press, 1984), 224–25.

10. FRIEDRICH SCHLEIERMACHER AND ROMANTIC THEOLOGY

1. For a characterization of the Romantic influence on theology, see Paul Tillich, *Perspectives on 19th and 20th Century Protestant Theology,* ed. C. Braaten (New York: Harper & Row, 1967), 76–89.

2. "Credo" first appeared on pages 109–11 in the journal *Athenaeum: Eine Zeitschrift,* edited by August Wilhelm Schlegel and Friedrich Schlegel, in 1798. The English translation is by Ruth Drucilla Richardson, whose correct translation of the third article (*Ich glaube an . . . Freundschaft der Maenner . . .* = friendship with men) we have expanded to read "friendship with men and women" in order to avoid misinterpretations of Schleiermacher's position.

3. "*10. Lass dich geluesten nach der Maenner Bildung, Kunst, Weisheit, und Ehre.*" (10. You shall desire for yourself the same education, art, wisdom, and honor that men can attain.) Schleiermacher did not, however, think that women should use their talents or learning in public life: see discussion below.

4. A Catholic theologian of the Romantic period, Franz von Baader (1765–1841), writes even more passionately than Schleiermacher about "infinite humanity" and "limitations of gender." For a discussion of von Baader, see the first edition of this *Women and Religion* sourcebook (New York: Harper & Row, 1977), 177–79, 187–90.

5. Friendship, for Schleiermacher, "originates in the reciprocal completion and confirmation of individuality." See *Lebenswelt der Romantik. Dokumente Romantischen Denkens und Seins,* ed. Richard Benz (Muenchen: Nymphenburger Verlag, 1948), 156.

6. See the excerpt from *Christmas Eve* below.

7. See the excerpt from *Christmas Eve* below. Richard R. Niebuhr argues, "The true function of Josef is not to negate or to affirm the various conceptions of the human spirit expounded, but to represent the common spirit uniting and

inspiriting the assembly." Richard K. Niebuhr, *Schleiermacher on Christ and Religion* (New York: Scribner's, 1964), 37–43. Our interpretation differs from Niebuhr's by stressing that Josef is paired specifically with Sophie and that his words should be regarded as expressing her feelings. Hence, in contrast to Niebuhr, we place a greater emphasis on the value of sheer childlikeness (and new birth) in Schleiermacher's thought.

8. "What is the celebration of Jesus' infancy, but the distinct acknowledgement of the immediate union of the divine with the being of a child . . . ?" See the excerpt from *Christmas Eve* below.

9. See the useful discussion and references in Patricia Guenther-Gleason, "Schleiermacher's Feminist Impulses in the Context of His Later Work," in *Schleiermacher and Feminism: Sources, Evaluations, and Responses,* ed. Iain G. Nicol (Lewiston/Queenston: Edwin Mellen Press, 1992), 114–18.

10. Schleiermacher's *Ten Commandments [On Sexual Love and Marriage]* were first published in *Athenaeum* (1798). The translation that appears in this volume was prepared by Ruth Drucilla Richardson. The editor has chosen to add "on sexual love and marriage" to the title in order to clarify the author's intention and context.

11. In Benz, ed., *Lebenswelt der Romantik,* 156.

12. Schleiermacher's *Ten Commandments* appeared as part of a larger text that he wrote specifically for "noble women" (*Idee zu Einem Katechismus der Vernunft Fuer Edel Frauen*). The word *edel* can have a mere psychological meaning ("high quality"), but behind *"edel"* there is the social group of *"Adel"* (nobility) whose interests are symbolized through class-appropriate behaviors.

13. Guenther-Gleason, "Schleiermacher's Feminist Impulses," 104, 106, 114–18; see also Sheila Briggs, "Schleiermacher and the Construction of the Gendered Self," in *Schleiermacher and Feminism,* 88, 93.

14. Guenther-Gleason, "Schleiermacher's Feminist Impulses," 125, cf. 127.

15. Dawn De Vries, "Schleiermacher's *Christmas Eve Dialogue:* Bourgeois Ideology or Feminist Theology?," *Journal of Religion* 69 (1989): 169–83, esp. pp. 180–82. De Vries argues against what she considers the excessively negative evaluation of Schleiermacher's views on women by Marilyn Chapin Massey, *Feminine Soul: The Fate of an Ideal* (Boston: Beacon Press, 1985), esp. pp. 136–46.

11. COMMUNITARIAN MOVEMENTS IN AMERICA: SHAKERS, THE ONEIDA COMMUNITY, AND MORMONS

1. Raymond Muncy, *Sex and Marriage in Utopian Communities—Nineteenth-Century America* (Bloomington: Indiana University Press, 1973), 8.

2. Lawrence Foster, *Women, Family, and Utopia: Communal Experiments of the Shakers, the Oneida Community, and the Mormons* (Syracuse: Syracuse University Press, 1991), 26–27.

3. Edward Deming Andrews, *The People Called Shakers: A Search for the Perfect Society* (Oxford: University Press, 1953; New York: Dover Publications, 1963), 5, 7–9, 11–12.

4. Stephen J. Stein, *The Shaker Experience in America: A History of the United Society of Believers* (New Haven/London: Yale University Press, 1992), xvi.

5. Stein, *The Shaker Experience,* 25.

6. Stein, *The Shaker Experience,* 43.

7. Stein, *The Shaker Experience,* 67.

8. Stein, *The Shaker Experience,* 76, 117.

9. Jean McMahon Humez, ed., *Gifts of Power: The Writings of Rebecca Jackson, Black Visionary, Shaker Eldress* (Amherst: University of Massachusetts Press, 1981).

10. Stein, *The Shaker Experience,* 256.

11. Calvin Green and Seth Y. Wells, *A Summary View of the Millennial Church or United Society of Believers (Commonly Called Shakers)* (Albany: Packard & Van Benthuysen, 1823), 9–10.

12. Green and Wells, *A Summary View,* 130. Adam and Eve's sexual sin appears to be that they were led into sexual intercourse "unseasonably" (pp. 130–31), a view that relates to Clement of Alexandria's understanding, as seen in Chapter 2 in this volume.

13. Green and Wells, *A Summary View,* 135. Note also the words of Shaker elder Frederick Evans in 1853: the "lust of generation is the one great evil that marred all the designs and works of God" (from Evans's *Tests of Divine Inspiration,* cited in Sally L. Kitch, *Chaste Liberation: Celibacy and Female Cultural Status* [Urbana/Chicago: University of Illinois Press, 1989], 51).

14. Green and Wells, *A Summary View,* 138.

15. Green and Wells, *A Summary View,* 162. For their interesting refutations of standard biblical verses appealed to by the supporters of marriage, see pp. 153–54, 157–59, 162. Likewise, Shakers rejected private property; inheriting land is appropriate only for those of "flesh and blood" who cannot "inherit the Kingdom of Heaven" (see Kitch, *Chaste Liberation,* 53).

16. Green and Wells, *A Summary View,* 216.

17. Green and Wells, *A Summary View,* 219.

18. Foster, *Women, Family, and Utopia,* 18–19.

19. Marjorie Proctor-Smith, *Women in Shaker Community and Worship: A Feminist Analysis of the Uses of Religious Symbolism* (Lewiston, N.Y.: Edwin Mellen Press, 1985), 162–63.

20. Foster, *Women, Family, and Utopia,* 31.

21. Constance Noyes Robertson, ed., *Oneida Community: An Autobiography, 1851–1876* (Syracuse: Syracuse University Press, 1970), 23.

22. *Circular,* March 21, 1870, in Robertson, *Oneida Community,* 283.

23. Noyes does not seem to have envisioned the adoption of homosexual relationships, however. See the selection that follows.

24. Richard J. DeMaria, "The Oneida Community's Concept of Christian Love," Ph.D. dissertation, University of Saint Michael's College, Toronto, Ontario, Canada, 1973.

25. Muncy, *Sex and Marriage,* 183. Later the community went in for scientific propagation or "stirpiculture," beginning in 1869. During the first ten years of the

program, fifty-eight children were born to selected couples at Oneida, nine of them fathered by Noyes himself. See Muncy, *Sex and Marriage,* 187–91, and Robertson, *Oneida Community,* 335–55. Noyes's own failure at "male continence" with a woman he presumably loved is described by Ernest R. Sandeen, "John Humphrey Noyes as the New Adam," *Church History* 40 (1971): 85–90.

26. Muncy, *Sex and Marriage,* 176–77.

27. Children were raised communally in an effort to rule out the notion of the parents' "ownership" of their offspring. See Robertson, *Oneida Community,* 311–34. Noyes believed that in traditional marriage, the wife and children were "owned" by the male head of the household; exalting "family spirit" merely made selfishness (insofar as owning personal property led to selfishness) appear to be a virtue. See Pierrepont B. Noyes, *A Goodly Heritage* (New York: Rinehart & Company, 1958), 4. Noyes's socialist views exerted a strong influence on his notions of marriage and the family.

28. Robertson, *Oneida Community,* chap. 10.

29. John Humphrey Noyes, *History of American Socialisms* (Philadelphia: J. P. Lippincott, 1870), 636.

30. Robertson, *Oneida Community,* 294.

31. Foster, *Women, Family, and Utopia,* 92.

32. *Circular,* March 18, 1872, in Robertson, *Oneida Community,* 284.

33. *Circular,* January 23, 1858, in Robertson, *Oneida Community,* 300.

34. Foster, *Women, Family, and Utopia,* 123–28, 153.

35. Foster, *Women, Family, and Utopia,* 196. The Mormon notion that marriage could be "spiritual" was rejected by the Shakers: see Kitch, *Chaste Liberation,* 85.

36. Foster, *Women, Family, and Utopia,* 131–33.

37. Foster, *Women, Family, and Utopia,* 134, quotation on p. 158, from a report of Eudocia Baldwin Marsh, "When the Mormons Dwelt Among Us," *The Bellman,* April 1, 1916, p. 375.

38. Foster, *Women, Family, and Utopia,* 158.

39. Foster, *Women, Family, and Utopia,* 187.

40. Joan Iverson, "Feminist Implications of Mormon Polygyny," *Feminist Studies* 10 (1984): 508; Julie Dunfey, "'Living the Principle' of Plural Marriage: Mormon Women, Utopia, and Female Sexuality in the Nineteenth Century," *Feminist Studies* 10 (1984): 529–32; for Mormon men's arguments, see David J. Whittaker, "The Bone in the Throat: Orson Pratt and the Public Announcement of Plural Marriage," *Western Historical Quarterly* 18 (1987): 308–10.

41. Foster, *Women, Family, and Utopia,* 199, 209–13.

42. Foster, *Women, Family, and Utopia,* 182.

43. Iverson, "Feminist Implications," 505, 510–12.

44. Foster, *Women, Family, and Utopia,* 235.

12. MOVEMENTS FOR RELIGIOUS AND SOCIAL REFORM IN NINETEENTH- AND TWENTIETH-CENTURY AMERICA

1. On the influence of Sarah Grimké's *Letters* on her contemporaries, see Elizabeth Ann Bartlett, *Liberty, Equality, Sorority: The Origins and Interpretation of*

American Feminist Thought: Francis Wright, Sarah Grimké, and Margaret Fuller (Brooklyn: Carlson Publishing, 1994), 5.

2. Gerda Lerner, *The Grimké Sisters from South Carolina: Pioneers for Woman's Rights and Abolition* (New York: Schocken Books, 1971), 187–88.

3. For Angelina's writings against slavery, see Angelina E. Grimké, *An Appeal to the Christian Women of the South* (Westport, Conn.: Negro Universities Press, 1970 [1836]); and see Sarah Grimké and Angelina Grimké, *The Public Years of Sarah and Angelina Grimké: Selected Writings, 1835–1839*, ed. Larry Ceplair (New York: Columbia University Press, 1991). On the radical religious elements of the Grimkés' opposition to slavery, see Frank G. Kirkpatrick, "From Shackles to Liberation: Religion, the Grimké Sisters, and Dissent," in *Women, Religion, and Social Change,* eds. Yvonne Yazbeck Haddad and Ellison Banks Findly (Albany: State University of New York Press, 1985), 433–55.

4. Lerner, *The Grimké Sisters,* 121.

5. Dorothy C. Bass, "'In Christian Firmness and Christian Meekness': Feminism and Pacifism in Antebellum America," in *Immaculate and Powerful: The Female in Sacred Image and Social Reality,* eds. Clarissa W. Atkinson, Constance H. Buchanan, and Margaret R. Miles (Boston: Beacon Press, 1985), 213–19.

6. For discussions of this episode, see Eleanor Flexner, *Century of Struggle: The Woman's Rights Movement in the United States* (New York: Atheneum Press, 1973), 45–49; and Blanche Glassman Hersh, "To Make the World Better: Protestant Women in the Abolitionist Movement," in *Triumph over Silence: Women in Protestant History,* ed. Richard L. Greaves (Westport, Conn.: Greenwood Press, 1985), 176–85.

7. G. H. Garnes and D. L. Drummond, eds., *Letters of Theodore Dwight Weld, Angelina Grimké Weld, and Sarah Grimké, 1822–1844* (New York: D. Appleton-Century Co., 1934), I: 424.

8. Garnes and Drummond, eds., *Letters,* 1:427.

9. Lerner, *The Grimké Sisters,* 203.

10. Hersh, "To Make the World Better," 192–93.

11. Lerner, *The Grimké Sisters,* 366.

12. See Bartlett, *Liberty,* 74–78.

13. For example, Grimké's assessment of Genesis 2 as a "recapitulation" of Genesis 1 demonstrates her lack of awareness of the scholarly opinion accepted later in the century that these chapters are the product of different authors. On Sarah's intellectual background, see Bartlett, *Liberty,* 61–67.

14. See the selection that follows.

15. For an extended discussion of Stanton's views on religion, see Mary D. Pellauer, *Toward a Tradition of Feminist Theology: The Religious Social Thought of Elizabeth Cady Stanton, Susan B. Anthony, and Anna Howard Shaw* (Brooklyn: Carlson Publishing, 1991), 15–152; Aileen Kraditor, *The Ideas of the Woman Suffrage Movement, 1890–1920* (Garden City: Doubleday, 1971), 65, 76 n. 2; and Elisabeth Griffith, *In Her Own Right: The Life of Elizabeth Cady Stanton* (New York: Oxford University Press, 1984), 210–13.

16. Elizabeth Cady Stanton, *Eighty Years and More: Reminiscences, 1815–1897* (New York: Schocken Books, 1971 [1898]), chap. 2.

17. Stanton, *Eighty Years,* 80.

18. Stanton, *Eighty Years,* 81.

19. Stanton, *Eighty Years,* 357.

20. Kraditor, *Ideas,* 75.

21. See William O'Neill, *Everyone Was Brave: The Rise and Fall of Feminism in America* (Chicago: Quadrangle Books, 1969), arguing that those who wanted to work only for suffrage overemphasized the changes that the vote would bring and neglected the psychological, social, and economic bonds that imprisoned women.

22. See Zillah R. Eisenstein, *The Radical Future of Liberal Feminism* (New York: Longman, 1981), 155–67.

23. See Rebecca Johnson, "A Historical Addendum," in *Women's Spirit Bonding,* eds. Janet Kalven and Mary I. Buckley (New York: Pilgrim Press, 1984), 76–80; Elizabeth V. Spelman, *Inessential Woman: Problems of Exclusion in Feminist Thought* (Boston: Beacon Press, 1988), 8, 12; and Griffith, *In Her Own Right,* 111, 119, 124, 129, 133–34, 205–6.

24. E. C. Stanton, S. B. Anthony, and M. J. Gage, eds., *The History of Woman Suffrage* (Rochester: Susan B. Anthony, 1881–1922), 1: 806.

25. See Ellen DuBois, "The Limitations of Sisterhood: Elizabeth Cady Stanton and Division in the American Suffrage Movement, 1875–1902," in *Women and the Structure of Society,* eds. Barbara J. Harris and JoAnn K. McNamara (Durham, N.C.: Duke University Press, 1984), 161–64; and Susan E. Hill, "The Woman's Bible: Reformulating Tradition," *Radical Religion* 3, no. 2 (1977): 23–30.

26. See Pellauer, *Toward a Tradition of Feminist Theology,* 22–49.

27. Stanton, *Eighty Years,* 390–93.

28. Griffith, *In Her Own Right,* 212.

29. See DuBois, "The Limitations of Sisterhood," 167.

30. Kraditor, *Ideas,* 69–70.

31. For an example of a contemporary adaptation of Stanton's hermeneutical stance, see Elisabeth Schüssler Fiorenza, "Toward a Feminist Biblical Hermeneutics: Biblical Interpretation and Liberation Theology," in *The Challenge of Liberation Theology: A First World Response,* eds. Brian Mahan and L. Dale Richesin (Maryknoll, N.Y.: Orbis Books, 1981), 91–112.

32. See, for example, Mary Maples Dunn, "Saints and Sisters: Congregational and Quaker Women in the Early Colonial Period," in *Women in American Religion,* ed. Janet Wilson James (Philadelphia: University of Pennsylvania Press, 1980), 27–46.

33. See especially Ann Douglas, *The Feminization of American Culture* (New York: Alfred A. Knopf, 1977).

34. See Martha Tomhave Blauvelt, "Women and Revivalism," in *Women and Religion in America—Volume I: The Nineteenth Century,* eds. Rosemary Radford Ruether and Rosemary Skinner Keller (San Francisco: Harper & Row, 1981), 1–45.

35. For a brief survey, see Janet Wilson James, "Women in American Religious History: An Overview," in *Women in American Religion,* 11–16.

36. Barbara Welter, "She Hath Done What She Could: Protestant Women's Missionary Careers in Nineteenth-Century America," in *Women in American Religion,* 111–25, esp. p. 119.

37. Mary Farrell Bednarowski, "Outside the Mainstream: Women's Religion and Women Religious Leaders in Nineteenth-Century America," *Journal of the American Academy of Religion* 48 (1980): 207–31. It is interesting to speculate whether women were pushed to the "outside" by virtue of their sex or whether they were attracted to these nonmainstream movements because the boundaries were more porous. (We thank Evelyn Kirkley for posing this problem in such an engaging way.)

38. See Bert James Loewenberg and Ruth Bogin, eds., *Black Women in Nineteenth-Century American Life: Their Words, Their Thoughts, Their Feelings* (University Park: Pennsylvania State University Press, 1976). For an overview of the history of black women in American Christianity, see Emilie M. Townes, "Black Women: From Slavery to Womanist Liberation," in Rosemary Radford Ruether and Rosemary Skinner Keller, eds., *In Our Own Voices; Four Centuries of American Women's Religious Writing* (San Francisco: HarperSanFrancisco, 1995), 151–205.

39. Jarena Lee, *Religious Experience and Journal of Mrs. Jarena Lee, Giving an Account of Her Call to Preach the Gospel* (Philadelphia, 1849 [1836]), 11–12.

40. Lee, *Religious Experience,* 18.

41. Lee, *Religious Experience,* 23.

42. Lee, *Religious Experience,* 23.

43. Lee, *Religious Experience,* 97.

44. Nancy Hardesty, Lucille Sider Dayton, and Donald W. Dayton, "Women in the Holiness Movement: Feminism in the Evangelical Tradition," in *Women of Spirit: Female Leadership in the Jewish and Christian Traditions,* eds. Rosemary Ruether and Eleanor McLaughlin (New York: Simon & Schuster, 1979), 226–54.

45. Phoebe Palmer, *Promise of the Father; or A Neglected Specialty of the Last Days* (New York: W. C. Palmer, Jr., 1872 [1859]), 23, 126–27.

46. Palmer, *Promise of the Father,* 37.

47. Palmer, *Promise of the Father,* 330.

48. Palmer, *Promise of the Father,* 1.

49. Palmer, *Promise of the Father,* 8.

50. Palmer, *Promise of the Father,* 1–2.

51. See the documents pertaining to White in *Women and Religion in America,* 79–81.

52. Susan Hill Lindley, "The Ambiguous Feminism of Mary Baker Eddy," *Journal of Religion* 64 (1984): 323.

53. Lindley, "Ambiguous Feminism of Mary Baker Eddy," 323.

54. Lindley, "Ambiguous Feminism of Mary Baker Eddy," 326–27. For other useful discussions of Mary Baker Eddy, see Susan M. Setta, "Denial of the Female— Affirmation of the Feminine: The Father-Mother God of Mary Baker Eddy,"

in *Beyond Androcentrism: New Essays on Women and Religion,* ed. Rita M. Gross (Missoula, Mont.: Scholars Press, 1977), 289–304; Christine Trevett, "Women, God, and Mary Baker Eddy," *Religion* 14 (1984): 143–53; Jean A. McDonald, "Mary Baker Eddy and the Nineteenth-Century 'Public' Woman," *Journal of Feminist Studies in Religion* 2 (1986): 89–111.

55. Daniel Mark Epstein, *Sister Aimee: The Life of Aimee Semple McPherson* (New York/San Diego/London: Harcourt Brace Jovanovich, 1993), 440.

56. Edith Blumhofer, *Aimee Semple McPherson: Everybody's Sister* (Grand Rapids, Mich.: William B. Eerdmans, 1993), 17, 190–91, 310.

57. Blumhofer, *Aimee Semple McPherson,* 263–64.

58. Blumhofer, *Aimee Semple McPherson,* 233–35.

59. Blumhofer, *Aimee Semple McPherson,* 16, 183, 233, 266–67.

60. Blumhofer, *Aimee Semple McPherson,* 382.

61. Blumhofer, *Aimee Semple McPherson,* 4.

62. Blumhofer, *Aimee Semple McPherson* 17, 387–88.

63. On nineteenth-century arguments concerning the ordination of women, see Barbara Brown Zikmund, "Biblical Arguments and Women's Place in the Church," in *The Bible and Social Reform,* ed. Ernest R. Sandeen (Philadelphia: Fortress Press, 1982), 85–104. For useful accounts of the history of women's ordination, see Rosemary R. Ruether, "Christianity and Women in the Modern World," in *Today's Women in World Religions,* ed. Arvind Sharma, intro. Katherine K. Young (Albany: State University of New York Press, 1994), 265–301; and Barbara Brown Zikmund, "Women and Ordination," in *In Our Own Voices,* 291–340.

64. For an interesting summary of the types of argumentation used in the nineteenth century by both "pro" and "anti" forces, see Barbara Brown Zikmund, "The Struggle for the Right to Preach," in *Women and Religion in America,* 208–41.

65. *Inter Insigniores, Acta Apostolicae sedis* 69 (1977): 98–116, passim. For essays sharply critical of nearly all aspects of the declaration, see Leonard Swidler and Arlene Swidler, eds., *Women Priests: A Catholic Commentary on the Vatican Declaration* (New York: Paulist Press, 1977).

66. *Ordinatio Sacerdotalis, Acta Apostolicae sedis* 86 (1994): 545–48; trans. in *The Pope Speaks* 39 (1994): 319–21.

13. TWENTIETH-CENTURY SEXUAL ISSUES: CONTRACEPTION, ABORTION, AND HOMOSEXUALITY

1. Augustine, *On Marriage and Concupiscence* 1.17.15; see Chapter 4.

2. On Sanchez, "ensoulment," and the church's use of new scientific knowledge regarding conception in the nineteenth century, see John T. Noonan, Jr., *Contraception: A History of Its Treatment by the Catholic Theologians and Canonists,* enlarged ed. (Cambridge, Mass.: Belknap Press of Harvard University Press, 1986), pts. 3 and 4. The Vatican continues to invoke modern biological and genetic science in its opposition to abortion. See John Paul II, *Evangelium Vitae,* section 60 (March 25, 1995).

3. The vulcanization of rubber in the midnineteenth century had made the mass availability of condoms a reality; later in the nineteenth century, the modern diaphragm was developed. See Noonan, *Contraception,* 469, 485.

4. For papal pronouncements on these and other themes, see William Faherty, S. J., *The Destiny of Modern Woman in the Light of Papal Teaching* (Westminster, Md.: Newman Press, 1950), chaps. 2–5.

5. Margaret Sanger, *My Fight for Birth Control* (New York: Farrar & Rinehart, 1931), 213–25.

6. Although a papal encyclical does not possess the same infallible status as does a dogmatic pronouncement—that is, the salvation of the individual does not depend on adherence to its precepts—the Vatican has always urged that faithful Catholics accept the teachings of the encyclicals as binding on their lives.

7. Such as "Woman's Duties in Social and Political Life," printed in *Catholic Mind,* December 1945; "Woman's Apostolate," in *Catholic Mind,* November 1949; and "Morality in Marriage," in *Catholic Mind,* January 1952.

8. The text of this famous speech can be found in *Catholic Mind,* January 1952.

9. For the discussion at Vatican II regarding contraception, see "The Church in the Modern World," *The Documents of Vatican II,* ed. Walter M. Abbott, S.J. (New York: Guild Press, 1966), 249–58. Also see Peter Riga, *Sexuality and Marriage in Recent Catholic Thought* (Washington, D.C.: Corpus Books, 1969) for a discussion.

10. The full texts of the Majority and Minority Reports and the *Humanae Vitae* are in Daniel Callahan, ed., *The Catholic Case for Contraception* (New York: Macmillan, 1969).

11. Paul VI, *Humanae Vitae,* citing from sections 4, 7, 10, 11, 14, 16.

12. John Paul II, *Evangelium Vitae,* citing from sections 2, 12, 13, 21, 57, 97, 100.

13. Articles by Catholic clergy and laypersons critical of the Vatican's position are in Callahan, *The Catholic Case for Contraception.* Especially recommended is Michael Novak's "Frequent, Even Daily, Communion," 92–102.

14. Pius XI, *Casti Connubii,* citing from sections 63, 64.

15. Paul VI, *Humanae Vitae* 14.

16. On John Paul II's role as archbishop of Cracow on the Vatican II study commission and his behind-the-scenes hand in the drafting of *Humanae Vitae,* see "The Polish Roots of 'Humanae Vitae,'" *Newsweek,* U.S. ed. (April 10, 1995).

17. John Paul II, *Evangelium Vitae,* citing from sections 44, 58, 62, 70, 72, 73.

18. See the selection that follows; see also Beverly Wildung Harrison, *Our Right to Choose: Toward a New Ethic of Abortion* (Boston: Beacon Press, 1983).

19. Internal note: The Christian natural-law tradition developed because many Christians understood that the power of moral reason inhered in humans beings *qua* human beings, not merely in the understanding that comes from being Christian. Those who follow natural-law methods address moral issues from the standpoint of what options appear rationally compelling, given present reflection, rather than from theological claims alone. My own moral theological method is congenial to certain of these natural-law assumptions. Roman

Catholic natural-law teaching, however, has become internally incoherent by insisting that in some matters of morality the *teaching authority* of the hierarchy must be taken as the proper definition of what is rational. This replacement of reasoned reflection by ecclesial authority seems to this Protestant to offend against what we must mean by moral reasoning on best understanding. I would argue that a moral theology cannot forfeit final judgment or even penultimate judgment on moral matters to anything except *fully deliberated contemporary communal consensus*. On the abortion issue, this of course would mean women would be consulted in a degree that reflects their numbers in the Catholic Church. No a priori claims to authoritative moral reason are ever possible and if those affected are not consulted, the teaching *cannot* claim rationality.

20. Internal note: See Paul D. Simmons' essay, chapter 18 in this book *[Abortion: The Moral Issues]*.

21. Internal note: H. Richard Niebuhr often warned his theological compatriots about abstracting acts from the life-project in which they are imbedded, but this warning is much neglected in the writings of Christian moralists. Cf. "The Christian Church in the World Crises," *Christianity and Society,* vol. VI, 1941.

22. Internal note: We know now that the birth control pill does not always work by preventing fertilization of the ova by the sperm. Frequently, the pill causes the wall of the uterus to expel the newly fertilized ova. The point here is that, from a biological point of view, there is no point in a procreative process that can be taken as a clear dividing line on which to pin neat moral distinctions.

23. Internal note: The most conspicuous example of corporate involvement in contraceptive failure was the famous Dalkan Shield scandal. Note also that the manufacturer of the Dalkan Shield is still dumping its dangerous and ineffective product on family-planning programs of so-called Third World (over-exploited) countries.

24. Internal note: Helmut Thielicke, *The Ethics of Sex* (New York: Harper & Row, 1964), 199–247. Compare pp. 210 and 226ff. Barth's position on abortion is a bit more complicated than I can elaborate here, which is why one will find him quoted on both sides of the debate. Barth's method allows him to argue that any given radical human act could turn out to be "the will of God" in a given context or setting. We may at any time be given "permission" by God's radical freedom to do what was not before permissible. My point here is that Barth exposits this possible exception in such a traditional, prohibitory context that I do not believe it appropriate to cite him on the pro-choice side of the debate. In my opinion, no woman could ever accept the convoluted way in which Barth's biblical exegesis opens the door (a slight crack) to woman's full humanity. His reasoning on these questions simply demonstrates what deep difficulty the Christian tradition's exegetical tradition is in with respect to the full humanity and moral agency of women. (See chapter 10 in this book *[Abortion: The Moral Issues].)*

25. Internal note: Cf. my "When Fruitfulness and Blessedness Diverge," *Religion and Life,* 1972. (My views on the seriousness of misogyny as an historical force have deepened since I wrote this essay.)

26. Internal note: Marie Augusta Neal, "Sociology and Sexuality: A Feminist Perspective," *Christianity and Crisis,* Vol. 39, No. 8 (May 14, 1979).
27. Internal note: For a feminist theology of relationship, see Carter Heyward, *Toward the Redemption of God: A Theology of Mutual Relation* (Washington, D.C.: University Press of America, 1982).
28. Internal note: Neal, "Sociology and Sexuality," op. cit. This article is of critical importance in discussions of the theology and morality of abortion.
29. Internal note: I am well aware that Catholic moral theology opens up several ways for faithful Catholics to challenge the teaching office of the Church on moral questions. However, I remain unsatisfied that these qualifications of inerrancy in moral matters stand up in situations of moral controversy. If freedom of conscience does not function de jure, should it be claimed as existent in principle?
30. Internal note: A theory is crassly utilitarian only if it fails to grant equal moral worth to all persons in the calculation of social consequences—as, for example, when some people's financial well-being is weighted more than someone else's basic physical existence. I do *not* mean to criticize any type of utilitarian moral theory that weighs the actual consequences of actions. In fact, I believe no moral theory is adequate if it does not have a strong utilitarian component.
31. For some recent works on this topic, see Michel Foucault, *The Use of Pleasure: Volume 2 of The History of Sexuality,* trans. Robert Hurley (New York: Pantheon Books, 1985); Foucault, *The Care of the Self: Volume 3 of The History of Sexuality,* trans. Robert Hurley (New York: Pantheon Books, 1986); David M. Halperin, *One Hundred Years of Homosexuality and Other Essays on Greek Love* (New York/London: Routledge, 1990); various essays in David M. Halperin, John J. Winkler, and Froma I. Zeitlin, eds., *Before Sexuality: The Construction of Erotic Experience in the Ancient Greek World* (Princeton, N.J.: Princeton University Press, 1990); John J. Winkler, *The Constraints of Desire: The Anthropology of Sex and Gender in Ancient Greece* (New York/London: Routledge, 1990); John Boswell, *Christianity, Social Tolerance, and Homosexuality: Gay People in Western Europe from the Beginning of the Christian Era to the Fourteenth Century* (Chicago/London: University of Chicago Press, 1980); and Boswell, *Same-Sex Unions in Premodern Europe* (New York: Vintage Books, 1995).
32. Thomas Aquinas, *Summa Theologica,* 2a.2ae.154.11–12.
33. *Declaration on Certain Questions Concerning Sexual Ethics* 8.
34. See Bruce Williams, O.P., "Homosexuality: The New Vatican Statement," *Theological Studies* 48 (1987): 260; critiqued by Gerald D. Coleman, S.S., "The Vatican Statement on Homosexuality," *Theological Studies* 48 (1987): 727–34, reprinted in *Homosexuality and Religion and Philosophy,* ed. Wayne R. Dynes and Stephen Donaldson (New York/London: Garland Publishing, 1992), 143–50.
35. *The Pastoral Care of Homosexual Persons,* citing from sections 7, 9, 17, 10, 11, 12.
36. Karl Barth, "The Doctrine of Creation," *Church Dogmatics* 3, sec. 4, ed. G. W. Bromiley and T. F. Torrance (Edinburgh: T. & T. Clark, 1961), 166.

37. For an historical overview of this reexamination, see Robert Nugent and Jeannine Gramick, "Homosexuality: Protestant, Catholic, and Jewish Issues—A Fishbone Tale," in *Homosexuality and Religion,* ed. Richard Hasbany (New York/London: Harrington Park Press, 1989), 7–46.
38. Nugent and Gramick, "Homosexuality," 21; and see Ralph W. Weltage, *The Same Sex: An Appraisal of Homosexuality* (Philadelphia: Pilgrim Press, 1969).
39. See John J. Carey, ed., *The Sexuality Debate in North American Churches, 1988–1995: Controversies, Unresolved Issues, Future Prospects* (Lewiston, N.Y.: Edwin Mellen Press, 1995).
40. "Report of the Commission on Homosexuality of the Episcopal Diocese of Michigan" (Detroit: Episcopal Diocese of Michigan, 1973), 4.
41. Resolution A–104sa, cited from *Episcopal Life,* 1991, p. 6. In 1994, the General Convention of the Episcopal Church discussed a study document on the subject of human sexuality that affirmed a traditional view of marriage but noted that there were discontinuities between the church's teaching and the experience of some Episcopalians.
42. The General Assembly Special Committee on Human Sexuality, Presbyterian Church (U.S.A.), "Keeping Body and Soul Together: Sexuality, Spirituality, and Social Justice." A document prepared for the 203rd General Assembly (1991), 19.023, 3, p. 168.
43. Division for Church in Society, Department for Studies of the Evangelical Lutheran Church in America, "The Church and Human Sexuality: A Lutheran Perspective" (Chicago: Evangelical Lutheran Church in America, 1993), 16.
44. For a broader discussion of feminist liberation theology, see Chapter Fourteen in this volume.
45. For examples, see Bernadette J. Brooten, *Early Christian Responses to Female Homoeroticism and Their Historical Context* (Chicago: University of Chicago Press, 1996); Robert L. Brawley, ed., *Biblical Ethics and Homosexuality: Listening to Scripture* (Louisville, Ky.: Westminster John Knox Press, 1996); Dale B. Martin, "Heterosexism and the Interpretation of Romans 1:18–32," *Biblical Interpretation* 3 (1995): 332–55; George R. Edwards, *Gay/Lesbian Liberation: A Biblical Perspective* (New York: Pilgrim Press, 1984); and Robin Scroggs, *The New Testament and Homosexuality: Contextual Background for Contemporary Debate* (Philadelphia: Fortress Press, 1983).
46. For examples, see James B. Nelson, *Embodiment: An Approach to Sexuality and Christian Theology* (Minneapolis: Augsburg Publishing House, 1978); D. J. Atkinson, *Homosexuals in the Christian Fellowship* (Grand Rapids, Mich.: William B. Eerdmans Publishing, 1979); Robert Nugent, ed., *A Challenge to Love: Gay and Lesbian Catholics in the Church* (New York: Crossroad, 1983); John McNeill, *The Church and the Homosexual,* 3rd ed. (Boston: Beacon Press, 1988); John McNeill, *Taking a Chance on God: Liberating Theology for Gays, Lesbians, and Their Lovers, Families, and Friends* (Boston: Beacon Press, 1988); Dynes and Donaldson, eds., *Homosexuality and Religion and Philosophy;* and Letha Dawson Scanzoni and Virginia Ramey Mollenkott, *Is the Homosexual My Neighbor?,* rev. ed. (San Francisco: HarperSanFrancisco, 1994).

47. See, for example, Beverly Wildung Harrison, *Making the Connections: Essays in Feminist Social Ethics,* ed. Carol S. Robb (Boston: Beacon Press, 1985); Carter Heyward, *Speaking of Christ: A Lesbian Feminist Voice,* ed. Ellen C. Davis (New York: Pilgrim Press, 1989); Heyward, *Our Passion for Justice* (New York: Pilgrim Press, 1984); Heyward, *Touching Our Strength* (San Francisco: Harper & Row, 1989); Heyward, *Staying Power: Reflections on Gender, Justice, and Compassion* (Cleveland: Pilgrim Press, 1995); Carter Heyward, Mary E. Hunt et al., "Lesbianism and Feminist Theology," *Journal of Feminist Studies in Religion* 2, no. 2 (Fall 1986): 95–106; and Mary E. Hunt, *Fierce Tenderness: A Feminist Theology of Friendship* (New York: Crossroad, 1991).

48. For further discussion of natural law as a basis of Christian theology, see the selection in Chapter 5.

49. Mary McClintock Fulkerson, "Gender—Being It or Doing It? The Church, Homosexuality, and the Politics of Identity," *Union Seminary Quarterly Review* 47 (1993): 30.

50. McClintock Fulkerson, "Gender," 31, 38–43, passim.

51. Internal note: For constructive moral epistemologies that build on creative insights from natural law tradition, see Beverly Wildung Harrison, *Making the Connections: Essays in Feminist Social Ethics,* edited by Carol S. Robb (Boston: Beacon, 1985), especially the introduction by Carol Robb and 3–21, 115–34, and 253–63; Anthony Battaglia, *Toward a Reformulation of Natural Law* (New York: Seabury, 1981); Daniel C. Maguire, *The Moral Choice* (New York: Doubleday, 1978); Margaret Farley, "New Patterns of Relationship: Beginnings of a Moral Revolution," in *Woman: New Dimensions,* edited by Walter J. Burghardt (New York: Paulist, 1976); and Barbara Hilkert Andolsen, Christine E. Gudorf, and Mary D. Pellauer, eds., *Women's Consciousness, Women's Conscience* (San Francisco: Harper & Row, 1985), especially 211ff.

52. Internal note: See Samuel Laeuchli, *Power and Sexuality: The Emergence of Canon Law at the Synod of Elvira* (Philadelphia: Temple University Press, 1972); Anne Llewellyn Barstow [*Witchcraze* (San Francisco: HarperSanFrancisco, 1994)]; and the classic, infamous, *Malleus Maleficarum (Hammer of Witches),* translated with introduction by the Rev. Montague Summers (New York: Dover, 1971). Written by monks Sprenger and Kraemer, it is indicative of the extent to which christian assumptions about the natural as moral are steeped in misogyny. See also Harrison on the relation between hatred of women and fear of homosexuality, "Misogyny and Homophobia: The Unexplored Connections," in *Making the Connections,* 135–51.

53. Internal note: At least one seminary (The Episcopal Seminary in Alexandria, Virginia) requires all of its students to sign a pledge that they will not engage in sexual activity outside of marriage while they are students at the seminary. And at least one psychiatrist who screens candidates for ordination in a liberal Episcopal diocese has indicated to those whom he interviews that their sexual behavior is *the* critical factor in his judging their fitness for ordination. While he expresses interest in hearing details of *heterosexual* lives, he makes no secret of his special disdain for gaymen and lesbians, who in his judgment,

as in the judgment of the Episcopal Church at large, are unfit for ordained ministry.

54. Internal note: For attention to interiorized spirituality as a moral problem, see Dorothee Sölle and Shirley A. Cloyes, *To Work and to Love: A Theology of Creation* (Philadelphia: Fortress, 1984), as well as other pieces by Sölle. This same theme is explored in the Amanecida Collective's *Revolutionary Forgiveness: Feminist Reflections on Nicaragua* (Maryknoll, N.Y.: Orbis, 1987); Gustavo Gutierrez, *The Power of the Poor in History*, translated by Robert Barr (Maryknoll, N.Y.: Orbis, 1983); and Phillip Berryman, *The Religious Roots of Rebellion: Christians in Central American Revolution* (Maryknoll, N.Y.: Orbis, 1984). In her essay "While Love Is Unfashionable: An Exploration of Black Spirituality and Sexuality," in Andolsen et al., *Women's Consciousness, Women's Conscience*, 121–41, Toinette M. Eugene examines connections between justice, sexuality, and spirituality in black experience.

55. Internal note: Friedrich Schleiermacher, *The Christian Faith*, edited by H. R. Mackintosh and J. S. Stewart, translation of 2d German edition (Philadelphia: Fortress, 1976), 332, 335.

56. Internal note: This is the position of many gay advocacy groups in religion. Alternatives to this theology are being given voice by such gay/lesbian activists as David Fernbach, *The Spiral Path: A Gay Contribution to Human Survival* (Boston: Alyson, 1981); Mary E. Hunt, *Fierce Tenderness: Toward a Feminist Theology of Friendship* [(New York: Crossroad, 1991)]; and Cherríe Moraga, *Loving in the War Years* (Boston: South End Press, 1983).

57. Internal note: See James Luther Adams, *On Being Human Religiously*, edited by Max L. Stackhouse (Boston: Beacon, 1976), especially 1–88; and Harrison, *Making the Connections*, 81–190, for interpretations of "freedom" and "rights" on the normative basis of justice.

58. Internal note: See Alison M. Jaggar, *Feminist Politics and Human Nature* (Totowa, N.J.: Rowman and Allanheld, 1983), especially 27–50 and 173–206.

59. Internal note: Important resources for grasping the extent of misogyny—and women's courage and creativity—in christian tradition include Kari Børreson, *Subordination and Equivalence: The Nature and Role of Women in Augustine and Thomas Aquinas* (Washington, D.C.: University Press of America, 1981); Rosemary R. Ruether and Eleanor McLaughlin, *Women of Spirit: Female Leadership in the Jewish and Christian Traditions* (New York: Simon & Schuster, 1979); Elizabeth A. Clark, *Jerome, Chrysostom, and Friends: Essays and Translations* (New York: Edwin Mellen Press, 1979); Elisabeth Schüssler Fiorenza, *In Memory of Her: A Feminist Reconstruction of Christian Origins* (New York: Crossroad Press, 1983); Phyllis Trible, *Texts of Terror: Literary-Feminist Readings of Biblical Narratives* (Philadelphia: Fortress, 1984). See Clarissa W. Atkinson, Constance H. Buchanan, and Margaret R. Miles, eds., *Immaculate and Powerful: The Female in Sacred Image and Social Reality* (Boston: Beacon, 1985), for similar themes within and beyond jewish and christian religions.

60. Internal note: It is interesting to me that in Thomist theology (in which the spiritual is the *super*natural and the "male principle" is in its image), femaleness is cast as "natural." But in modern liberalism's equation of the natural with the divine process, the construct of female "nature" (receptive, passive) is set as different from the male "nature," which is normative for a fully human life. Femaleness is thus "unnatural" in liberal theology, as are sexual acts that run contrary to human (and divine) "nature." Whether "natural" (beneath the supernatual God-man) or "unnatural" (beneath the natural·God-man), women are objects rather than subjects of moral agency in christian history. Liberalism thus has changed nothing with regard to classical christianity's sacred contempt for women. Homosexual men, of course, have a very different history. As long as they have been "discreet," they have maintained heterosexist benefits of male privilege and domination. Openly gay men—not closeted homosexuals—receive scorn and contempt in christian history.

61. Internal note: For help in understanding the politics of this dynamic, see Zillah R. Eisenstein, *The Radical Future of Liberal Feminism* (New York: Longman, 1981); Beverly Wildung Harrison, *Our Right to Choose: Toward a New Ethic of Abortion* (Boston: Beacon, 1983); and Jaggar, *Feminist Politics and Human Nature*.

62. Internal note: John Boswell explores this in *Christianity, Social Tolerance, and Homosexuality: Gay People in Western Europe from the Beginning of the Christian Era to the Fourteenth Century* (Chicago: University of Chicago Press, 1980).

63. Internal note: Margaret C. Huff, "The Interdependent Self: An Integrated Concept from Feminist Theology and Feminist Psychology," in *Philosophy and Theology*, No. 2, pp. 160–72.

14. FEMINIST LIBERATION THEOLOGIES

1. For a useful overview of the history of American women, see Sara M. Evans, *Born for Liberty: A History of Women in America* (New York: Free Press, 1989).

2. See William O'Neill, *Everyone Was Brave: The Rise and Fall of Feminism in America* (Chicago: Quadrangle Books, 1969).

3. Elizabeth Farians, "Justice: The Hard Line," *Andover Newton Quarterly* 12 (March 1972): 199.

4. Mary McClintock Fulkerson, *Changing the Subject: Women's Discourses and Feminist Theology* (Minneapolis: Fortress Press, 1994), 31.

5. For a discussion of lesbian liberation theology and excerpts from Carter Heyward, see Chapter Thirteen.

6. For a useful account of the genealogy of liberation theology, see Robert McAfee Brown, *Theology in a New Key: Responding to Liberation Themes* (Philadelphia: Westminster Press, 1978), 27–74; for an account of the emergence of liberation theology and the reaction against it, see Penny Lernoux, *People of God: The Struggle for World Catholicism* (New York: Viking, 1989).

7. For a classic statement of these themes, see Gustavo Gutiérrez, *A Theology of Liberation: History, Politics, and Salvation*, trans. and ed. Caridad Inda and John Eagleson (Maryknoll, N.Y.: Orbis, 1973).

8. Mary Daly, *The Church and the Second Sex* (New York: Harper & Row Publishers, 1975 [1968]).

9. Mary Daly, *Beyond God the Father: Toward a Philosophy of Women's Liberation* (Boston: Beacon Press, 1973), 9.

10. Daly, *Beyond God the Father,* 19.

11. Daly, *Beyond God the Father,* 19.

12. Daly, *Beyond God the Father,* 67–68.

13. Daly, *Beyond God the Father,* 72.

14. Daly, *Beyond God the Father,* 55.

15. Daly, *Beyond God the Father,* 50.

16. See Mary Daly, *Gyn/Ecology: The Metaethics of Radical Feminism* (Boston: Beacon Press, 1978); Daly, *Pure Lust: Elemental Feminist Philosophy* (Boston: Beacon Press, 1984); Daly, *Websters' First New Intergalactic Wickedary of the English Language* (Boston: Beacon Press, 1987); and Daly, *Outercourse: The Be-Dazzling Voyage* (San Francisco: HarperSanFrancisco, 1992).

17. See Rosemary Radford Ruether, *Women of Spirit: Female Leadership in the Jewish and Christian Traditions* (New York: Simon & Schuster, 1979); Ruether and Rosemary Skinner Keller, eds., *Women and Religion in America* (San Francisco: Harper & Row, 1981); Ruether, *Womanguides: Readings Toward a Feminist Theology* (Boston: Beacon Press, 1985); Ruether, *Women-church: Theology and Practice of Feminist Liturgical Communities* (San Francisco: Harper & Row, 1985); and Ruether, *Gaia and God: An Ecofeminist Theology of Earth Healing* (San Francisco: HarperSanFrancisco, 1992).

18. Elisabeth Schüssler Fiorenza, *Bread Not Stone* (Boston: Beacon Press, 1984), 15–22; and see Elisabeth Schüssler Fiorenza, *But She Said: Feminist Practices of Biblical Interpretation* (Boston: Beacon Press, 1992), 142–43. See also McClintock Fulkerson, *Changing the Subject,* 34–35.

19. Ruether, *Sexism and God-Talk: Toward a Feminist Theology* (Boston: Beacon Press, 1983), 21–22.

20. For a valuable critique of Ruether's methodology, particularly with respect to its underlying notions of experience and subjectivity, see McClintock Fulkerson, *Changing the Subject,* 54–56.

21. See also Ruether, *To Change the World: Christology and Cultural Criticism* (New York: Crossroads Publishing, 1981).

22. For other prominent examples, see Gayraud Wilmore and James Cone, eds., *Black Theology: A Documentary History* (New York: Orbis Books, 1979); Katie G. Cannon, *Black Womanist Ethics* (Atlanta: Scholars Press, 1988); and Delores Williams, *Sisters in the Wilderness: The Challenge of Womanist God-talk* (Maryknoll, N.Y.: Orbis Books, 1993).

23. Alice Walker, *In Search of Our Mother's Gardens* (New York: Harcourt Brace Jovanovich, 1983), xi–xii.

24. Barbara Smith, *Home Girls: A Black Feminist Anthology* (Latham, N.Y.: Kitchen Table—Women of Color Press, 1983), xxiv–xxvi.

25. Jacquelyn Grant, *White Women's Christ and Black Women's Jesus: Feminist Christology and Womanist Response* (Atlanta: Scholars Press, 1989), 205.

26. For an account of the emergence of African-American feminist theology, see Kelly D. Brown, "The Emergence of a Black Feminist Theology in the United States," in *We Are One Voice*, eds. Simon S. Maimela and Dwight N. Hopkins (Braamfontein, South Africa: Skotaville Publishers, 1989), 61–71.

27. Grant, *White Women's Christ*, 210.

28. Grant, *White Women's Christ*, 217.

29. Internal note: Cecil Wayne Cone, *Identity Crisis in Black Theology* (Nashville, Tennessee: African Methodist Episcopal Church, 1975), passim, especially Chapter II.

30. Internal note: Olive Gilbert, *Sojourner Truth: Narrative and Book of Life* (1850 and 1875; reprint ed., Chicago: Johnson Publishing Co., Inc., 1970), p. 83.

31. Internal note: Harold A. Carter, *The Prayer Tradition of Black People* (Valley Forge: Judson Press, 1976). Carter, in referring to traditional Black prayer in general, states that Jesus was revealed as one who "was all one needs!" p. 50.

32. Internal note: Ibid.

33. Internal note: J. D. Roberts, *A Black Political Theology* (Philadelphia: The Westminster Press, 1974), p. 138. See especially Chapter 5. See also Noel Erskine, *Decolonizing Theology: A Caribbean Perspective* (New York: Orbis Books, 1980), p. 125.

34. Internal note: Roberts, *A Black Political Theology*, p. 133.

35. Internal note: Albert Cleage, *The Black Messiah* (New York: Sheed and Ward, 1969), p. 92.

36. Internal note: [James] Cone, *God of the Oppressed* [New York: Seabury Press, 1975], p. 134.

37. Internal note: Jarena Lee, *Religious Experiences and Journal of Mrs. Jarena Lee* (Philadelphia, 1849), pp. 15–16.

38. Internal note: Ibid., p. 16.

39. Ada María Isasi-Díaz, "*Mujeristas:* A Name of Our Own," in *Yearning to Breathe Free: Liberation Theologies in the United States*, eds. Mar Peter-Raoul, Linda Rennie Forcey, and Robert Frederick Hunter Jr. (Maryknoll, N.Y.: Orbis Books, 1990), 121–22.

40. Isasi-Díaz, "*Mujeristas*," 122.

41. Isasi-Díaz, "*Mujeristas*," 122.

42. See, for example, María Pilar Aquino, *Our Cry for Life: Feminist Theology from Latin America*, trans. Dinah Livingstone (Maryknoll, N.Y.: Orbis Books, 1993); Allan Figueroa Deck, *Frontiers of Hispanic Theology in the United States* (Maryknoll, N.Y.: Orbis Books, 1992); and Virginia Fabella and Mercy Amba Oduyoye, eds., *With Passion and Compassion: Third-World Women Doing Theology* (Maryknoll, N.Y.: Orbis Books, 1988).

43. Internal note: Ada María Isasi-Díaz, "Toward an Understanding of *Feminismo Hispano* in the U.S.A.," in *Women's Consciousness, Women's Conscience,* ed. Barbara H. Andolsen, Christine E. Gudorf, and Mary D. Pellauer (New York: Winston, 1985), pp. 51–61.

44. Internal note: Ada María Isasi-Díaz and Yolando Tarango, *Hispanic Women: Prophetic Voice in the Church* (San Francisco: Harper & Row, 1988).

45. Internal note: José Míguez Bonino, "Nuevas Tendencias en Teología," *Pasos* (1985), p. 22.

46. Internal note: Charles Curran, *Catholic Moral Theology in Dialogue* (Notre Dame, Ind.: Fides, 1972), p. 53.

47. Internal note: Juan Luis Segundo, *The Liberation of Theology* (Maryknoll, N.Y.: Orbis Books, 1982), p. 118.

48. Internal note: Norman K. Gottwald, "Socio-Historical Precision in the Biblical Grounding of Liberation Theologies" (unpublished address to the Catholic Biblical Association of America, San Francisco, August 1985), p. 11.

49. Internal note: Virgilio Elizondo, *Galilean Journey* (Maryknoll, N.Y.: Orbis Books, 1984).

50. Internal note: The best-known examples of this are the four volumes of *The Gospel of Solentiname* (Maryknoll, N.Y.: Orbis Books, 1982).

51. Internal note: Segundo, *Liberation,* p. 121.

52. Internal note: Ibid., p. 119.

53. Internal note: [Charles] Curran, *Moral Theology [Catholic Moral Theology in Dialogue,* Notre Dame: Fides, 1972], p. 64.

54. Internal note: Stanley Hauerwas, "The Moral Authority of Scripture: The Politics and Ethics of Remembering," in *The Use of Scripture in Moral Theology,* ed. Charles E. Curran and Richard A. McCormick (New York: Paulist Press, 1984), p. 245.

55. Internal note: Isabel Allende, *The House of the Spirits* (New York: Knopf, 1985), pp. 358–68; Charlotte Bunch, *Passionate Politics* (New York: St. Martin's Press, 1987); Nancy Hartsock, *Money, Sex, and Power* (Boston: Northeastern University Press, 1985); and Carter Heyward, *The Redemption of God* (Washington, D.C.: University of America Press, 1984).

◆ Suggestions for Further Reading

1. THE NEW TESTAMENT AND CHRISTIAN ORIGINS

Brooten, Bernadette. "Early Christian Women and Their Cultural Context: Issues of Method in Historical Reconstruction." In *Feminist Perspectives on Biblical Scholarship*, ed. Adela Yarbro Collins, 65–91. Chico, Cal.: Scholars Press, 1985.

———. "Paul's Views on the Nature of Women and Female Homoeroticism." In *Immaculate and Powerful: The Female in Sacred Image and Social Reality*, eds. Clarissa W. Atkinson, Constance H. Buchanan, and Margaret R. Miles, 61–87. Boston: Beacon Press, 1985.

———. *Early Christian Responses to Female Homoeroticism and Their Historical Context*. Chicago: University of Chicago Press, 1996.

Fiorenza, Elizabeth Schüssler. *Bread Not Stone: The Challenge of Feminist Biblical Interpretation*. Boston: Beacon Press, 1984.

———. *But She Said: Feminist Practices of Biblical Interpretation*. Boston: Beacon Press, 1992.

———. *In Memory of Her: A Feminist Theological Reconstruction of Christian Origins*. New York: Crossroad, 1983.

Kraemer, Ross Shepard. *Her Share of the Blessings: Women's Religions Among Pagans, Jews, and Christians in the Greco-Roman World*. New York/Oxford: Oxford University Press, 1992.

MacDonald, Dennis Ronald. *The Legend and the Apostle: The Battle for Paul in Story and Canon*. Philadelphia: Westminster Press, 1983.

Martin, Dale B. *The Corinthian Body*. New Haven: Yale University Press, 1995.

Yarbrough, O. Larry. *Not Like the Gentiles: Marriage Rules in the Letters of Paul*. SBL Dissertation Series 80. Atlanta: Scholars Press, 1985.

2. CLEMENT OF ALEXANDRIA AND THE GNOSTICS

Buckley, Jorunn Jacobsen. *Female Fault and Fulfillment in Gnosticism*. Chapel Hill/London: University of North Carolina Press, 1986.

Hunter, David G. "The Language of Desire: Clement of Alexandria's Transformation of Ascetic Discourse." *Semeia* 57 (1992): 95–111.

Kinder, Donald. "Clement of Alexandria: Conflicting Views on Women." *The Second Century* 7 (1989–90): 213–20.

King, Karen L., ed. *Images of the Feminine in Gnosticism*. Philadelphia: Fortress Press, 1988.

Pagels, Elaine. *The Gnostic Gospels*. New York: Random House, 1979.

Robinson, James M., ed. *The Nag Hammadi Library*. 2nd ed. San Francisco: Harper & Row, 1981.

Torjesen, Karen Jo. *When Women Were Priests: Women's Leadership in the Early Church and the Scandal of Their Subordination in the Rise of Christianity*. San Francisco: HarperSanFrancisco, 1993.

3. JEROME: THE EXALTATION OF CHRISTIAN VIRGINITY

Brown, Peter. *The Body and Society: Men, Women, and Sexual Renunciation in Early Christianity*. New York: Columbia University Press, 1988.

Castelli, Elizabeth. "Virginity and Its Meaning for Women's Sexuality in Early Christianity." *Journal of Feminist Studies in Religion* 2 (1986): 61–88.

Clark, Elizabeth A. "Antifamilial Tendencies in Ancient Christianity." *Journal of the History of Sexuality* 5 (1995): 356–80.

——. *Ascetic Piety and Women's Faith: Essays on Late Ancient Christianity*. Lewiston, N.Y.: Edwin Mellen Press, 1986.

——. *Jerome, Chrysostom, and Friends: Essays and Translations*. New York/Toronto: Edwin Mellen Press, 1979.

Cooper, Kate. *The Virgin and the Bride: Idealized Womanhood in Late Antiquity*. Cambridge, Mass.: Harvard University Press, 1996.

Elm, Susanna. *"Virgins of God": The Making of Asceticism in Late Antiquity*. Oxford: Clarendon Press, 1994.

Hunter, David G. "Helvidius, Jovinian, and the Virginity of Mary in Late Fourth-Century Rome." *Journal of Early Christian Studies* 1 (1993): 47–71.

——. "Resistance to the Virginal Ideal in Late Fourth-Century Rome: The Case of Jovinian." *Theological Studies* 48 (1987): 45–64.

Kelly, J. N. D. *Jerome: His Life, Writings and Controversies*. New York: Harper & Row, 1976. Esp. chaps. 6, 10–13, 17.

Miller, Patricia Cox. "The Blazing Body: Ascetic Desire in Jerome's Letter to Eustochium." *Journal of Early Christian Studies* 1 (1993): 21–45.

Wimbush, Vincent, ed. *Ascetic Behavior in Greco-Roman Antiquity: A Sourcebook*. Minneapolis: Fortress Press, 1990.

4. AUGUSTINE: SINFULNESS AND SEXUALITY

Børresen, Kari Elisabeth. *Subordination and Equivalence: The Nature and Rôle of Woman in Augustine and Thomas Aquinas*. Trans. Charles H. Talbot. Part 1. Washington, D.C.: University Press of America, 1981.

Brown, Peter. "Augustine and Sexuality." The Center for Hermeneutical Studies in Hellenistic and Modern Culture, Colloquy 46. Berkeley: The Center for Hermeneutical Studies in Hellenistic and Modern Culture, 1983.

———. *The Body and Society: Men, Women, and Sexual Renunciation in Early Christianity.* Chap. 19: "Augustine: Sexuality and Society." New York: Columbia University Press, 1988.

———. "Sexuality and Society in the Fifth Century A.D.: Augustine and Julian of Eclanum." In *Tria Corda: Scritti in onore di Arnaldo Momigliano,* ed. E. Gabba, 49–70. Como: New Press, 1983.

Clark, Elizabeth A. "'Adam's Only Companion': Augustine and the Early Christian Debate on Marriage." *Recherches Augustiniennes* 21 (1986): 139–62.

———. "Vitiated Seeds and Holy Vessels: Augustine's Manichean Past." In (1) Clark, *Ascetic Piety and Women's Faith: Essays on Late Ancient Christianity,* 291–349. New York/Toronto: Edwin Mellen Press, 1986; and (2) *Images of the Feminine in Gnosticism,* ed. Karen King, 367–401. Philadelphia: Fortress Press, 1988.

Pagels, Elaine. *Adam, Eve, and the Serpent.* Chaps. 5 and 6. New York: Random House, 1988.

Rees, B. R. *The Letters of Pelagius and His Followers.* Woodbridge: Boydell Press, 1991.

Shaw, Brent D. "The Family in Late Antiquity: The Experience of Augustine." *Past and Present* 115 (1987): 3–51.

5. THOMAS AQUINAS AND THE SCHOLASTIC WOMAN

Allen, Prudence. *The Concept of Woman: The Aristotelian Revolution, 750 B.C.–A.D. 1250.* Montreal: Eden Press, 1985.

Børresen, Kari Elisabeth. *Subordination and Equivalence: The Nature and Rôle of Woman in Augustine and Thomas Aquinas.* Trans. Charles H. Talbot. Part 2. Washington, D.C.: University Press of America, 1981.

Brundage, James A. *Law, Sex, and Christian Society in Medieval Europe.* Chicago/London: University of Chicago Press, 1981.

Hartel, Joseph Francis. *Femina Ut Imago Dei in the Integral Feminism of St. Thomas.* Analecta Gregoriana 260. Rome: Editrice Pontificia Università Gregoriana, 1993.

McLaughlin, Eleanor Commo. "Equality of Soul, Inequality of Sexes: Women in Medieval Theology." In *Religion and Sexism: Images of Woman in the Jewish and Christian Traditions,* ed. Rosemary R. Ruether, 213–66. New York: Simon & Schuster, 1974.

Milhaven, John Giles. "Thomas Aquinas on Sexual Pleasure." *Journal of Religious Ethics* 5 (1977): 157–81.

Williams, Cornelius. "The Hedonism of Aquinas." *The Thomist* 38 (1974): 257–90.

6. WOMEN RELIGIOUS OF THE MIDDLE AGES

Atkinson, Clarissa W. *Mystic and Pilgrim. The Book and the World of Margery Kempe.* Ithaca/London: Cornell University Press, 1983.

Bynum, Caroline Walker. *Holy Feast, Holy Fast: The Religious Significance of Food to Medieval Women.* Berkeley: University of California Press, 1987.

Newman, Barbara. *Sister of Wisdom: St. Hildegard's Theology of the Feminine.* Berkeley: University of California Press, 1987.

Nichols, John A., and Lillian Thomas Shank, eds. *Distant Echoes: Medieval Religious Women.* Vol. 1. Kalamazoo: Cistercian Publishers, 1984.

Petroff, Elizabeth Alvilda. *Body and Soul: Essays on Medieval Women and Mysticism.* New York/Oxford: Oxford University Press, 1994.

———, ed. *Medieval Women's Visionary Literature.* New York/Oxford: Oxford University Press, 1986.

Schulenberg, Jane Tibbets. "Women's Monastic Communities, 500–1000: Patterns of Expansion and Decline." In *Sisters and Workers in the Middle Ages,* eds. Judith M. Bennett et al., 208–39. Chicago/London: University of Chicago Press, 1989.

Shank, Lillian T., and John A. Nichols, eds. *Peaceweavers: Medieval Women Religious.* Vol. 2. Kalamazoo: Cistercian Studies, 1987.

Stuard, Susan Mosher, ed. *Women in Medieval History and Historiography.* Philadelphia: University of Pennsylvania Press, 1987.

Wiethaus, Ulricke, ed. *Maps of Flesh and Light: The Religious Experience of Medieval Women Mystics.* Syracuse: Syracuse University Press, 1993.

7. WOMAN AS WITCH

Ankarloo, Bengt, and Gustav Henningsen, eds. *Early Modern European Witchcraft: Centres and Peripheries.* Oxford: Clarendon Press, 1993.

Barstow, Anne Llewellyn. *Witchcraze: A New History of the European Witch Hunts.* San Francisco: HarperSanFrancisco/Pandora, 1994.

Brown, David. C. *A Guide to the Salem Witchcraft Hysteria of 1692.* Pittsburgh: D. C. Brown, 1984.

Godbeer, Richard. *The Devil's Dominion: Magic and Religion in Early New England.* Cambridge: Cambridge University Press, 1992.

Gragg, Larry Dale. *The Salem Witch Crisis.* Westport, Conn.: Praeger, 1992.

Karlsen, Carol F. *The Devil in the Shape of a Woman: Witchcraft in Colonial New England.* New York: Vintage Books, 1987.

Levack, Brian P. *Articles on Witchcraft, Magic, and Demonology.* Vols. 3 and 5. New York: Garland Publishing, 1992.

Quaiffe, G. R. *Godly Zeal and Furious Rage: The Witch in Early Modern Europe.* London: Croom Helm, 1987.

Roper, Lyndal. *Oedipus and the Devil: Witchcraft, Sexuality, and Religion in Early Modern Europe.* New York: Routledge, 1994.

Williams, Selma R., and Pamela Williams Adelman. *Riding the Nightmare: Women and Witchcraft from the Old World to Colonial Salem.* New York: HarperCollins, 1992.

8. THE PROTESTANT REFORMATIONS AND THE CATHOLIC RESPONSE

Bainton, Roland. *Women of the Reformation in France and England.* Boston: Beacon Press, 1973.

Bainton, Roland. *Women of the Reformation in Germany and Italy.* Boston: Beacon Press, 1971.

Douglass, Jane Dempsey. "Women and the Continental Reformation." In *Religion and Sexism: Images of Woman in the Jewish and Christian Traditions,* ed. Rosemary Radford Ruether, 292–318. New York: Simon & Schuster, 1974.

———. *Women, Freedom, and Calvin.* Philadelphia: Westminster Press, 1985.

Irwin, Joyce L. *Womanhood in Radical Protestantism, 1525–1675.* New York: Edwin Mellen Press, 1979.

Marr, Lucille M. "Anabaptist Women of the North: Peers in the Faith, Subordinates in Marriage." *Mennonite Quarterly Review* 61 (1987): 347–62.

Roper, Lyndal. *The Holy Household: Women and Morals in Reformation Augsburg.* Oxford: Oxford University Press, 1989.

———. *Oedipus and the Devil: Witchcraft, Sexuality, and Religion in Early Modern Europe.* London/New York: Routledge, 1994.

Thompson, John L. "*Creata Ad Imaginem Dei, Licet Secundo Gradu*: Woman as the Image of God According to John Calvin." *Harvard Theological Review* 81 (1988): 125–43.

Wiesner, Merry E. "Luther and Women: The Death of Two Marys." In *Disciplines of Faith: Studies in Religion, Politics, and Patriarchy,* eds. Jim Obelkevich, Lyndal Roper, and Raphael Samuels, 295–308. London: Routledge & Kegan Paul, 1987.

———. "Nuns, Wives, and Mothers: Women and the Reformation in Germany." In *Women in Reformation and Counter-Reformation Europe: Public and Private Worlds,* ed. Sherrin Martin, 8–28. Bloomington/Indianapolis: Indiana University Press, 1989.

9. JOHN MILTON

Aers, David, and Bob Hodge. "'Rational Burning': Milton on Sex and Marriage." *Milton Studies* 13: 3–33. Pittsburgh: University of Pittsburgh Press, 1979.

Halkett, John. *Milton and the Idea of Matrimony: A Study of the Divorce Tracts and Paradise Lost. Yale Studies in English* 173. New Haven/London: Yale University Press, 1970.

Johnson, James Turner. *A Society Ordained By God: English Puritan Marriage Doctrine in the First Half of the Seventeenth Century.* Nashville/New York: Abingdon Press, 1970.

McColley, Diane Kelsey. *Milton's Eve.* Urbana/Chicago/London: University of Illinois Press, 1983.

Walker, Julia M., ed. *Milton and the Idea of Woman.* Urbana/Chicago: University of Illinois Press, 1988.

Wittreich, Joseph. *Feminist Milton.* Ithaca/London: Cornell University Press, 1987.

10. FRIEDRICH SCHLEIERMACHER AND ROMANTIC THEOLOGY

Briggs, Sheila. "Images of Women and Jews in Nineteenth- and Twentieth-Century German Theology." In *Immaculate and Powerful: The Female in Sacred*

Image and Social Reality, eds. Clarissa W. Atkinson, Constance H. Buchanan, and Margaret R. Miles, 226–59. Boston: Beacon Press, 1985.

De Vries, Dawn. "Schleiermacher's *Christmas Eve Dialogue*: Bourgeois Ideology or Feminist Theology?" *Journal of Religion* 69 (1989): 169–83.

Hausen, Karin. "Family and Role Division: The Polarization of Sexual Stereotypes in the Nineteenth Century—An Aspect of the Dissociation of Work and Family Life." In *The German Family: Essays on the Social History of the Family in Nineteenth- and Twentieth-Century Germany,* eds. Richard J. Evans and W. R. Lee, 51–83. London: Croon Helm; Totowa, N.J.: Barnes and Noble, 1981.

Massey, Marilyn Chapin. *Feminine Soul: The Fate of an Ideal.* Boston: Beacon Press, 1985.

Nicol, Iain G., ed. *Schleiermacher and Feminism: Sources, Evaluations, and Responses.* Schleiermacher: Studies-and-Translations 12. Lewiston/Queenston/Lampeter: Edwin Mellen Press, 1992.

Pattison, George. "Friedrich Schlegel's *Lucinde:* A Case Study in the Relation of Religion to Romanticism." *Scottish Journal of Theology* 38 (1985): 545–64.

Richardson, Ruth Drucilla. *The Role of Women in the Life and Thought of the Early Schleiermacher (1768–1806): An Historical Overview.* Lewiston, N.Y.: Edwin Mellen Press, 1991.

Schleiermacher, Friedrich. *On Religion: Speeches to Its Cultured Despisers.* Trans. John Oman. New York: Harper & Row, 1958.

———. *Servant of the Word: Selected Sermons of Friedrich Schleiermacher.* Trans. and intro. Dawn De Vries. Philadelphia: Fortress Press, 1987.

11. COMMUNITARIAN MOVEMENTS IN AMERICA

Beecher, Maureen Ursenbach, and Lavinia Fielding Anderson, eds. *Sisters in Spirit: Mormon Women in Historical and Cultural Perspective.* Urbana/Chicago: University of Illinois Press, 1987.

Braude, Ann. *Radical Spirits: Spiritualism and Women's Rights in Nineteenth-Century America.* Boston: Beacon Press, 1989.

Dunfey, Julie. "'Living the Principle' of Plural Marriage: Mormon Women, Utopia, and Female Sexuality in the Nineteenth Century." *Feminist Studies* 10 (1984): 523–36.

Foster, Lawrence. *Women, Family, and Utopia: Communal Experiments of the Shakers, the Oneida Community, and the Mormons.* Syracuse: Syracuse University Press, 1991.

Humez, Jean McMahon. *Mother's First-Born Daughters: Early Shaker Writings on Women and Religion.* Bloomington: Indiana University Press, 1993.

Iverson, Joan. "Feminist Implications of Mormon Polygyny." *Feminist Studies* 10 (1984): 504–36.

Kitch, Sally L. *Chaste Liberation: Celibacy and Female Cultural Status.* Urbana/Chicago: University of Illinois Press, 1989.

Muncy, Raymond. *Sex and Marriage in Utopian Communities:19th Century America.* Bloomington: Indiana University Press, 1991.

Robertson, Constance Noyes, ed. *Oneida Community: An Autobiography,*
 1851–1876. Syracuse: Syracuse University Press, 1970.
Ruether, Rosemary Radford, ed. "Utopian and Communal Societies." In *In Our*
 Own Voices: Four Centuries of American Women's Religious Writings, eds.
 Rosemary Radford Ruether and Rosemary Skinner Keller, 341–82. San
 Francisco: HarperSanFrancisco, 1995.
Stein, Stephen J. *The Shaker Experience in America: A History of the United Society*
 of Believers. New Haven/London: Yale University Press, 1992.
Wessinger, Catherine, ed. *Women's Leadership in Marginal Religions: Explorations*
 Outside the Mainstream. Urbana/Chicago: University of Illinois Press, 1993.

12. MOVEMENTS FOR RELIGIOUS AND SOCIAL REFORM IN NINETEENTH- AND TWENTIETH-CENTURY AMERICA

Bartlett, Elizabeth Ann. *Liberty, Equality, Sorority: The Origins and Interpretation*
 of American Feminist Thought: Frances Wright, Sarah Grimké, and Mar-
 garet Fuller. Brooklyn: Carlson Publishing, 1994.
Church of England, General Synod. *The Ordination of Women to the Priesthood:*
 The Synod Debate, 11 November 1992, The Verbatim Record. London:
 Church House Publishing, 1993.
Griffith, Elisabeth. *In Her Own Right: The Life of Elizabeth Cady Stanton.* New
 York: Oxford University Press, 1984.
James, Janet Wilson. *Women in American Religion.* Philadelphia: University of
 Pennsylvania Press, 1980.
Loewenberg, Bert, and Ruth Bogin, eds. *Black Women in Nineteenth-Century Amer-*
 ican Life: Their Words, Their Thoughts, Their Feelings. University Park:
 Pennsylvania State University Press, 1976.
Lutz, Alma. *Crusade for Freedom: Women of the Antislavery Movement.* Boston:
 Beacon Press, 1968.
Pellauer, Mary D. *Toward a Tradition of Feminist Theology: The Religious Social*
 Thought of Elizabeth Cady Stanton, Susan B. Anthony, and Anna Howard
 Shaw. Brooklyn: Carlson Publishing, 1991.
Ruether, Rosemary Radford, and Rosemary Skinner Keller, eds. *In Our Own Voices:*
 Four Centuries of American Women's Religious Writing. San Francisco:
 HarperSanFrancisco, 1995.
Stanton, Elizabeth Cady. *The Elizabeth Cady Stanton–Susan B. Anthony Reader:*
 Correspondence, Writings, Speeches. Ed. Ellen Carol DuBois. Rev. ed.
 Boston: Northeastern University Press, 1992.

13. TWENTIETH-CENTURY SEXUAL ISSUES

Brawley, Robert L., ed. *Biblical Ethics and Homosexuality: Listening to Scripture.*
 Louisville, Ky.: Westminster John Knox Press, 1996.
Brooten, Bernadette. *Early Christian Responses to Female Homoeroticism and Their*
 Historical Context. Chicago: University of Chicago Press, 1996.
Callahan, Daniel, ed. *The Catholic Case for Contraception.* New York: Macmillan
 Company, 1969.

Carey, John J., ed. *The Sexuality Debate in North American Churches, 1988–1995: Controversies, Unresolved Issues, Future Prospects*. Lewiston, N.Y.: Edwin Mellen Press, 1995.

Dynes, Wayne R., and Stephen Donaldson, eds. *Homosexuality and Religion and Philosophy*. New York: Garland Publishing Company, 1992.

Harrison, Beverly Wildung. *Our Right to Choose: Toward a New Ethic of Abortion*. Boston: Beacon Press, 1983.

Hunt, Mary E. *Fierce Tenderness: A Feminist Theology of Friendship*. New York: Crossroad Publishing Company, 1991.

McClintock Fulkerson, Mary. "Gender—Being It or Doing It? The Church, Homosexuality, and the Politics of Identity." *Union Seminary Quarterly Review* 47 (1993): 29–46.

Noonan, John T., Jr. *Contraception: A History of Its Treatment by the Catholic Theologians and Canonists*. Enlarged ed. Cambridge, Mass.: Belknap Press of Harvard University Press, 1986.

Nugent, Robert, ed. *A Challenge to Love: Gay and Lesbian Catholics in the Church*. New York: Crossroad Publishing Company, 1983.

14. FEMINIST LIBERATION THEOLOGIES

Chopp, Rebecca S. *The Power to Speak: Feminism, Language, God*. New York: Crossroad, 1989.

Christ, Carol, ed. *Womanspirit Rising*. San Francisco: HarperSanFrancisco, 1979, 1992.

Fabella, Virginia, and Sergio Torres, eds. *Irruption of the Third World: Challenge to Theology*. Maryknoll, N.Y.: Orbis Books, 1983.

Fulkerson, Mary McClintock. *Changing the Subject: Women's Discourses and Feminist Theology*. Minneapolis: Fortress Press, 1994.

Gnanadason, Aruna. *Towards a Theology of Humanhood: Women's Perspectives*. Delhi: I.S.P.C.K. for All India Council of Christian Women, 1986.

Isasi-Díaz, Ada María, and Fernando F. Segovia. *Hispanic/Latino Theology: Challenge and Promise*. Minneapolis: Augsburg Fortress Press, 1996.

King, Ursula, ed. *Feminist Theology from the Third World: A Reader*. London: Society for Promoting Christian Knowledge, 1994.

Pobee, John S., and Bärbel von Wartenberg-Potter. *New Eyes for Reading: Biblical and Theological Reflections by Women from the Third World*. Quezon City, Philippines: Claretian Publications, 1987.

Russell, Letty, et al., eds. *Inheriting Our Mother's Gardens: Feminist Theology in Third-World Perspective*. Philadelphia: Westminster Press, 1988.

Williams, Delores. *Sisters in the Wilderness: The Challenge of Womanist God-talk*. Maryknoll, N.Y.: Orbis Books, 1993.

∿ Permissions Acknowledgments

Grateful acknowledgment is made for the selections in this volume used as noted, with the permission of the following publishers.

Arno Press, Inc., for selections from Elizabeth Cady Stanton, *The Woman's Bible,* Parts 1, 2, and Appendix. New York: Arno Press, Inc., 1972.

Beacon Press, for selections from Rosemary Radford Ruether, *Sexism and God-Talk: Toward a Feminist Theology.* Boston: Beacon Press, 1983, 1993.

Concordia Publishing House, for selections from Martin Luther, *Luther's Works,* Vol. 1, ed. Jaroslav Pelikan. Saint Louis: Concordia Publishing House, 1958.

Fortress Press, for selections from Martin Luther, "The Estate of Marriage" in *Luther's Works,* Vol. 45, *The Christian in Society II,* ed. Walther I. Brandt. Philadelphia: Fortress Press, 1962.

HarperCollins Publishers, Inc., for selections from Carter Heyward, *Touching Our Strength: The Erotic as Power and the Love of God.* New York: Harper & Row, 1989. For selections from Julian of Norwich, *The Revelations of Divine Love,* trans. James Walsh. Harper & Row, 1961. And for selections from "The Gospel of Mary" in *Gnosticism: A Sourcebook of Heretical Writings from the Early Christian Period,* ed. Robert M. Grant. New York: HarperCollins Publishers, Inc., 1961.

Harvard University Press, for selections from Jerome, *Letter 22,* "To Eustochium: The Virgin's Profession" in *Select Letters of St. Jerome,* trans. F. A. Wright. Loeb Classical Library, Cambridge: Harvard University Press, 1933.

John Knox Press, for selections from *Christmas Eve* by Friedrich Schleiermacher, trans. Terrence N. Tice. Richmond: John Knox Press, 1967.

Jonathan Cape Ltd., for selections from Margery Kempe, *The Book of Margery Kempe,* 1426, ed. W. Butler-Bowen. London: Jonathan Cape, 1936.

Medieval and Renaissance Texts and Studies, for selections from *The Letters of St. Catherine of Siena,* trans. Suzanne Noffke. Binghamton: Medieval and Renaissance Texts and Studies, 1988.

Orbis Books, for selections from Ada María Isasi-Díaz, "*Mujeristas:* A Name of Our Own," in *Yearning to Breathe Free: Liberation Theologies in the United States,* ed. Mar Peter-Raoul et al. Maryknoll, N.Y.: Orbis Books, 1990.

Paulist Press, for selections from *Angela of Foligno: Complete Works,* trans. Paul Lachance. New York/Mahwah: Paulist Press, 1993.

Pilgrim Press, for selections from Beverly Wildung Harrison's "A Theology of Pro-choice: A Feminist Perspective," in *Abortion: The Moral Issues,* ed. Edward Batchelor Jr. New York: Pilgrim Press, 1982.

The Pushkin Press, for selections from J. Sprenger and H. Kramer, *Malleus Maleficarum,* trans. Montague Summers. London: The Pushkin Press, 1948.

The Religious Education Association of the United States and Canada, for Mary Daly's "The Women's Movement: An Exodus Community." Reprinted from the September/October 1972 issue of *Religious Education* by permission of the publisher, the Religious Education Association, 409 Prospect St., New Haven, CT 06510. Membership or subscription available on request.

Scholars Press, for selections from Jacquelyn Grant, *White Women's Christ and Black Women's Jesus: Feminist Christology and Womanist Response.* Atlanta: Scholars Press, 1989.

University Press of America, for selections from Carter Heyward, "Coming Out and Relational Empowerment," in *No Easy Peace: Liberating Anglicanism,* eds. Carter Heyward and Sue Phillips. Lanham, Md.: University Press of America, 1992.

The Westminster Press, for selections from *Alexandrian Christianity,* Vol. 2, The Library of Christian Classics, Ed. Henry Chadwick and J. E. L. Oulton. Used by permission of The Westminster Press. Philadelphia, The Westminster Press, 1954.